# The World of Storytelling

# The World of Storytelling

## Expanded and Revised Edition

*by Anne Pellowski*

The H.W. Wilson Company 1990

Published by TheH.W. Wilson Company
950 University Avenue
Bronx, NY 10452

Copyright notices of publishers granting permission to reprint material are listed in the Acknowledgments section of this book.

Library of Congress Cataloging in Publication Data
Pellowski, Anne.
    The world of storytelling / by Anne Pellowski.—Expanded and rev. ed.
        p.    cm.
Includes bibliographical references
ISBN 0-8242-0788-2
1. Storytelling.   2. Tales—History and criticism.   I. Title.
LB1042.P44    1990
808.5′43—dc20                                    90-31151
                                                      CIP

*To Sister Bernetta Quinn, who taught me*
*so much about writing stories,*
*and to Mrs. Augusta Baker, who helped me*
*develop my talent in telling stories.*

# CONTENTS

# ILLUSTRATIONS

# PREFACE

This work is intended for all who are interested in storytelling. It is not just for those who wish to become storytellers for children and adults, but also for those who already are storytellers in libraries, schools, museums, parks, religious institutions, camps, homes, or other social or cultural institutions, and wish to know more about the historical traditions of this art and craft. It is meant, too, for students of children's literature as a source of information about the oral traditions out of which much literature for children grew.

This book is not intended for folklorists and ethnologists, although I shall be pleased if they find it of some interest. One may wonder about this seeming contradiction, especially since I have taken information for many parts of the book from the work of folklorists and ethnologists. To explain, I shall resort to personal experience.

When I first came to the New York Public Library and took the in-service storytelling seminar from Augusta Baker, I immediately sensed that I was embarking on something for which I had a natural talent and interest. The greater my involvement became in storytelling, the greater my desire became to learn more about its history and contexts, and about the sources of stories. I began reading about myth and folklore and about the peoples among whom such stories had been, and still are being, recorded.

To my dismay, I realized that folklorists, in general, have a very poor opinion of story compilers and storytellers for children. They criticize them for poor scholarship, for watering down and changing original stories, and for the artificial manner in which they learn and tell stories. This is enough to put any storyteller on the defensive!

But, as I continued to read a great deal in the fields of folklore and ethnography, I learned some of the reasons behind the careful recording of informants, and began to realize that in many of the published collections from which tellers were selecting their stories, the subtleties and nuances of the source cultures had certainly been changed, if not completely lost. Also, I had to admit that storytelling practiced in public institutions, in a number of instances, took on a decidedly formal, studied, and artificial air.

On the other hand, I also observed and took part in many fine storytelling sessions organized by various institutions or individuals. The best were characterized by telling of a very high order with great similarity, in the mood created between audience and teller, to that described by various observers of folk storytelling. To me it seemed distinctly narrow-minded on the part of folklorists and ethnologists to disdain such storytelling as unworthy of comparative study.

Subsequently, I myself was able to travel to many parts of the world where oral narration events are still a major form of entertainment and a cultural and social force of considerable significance. Once again, either as an audience participant or as an observer, I was struck by the similarity in mood and feeling to that of my best earlier storytelling experiences. This occurred in spite of the fact that the physical conditions, the stories, and the manner of telling were all quite different from any I had previously encountered.

My conclusion was that, as in so many professions or crafts, a good storyteller recognizes his or her own peer, and it matters very little whether the stories have been learned entirely from oral sources or from printed or mechanically recorded versions. However, I was usually able to participate only in a limited number of storytelling events in many of the places I visited. There was no way of telling whether such events were typical or one-of-a-kind. It seemed better to defer to the descriptions of folklorists, ethnographers, linguists, and others who had had the opportunity to observe and live in the different cultures for much more extended periods of time than I had.

As so many of these scholars have pointed out, even after long and careful first-hand study, one can still misinterpret the stories and storytelling contexts of other peoples. I hope I have avoided this as much as possible by citing the work of observers from within the cultures, when available, as well as the work of outside observers.

Institutional or professional storytellers for children usually refer to another's stories as folktales or fairy tales (or the equivalent in other languages). This is in direct contradiction to the use of these same terms by most folklorists, who tend to follow rules such as that set by Sean O'Sullivan in *A Handbook of Irish Folklore* (p. 555): "Be sure to determine whether the storyteller has learned his/her stories only through oral sources, for if this is not the case, it is not folklore."

*The World of Storytelling* does not question the folklorists' definitions of folktale, fairy tale, or any other type of oral literature. However, such terms are used in a much broader sense in this book, incorporating stories narrated by tellers of all kinds, whether they use oral, printed, or visual sources. Insofar as is possible, in each case the term used by a particular storyteller to describe story material is retained; and, when possible, it is pointed out where folklorists and ethnologists might disagree on the usage of these terms.

This book is also an attempt to rectify the relative obscurity of storytellers, especially the great ones. This is an area in which folklorists are likely to be in agreement, for of late there have been many criticisms of their past failure to record not only the name of the storyteller, but the specifics of style, manner of delivery, and the general ambiance or specific contexts of storytelling occasions. Richard Dorson pointed this out some fifteen years ago in the introduction to his book *Folktales Told around the World*.

In the past, it was generally believed that folktales in and of themselves were such strong and meaningful stories that they were the product of a collective consciousness in a given culture, and all of them were automatically passed down from one generation to the next. More and more evidence suggests that this is not necessarily so. In all likelihood, many a story stays alive precisely because there was or is a gifted individual telling it frequently and well, often changing it subtly to suit the place and time. Those stories no longer told with artistry and style, or whose message no longer fits the context, often die out for lack of interest on the part of the listeners. There are many discussions of this point in books and articles written by folklorists and ethnologists. For a general review see the articles under "Folklore" and "Folktale" in the *Standard Dictionary of Folklore Mythology and Legend*, edited by Maria Leach and Jerome Fried, or the books by Richard Bauman and Emma E. Kiefer cited in the bibliography of this book.

Individual versions of folktales and fairy tales should be considered as much a cultural property of the storyteller as written fictional stories are of the author. This poses many ethical questions for the publisher of folktales and fairy tales, for the compiler and editor, and for the storyteller using printed versions of stories as a source. Among traditional storytellers there has generally been a very strong ethical reluctance to use another teller's material. In *Folktales and Society*, Linda Dégh reported that among the Hungarian Szekler villagers there was great reservation about the use of another teller's stories. If stories "belonged" to one individual, they were not told by another, unless they were passed on with permission or through inheritance. There are numerous other examples of such restraint, some of which were mentioned by Robert Lowie in *Social Organization* (pp. 141–134), by Bronislaw Malinowski in the chapter "Myth in Primitive Psychology" in his book *Magic, Science and Religion and Other Essays* (p. 102), and by Paul Radin in *The Trickster* (p. 122).

Unfortunately, many modern compilers, editors, and publishers fail to note the precise sources of the stories in the collections they publish. This is especially true of collections destined for use by and with children. It is hoped that this book will encourage those who produce such collections to give more recognition to the specific storytellers from whom the tales were recorded; also, to include more about the context of the stories, and the background of the society and culture within which they were (or are) told. Those who review such collections for purchase and use in schools and libraries may possibly find some guidance in this book, and in the many items cited in its bibliography.

Finally, this book is intended as a stimulus to social scientists, educators and psychologists, especially those working in comparative educational theory. It now seems obvious, from the evidence presented in numerous studies, that story (in all its forms and however defined) has a generally powerful influence on the development of personality and world view. But, as many storytellers have observed from personal experience, the orally told story has a dramatically different impact from the story read in a book or seen on a television screen. While there has been a great increase in research on story, its meaning, and its impact on the education of children, there has been very little on the relative merits of oral, written and visual formats of story. Chapter 15 in this book is an attempt to point out some of the directions educators, social scientists, psychologists and others might pursue in a more thorough examination of the role the storyteller (as contrasted to the story writer or story filmmaker) might play in the education of children.

Regrettably, because of space and time limitations, the "Multilingual Dictionary of Storytelling Terms" in the first edition could not be updated and included in this edition. It is hoped that the Dictionary can be revised and expanded into a separate publication in the future.

# ACKNOWLEDGMENTS

Thanks are due to the following persons who provided assistance in collecting material used in the first edition and carried over to the second:

Amy Kellman, Carnegie Library of Pittsburgh; Marilyn Berg Iarusso and the staffs of the Office of Children's Services, Central Children's Room, Picture Collection, Oriental and Slavonic Divisions, Rare Book Room, and Wertheim Room, all at The New York Public Library; Eva L. Kiewitt and Polly Grimshaw, Indiana University Library, Bloomington; Harold Scheub, University of Wisconsin, Madison; Christa A. Sammons, Beineke Library, Yale University; Verna Aardema Vugteveen; Joan and Henry Ferguson; Lucia Binder, Vienna; Dr. Bernhard Bischoff, Munich; Rolf W. Brednich, Seminar für Volkskunde, Gottingen; Fritz Nötzoldt, Heidelberg; Koji Kata, Morio Kita, and Kiyoko Toyama of Tokyo.

For additional material in this second edition the author wishes to acknowledge the help of:

Lynn Ager Wallen, Juneau, Alaska; Stuart H. Blackburn, San Francisco; Joseph C. Miller, Jr., Conshohocken, Pennsylvania; Nancy Munn, University of Chicago; Jerry Peters, Milwaukee Public Library; George Shannon, Eau Claire, Wisconsin; Joel Sherzer, University of Texas; Jimmy Neill Smith, NAPPS; Cathy Spagnoli, Seattle; Kate Stevens, Toronto; Ruth Stotter, Dominican College, San Rafael, California; Andrew Tracey, International Library of African Music, Grahamstown, South Africa; reference and interlibrary loan staff, Golda Meir Library, University of Wisconsin-Milwaukee; reference staff, Butler Library, Columbia University; reference staff, Sterling Library, Yale University.

Very special thanks are due to Victor Mair, University of Pennsylvania, for guidance in the use of Asian sources; and to Dean Mohammad Aman and Assistant Dean Wilfred Fong of the Graduate School of Library and Information Science, University of Wisconsin-Milwaukee, for providing generous office space and word-processing facilities.

The author is grateful to the publishers of the following works for permission to quote selections:

"Translations of Buddhist Literature" and "Tun-huang Texts" from the *Dictionary of Oriental Literatures*, Vol. 1: *East Asia*, edited by Jaroslav Průšek and Zbigniew Słupski. London: Allen & Unwin; New York: Basic Books, 1974.

*The Content and Style of an Oral Literature* by Melville Jacobs (1959); *The Legends of the Hasidim* by Jerome Mintz (1968); *Folktales Told Around the World*, edited by Richard Dorson (1975); all published by the University of Chicago Press.

*Folktales and Society* by Linda Dégh, translated by Emily M. Schlossberger. Bloomington: Indiana University Press, 1969.

*The Book of the Gods and Rites* and *The Ancient Calendar* by Fray Diego Durán, translated by Fernando Horcasitas and Doris Heyden. Norman: University of Oklahoma Press, 1971.

*The Xhosa Ntsomi* by Harold Scheub (1975); *Shinqiti Folk Literature and Song* by H. T. Norris (1968); *The Content and Form of Yoruba Ijala* by S. A. Babalola (1966); all published by Oxford University Press.

*Growing Up in Dagbon* by Christine Oppong. Accra: Ghana Publishing Corporation, 1973.

*Nireke No Hitobito* by Morio Kita. Tokyo: Shincho-Shi Publishers, 1964.

American Council of Learned Societies, for short selections from *Russian Folklore* by Yuri M. Sokolov. New York: Macmillan, 1950.

*Kuna Ways of Speaking* by Joel Sherzer (1983); *An Epoch of Miracles* by Allen F. Burns (1983); both published in Austin by the University of Texas Press.

*Literature as Recreation in the Late Middle Ages* by Glending Olson. Ithaca: Cornell University Press, 1982.

I am truly grateful for the meticulous editing done by Judith O'Malley; I know my thanks can never be adequately expressed in lower case, but she will be insistent on maintaining that form.

Last but not least, thanks to John, David, and Michael Collard for their help in indexing.

# A Note on Abbreviations and Spelling

The reader of this book will find inconsistencies in spelling, in the transliteration of terms from non-Roman alphabets, and in the use of diacritic marks. This results from the fact that terms are generally used in the form in which they are found in the particular source being cited. For example, *ceilidhe* may appear in one source, while other sources use *ceilidh* or *celidh*. Exceptions to this are the four terms "folklore," "folktale," "storyteller," and "storytelling." For ease of editing they are always used as single words without a hyphen, regardless of the form in which they are used by the authors quoted or cited in this work. When searching in data bases for titles beginning with these words, it is usually better to search under the author's or editor's name first.

Abbreviations have been used as follows:
ALA—American Library Association
B.C.E.—Before the Common Era
C.E.—Common Era
c.—circa
IBBY—International Board on Books for Young People
L.C.L.—Loeb Classical Library, Harvard University Press
NAPPS—National Association for the Preservation and Perpetuation of Storytelling
p.—page
pp.—pages
Pr.—Press
S.B.E.—Sacred Books of the East
Univ.—University
vol.—volume

# I

## *Introduction*

**Figure 1**   *Detail from the bull's head lyre from Ur, c. 3000 B.C.E. Photo courtesy of the University Museum, Philadelphia.*

# CHAPTER 1

# *History and Definition of Storytelling*

Most modern dictionaries define a storyteller, first, as one who tells or writes stories and, second, as one who tells fibs or falsehoods. This order is relatively recent. Until well into the nineteenth century, the more frequent use of the word was in the latter sense. The first definition generally was reserved for describing storytellers in non-English-speaking areas of the world.

The earliest use of the English term "storyteller" that is cited in the Oxford English Dictionary occurred in 1709, by Steele in the *Tatler*, but it is likely that the word was used widely long before that date. The same dictionary, under the entry for "story," cites a line from William Dunbar's *Poems* (c. 1500–1520 C.E.): "Sum singis, sum dancis, sum tellis storeis." Whether or not the terms "story" and "storytelling" were in use, in English or in other language equivalents, the telling of tales was commonly recognized as a form of entertainment from ancient times up to the present.

There are a number of early examples of stories or story fragments in texts from ancient Babylonian, Canaanite, Hittite, Sumerian, Egyptian, Chinese, and Sanskrit. However, many of these contain no indication as to who told the stories, to whom they were told, and how or why. Some artifacts indicate that storytelling was an early entertainment. The beautiful lyre that was made at Ur more than 5,000 years ago has an inlay showing animals acting like men. Frankfort speculates that this type of illustration must have had something to do with the reciting or recording of myths or fables (fig. 1).[1] The first written description of an action that at least vaguely resembles storytelling appears to be in the Egyptian papyrus known as the Westcar Papyrus, recorded sometime between the twelfth and eighteenth dynasties (2000–1300 B.C.E.). It describes an encounter between Khufu (Cheops) and his sons:

"Know ye a man who can tell me tales of the deeds of magicians?" Then the royal son Khafra stood forth and said, "I will tell thy Majesty a tale of the days of thy forefather Nebka. . . ."[2]

After Khafra has told his tale, another son, Baiufra, tells one from the time of Seneferu (father of Cheops) and the third son, Herutatef, concludes with a contemporary tale.

Another papyrus of approximately the same date, known as the Golenischeff Papyrus and now in the Hermitage in Leningrad, gives an account of the conversation between a nobleman and a sailor. The nobleman has returned from an unsuccessful mission and is reluctant to report to the ruling powers. The sailor, to convince the nobleman that he should not be afraid, then narrates his adventures as a kind of "proof" that such things can befall anyone! This has come to be known as the story of "The Shipwrecked Sailor."[3]

The Bible has, as Ranke puts it, "most of the forms of folktales in some shape or other, complete or incomplete."[4] But in the Old Testament there are few descriptions of actual storytelling occasions. The most striking one is in Judges 9:7, where Jotham tells a tale to convince the people of Shechem of the terrible deeds done by Abimelech, their ruler. The Chadwicks believe that this and other passages (Deut. 11:29, and Josh.: 8:33, among others) reflect a custom followed by Hebrew prophets or orators on public occasions. Their general conclusion is that "we cannot recall any recitation for the sake of entertainment" in early Hebrew literature.[5]

Sanskrit scripture, on the other hand, does have a number of passages that indicate storytelling was practiced for religious and secular reasons. In the *Kaushitaki Brahmana Upanishad*, Part III (c. 500 B.C.E.), at the end of a story about Soma (a Hindu god), the narrator remarks that "it is thus told us by those versed in legend *(âkhyânavidah).*"[6] Later, in several of the *Grihya-Sūtras*, or *Rules of Vedic Domestic Ceremonies* (c. 200 B.C.E.), appropriate times are mentioned for telling tales. Two examples are:

> They who have lost a Guru by death, or are afflicted by other misfortune, should perform on the new-moon day an expiatory ceremony. . . . Keeping that (fire) burning, they sit till the silence of the night, repeating the tales of the aged, and getting stories of auspicious contents, Itihasas and Puranas, told to them.
> *Āsvalāyana-Grihya Sūtra,* IV Adhyâya 6 Kândikâ 1,6,
> trans. by Hermann Oldenburg[7]

> [In preparation for a festival] therefore (husband and wife) should eat fast-day food which is pleasant to them. Let them sleep that night on the ground. They should spend that night so as to alternate their sleep with waking, entertaining themselves with tales or with other discourse.
> *Grihya-Sūtra of Gobhila,* I Prapâthaka 6 Kândikâ 4,5,6,
> trans. by Hermann Oldenburg[8]

There is also fairly good evidence that some early forms of storytelling in India were accompanied by pictures. A number of scholars conclude that brief descriptions in the *Sūtras* of Panini (sixth or fifth century B.C.E.), in the *Mahabhasya* of Patanjali (160–140 B.C.E.) and in numerous other texts are probably referring to the recitation of tales while showing individual pictures or a sequence of pictures on a scroll or cloth.[9]

Buddhist teaching, from early times to the present day, makes use of stories.

The *Tripitaka*, part of the sacred scriptures of Buddhism, contains many passages in which some storytelling device is used to make a point. The part known as the fift *Nikaya*, which contains fifteen books, is full of dialogues, lives of sages and saints, fables, the birth stories (Jatakas), and numerous tales of all types. The recitation of these stories was looked on with favor by the Buddhist authorities, and continued to be so regarded throughout the later centuries of Buddhist expansion and development. In a work that probably dates to around 300–400 C.E., *The Questions of King Milinda*, the sage Nagasena reassures the king that the recitations are a good practice.[10]

Taoism and Confucianism did not have quite this richness of oral narrative, but they, too, probably used story to spread or reinforce belief. The *Tao-te-Ching* (c. 300 B.C.E.) contains little in the way of narrative, but the writings of Chuang-Tze (c. 100 B.C.E.) are full of parables, narratives, and short tales of all kinds. Chuang-Tze's work cannot be taken as literal history, since it describes encounters and confrontations between Confucius, Lao-Tze, and a host of other sages, heroes, and characters that could not possibly have taken place. However, it is quite possible, and even likely, that Chuang-Tze did not invent the parables and tales he wrote down, but simply recorded many from the oral tradition extant in his time. In describing how he believes Lao-Tze and Confucius told their parables and proverbs, Chuang-tze was probably recording some of the ways he had heard tales told by members of the two philosophical systems.

Early Greek writing makes frequent reference to the art of telling stories, either through implication or by actually describing when and by whom it was done. Euripides, in the play *Heracles* (c. 423 B.C.E.), puts such a description in the mouth of Amphitryon. Advising his daughter-in-law Megara on how to spend the time waiting for her husband's return, Amphitryon says:

> Be calm;
> dry the living springs of tears that fill
> your children's eyes. Console them with stories,
> those sweet thieves of wretched make-believe.
> *Heracles*, lines 97–103, trans. by Gilbert Murray[11]

Aristophanes also refers to storytelling in his plays. In *Lysistrata* (c. 411 B.C.E.) the chorus of old men says:

> I want to tell you a fable they used to relate to me when I was a little boy.
> *Lysistrata*, line 718, trans. unknown[12]

The old men proceed to tell the story of Atalanta and how she fled from marriage to Melanion, except that they reverse the action of the characters to make their point with the women.

In an amusing scene in *The Wasps* (c. 422 B.C.E.), Bdelycleon is trying to instruct Philocleon as to how to behave and talk in polite society. Philocleon then announces that he will tell the legend of Lamia, whereupon the following exchange takes place:

> Bdel.: Come, no fabulous tales, pray! talk of realities, of domestic facts, as is usually done.
> Phil.: Ah! I know something that is indeed most domestic. Once upon a time there was a rat and a cat. . . .
> *The Wasps*, lines 1178–1180, trans. unknown[13]

Earlier in the same play (line 566) is the statement: "Others tell us anecdotes or some comic story from Aesop [to get on their good side]."

In *The Republic* (c. 400 B.C.E.) Plato writes:

> . . . we begin by telling children stories which though not wholly destitute of truth, are in the main fictitious; and these stories are told them when they are not of an age to learn gymnastics. . . . the beginning is the most important part of any work, especially in the case of a young and tender thing; for that is the time at which the character is being formed and the desired impression is more readily taken.
>
> *The Republic*, Book 2, trans. by Benjamin Jowett[14]

Aristotle, in his *Politics*, Book 7, Part 1336 (c. 322 B.C.E.), mentions that "educational directors, as they are called, should be careful what tales, fact or fiction, children hear." Two centuries later the Greek writer Dio Chrysostom imagines the following dialogue to have taken place between Alexander and Diogenes:

> Have you not heard the Libyan myth? And the king replied that he had not. Then Diogenes told it to him with zest and charm, because he wanted to put him in a good humour, just as nurses, after giving the children a whipping, tell them a story to comfort and please them.
>
> Discourse, 4, 74, trans. by J. W. Cohoon[15]

Ovid's *Metamorphoses* (c. 7 C.E.) depicts a scene of storytelling that would be seen later throughout Europe and the British Isles, namely that of women sewing or spinning and telling tales to make the work move more swiftly. He is here describing the daughters of Minyas, who do not wish to go out and celebrate the feast of Bacchus:

> Then one of them . . . says: While the other women are deserting their tasks and thronging this so-called festival, let us also, who keep Pallas, a truer goddess, lighten with various talk the serviceable work of our hands, and to beguile the tedious hours, let us take turns in telling stories, while all the others listen. The sisters agree and bid her be first to speak. She mused awhile which she should tell of many tales, for very many she knew.
>
> *Metamorphoses*, Book 4, 36–44, trans. by F. J. Miller[16]

The historian Strabo in his *Geography* (c. 7 B.C.E.–18 C.E.) does not depict one particular storytelling scene, but in several places implies that tale telling was a common human experience:

> Man is eager to learn and his fondness for tales is a prelude to this quality. It is fondness for tales, then, that induces children to give their attention to narratives and more and more to take part in them. The reason for this is that myth is a new language to them—a language that tells them, not of things as they are, but of a different set of things. And what is new is pleasing, and so is what one did not know before, and it is just this that makes men eager to learn. But if you add to this the marvellous and the portentous, you thereby increase the pleasure, and pleasure acts as a charm to incite to learning. At the beginning we must needs make use of such bait for children. . . .
>
> Geography, Book 1, Part 2, 8, trans. by Horace L. Jones[17]

Even pre-Christian Latin literature includes a few brief mentions of storytelling occasions. In one of Cicero's works (c. 45 B.C.E.) we find one of the earliest denigrations of the fairy tale:

> . . . as for your school's account of the matter, it is the merest fairy-story, hardly
> worthy of old wives at work by lamplight.
>
> *De natura Deorum*, I, 34, trans. by H. Rackham[18]

Cicero does not say so directly, but he certainly implies that one of the things done by "old wives at work by lamplight" is storytelling, probably to make the task go faster.

Horace, in one of his satires (c. 30 B.C.E.), is much more specific in describing a storytelling scene:

> O evenings, and suppers fit for the gods! with which I and my friends regale
> ourselves in the presence of my household gods. . . . Then conversation arises, not
> concerning other people's villas and houses, nor whether Lepos dances well or not;
> but we debate on what is more to our purpose, and what it is pernicious not to
> know. . . . Meanwhile, my neighbor Cervius prates away old stories relative to the
> subject.
>
> *Satires*, Book II, 6, trans. by Christopher Smart[19]

One of the stories that Cervius "prates away" is "The Country Mouse and the City Mouse." This entire passage gives a vivid picture of one type of entertaining storytelling among well-to-do Romans.

The above examples would suggest that folktales and legends and myths were clearly perceived as entertainment (and sometimes education) to be enjoyed by adults and children. They were told by anyone who felt so inclined and in a variety of situations.

But what about the professional storytellers and reciters—the bards, minstrels and *rhapsodes*—also described in some detail in early literature, especially Greek? The *Odyssey* (seventh or sixth century B.C.E.) has numerous references to bards, the occasions on which they perform, and the content of their stories. These examples are from Book 1:

> Now when the wooers had put from them the desire of meat and drink, they
> minded them of other things, even of the song and dance, for these are the crown
> of the feast. And a henchman placed a beauteous lyre in the hands of Phemius, who
> was minstrel to the wooers despite his will. . . .

Phemius starts to sing of the return of the Achaeans. Penelope hears him, enters, and says to him:

> "Phemius, since thou knowest many other charms for mortals, deeds of men and
> gods, which bards rehearse, some of these do thou sing. . . ."

Later, Telemachus answers:

> ". . . men always prize that song the most, which rings newest in their ears."
>
> *Odyssey*, trans. by S. H. Butcher and Andrew Lang[20]

Pindar, in one of his *Nemean Odes* (c. 485 B.C.E.) gives a picture of one of the ways in which the bard found narrative subjects for his tales in song:

> Even as the sons of Homer, those singers of deftly woven lays, begin most often with
> Zeus for their prelude; even so hath our hero laid a first foundation for a tale of
> achievements in the sacred games by receiving a crown in the sacred grove of
> Nemean Zeus.
>
> *Odes*, II, 1–5, trans. by Sir John Sandys[21]

Plato's *Ion* (c. 400 B.C.E.) gives an excellent picture of the *rhapsode* (the reciter-type bard) and his position in society. Although it is colored by Plato's irony and his poking fun at the pretensions of some *rhapsodes*, it can still tell us much about this type of storyteller:

> I often envy the profession of a *rhapsode*, Ion, for you have always to wear fine clothes, and to look as beautiful as you can is a part of your art. . . . you are obliged to be continually in the company of many good poets.
> Trans. by Benjamin Jowett[22]

A form of bardic storytelling is probably being referred to in this passage from the *Śatapatha-Brāhmāna*, part of Sanskrit scriptures (c. 500 B.C.E.):

> And on the following day, he goes out to the house of the *Sûta* (court minstrel and chronicler), and prepares a barley pap for Varuna; for the *Sûta* is a spiriter. . . . And he, the *Sûta*, assuredly is one of his jewels: it is for him that he is thereby consecrated; and him he makes his own faithful [follower].
> V Kanda 3, Adhyâya, 1 Brâhmana 5, trans. by Julius Eggeling[23]

There are even very early descriptions of the bard's position among the Gauls. Diodorus of Sicily, writing in Greek (c. 50 B.C.E.), comments:

> The Gauls are terrifying in their aspect and their voices are deep and altogether harsh; when they meet together they converse with few words and in riddles, hinting darkly at things for the most part and using one word when they mean another. . . . Among them are also to be found lyric poets whom they call Bards. These men sing to the accompaniment of instruments which are like lyres, and their song may be either of praise or of obloquy.
> *Library of History*, V, 31, trans. by C. H. Oldfather[24]

The question has often been asked: Did these bards, minstrels, *rhapsodes*, and the like precede or follow the telling of tales by persons not looked on as professionals? Did this special career develop as a secularization of originally priestly or religious functions? Or were the first storytellers merely the best from those who entertained their particular social group informally, then realized their special talents and power, and gradually sought to protect their status by devising systems regulating training, practice, and performance?

Going back to Strabo, we find that he has this to say:

> . . . the fact that the ancients used the verb "sing" instead of the verb "tell" bears witness to this very thing, namely, that poetry was the source and origin of style. . . . For when poetry was recited, it employed the assistance of song. . . . Therefore since "tell" was first used in reference to poetic "style" and since among the ancients the poetic style was accompanied by song, the term "sing" was to them equivalent to the term "tell."
> *Geography*, Book 1, Part 2, 6, trans. by Horace L. Jones[25]

The modern philosopher Johan Huizinga would agree with this. In *Homo Ludens: A Study of the Play Element in Culture*, he begins:

> Play is older than culture, for culture, however inadequately defined, always presupposes society, and animals have not waited for man to teach them their playing.[26]

Later he writes:

Poetry everywhere precedes prose. . . . All poetry is born of play. . . . Gradually the poet-seer splits up into the figures of the prophet, the priest, the soothsayer, the mystagogue and the poet as we know him; even the philosopher, the legislator, the orator, the demagogue, the sophist and the rhetor spring from that primordial composite type, the *vates*. The early Greek poets all show traces of their common progenitor. Their function is eminently a social one; they speak as the educators and monitors of the people. They are the nation's leaders. . . .[27]

In light of these passages and others, Huizinga might well have answered the question like this: Storytelling was first practiced by ordinary persons gifted in poetic speech, which had been discovered in their play; gradually this playful aspect of poetic tale telling was grafted onto religious rituals, historical recitations, epic compositions, educational functions, and the like.

The Chadwicks, scholars in the history of literature, divided oral literature into five types. They were unwilling to state definitely that Type D (oral literature of celebration, including religious ritual) followed or preceded Type A (narrative poetry or saga designed for entertainment). They found too many instances in which the order apparently could have evolved in either direction. However, they imply that narration for entertainment preceded other types in quite a number of other cultures. They do not speculate on whether the professional bard preceded the popular, nonprofessional poet-reciter.[28]

Arthur Ransome, in his chapter on the origins of storytelling, states unequivocally:

At first there would be no professional storytellers. But it would not be long before . . . there would be found some one whose adventures were always the pleasantest to hear, whose deeds were the most marvelous, whose realistic details the most varied.[29]

A. B. Lord and his mentor and predecessor Milman Parry, both important scholars of oral epic narrative, analyzed the performances of Serbo-Croatian oral epic singers. They developed a system whereby texts could be examined for repeated phraseologies and parallelisms, similar to those they had found in readings of the Homeric epics. This led them to speculate that the twentieth century oral epic performers were following language patterns close to those of ancient Greek performers, and also using music and poetic rhythm in the same way. They do not theorize about whether this bardic type preceded or followed folk storytelling, although they do firmly state their belief that written literature supplanted the oral but did not grow out of it directly.[30]

G. S. Kirk, in *The Songs of Homer*, came up with the premise that Greek oral epic performers were "corrupted" once they began to rely on written texts. That is, he believed that no true bards or minstrels could be called by those names if they were once exposed to writing and reading. The *Iliad* and the *Odyssey*, he contended, were oral epics, written down, and virtually all that came after them was no longer truly oral-based. But Kirk also left out of his discussion the possible role and influence folk storytellers might have had on oral epic performers, and vice versa. Nor did he comment much on the ability of folk tellers to maintain extensive repertoires that used the special language of orality, even after they had been exposed to literacy.

In the past two decades, the discussions about orality and literacy have been greatly expanded by the work of many thinkers and scholars. Eric A. Havelock summed up his life-long preoccupation with this theme in his book *The Muse Learns to Write*. His basic conclusion was that the unique quality of the Greek alphabet (which he believed to be the only true ancient alphabet), changed not only the basic means of communication, but also the shape of Greek consciousness, and European consciousness when that area of the world came to adapt and use the Greek alphabet for its languages. It was not only the story crafters and tellers whose lives were dramatically changed by the appearance of a system that enabled human speech to be recorded in an accurate and easy manner, capable of being learned even by children; all levels of society were affected by this revolutionary device, and they began thinking and acting in different ways because they no longer had to keep in memory everything they knew.

Havelock implied that this had as dramatic an effect as the discovery of human speech. The brain was freed from the heavy responsibility of memorization and could expand in creative, new directions. Furthermore, the Greek alphabet, he believed, brought about what is commonly called "logical" and "categorical" modes of thinking. Storytelling was forever changed, even for those who themselves did not become literate, because the surrounding society had been transformed. But he did not imply that this was necessarily a superior way of thinking or that oral-based civilizations of an equally complex character did not exist. On the contrary, he stated that "Not creativity, whatever that may mean, but recall and recollection pose the key to our civilized existence."[31]

Walter J. Ong is another scholar who has explored this question extensively. He defined orality in a number of ways, and described "primary orality" as being the means of communication in societies that are totally nonliterate; but this orality is as much a shaper of complex social consciousness as is literacy. It is simply different. In his view, there can be no such thing as "oral literature" because it is a contradiction in terms. There is literature which is sometimes recited or interpreted by speaking it aloud, and there is the oral performance and passing down of narrative, history, laws, customs, and other communications that have never been written down.[32]

Other scholars in this century (anthropologists, archeologists, folklorists, philologists, semioticians, and others who study linguistics and literature), have attempted to find evidence for one theory or another by studying peoples not yet touched by written cultures, especially those using linear alphabets; or they examine still further the earliest examples of pictures, signs, writing, memory aids and artifacts from ancient and even more recent civilizations. Out of this research has come much speculation about the ways in which humans have told stories in the past, their reasons for doing so, and how this changed with the gradual spread of composition in writing.

The best one can say about the earliest origins of storytelling is that there is evidence to support many theories:

1. That it grew out of playful, self-entertainment needs of humans.
2. That it satisfied the need to explain the surrounding physical world.
3. That it came about because of an intrinsic religious need in humans to honor or propitiate the supernatural force(s) believed to be present in the world.
4. That it evolved from the human need to communicate experience to other humans.
5. That it fulfilled an aesthetic need for beauty, regularity, and form through expressive language and music and body movement.

6. That it stemmed from the desire to record the actions or qualities of one's ancestors or leaders, in the hope that this would give them a kind of immortality.
7. That it encoded and preserved the norms of social interaction that a given society lived by.

Documentation for the same kinds of storytelling, such as those cited above, continues up to the time of printing by movable type. It can be found in Sanskrit, Chinese, Parthian, Greek, Latin, Anglo-Saxon, Old German, Icelandic, Old Slavonic, and probably in many of the other written languages in use during that period. For example, depictions of bardic storytelling (see definition, page 21) are to be found in Lucan's *Pharsalia* (c. 60 C.E.), Athenaeus' *Deipnosophistae* (c. 200 C.E.), in *Beowulf* (c. 700 C.E.), in Bede's *Ecclesiastical History of the English People* (c. 700 C.E.), in Asser's *Life of King Alfred* (c. 970 C.E.), and in the narrative poem *Deor* (c. 1000 C.E.), describing an Old Teutonic minstrel. These are, of course, different types of bards, and some suffered a decline in legal or social position before the arrival of mass printing. However, it appears as though all of them used narratives with a heroic/poetic content, and a formal style of presentation seems to have been common to all of them.

As for the professional storytellers in civilizations for which there is little or no written record, such as the Incan and some of the early African kingdoms, we must base our suppositions on other surviving artifacts. Scholars and researchers are now only in the beginning stages of examining the impact of primary orality on these cultures. Also, there must be much more intensive study of the performances of tellers who were recorded shortly after they came into contact with persons from literate cultures.

Descriptions of folk storytelling in the home, work place, street or other public venue are encountered in numerous sources, as will be noted in Chapter 4. The occasions remained essentially the same as those in classical times. Storytelling as a means of educating and socializing the child continued to be mentioned, just as it had been in the works of Plato and Aristotle. Quintillian (C.E. 35–100) wrote:

Their pupils should learn to paraphrase Aesop's fables, the natural successors of the fairy-stories of the nursery, in simple and restrained language and subsequently to set down this paraphrase in writing with the same simplicity of style.
*Institutio Oratoria*, Book 1, ch. 9, pt. 2,
trans. by H. E. Butler[33]

In the opening part of the *Panchatantra* (c. 400 C.E.), compiled for the education and enlightenment of the royal children of India, there is this "guarantee" of the efficacy of storytelling, with the use of tales from that collection:

Whoever learns the work by heart,
Or through the storyteller's art
Becomes acquainted;
His life by sad defeat—although
The king of heaven be his foe—
Is never tainted.
Trans. by Arthur W. Ryder[34]

Strabo mentioned that Parthian teachers rehearsed their pupils "both with song and without song" in narratives about their gods and noble men.[35]

Only in what shall be called religious storytelling in this book (see definition, page 44) are there documented changes in the approach to storytelling style that can be called dramatic. The sacred scriptures of the Judaic, Christian, and Islamic religions are obviously based on much that was orally passed down, and included narratives that can be said to have entertaining as well as moral or didactic power. However, shortly after these texts became fairly fixed, there appears to have been a change in attitude to storytelling. It was frowned upon by the orthodox religious authorities because it resulted in versions or interpretations of the sacred texts that were not "true." Priests, monks, rabbis, imams and other recognized teachers of these religions were expected to read or recite word for word, or at least paraphrase closely the original text. Of course, this did not prevent some of them, or members of the laity, from passing down orally their own versions of their religious experiences, and their own interpretations of stories in the scriptures.

Hindu and Buddhist religious authorities, on the other hand, seemed to tolerate and even encourage the use of storytelling. The belief in the superiority of the spoken word over the written word has always been very strong in India, and survives to this day.[36] However, there is evidence that in some sects in these religions, too, a certain inflexibility set in, once certain sacred story texts were regarded as fixed.

In any case, long before the advent of mass printing and distribution, there was a gradual secularization of both the style and content of many stories from all of these religions. Storytellers were telling them in public, for purely entertaining purposes, and they probably changed a bit with each telling, while the scriptural versions stayed pretty much the same.

Mass distribution of printed stories and tales began in Asia and Europe at approximately the same time: the late fifteenth and the beginning of the sixteenth century. Print did not so much usurp the place of the storyteller as use the devices of storytelling to advertise. Bardic performances did suffer a decline in those areas saturated by print where a sizable number of the populace learned to read, or had occasions to hear things read aloud. Their place was partly taken up by street and marketplace storytelling, usually promoting the sale of narrative ballads or news sheets or cheaply printed chapbooks. Sometimes these street performers tried to evoke the same kinds of heroic and high-minded feelings as had the bards, but they usually succeeded in appealing more to the curiosity of the folk. And they certainly never attained the professionalism and social position that bards, and even wandering minstrels, had enjoyed in earlier centuries.

The market storytellers in the Arabic-speaking world continued to relate the elaborate tales-within-frameworks that had entered their oral repertoires from India via Persia, but they also added other elements that had evolved from Islamic tradition. In the Hindu- and Buddhist-influenced areas of Asia, the differences among Vedic, classical, and folk myths and tales had always been difficult to perceive. With the spread of Buddhism under Aśoka and, later, the increasing influence of the Moghul Empire, trade and travel increased so much that peoples in all parts of Asia began to hear stories that once had been confined to a relatively fixed area. It became virtually impossible to sort out all of the origins of Hindu- and Buddhist-inspired tales.

There is little doubt that many of these stories passed rapidly into China and East Asia, and later into Europe via Persia and through the Arabs living in North Africa and Spain.[37] Many scholars agree that certain elements now present in folktales throughout Europe entered during some period of trade with or conquest by Asian peoples. Some claimed that Manichaeism was the strongest force in the movement of Hindu-Buddhist story elements from Asia to the Middle East and Europe.[38] The method of entry may have been oral, but the stories were quickly converted into print. What is still widely debated, however, is whether there was a reverse flow, and to what extent European stories influenced those in Asia in the periods prior to the nineteenth century.

Europe was also enriched by the firsthand, tale-bearing accounts of exploration and colonization coming from Africa and the Americas. Unfortunately, most of the manuscripts and many of the other records extant among the Aztecs, the Maya, the Incas, and other Native American groups were destroyed by the colonizing powers. The only documentation one can find for storytelling is in some artifacts, and in those records that were re-created from memory decades or even hundreds of years after the destruction of the originals. Accounts of some of the more sympathetic explorers and missionaries also contain descriptions of myth, ritual, and legends, as well as information about how and when they were told. A good example of the latter is in Fray Diego Durán's *The Ancient Calendar* (1579 C.E.), describing the ceremony after the birth of the Aztec child, subsequent to the use of prophetic pictures by the astrologer:

> The parents or kinsmen were told about these many things, having first listened to assurances and then to long, flowery speeches. After this the soothsayers told two dozen lies and fables.
> Trans. by Fernando Horcasitas and Doris Heyden[39]

One must take into account, of course, that it is a foreign missionary who calls the tales told "lies and fables." It may well be that the stories were embedded with important beliefs that were not apparent to the outsider.

The *Popol Vuh* of the Maya was also written down again shortly after the conquest, from the memories of those who had preserved it, probably through continued oral recitation. It is replete with myths, parables, and tales, but no actual storytelling occasions are depicted.

In Africa, storytelling obviously had been commonly practiced in many areas. There do not appear to be any written descriptions prior to the arrival of Arabic and European traders, but oral tradition speaks of the practice as being an ancient one. Ben-Amos finds at least tentative evidence of storytelling in the appearance of the *akpata* players in two of the Benin bronzes from the seventeenth century (fig. 2). He theorizes that it is as likely as not that these performers accompanying the *Oba* (ruler) did praise singing and ritual-narrative singing. The *akpata* has lost most of its ceremonial meaning and use but it is still employed by professional storytellers in present-day Nigeria.[40]

Whether or not this form of storytelling was practiced in the seventeenth century kingdom of Benin, there is evidence from the works of Leo Africanus (c. 1600 C.E.) and from a number of European travelers and traders that both heroic/poetic and folk stories were recited on occasion in different parts of Africa. Such accounts, together with those coming from the Americas and those that had already come from Asia, enriched the possibilities of fantasy and imaginative speculation for the European storyteller. As the folklorist Linda Dégh has pointed out, the storyteller is generally experienced and widely traveled, knowledgeable, and well-versed in the ways of the world. The storyteller attracts new narrative material "like a magnet."[41]

People tend to clarify their own identities in learning how others differ from

**Figure 2**  *A Benin bronze from the seventeenth century showing an* akpata *player (small figure, lower right). Photo courtesy of The British Library.*

them. It is no wonder then that, following their fascination with other parts of the world during the preceding centuries, the Europeans of the nineteenth century began to look more closely at their own traditions. The French critic of children's literature Isabelle Jan states that "there is a time in the evolution of every nation when it will seek to assert its specific identity by means of folklore."[42] For many of the European nations, this time was the nineteenth century.

Among the educated and highly literate classes, oral narration as a form of entertainment for adults had died out by the late eighteenth century. True, the same kinds of tales that delighted the listening audience among the folk were appreciated by the reading audience, but in polished form, as in Perrault or in the elegant versions of the Arabian Nights. For children, it was another matter. Folktales, legends, and myths were still commonly being told to them orally, more for didactic than for entertainment purposes. Paraphrasing Lucretius, Francis Bacon wrote:

> Men fear death, as children fear to go in the dark; and as that natural fear in children is increased with tales, so is the other.
>     *Essays* 2, "Of Death"[43]

In one of his plays, Schiller is probably transfering his own childhood feelings to the character of idealistic young Max Piccolomini. Max reassures Thekla, daughter of Wallenstein, and says that her father's fascination with the supernatural is common to many people. He tells her:

> Not only human pride fills the air
> With ghosts, with secret forces;
> Also for a loving heart is this ordinary
> World too narrow, and deeper meaning
> Lies in the fairy tales of my childhood
> Than in the truths that life has taught.
>     *Die Piccolomini*, III, 4[44]

It was the appearance of the Grimm Brothers' *Kinder- und Hausmärchen* (1812–1815) that excited the educated and involved the literate adult population once again with oral tradition. After the erudite Jakob Grimm and the poetic Wilhelm Grimm had published their versions of the tales, complete with notes and comments, they made such "collecting" acceptable as an academic discipline. The tales became the rage of scholar and dilettante alike. It was probably fashionable to visit one's childhood nurse, listen to her tales, and report on them to one's intellectual and social peers at the next gathering. For the traveler, it became *de rigeur* to report on storytelling "among the natives." The only trouble was that all too often the stories and the manner of telling them were recorded and presented in such a refined and literary language that the flavor and style of the oral originals was practically gone. By 1891 Hartland was writing:

> To sum up it would appear that national differences in the manner of storytelling are for the most part superficial.[45]

Nothing could have been further from the truth. There were and still are enormous differences in the manner of telling tales.

Modern scholars agree that most folktale or storytelling research of the nineteenth or early twentieth century is not valid in terms of present-day standards. The tales taken down in this period by missionaries, travelers, anthropologists, philologists, social scientists, psychologists, and folklorists are still studied and compared with later versions recorded under more stringent controls and with greater care for the entire context. But they are rarely accepted now as the authoritative versions, as was often the case formerly.

Nevertheless, in spite of their disfavor among some scholars, the Grimm Brothers' tales must be considered as the single most important group of folktales that affected storytelling for children. Their widespread appeal and their contemporaneous legitimacy helped educated European parents to believe it was important to continue telling such stories to children, even though, in many cases, there was opposition from formal educational authorities. In the United States, with the public library just beginning to expand its work with children, the first children's librarians looked to such collections, and many later ones inspired by or modeled on that of the Grimm Brothers, to justify the need for the story hour as a part of the regular work of every children's library. It is doubtful that this could have happened without the apparent mantle of scholarship and prestige spread over the folktale collections of the Brothers Grimm, and later of Afanas'ev, Asbjørnsen and Moe, and others.

It did not take long for this institutionalized type of storytelling to take hold. By 1927 it was an established part of most public library programs. Furthermore, it had also spread to municipal recreation departments. When these institutions inspired the establishment of similar ones in Canada, England, Denmark, Sweden, Norway, Australia, and other countries, it was quite natural that the storytelling component would be carried along.

Storytellers in such cases were usually trained during in-service seminars and learned their stories from books more often than from oral sources. Not one of the more than fifty storytelling manuals published in the United States from 1900–1975 suggests that the novice storyteller learn stories only (or principally) from oral sources. In fact, most of them have lists of suggested books from which it is good to learn stories.

## Toward a Definition of Storytelling

For whatever reasons—training, limitations of time and opportunity, or their own frame of reference—librarian-storytellers tended to focus on already published stories as sources of story hour material. They saw storytelling, for the most part, as an introduction to books and a means of encouraging children to read. A definition of storytelling widely used in library courses and workshops was the following:

> Storytelling as an art means recreating literature—taking the printed words in a book and giving them life.[46]

However, there are recent indications that librarians and other institutional storytellers are beginning to regard oral storytelling as a medium in its own right, and do not restrict it to the retelling of written literature.

Among literature specialists, Mia Gerhardt, in her masterful study of The Thousand and One Nights, uses the term storyteller to encompass "those who created the stories, and those who repeated them, the narrators who worked them over, the redactors who wrote them down, the compilers who collected them, and the translators who made them accessible in other languages."[47]

The literary critic Walter Benjamin defined storytelling by contrasting it to the sharing of information. Information has value only for the moment it is new, but storytelling is capable of releasing information even when the story is very old. He concluded that:

> ... nothing ... commends a story to memory more effectively than that chaste compactness which precludes psychological analysis. And the more natural the process by which the storyteller forgoes psychological shading, the greater becomes the story's claim to a place in the memory of the listener. . . .[48]

But Benjamin then goes on to equate this essentially oral craft with the craft of the writer, and makes little distinction between the two very different processes of composing stories orally and in written form.

The above definitions are not acceptable to folklorists, ethnologists, anthropologists, philologists, and others who are interested mostly in orally learned and transmitted stories. They use definitions developed in their own frame of reference. Axel Olrik, the folklorist who coined the phrase "epic laws of folk literature," believed that the folk narrator was one who told tales by unconsciously obeying such epic laws as the "law of opening and closing," the "law of repetition," and others.[49] William Jansen, on the other hand, wrote that the folk storytelling performance may be "at various times and for various reasons, an art, a craft, a common skill, or a universal and general capability."[50] Harold Scheub, a folklorist with extensive field experience in Africa, defines the type of storytelling he observed as "the creation of a dramatic narrative whose conflict and resolution are derived from . . . remembered core cliches and shaped into a plot during performance."[51]

Dell Hymes[52] and Robert Georges[53] both describe at length the "communicative event," a culturally defined social event that is appropriate for certain forms of communication. Georges draws up a set of postulates that are contained in his definition of a "storytelling event," and one of these postulates is that the storyteller is an "encoder" who uses linguistic, paralinguistic, and kinesic codes to formulate, encode, and transmit the message of the story.[54] Linda Dégh believes that the teller is the bearer of tradition (or the communal contribution of past bearers of tradition) to the storytelling community of which she or he is a part.[55]

Dennis Tedlock emphasizes the totality of the storytelling experience and finds it important to distinguish orally composed texts from those composed in written form. The teller, he contends, learned language structure and meaning, plot structure and characterization, the art of telling, and everything else that comprises the storytelling act, as a totality, not in bits and pieces as the modern student tends to learn about written literature. He believes the orally told story is not a genre, but "a complex ceremony in miniature."[56] He has devised his own method for writing down oral performances.

Those who use storytelling for religious reasons today would probably formulate still another set of definitions, as would those who have developed an elaborate style of theatrical storytelling.

Since all of these kinds of storytelling are still going on in different parts of the world, it was necessary to draft a new definition that would embrace the institutional and theatrical storyteller's conception of storytelling, as well as that of the folklorist, the ethnographer, the semiotician, and the linguistics scholar.

There is not only much disagreement about the words "tell," "teller," and "telling" and their use to describe both oral and written processes; the term "story" is also the subject of much discussion. In recent years, so much research has focused on the meaning of story, the process through which humans learn to use story, and the various forms of story, that it would take a book longer than this one to summarize all the theories and examples. In this book, the term "story" will refer to any connected narrative, in prose or poetry or a mixture of the two, that has one or more characters involved in a plot with some action and at least a partial resolution. It may or may not have fictional aspects.

The definition of storytelling used here is: the entire context of a moment when oral narration of stories in verse and/or prose, is performed or led by one person before a live audience; the narration may be spoken, chanted, or sung, with or without musical, pictorial, and/or other accompaniment, and may be learned from oral, printed or mechanically recorded sources; one of its purposes must be that of entertainment or delight and it must have at least a small element of spontaneity in the performance.

# II

*Types of Storytelling:*

*Past and Present*

# CHAPTER 2

# *Bardic Storytelling*

In the previous chapter, a number of references to bardic storytelling were cited. The term "bard" is of Celtic origin, so, strictly speaking, bardic storytelling should refer only to a specific type practiced in Ireland, Wales, Scotland, and parts of Brittany. However, bard has come to be the commonly accepted English word for any poet/singer/performer. For purposes of this book, the term will mean a storyteller whose function is to create and/or perform poetic oral narrations that chronicle events or praise the actions of illustrious forbears and leaders of a tribal, cultural or national group. In performance, the bard is usually, but not necessarily, accompanied by one or more musical instruments, either self-played or played by others.

If one accepts the above definition, there were and still are bards in many parts of the world. A quick scanning of the dictionary in the first edition of this book will show more than fifty different types. Some scholars would differ on whether or not to translate all of these as bard. Here they will all be treated as belonging to the bardic group. Only a few of the specific ways in which they can be differentiated will be covered here.

In many instances it is extremely difficult to separate bardic storytelling from religious storytelling, because the performances honor heroes who have some religious significance or connection. This problem will be pointed out in the relevant sections, and will be discussed further in the chapter on religious storytelling.

The earliest recorded verbal depiction of a bard is probably among those to be found in Homer (see Chapter 1) or those found in the Sanskrit scriptures. One of the latter is cited on page 8. Another, taken from the same *Śatapatha-Brāhmāna*, is an even more explicit account of the probable role of the bard in early India:

(In telling) this revolving (legend), he tells all royalties, all regions, all Vedas, all gods, all beings; and, verily, for whomsoever the Hotri knowing this, tells this revolving legend, or whosoever even knows this, attains to fellowship and communion with these royalties, gains the sovereign rule and lordship over all people, secures for himself all the Vedas, and by gratifying the gods, finally establishes himself on all beings.

XIII Kânda, 4 Adhyâya, 3 Brāhmana, 15, trans. by Julius Eggeling [1]

This passage refers to the elaborate preparations for the special ceremonies conducted every ten years in a Horse-Sacrifice Year.

The bard mentioned above and in Chapter 1, in the citations from Sanskrit scriptures, was usually referred to by the term *sûta*. There was, however, another early Indian bard called *māgadha*. This term actually meant a place and a people in ancient India. Magadha is mentioned very often in the early Hindu and Buddhist scriptures, frequently as the source of the best wandering bards. Eventually, the place name came to refer to a bard or minstrel in general. Magadha was later most famous as a great center of Buddhism, under the ruler Aśoka (c. 260–230 B.C.E.).[2]

Actually, although both these Greek and Sanskrit sources date to approximately 500 B.C.E., pictorial evidence and indirect verbal evidence can be found in earlier civilizations. The Sumerian myth of Enki and Eridu speaks of the gods feasting and banqueting until finally one god pronounces his blessing, and in so doing, speaks of "this house directed by the seven lyre-songs, given over to incantations with pure songs. . . ."[3] There are several mosaics, tablets and sculptures with representations of harpists or lyre players who seem to be reciting. The Standard of Ur, dating to approximately the third millenium B.C.E. and now in the British Museum, shows a woman singer or reciter in one corner, on the side referred to as "Peace." Next to her is a lyre player. She is probably a bard, singing of the battle depicted on the other side of the standard, while being accompanied by music. In the Damascus Museum can be found a Sumerian statue known as Ur-Nina, found in a temple at Mari, and dating to about the same time. Scholars speculate that the woman depicted was a religious bard.[4]

Egyptian art from several early periods shows different scenes in which musicians and singers seem to be declaiming or reciting in front of a ruler or group of people. The beautifully clear relief from the tomb of Pa-Aton-em-heb that depicts a blind harpist reciting may well be one of the reasons behind the widespread belief that early bards were all blind.[5] This is romantic speculation, as Lord and the Chadwicks both convincingly show that there were numerous and gifted bards who were not blind. They also point out that, although a number of blind persons turned to this occupation because it was one that their handicap permitted, their blindness did not necessarily make them skilled singers and narrators.[6]

It is safe to speculate that the ancient peoples who preserved any records at all probably experienced their history, both past and recent, as stories told orally by someone specializing in that art. For purposes of this book, these bardic performers will be divided into two types and referred to as chronicler-historians or praise singers. The chronicler-historian generally narrates what is called the oral epic or historical ballad. The heroes in these are not necessarily praised; sometimes they are shown with all of their human flaws. The praise singer recounts and glorifies the names and deeds of one or more persons, living or dead, associated with the group from which the praise singer comes and for which he or she performs. Both the chronicler-historian and the praise singer performed most often in a chanted or sung type of verse, sometimes with prose interludes. Both of these bardic groups can be subdivided into two types: one who recites and performs existing texts with only minimal changes, and another who composes anew each time a narrative event takes place, using formulaic expressions and repeated themes, but combining them in different patterns with each performance.

The two types of chronicler-historians are best exemplified by the Greek *aoidos* and the *rhapsode*. The former is the term used in Homer to designate the poet-singer who composed spontaneously as he performed. The latter term came into later use and denotes one who performs Homeric poems. The recitation of the *rhapsode* was studied, rather than spontaneous, and was judged by how well it corresponded to the previously composed texts, either written or handed down in memorized form. Plato's *Ion* gives us a good picture of the life and style of the *rhapsode* (fig. 3).

The two types of praise poets are best observed in the different parts of Africa where some can be found performing even up to the present time. The Yoruba, Mande, Hausa, Sotho, Xhosa and Zulu are among those who have praise singers who compose and perform; once the narrative is well known and respected, however, it is supposed to be repeated without significant changes. There are thus praise singers who can be known for their performance of the praise epics composed by others.

Not all of the performances of these various types of performers can be classified as storytelling events in terms of the definition given in Chapter 1, because some had mostly descriptive rather than narrative content. But indications are that quite a number of them can be called storytelling.

## Origin of the Term Bard

It was really the classic Greek and Roman writers who introduced the term bard into the English language, but in an indirect way. In Greek, Diodorus (see Chapter 1) and Strabo were the first to use the term to describe a person with a certain position among the Gauls. Writing some time near the beginning of the Common Era, Strabo says:

> Among the Gallic peoples, generally speaking, there are three sets of men who are held in exceptional honour: the Bards, the Vates and the Druids. The Bards are singers and poets; the Vates, diviners and natural philosophers; while the Druids, in addition to natural philosophy, study also moral philosophy. . . .
> *Geography*, 4, 4, 3–4, trans. by Horace L. Jones[7]

A few decades later, the Roman Lucan wrote this comment on the bards of Gaul:

> The Gallic bards, who compose elegies for heroes fallen in battle, and transmit these to posterity, were once more free to declaim their verses.
> *Pharsalia* 1, 447ff, trans. by Robert Graves[8]

Around 200 C.E., the Greek writer Athenaeus, who lived in Rome, put these words in the mouth of a supposed visitor to the Celts in Gaul:

**Figure 3** *A rhapsode with his rhabdos, from an Attic red-figure amphora, c. 400 B.C.E. British Museum No. E 270. Photo courtesy of The British Library.*

After he had set a limit to the feast, one of the native poets arrived too late; and meeting the chief, he sang the praises in a hymn extolling his greatness. . . . And the chief, delighted with this, called for a bag of gold and tossed it to the bard as he ran beside him.

*Deipnosophistae*, IV, 152, trans. by Charles B. Gulick[9]

Following this early mention of bards among the Celtic peoples, the term seemed to disappear about the fifth century in the written records concerning the Celtic and Teutonic peoples and did not come into widespread use again until the thirteenth century. By that time, the bards seem to have become so highly professional that there were many ranks of them, and the lowest one, called bard, was disdained by the higher ranks. In the Celtic *Leabhar na g-ceart or The Book of Rights* (c. 1400) one of the passages can be translated:

It is not known to every prattling bard;
It is not the right of a bard, but the right of a poet (*fili*)
To know each king and his right.[10]

On the other hand, the *ollam*, or highest ranking *fili*, was looked on as the poet laureate of his day. He was entitled to wear a *tugen* (also called *tuighean* or *taeidhean*) that apparently was made of feathers and must have looked very impressive:

For it is of skins of birds white and many-colored that the poets' toga is made from their girdle downwards, and of their crests from the girdle upwards to their neck.[11]

The *ollam* had a retinue of twenty-four persons, a repertoire of seven times fifty stories, and sometimes sat in an official chair.[12]

Walker quotes an entry from the code of laws of an early Irish king, Mogha Nuadhad, that lists clothing due to the various bards (fig. 4):

Three milch cows is the value of a free Poet's clothing, and of his wife's; it is the same from the chief Bard of a Petty Prince to the Ollamh; and the value of their wive's (sic) clothing is the same.[13]

Later, in a law called *Ilbreachta*, J.C. Walker noted that whereas all other persons could wear clothing of one, two, three, or four colors, depending on their rank or social standing, the *ollam* could wear five colors, only one less than royalty, who wore six.[14]

In Wales, the word bard is found at several points in the laws of Howel Dda, a Welsh king who died about 950. The earliest known manuscript containing these laws, however, is dated about 1200. Since these laws were constantly being changed and recodified, the later year must be accepted as more valid for the descriptions of the ranks of bard and *pencerdd*. The bard of the household or *bardd teulu* was one of the twenty-four officers in the court of the king. He received a steer out of every spoil that was captured while he was in service to the household. In return he had to sing the "Monarchy of Britain" before the warriors on the day of battle. (This was probably a praise epic celebrating the lives and deeds of British rulers.) He received his harp and gold ring from the queen and sat second nearest to the chief of the household.[15]

On the other hand, the *pencerdd*, who was the chief of song, sat to the left of the chief of the household. He always sang first, followed by the *bardd teulu*. He

**Figure 4** *Irish bard. Reproduced from Joseph C. Walker,* A Historical Essay on the Dress of the Ancient and Modern Irish *(Dublin: J. Christie, 1818). This was either a left-handed bard or the plate was reversed in the process of printing. Most sources agree that the harp was held against the left shoulder. Photo courtesy of the Metropolitan Museum of Art.*

became a *pencerdd* when he had "won his chair," states the law, but it does not stipulate how he went about doing this.[16]

In addition to the *bardd teulu* and the *pencerdd*, there was a bard in Wales lower in rank, called a *cerddor*. Not all scholars agree that this was one of the bardic group. He tended to be a wandering minstrel, rather than being attached to one household.[17] The *cerddor* gradually came to be associated with the telling of the popular tales, called *cyfarwyddyd*. Eventually, according to some authorities, the *cerddor* came to be called *cyfarwyddiaid*.[18] They are probably the closest equivalent to the Irish *seanchaidhe* (folk storytellers) that the Welsh had, and could well be classified as folk tellers rather than as bards.

Nash and Toland both placed the *cler* among the bardic group, calling him a poet-minstrel whose "circuit was among the yeomen of the country."[19] Nash further mentioned that the *cler* "maintained his ground against pressure from bards to come under their control," implying that the *clerwr* (pl. of *cler*) were not trained in the bardic schools and did not belong in the hereditary group.[20] Gwynn Williams placed the *clerwr* in Wales from the sixteenth through the eighteenth centuries and called them the counterpart to the continental *clerici vagantes* or *goliardi*.[21] However, current scholarship tends toward the belief that all of these were poets who composed in written rather than in oral form, and therefore they cannot be called storytellers according to the definition used in this book.

It can be seen that both Welsh and Irish bards had precise positions in their society, and at least some of the ranks seemed to coincide. The *fili* apparently did not have a Welsh equivalent. The Chadwicks speculate that the Irish *fili* had some connection with the Gaulish *vates*, mentioned in the quote from Strabo on page 23. They point out that there is an Irish word, *fáith* (prophet), that corresponds roughly to the *vates*. Perhaps at some point the function of the *fáith* was assumed by a bardic type, who then became known as a *fili*.[22]

In any case, from the thirteenth century onwards there are numerous mentions of bards in both Irish and Welsh manuscripts and documents. As the years passed, their positions and duties seemed to change somewhat, mainly in the fact that they began to inherit their posts. Bardic composition and recitation in Wales were formulized to such an extent that, starting in the late twelfth century, a gathering known as the eisteddfod was established as an annual (or fairly regular) competition. In a modern form, it exists up to today.

## The Minstrel Type of Bard

In the period between the time when Strabo, Lucan, and others wrote about the bards in Gaul, and the twelfth century when they again appear under that name in Irish and Welsh literature, there were other poet-singers who had positions similar to the bard. The Anglo-Saxons used the terms *scop* or *gleoman* to designate such a person. Most of our information about the *scop* comes from three sources: *Beowulf*, *Widsith*, and *Deor*.

In *Beowulf*, Hrothgar is shown to have an official *scop* attached to his court:

> There was singing and music together in accompaniment in presence of Healf-dane's war-like chieftan; the harp was played and many a lay rehearsed, when Hroth-gar's bard (*scop*) was to provide entertainment in hall along the meadbench. . . .
> *Beowulf*, trans. by J. R. C. Hall[23]

*Deor* tells of a *scop* who had a similar position:

Of myself I will say this much, that once I was minstrel of the Heodeningas, my master's favorite. My name was Deor. For many years I had a goodly office and a generous lord, till now Heorrenda, a skilful [sic] bard, has received the estate which the protector of warriors gave to me in days gone by.

Deor, trans. by Bruce Dickins[24]

*Widsith* lists a resume of the life of a composite wandering *gleoman*: It ends on a professional note, implying that gleemen should be treated well, for it is they who are the real voice of fame:

So wandering far, / by fate are driven
the gleemen of men / through many lands,
to say their need / and to speak their thanks.
Ever south or north, / some one is found,
Wise of word / and liberal of gifts
Who before the court wishes / to exalt his fame,
To honor his earlship, / until all is scattered,
Light and life together; / he gains laud,
He holds under the heavens / a high and fast fame.[25]

The *scop* recited or sang not only sagas, but also poems on a variety of subjects. He was generally well traveled and could therefore comment on many things. Whereas many at the feasts were expected to pick up the harp and perform, it was the *scop* or *gleoman* who was expected to set the highest standards and be the most original. It is not known whether the *scop* accompanied leaders into battle, as did the Welsh and Irish bards.[26] From various passages in all three poems, we know that the scop did have a high position of honor and that his influence was considerable.

In *Beowulf*, another term used is *thyle*. This is usually translated as "spokesman" or "orator." In the early Norse of the Edda poems, it is *thulr* and seems to mean "poet." The Chadwicks also cite other meanings, that depend on the context in which the word is used, and believe that the position of the *thyle* or *thulr* may have been a close approximation of the *fili*.[27] In any case, they obviously did occasionally recite poetry of a bardic nature.

The old Norse and Icelandic *skáld* was quite clearly the equivalent of the Anglo-Saxon *scop*. *Skáld* literally means poet. From quite early on, that is, well before the year 1000, it had become a regular practice for poets to recommend themselves to some noble patron in one or another of the areas now comprising the Scandinavian countries. More often than not, this poet was a traveling Icelander, because it was his language that was spoken and understood throughout the region. In the second half of the tenth century, the practice began to decline in Norway, but there were still a great number of *skálds* in Iceland during both the tenth and eleventh centuries. They did not begin to disappear until the late thirteenth century.[28] Snorri Sturluson, in his prologue to *Heimskringla* (c. 1225), wrote:

There were *skálds* with Harald the Fairhaired and men still know their poems, and the poems about all the kings who have since ruled Iceland. And we make our statements most of all from what is said in those poems.[29]

The *skáld* is not to be confused with the prose *saga* (pl. *sögur*) teller, even though some of his poetic compositions have been called sagas in English or

German, and many were later taken up and incorporated into the prose family *sögur*. The *skáld* composed and recited a unique type of story in poetry of a strictly syllabic character different from the poetry of the Eddas and very different from the prose of the *sögur*. The *skáld* was not a prose storyteller.[30]

## Origin of the Term Minstrel

Starting about the fourteenth century, the terms "bard" and "minstrel" replaced *scop* and *gleoman* in the English language. There is much disagreement among scholars as to how and why this exchange of terms took place. Bard was apparently picked up by educated persons who read the Greek and Roman classics and found the term used there. The term minstrel came from France. The most widely accepted view seems to be that some *jongleurs* who gave up wandering attached themselves to specific courts, began performing the works of *troubadours* and *trouvères* (depending upon whether they went south or north, respectively), and then set up guilds to train others and thus protect their ranks. These performers were initially called *ménétriers* and then *ménéstrels*. They eventually spread all over Europe, and the accepted English term for them became minstrel. In German, it became *Spielmann*.

Before one can take up the question of the minstrels, one must consider first the development of the term *jongleur*, and the special position the *jongleurs* had in performing and spreading not only the poems of the *troubadours* and *trouvères*, but legends surrounding the lives of these two groups. The French scholar de La Rue believed the *jongleurs* were the continuation of the *bardi*, mentioned by classical writers as being prevalent among the early Gauls.[31] He believed that the Roman influence brought the Latin term *joculator* to the Gauls, applying it to the men who performed on instruments, perhaps accompanying the real *bardi*. Slowly, they came to add other entertainments to their repertoire, such as juggling, miming, magic tricks, tumbling and more. The term *joculator* was gradually transformed into various medieval French terms, such as *jugler, jugleours, jongleors,* and finally *jongleur*. According to de La Rue, these changes began under the kings of the second dynasty (987–1328).[32]

Faral was of the opinion that there was no serious proof of this and that the connection could not be taken into consideration. He also disagreed with those who considered the *jongleur* to be the direct descendant of the Anglo-Saxon *scop*. If the *jongleur* has an ancestor or predecessor at all, he felt it was more likely to have been the Roman mime (*mimus* or *histrio*). These were semitheatrical performers who were quite common in decadent Rome. Faral believed they may well have seen opportunities for support declining among the Romans, so they went north to other parts of the empire. He cited quite a number of documents from the ninth, tenth, and eleventh centuries that mention the *mimus* and the *jongleur* in the same place, as though they were similar in nature.[33]

Regardless of which group they might have descended from, the *jongleurs* were to be found throughout the Latin countries from the ninth century on, but especially in France. The Roman Catholic Church tried to get rid of them and passed decrees forbidding lay persons, clerics, and monks to have anything to do with their amusements. During the eleventh and twelfth centuries, some of them were tolerated because they began performing the heroic *chansons de geste*, sometimes in churches at special feasts. On occasion, they also recited the lives of saints in verse.[34]

But their "golden age" was the thirteenth century. There were literally thousands of them, and they were to be found throughout Europe. There were even female *jongleresses*. Not all of them recited epics or told stories, so only a fraction of these performers can be considered storytellers.[35]

When the custom of composing lyric verse began at the turn of the twelfth century, the ultimate in performance at the elegant courts and wealthy homes was the singing or chanting of these lyrics. The composers, called *troubadours* or *trouvères*, were of a completely new tradition. This was not narrative poetry of the types previously extant. It was lyric verse. The work of the *troubadours* and *trouvères* attracted the more talented *jongleurs* and *jongleresses* who were already performing in all the courts, and they either were hired by or attached themselves to the *troubadours* and *trouvères*. Sometimes they found they were themselves capable of composing this new form of poetry, and thus they raised their position within the court to that of *troubadour* or *trouvère*.[36]

According to the definition used in this book, the *troubadours* and *trouvères* were not storytellers, with the exception of a few who might be classified as bardic praise singers. The characteristic that most distinguished their poetry from earlier types was precisely that it was lyric and only incidentally narrative, if at all. It did not concern itself with telling stories, as did heroic or epic poetry. So the romantic view that *troubadours* were the antecedents of later storytellers is simply not the case. They are discussed here in detail because this confusion exists and because they were the inspiration for, and the subjects of, later stories used by *jongleurs* and minstrels. The notion that they belong in the ranks of early storytellers must be dispelled. Even illustrations of a number of types labeled as *troubadours* or *trouvères* must be looked at skeptically, for there are almost no contemporary depictions that show the difference between bards, *scops*, minstrels, gleemen, and *jongleurs*, who often were storytellers, and the *troubadours* and *trouvères*, who were not (figs. 5, 6, and 7).

Once having settled permanently in a court, the *jongleurs* took on a new aspect, that of ministering to the whims of one master or mistress. It is from the Latin root word *ministerialis* or *menestralis* that the words *ménétrier* and *ménéstral* probably were formed. They were first used in a general way and then came to mean a domestic *jongleur*, that is, one permanently attached to the household, with a salary and perquisites. It was this practice that spread throughout Europe, as mentioned previously. By the year 1300, most of the *troubadours* and *trouvères* had vanished. The *Minnesänger*, who were a close German equivalent, survived only a little longer.[37]

The minstrel, by whatever name he or she was known, did continue to narrate stories in verse, chant, or song, as one of a number of entertainments. Other skills they displayed included juggling, tumbling and acrobatics, and short dramatic skits. They usually traveled in groups, and sometimes one in the group was more adept at tale telling, whereas another might be more talented at playing musical instruments, and still another was better at tumbling and juggling. The stories they told can often be classified as bardic because of their subject matter, which was related to the noble families and frequently mentioned real personnages who had lived in earlier times, although the accounts by then were highly fictionalized. It would probably be equally correct to classify them as folk storytellers, because their repertoires included tales that had come from the common folk, mostly because they had begun performing more and more in public places and less and less in the courts and homes of the wealthy.

## Russian and South Slavic Bards

To a great degree, the same process took place in Russia with the *gusliari*, the *veselÿe lyudi*, the *skomorokhi*, and the *skaziteli*. However, although the performances passed back and forth between the homes of royalty and the wealthy and the homes of the peasantry, the subjects of the stories remained essentially the same. From the *byliny*, oral epics chanted or sung by the Russian minstrels, we get bits of information about the performers themselves. But most of the contemporaneous descriptions of the early Russian minstrels are to be found in other historical sources. *Russian Minstrels* by Russell Zguta, the second volume of *The Growth of Literature* by the Chadwicks, and *Russian Heroic Poetry* by Nora K. Chadwick record and discuss these historical references. These three books are the principal sources for the summary that follows.

The *gusliari* were minstrels attached to the courts at Kiev. They sang epic poems of such heroes as Alexander Nevskii and Iaroslav the Wise, while accompanying themselves on the stringed instrument known as the *gusli*. When patronage by their royal supporters began to decline, they either disappeared or transformed themselves into *skomorokhi*, who performed for much wider audiences.

*Veselÿe lyudi* means literally "joyous people," and this term, and the term *skomorokhi*, are the ones most frequently encountered in the early histories to describe entertainers that appear remarkably like the minstrels of Western Europe. The two terms were used more or less interchangeably, except that the latter seem to be referred to as being more organized and more likely to be settled permanently in one place. The *skomorokhi* are defined by the Chadwicks as "a confraternity of public entertainers, actors, wandering minstrels, dancers, singers, wrestlers and buffoons."[38] Zguta, on the other hand, feels this definition is one-sided for it reduces all *skomorokhi* to one type. He points out that there were registered *skomorokhi* who settled in specific cities, towns, and villages; they achieved a social position that was quite respectable. They payed taxes and owned property. Their work included overseeing wedding arrangements. They played a prominent part in all festivals.[39]

In the *Odyssey*, *Beowulf*, the *Mabinogion*, and other oral epics there are descriptions of kings, nobles, and wealthy persons trying their hands and voice in the performance of heroic poetry as amateurs. One can find similar indications in the *byliny* that this was done by the czars, the nobles, and the wealthy in Russia, sometimes in disguise. But most of the performances of the oral epic poems were by the professional *gusliari*. Later, the *veselÿe lyudi* and the *skomorokhi* took over some of the professional recitation of the *byliny* and other heroic verse. Like the *aoidoi*, the *rhapsode*, the *scop*, the *ollam* and the *pencerdd*, some of the *skomorokhi* seemed to acquire honored positions in well-to-do homes, being regarded as equals. But, for the most part, they performed for the entire community at large.

They were not treated with much respect by the church authorities, who found their unruly ways and their defiance of conventions a menace to ecclesiastical authority. Zguta believes that the main reason the church authorities did not like them was because the roots of their practices dated to pre-Christian times. He believed that they may well have been descended from earlier shamans. In the sixteenth and seventeenth centuries there were a number of repressive decrees directed at curtailing their power. There was even a proverb that said "*skomorokh* and priest are no comrades." The czars and civil authorities did not seem to pay

**Figure 5** *An early court minstrel or* scop *(often incorrectly labeled as a* troubadour). *Segment from* Münchener Bilderbogen, *No. 9, "Zur Geschichte der Costüme" (originally published by Braun and Schneider, mid-nineteenth century). Picture courtesy of The New York Public Library, Picture Collection.*

**Figure 6**   *Theatrical setting sometimes associated with* troubadours, *but more often with minstrels; Arles, France, 1622. Picture courtesy of The New York Public Library, Picture Collection.*

**Figure 7**   Trouvère *accompanying himself on the violin; sculpture from the portico of the Abbey of St. Denis, twelfth century. Picture courtesy of The New York Public Library, Picture Collection.*

too much attention to the church persecution until Alexis, father of Peter the Great, began to back up the position of the religious authorities. He wanted a spiritual reform and believed this could only take place if the influence of the *skomorokhi* were to be weakened. He passed two edicts in December 1648 railing against the frivolous and "pagan" practices of the *skomorokhi*. From this date on the *skomorokhi* were oppressed in earnest. Alexis stipulated that those *skomorokhi* caught repeatedly in performance were to be exiled to the border regions. By the end of the century, references to the *skomorokhi* grow rare and virtually disappear.[40] This persecution did not affect the *kalêki*, the religious counterpart of the *skomorokhi*.

In the next century there began to appear collections of *byliny* gathered from the peasant class. Many scholars thus speculate that the *skomorokhi* had gone "underground," that is, to the rural areas where people might be likely to protect them from the authorities. There, they had passed on their *byliny* to the peasants. Others surmise that they were forced into exile to Siberia and other remote places. In such isolation they could still carry out some of their performances, and the singing of oral narratives was apparently one of the skills they continued to practice for the enjoyment of common people.

The peasants who sing, chant, or recite these oral narratives, called *byliny* if they are metrical, and *pobyvalshchiny* if they are non-metrical, are known as *skaziteli* (male) or *skazitelnitsy* (female). They come from the most humble origins and were and are to be found only in the very remote rural regions of Russia. They were usually of the artisan class, since it was easier to perform while working at such crafts as net making, cobbling, or tailoring than while farming or working in the fields. Most of those recorded in the last one hundred and fifty years were found in the region of Olonets, but they have been found in smaller numbers in almost all rural regions of Russia.

In the Serbo-Croatian part of Yugoslavia, the counterparts of the *skaziteli* are the *guslari* and the equivalents of the *byliny* are called *narodne pjesme* or *bugarštice*, depending on their meter. It was the study of these minstrels and their performances that enabled Milman Parry to come to the extraordinary conclusion that the Homeric poems were not written literature, but more likely the record of performances of oral epic poets. His work, and that of his follower Albert Lord, literally turned upside down the thinking about orality and literacy, and oral composition as opposed to written composition. The study of all bardic performance, and the poetry that results from it, was completely changed after the publication of their works.

The *guslari* in Yugoslavia was, until recently, the chief entertainer in small towns and villages, at least for the male population. In the really small villages, where there was no public gathering place, the singer was likely to perform in a private home. In such cases, it was likely that the women and children could also listen. In the bigger towns or villages, where there was a *kafana* (coffee or tea house), the performances were usually given in that public place. This was especially the case for Moslems during the month of Ramadan, the time of fasting. In non-Moslem areas, or in areas where Moslems and non-Moslems both lived, there were performances in taverns and inns. No women or children were allowed. Another occasion where people might well have had the opportunity to listen to the singers was at weddings. However, there was often such confusion and merriment at these feasts that it was considered difficult to perform well without interruption.

Skendi reported that similar conditions prevailed in Albania. In that area the epic songs were called *këngë pleqërishte* or *këngë trimash*.[41]

## Asian Bards

The *gosan* was a Parthian bard who practiced in ancient Persia up to and even beyond the Sassanian era. The *gosan* entertained both king and commoner. References to this type of bard indicate he was "eulogist, satirist, storyteller, musician; recorder of past achievements and commentator of his own times. . . . sometimes a solitary singer and musician, and sometimes one of a group, singing or performing on a variety of instruments."[42] He was succeeded by other types of bards and minstrels, many of whom achieved high rank in the court. They were called on to perform at state banquets, on special occasions, and at festivals such as Nauruz, the Iranian New Year.[43]

In Turkey, Iran, and the Asian parts of Russia there are still bards and minstrels who perform oral epics, but these epics tend to differ from those told in Russia and the Balkan areas. The *halk hikâyeleri* of Turkey are a mixture of prose and poetry, and the characters are heroic types rather than named, historical individuals. Eberhard[44] does not give the Turkish name for these minstrels, but it is surely similar to the Azerbaijani *ašyq* reported by Winner,[45] the Persian *aushek* referred to by Chodzko[46] and the Armenian *ashough* mentioned by Hoogasian-Villa.[47]

The minstrels accompany themselves on an instrument. Since their works contain many Persian words, it is believed that they were influenced more by Asian sources than by European. The fact that their style is prosimetric indicates that there was probably an Indian influence as well, brought to the area by the spread of Buddhism. However, these minstrels do parallel very closely those in medieval Spain and France.

The epics these minstrels performed in more recent times were not the same as those composed and recited for nobles at a court or for a ceremonial meeting of a religious or shamanistic group. Such epics are known to have existed in these areas in the past, and they were probably entirely in verse, much like the Homeric epics. Or, if they are in prosimetric style, it means they were probably influenced by Buddhism. The epic of King Kesar and his wars against the Turkish tribes of Central Asia is a good example. It was still being performed in Tibet during the first half of this century. The recital took from three to ten days, and the bard who sang it was often a professional who wore a most impressive costume: a high pointed white hat adorned with images of the sun and the moon and a white coat. The presentation was made even more effective by the use of a painted image of important moments in the life of King Kesar which the bard pointed to at regular intervals. The story of the epic had both European and Asian elements, and some scholars concluded it had its origins among Turkish tribes of Central Asia.[48]

The newer minstrel epics, on the contrary, were and occasionally still are performed for ordinary people in tea or coffee houses, at weddings, and in public places in small towns and villages. Their format and style are different from the Russian and Serbo-Croatian epics. The Turkish, Azerbaijani, and Armenian minstrels can introduce improvisations to both the prose and poetry segments of the epic. Sometimes the epics are performed in their entirety; at other times only segments are recited.

Kazakh bards are called either *aqyn* or *dsyrsy*. The terms are virtually synonymous. They improvise songs and epics as well as reciting those they have collected from already existing sources. They are among the performers appearing at the *ajtys*, a kind of singing competition that used to be part of every large Kazakh celebration. Like the eisteddfod in Wales, the *ajtys* is kept alive in modern times by certain national groups. Other activities at the *ajtys* include wrestling, horse races and games. On such occasions, however, the bards do not perform recitations of previously composed epics, because the *ajtys* is totally spontaneous. It is a kind of singing duel in which the words, but not the tunes, have to be improvised on the spot, with one party starting the verse, and the other party alternating. Amateurs can also take part and, if they perform well, they can eventually become professionals.[49]

A similar custom used to be common among peoples living on the Arabian peninsula. There, a poetic duel, called *riddiyyih*, is exchanged by the two poets, with the audience clapping hands to keep time with them. Many of these poems are lyric rather than narrative in nature, but once the poet has learned to master the performance techniques, he is expected to give a prose narrative introduction to the poem, a kind of story prelude.[50]

Novice Afghan bards were called *dum*, and when they had succeeded in reaching master status, they were called *ustad*. These bards were, for the most part, people of an Indian caste that had become Islamicized and moved to Afghanistan. They sang to various instruments when performing. In the late nineteenth century, some of the successful ones were known to have become very rich.[51]

The Kirghiz people obviously had a similar bard, for the Chadwicks cite four references to a minstrel called an *akin*. Various travelers and visitors at the courts of Kirghizi sultans in the late nineteenth and early twentieth centuries commented on them.[52]

The Yakuts of eastern Siberia also had bards, but no name or current description could be located for them. Shklovsky gave only a brief account of a woman bard he encountered, who performed at weddings. She may well have been a descendant of a banished *skomorokhi*.[53]

All of these forms of bardic storytelling were probably influenced by early Indian forms. Religious forms of bardic storytelling were very prevalent in India, and when Buddhism began its spread in all directions out of India, it was only natural that its unique prosimetric style of oral narration would be noticed wherever the itinerant religious tellers went. Furthermore, the tales they told soon became secularized.

Ancient bardism in India practiced by the *sûta* was almost exclusively religious, but modern forms are both religious and secular. Some of them are a curious mixture of both. Many of them use pictures, music and other adjuncts to their storytelling. These aspects are covered in greater detail in Chapters 11 and 12.

There were and still are so many bardic groups in India that this short review can only highlight a few of them. For example, in Gujarat alone, there are eighteen castes listed as bardic. Some kept written records and others used only oral memory as their source of material. Scholars have occasionally used this material for the reconstruction of periods of Indian history.[54] Shah and Shroff describe a few of these castes in some detail. The Bhats and Carans performed all types of bardic material, and folktales as well. They kept no written records. The Vahivancas, on the other hand, did and still do keep written records, which are used as memory aids in the recitation of a particular family history.[55]

The Bengali *kathak*, or reciter, was not the exact equivalent of the Greek *rhapsode* because he often interspersed his own comments or additions among the couplets of classic text that he might have memorized. Depending on his audience, he might add a local folktale, or a popular legend, or even a bit of vulgar humor. The religious, spiritual and philosophical aspects of the text on which he was supposed to comment were often left out, if he felt they would not be understood by his listeners. In fact, it is not at all unlikely that the prosimetric style was born of this practice. Bards were expected to perform the oral epics, such as the *Ramayana* and the *Mahabharata* or segments of the *Puranas*, by rote in verse form; however, like humans in that situation in many parts of the world, they probably could not resist putting in their own comments, which would have been easier to do in prose format. The more successful they were in adding material of appeal to the public, the more they would have been likely to continue the practice. Yet their public would probably have felt cheated if they had not heard at least a part of what sounded like the original epic in verse. This was what gave the performance legitimacy.

The *kalamkari* bards of Andhra Pradesh in southeastern India straddle both religious and secular types. They carry their large cloths, spread them out, and then narrate in epic form the *Ramayana* or portions of the *Mahabharata*. The pictorial images of the gods and heroes are believed to be sacred, and in many cases, a necessary part of the performance. Of course, they also help as memory aids and as devices to attract and hold an audience. Narration is in the vernacular languages.[56]

The *par* are scrolls telling mostly secular tales of heroes from various regions of Rajasthan. They are used by *bhopo* or *bhopi*, male or female bards who find patrons to buy the scrolls from the artist families that produce them. The hero may have different names, but he looks much the same in many of the scrolls. A typical narrative will cover his birth, his adventures as a young man, his marriage, his fight with an enemy, and his eventual death.[57]

In Bengal the term for such a storytelling cloth or scroll is *pat*; its content is almost always related to the *Ramayana*, but not the traditional classic version of Valmiki. Rather, the *patuas* (the artists who produce the scrolls) have passed down for generations their own oral versions of some of the segments of the *Ramayana*. Like the *kathaks*, they are very free in their interpretation of the texts.

Other bards of present-day India include those who perform with musical accompaniment and choral speaking groups to echo their refrains. Many of these performances are part of religious ritual and are described in Chapter 3.

Chinese bards of the past included the *tze-ti*. They performed in wealthy homes during the Ch'ing dynasty (1641–1911 C.E.) only for the honor of doing so and never for remuneration.[58] They sometimes were accepted into the storytellers' guilds or schools and came under their protection.[59] Although a considerable number of the storytellers in these guilds, in China and Japan, could possibly be termed bardic because of the type of stories they narrated, they will be discussed together with other theatrical guild storytellers in Chapter 5.

Barbara Ruch, who has written an interesting study of the medieval *jongleurs* of Japan, believes that one must call their literature "vocal" as distinct from "oral." This is because the performances were based on written texts. The audiences for these performances ranged from scholar-aristocrats to illiterate beggars.[60] There were picture-reciting bards, both religious and secular. There were *goze*, women (often blind) who played the *tsuzumi* and chanted long narratives. There were other religious bards (see Chapter 3) and secular bards like the *biwa-hoshi*, blind narrators who played a lute called the *biwa* and told the long narratives that gradually evolved into such classics as *Heike monogatari, Hogen monogatari, Heiji monogatari*, and others.[61] This last-named group in the latter half of the fourteenth century formed a guild known as *Todoza*; members were classified into four groups, from beginner to master.[62]

An unusual form of bardism in Japan was practiced by the Ainu, a light-skinned people who live in the northern part of the islands, and who are quite distinct racially from all other peoples in the region. Their language is unrelated to Japanese and Chinese. Their epics were recited sometimes by women, more often by men. The occasions could be connected with religious ceremonies, while waiting for a fish to bite, or around a fireside at home on winter nights. In other words, they practiced all-purpose bardism! How ancient this practice is one can only speculate, since the best-known epic was not written down until the 1920s, and Wakarpa, the bard who recited it, knew only that he had learned it from his predecessor. It is in the first person, which is the case for Ainu folktales as well.[63]

The Achehnese (or Achinese) of the island of Sumatra had epic poetry that concerned both ancient and more modern heroes. By 1900, the public recitation of these epics was rare. Yet new ones were still being composed at that time, so it was possible to document how such heroic poems came into being:

> Some one man, who . . . knows by heart the classic descriptions of certain events and situations as expressed in verse by peoples of olden times, but whose knowledge . . . is somewhat greater than that of others; . . . who is endowed, besides, with a good memory and enthusiasm . . . puts his powers to the test by celebrating in verse the great events of more recent years. . . . The events of which he sings have not yet reached their final development, so he keeps on adding, as occasion rises, fresh episodes to the poem.[64]

Snouck Hurgronje shows a photo of Dōkarim, a bard whom he observed and studied at great length, as he went about the process of composing and refining an epic poem having to do with the wars against the Dutch.[65]

## Bards in the Pacific Islands

Throughout Melanesia, Micronesia, and Polynesia there have been, and in a few cases still are, performers of a bardic nature. The Polynesians have an especially rich history of such epic styles. As Katherine Luomala has stated, they "had a name for every narrative and poetic form, and each had its proper time and place."[66] The Maori of New Zealand had the most complex of all Polynesian narrative epics. In a sense, every mother had to be a bard because she was expected to sing *oriori*, lullabies and songs full of historical allusions, so her children, while still young, could learn about their ancestors.[67] The Samoans were famous for their "talking chiefs" who were skilled in composing and reciting traditions, genealogies, myths and legends.[68] The *tohunga*, common to most parts of Polynesia, must be considered more a religious storyteller than a secular bard because of the sacred nature of his training and responsibilities in ritual.

Among the Melanesians, too, there were bards, apparently similar to the Samoan "talking chiefs." The Marandas reported that Timoti Bobongi, chief of a clan in the Solomon Islands, "is an acknowledged singer of tales and is often invited to sing myths in the memorial feasts. . . . He has also mastered genres other than myth and is a competent performer of songs."[69] Some of these songs had all of the characteristics of epics.

Mitchell states that, on the whole, "Micronesia lacks the complex mythologies found in Polynesia."[70] Nevertheless, there was the *sou fòs*, the person skilled in narrating *uruwo*, legend or history. *Uruwo* was often chanted in a special language, called *itang*, and had to be learned exactly.[71] These are some of the characteristics of bardic material.

## Native American Bards

Durán gave us a picture of Aztec bards that could apply to almost any of the preceding peoples mentioned in this chapter.

> All these had their singers who composed chants about their own glorious deeds and those of their ancestors. . . . In their kingdoms songs had been composed describing their feats, victories, conquests, genealogies, and their extraordinary wealth. I have heard these lays sung many a time at public dances, and even though they were in honor of their native lords, I was elated to hear such high praise and notable feats.
>
> *Book of the Gods and Rites*, trans. by Fernando Horcasitas and Doris Heyden[72]

Durán lived and wrote in Mexico in the sixteenth century, less than one hundred years after the arrival of the first Spanish, so it is likely that the Aztec bards were still performing much as they had before the conquest.

The Incas of Peru did not seem to have the praise singer type of bard, but rather the chronicler-historian type. The *amauta* were oral specialists who decided what oral history was to be taught and which episodes of each Inca ruler's past were to be popularized and remembered. They were also involved in the selection and training of the *quipu-kamayoq*, the professional interpreters and reciters of the *quipu*,[73] a knotted cord that served as a memory device for historical traditions as well as being used for an accounting system (fig. 8).

## African Bards

It is in Africa that one encounters the richest variety of bards for the post-medieval period. There is disagreement as to whether many of the performers are truly bardic. Finnegan disputes the use of the term "epic" to describe most of the praise songs or chronicles of African heroes. She finds little that is both narrative and epic.[74] Jordan does not express the belief that there are no bards, but simply states that the African performers have no exact parallels in classical or modern Western societies.[75]

Mafeje, Biebuyck, Okpewho, Opland, and others, on the contrary, present fairly convincing arguments to show that there are African bards who are not very different from those in Celtic or classical history.[76] Their functions, their social position, and the content of their performances are all similar to those of early Anglo-Saxon, Teutonic and Celtic bards.

Regarding the Nyanga people of the Congo Republic, Biebuyck points out the differences between *muşínjo*, their praise recitations for chiefs or headmen given on state occasions, and the *kárışı*, their true epics. The former are recited without any musical accompaniment and are relatively short. The latter are first sung, then narrated, usually with rattles, bells, and percussion sticks as background sounds. The bard performs the *kárışı* in episodes, rarely narrating the entire epic

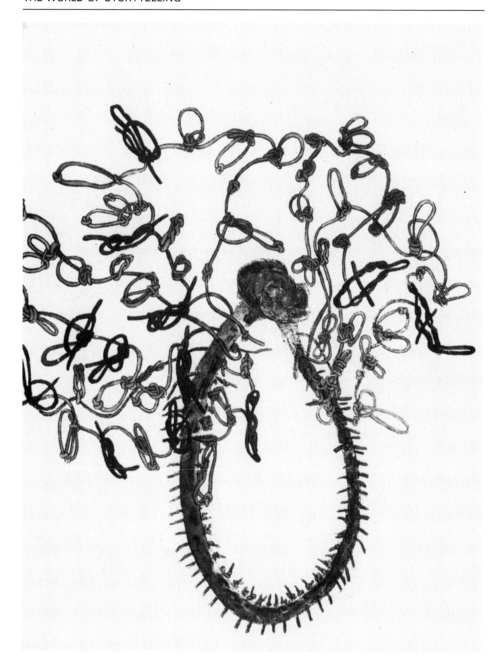

**Figure 8**  Quipu *knotted in such a way that it could be used as a memory aid by historical narrators of the Incas of Peru. Reproduced from Lord Kingsborough,* Antiquities of Mexico. . . . *(London: Robert Havell, 1831), vol. 4. Photo courtesy of Library of Congress.*

at one time, but sometimes it is done on consecutive evenings. The bard receives only very small amounts of money for this service, but often accepts food and beer for himself and his assistants. For the bard, the act of reciting the epic has some religious significance, but the audience would generally consider the session a socially uplifting and entertaining experience rather than a religious one.[77]

The situation is essentially the same for the Lega, a neighboring people in the area. For them, the epic is called *lugano*. The bard is called *mugani wa lugano*.[78]

The *imbongi* of the Xhosa in South Africa is a self-appointed bard, but he could not remain so if he did not reflect in his poetry the feelings, aspirations, and interests of the group from which he comes and for whom he performs. His duties are to celebrate victories, chant the laws and customs of the nation, recite the genealogies of the royal families, and criticize the abuse of power or neglect of responsibility on the part of a chief or ruler. Mafeje recorded a modern bard of this type as he composed and performed his account of the history and politics of the Xhosa and the South African government.[79] Opland examined all available material on living and deceased bards of this type, and describes in some detail the performance techniques and style they had in common, and the ways in which they can be compared to European bards. Traditionally, this bard wears a cloak and hat of animal skins and brandishes one or two knobbed sticks or spears.[80]

In Rwanda and Burundi, Vansina found as many different types of oral narratives and performers as Luomala found in Polynesia. Burundi mothers, just like Maori mothers, sing lullabies that border on the bardic, they are so full of references to family history.[81] Once a month, at the new moon, it was customary to publicly perform *ncyeem ingesh*, dynastic songs. Artistic, historical narratives called *ncok* are sung while persons who are about to take part in a masked dance are getting dressed and decorated.[82]

In Rwanda, there are both oral dynastic poems of a family nature and warriors' epic poems. It was the *abateekerezi* who had the tasks of composing, memorizing, and chanting the most important events of each reign, while the *abacurabwenge* added to and memorized the genealogies and other historical tales. The *abasizi* were similar to *rhapsodes*, reciting from memory the praise poems of earlier poets.[83]

The Swahili *utenzi*, a long epic-like poem, is now a literary genre, but it was once composed and recorded through oral means for entertainment and inspiration.[84] It usually treated of the deeds of Moslem heroes, but more recently some *utenzi* were composed and recited on such occasions as the inauguration of the first presidents of the newly independent nations of East Africa. These *utenzi* naturally celebrated the lives of these new heroes.[85]

Because of the great amount of travel by explorers and missionaries into the region of the Baganda, their bards were described in detail quite early in British reports. Speke and Roscoe both gave verbal pictures that seem quite explicit:

> I found him [the chief] sitting on the ground with several elders; whilst Wasoga minstrels played on their lap-harps, and sang songs in praise of their king . . . and the noble stranger who wore fine clothes. . . .[86]
>
> The old harp used at the court of the King and the chiefs used to be accompanied by songs belauding the King's power and benevolence, praising him and belittling his enemies. The words were made to fit the tunes at a moment's notice, and were suited to passing events. . . . The older and more popular songs were the traditions and legends of the nation, sung in a minor key.[87]

The Baganda lost their kingdom in the twentieth century, and bardic singing among them went into a decline. But there were bardic performances still in recent times in Uganda. Morris describes the *omwevugi*, a praise poet he encountered who recited in the Runyankore language.[88]

In West Africa there are many epic bards and there are hunters' bards. The latter are performers whose original function was to prepare and accompany groups of hunters in order to bring them good luck in their search for game. The hunters' groups are now largely symbolic, but still quite active in social and cultural contexts. The chief occasion on which their bards perform for them— for the Yoruba groups, particularly—is the annual celebration of the Ogun festival.[89] This falls sometime in the dry season between December and April. Each compound or village in which the hereditary members of the hunters' groups live decides on its own appropriate days for celebration. Other times when the bards are asked to perform are for the wake of a deceased member, for a housewarming, to celebrate a new farm purchase, or for a child-naming or marriage ceremony. The latter two occasions are now used by the general public, even those not members of the hunters' groups, as a time for inviting the bards to perform, simply for aesthetic satisfaction and enjoyment. The bards themselves are rarely members of the hunters' groups, and their office is not hereditary. In Yoruba, the bard is called *oníjàlá*, and the narratives are called *ijálá*.[90] In the Mande language, the bard is called a *donso-jeli*, partly after the six-stringed instrument with which he accompanies himself.[91] The training of these hunters' bards is fairly lengthy and is described in more detail in Chapter 14. Some aspects of their performance style are discussed in Chapter 10.

The epic bards are known by a score or more of names throughout present-day West Africa, but the most commonly recognized term for them is *griot*. This is especially true since the appearance of the book *Roots* by Alex Haley, based in part on the recitations of a modern *griot* from Gambia. Other terms for the *griot* include *gêwel*, *gawlo*, *īggīw* (male) and *tīggiwīt* (female), *diaré*, and *mbom mvet*. Charles Bird discusses the fine differences between the epic bard and the hunters' bard in West Africa.[92] The chief difference is the fact that the epic bard is generally a hereditary type, while the hunters' bard is not. For some reason, Mafeje did not recognize or take note of this point, because he wrote that one of the differences between Celtic bards and those of modern Africa was that the latter are never hereditary.[93] In South Africa, the situation with which Mafeje was most familiar, these are not inherited positions; but in West Africa the entire group of epic bards receives its training and social position solely through inherited means. In fact, among the Malinke, these *griots* belong to a special caste, and cannot marry outside it. Some scholars speculated that this caste of *griots* were descended from Jews who had settled in Mali in ancient times.[94] These West African bards satisfy all the conditions Mafeje cited as necessary in order to be called bards. And like the South African *imbongi*, the *īggīw*, *tīggiwīt*, and *diaré* had a right to say what they liked with impunity.[95]

It is curious that one can find female epic bards among the Saharan and Sahelian peoples. In spite of the fact that most of these peoples are Islamic, the women bards always perform in public, to mixed audiences:

> He who loves to listen, goes to them in their homes, and they sing to him, both their male and their female, their youth and their elder, and not one of them has any feeling of embarrassment in front of the other.[96]

This custom probably was inherited from pre-Islamic times. In Mauritania, for example, the musicians' families are so ancient in lineage that they can usually be traced back to time before the arrival of Islam. In fact, most of the hereditary bards of this region are a mixture of early Arab, Berber, and Sudanic cultures, and the Islamic tradition for them is relatively recent.

In Ethiopia, which has both Sudanic and Coptic cultural influences, there were a group of professional minstrels called *azmaris* who sang, danced, told tales and did improvisations, usually to a one-stringed instrument called the *leqso*. They can be compared to the *skomorokhi* of Russia, or the medieval minstrels of Europe. The subjects of their songs were usually contemporary events or the personal history and background of someone prominent in their audience. The songs were usually complimentary, but were sometimes outrageous or even offensive. *Azmaris* date back to at least the sixteenth century, when they were attached to courts much as were the early minstrels of Europe.[97]

There was a female type of bard in Ethiopia, similar to the *azmari*, but called a *mungerash*. A French musicologist recorded a vivid picture of one in the 1920s:

> There is one in Abyssinia named Tadigê, renowned in court and city . . . she was much sought after . . . she took part in official ceremonies on horseback, letting her long blue mantle flow behind her on the wind, while with an excited gesture she would accentuate the war songs or the praise songs in honor of Menelik and his illustrious guests.[98]

Both the *azmari* and the *mungerash* were known to have rather loose reputations, yet their social position was often stronger than it might have appeared outwardly because people feared their power to criticize.[99]

Among the Arabic-speaking peoples there is also disagreement as to whether they possess a truly bardic literature. The *siyar* (sing. *al-sira*) are legendary biographies of pre-Islamic poet warriors, Bedouin knights, princes, and tribes. According to Connelly, a fairly typical attitude is that the long, sung *siyar* still extant are "coarse vulgarities, ignorant of authorship, anonymous, wretched in language and style, a register of the conditions of the vulgar, deprived of color and literary splendor."[100]

Connelly does not agree with this and believes this attitude has developed over the years because of the general suppression of fiction, oral story, music, and representational art on religious, social, and political grounds.[101] In her study of the performers of one epic in Egypt, she attempts to show that the *siyar* may be composed and performed by and for the folk, rather than the elite, but they are epics in every sense of the word, although not the exact counterparts of medieval *chansons de geste*, to which they are frequently compared. They are their own unique form of epic, orally transmitted, with extensive use of formulaic language, and performed to the accompaniment of a *rabab*.

This brief survey of bardism throughout the world has probably omitted many types, for there was neither time nor space to trace each and every bardic group. Appropriately, the survey ends in Egypt, where, as mentioned, some of the earliest pictorial depictions of the bard are to be found. Bardic storytelling seems to be the type that succumbs soonest in areas that become attached to and dependent on the printed word. It remains to be seen whether these last performing groups of bardic tellers will survive or not.

# CHAPTER 3

# *Religious Storytelling*

Religious storytelling is that storytelling used by official or semi-official functionaries, leaders, and teachers of a religious group to explain or promulgate their religion through stories, rather than exclusively through memorization of laws, scripture, catechisms and the like. Such storytelling employs at least a few elements that are dramatic and entertaining, so as to capture and hold the interest of the audience. It does not include the telling of religious tales by ordinary folk in everyday, non-ritualistic situations. Some readers might find this definition unnecessarily narrow, since a religion cannot be separated easily from the mass of common people who practice it; and their ways of interpreting their religious belief and passing it on often have as much effect on the survival of religious practices as those methods dictated by the leaders or hierarchy of the religion. Some would even go so far as to say that the validity of the interpretations of common folk is equal to or greater than that of orthodox religious authorities. However, to include in this chapter a discussion of storytelling in what is often called "folk religion" would necessitate covering such a range of differing opinions and theories that there would be little space left for the orthodox points of view. Therefore, such folk religious storytelling is mentioned only in passing here, and is covered in the chapter on folk storytelling.

## Hindu Storytelling

In the Hindu religion, the *Brahmanas* are prose commentaries explaining the relationship between the Vedas (the most ancient sacred texts) and the ceremonies that had grown up around the early rituals of this religion. Although at first they were not considered as sacred revelation, in time they came to be regarded as such. In the *Brahmanas*, there are many myths and a large number of stories. Eggeling, one of the scholar-translators of these texts, believed that many of the stories were "invented by the authors ... for the purpose of supplying some kind of traditional support for particular points of ceremonial. ... The style of the narrative and the archaic mode of diction which they affect, readily lend themselves to syntactic turns of expression rarely indulged in by the authors in the purely explanatory or exegetic parts of their works."[1]

In other words, as in so many cases both ancient and modern, the orally told story had the ability to engage the interest of the listener and to express symbolic meaning in a readily understandable way. It was seized on as a logical device to use in the promulgation of religion. The orality of some of the narratives survives in many of the written sacred texts. The stories attached to certain ceremonials in the Hindu religion (such as the marriage ceremony) remain in use up to the present day. Sometimes they are used in word-for-word memorized style, and sometimes the core events and motifs are reworked by the teller. Although many were first written down approximately 500 B.C.E., it is likely they are much, much older.

But the elite Brahmin caste was not the only one to have its popular interpretations of the Vedas. For the ordinary mass of people there were recitations of *itihâsas* (ancient tales) and *puranas*. The *puranas* are "legends and annals of ancient times, as well as allegories and stories seeking to present the deeper truths of Indian religion in a popular garb. ..."[2] There are eighteen of them, and the *Vishnu Purana* is one of the most widely recognized. It opens with a hymn of praise, and then the narrator states that he will give an account of the origin of the world. Following praise and description of Vishnu as the creator, comes the appearance of various forms (spirit, time, matter, visible substance) and principles (nature, intellect, etc.).

> Intellect and the rest ... formed an egg, which gradually expanded like a bubble of water. This vast egg ... compounded of the elements and resting on the waters, was the excellent natural abode of Vishnu in the form of Brahma; and there Vishnu, the lord of the universe, whose essence is inscrutible, assumed a perceptible form, and even he himself abided in it in the character of Brahma. Its womb, vast as the mountain Meru, was composed of the mountains; and the mighty oceans were the waters that filled its cavity. In that egg ... were the continents and seas and mountains, the planets and divisions of the universe, the gods, the demons and mankind. And this egg was externally invested by seven natural envelopes, or by water, air, fire, ether, and Ahankara, the origin of the elements ... next came the principle of Intelligence; and finally, the whole was surrounded by the indiscrete Principle: resembling thus the coco-nut, filled interiorly with pulp, and exteriorly covered by husk and rind.[3]

The scholar Raghavan states that according to the preface of all the *itihâsas* and *puranas*, they were told "to vast congregations of people ... by a class of reciters called *suta-pauranikas*." He continues by stating that "evidence of numerous inscriptions establishes the fact of continuity of this practice ... all through the course of Indian history."[4]

According to Raghavan, "there developed, in later historical periods, centers of spiritual endeavor called *mathas*, which were originally natural habitations in the form of mountain caves . . . , but were later enlarged into structural buildings." These *mathas* were the site for much religious storytelling.[5] It may well be that the artist of the drawing in figure 9 was attempting to depict a *matha*.

In the state of Kerala, in southwestern India, a caste known as *chakkiyars* had as its special duties the narration of *itihasas* and *puranas*. This was always done in temples or in the *kuttumbalam*, a special building outside the temple. The dramatic and serious performance was sometimes interspersed with amiable criticism of officials present in the audience, who were required to take the chaffing in silence.[6]

Vyasa, the generic name given to the "composer" of the epic *Mahabharata* (c. 600–300 B.C.E.), opens one of the early segments by stating that this work was intended to introduce the Vedas to the people. The same could be said of the sage Valmiki, who composed the *Ramayana* (c. 300–200 B.C.E.). These two great epics form the substance of much of the religious storytelling practiced in India down through the ages.

Pictures were sometimes used to accompany the telling of these religious tales in ancient India. Some of the first references to such storytelling are not too clear, so we can only speculate as to how it was done, and why the use of pictures should be added to oral narrative. Some of the later descriptions, however, give us a very good idea of at least one type of religious picture storyteller. Some Brahmanical teachers used a portable frame or scroll on which were drawn very graphic pictures showing what would happen if one did this good deed or that evil one. The more popular of these tellers were called *yamapattaka*, for they used a picture or scroll dominated by Yama, God of the Underworld. Here is how the seventh century (C.E.) poet Bana describes such a teller as he performs in a marketplace:

> . . . in the bazaar street amid a great crowd of inquisitive children he observed a *yamapattaka*, in whose left hand was a painted canvas stretched out on a support of upright rods and showing the lord of the dead mounted on his dreadful buffalo. Wielding a reed-wand in his other hand, he was expounding the features of the next world. . . .[7]

Some game historians speculate that the performance pictures of the Brahmanical teachers and the *yamapattaka* evolved into individual teaching pictures and eventually into the game of *Snakes and Ladders*. However, the *yamapattaka* performers continued their work even into the nineteenth and twentieth century. They obviously had mass appeal, despite the moralistic tone that was probably used in telling stories to match the scenes depicted.

The scholar Coomaraswamy cites many references to early Indian manuscripts and printed works that refer to picture storytelling.[8] Many of the short descriptions he located in ancient sources could easily be used to describe as well the modern Indian storytellers who wander about their districts, reciting and illustrating their narratives with cloths, scrolls, wooden panels, palm-leaf books, picture sheets and the like. A large percentage of these performances are part of religious ritual.

Typical of such ritual use are the Saurashtra temple cloths, *mata ni pachedi*, used exclusively in worship to honor the Mother Goddess. Joan Erickson gives an explanation of the long process by which these cloths are made. They usually contain images of the Mother Goddess surrounded by groups of worshipers, other gods, animals, warriors, hunters, and many symbols of one kind or

**Figure 9** *Reproduction of a painting from the Kanora school, India, which is probably a representation of Valmiki, teaching the Vedas or reciting a segment from the* Ramayana. *Picture courtesy of New York Public Library, Picture Collection.*

another, calling to mind the myths and legends associated with that particular Mother Goddess. These cloths are painted by artists working in guild-like groups, but the narration of the stories in them is done by others.[9]

Hindu and Buddhist scriptures were often written on palm-leaf books, and these were frequently illustrated with narrative scenes (fig. 10). There is still disagreement as to which of these types were designed for use in storytelling, but it is likely that those books with the pictures on the front and the texts on the back were used in recitations or picture storytelling. The texts on the reverse of these picture sets are most often excerpts, rather than entire scriptural passages, indicating that they may have been used as memory aids. A large sculptural relief from Sri Lanka, dating from approximately the twelfth century (C.E.), shows a sage reading or reciting from one of these palm-leaf books.[10]

Palm-leaf books are still an integral part of the performance of oral story poems recited by performers in certain rituals in Tamil Nadu, at the very southern tip of India. The narratives of these bow-song performers are inserted into, and become an integral part of, a three-day ritual festival held sometime between January and May, and honoring the special gods and goddesses worshiped by the particular community organizing the festival (fig. 11). Blackburn has given us an excellent description of all aspects of the festival, and the performances that take place. An unusual aspect is that the palm-leaf manuscripts, written down by bards one or two hundred years ago, are deemed a necessary part of the ritual. "A performance is thought to successfully summon deities only when their stories are accurately presented, and palm-leaf manuscripts are considered the most authentic form of a story."[11] The manuscripts may not be directly used in the performance, but they at least must be placed on the platform to show authenticity. Newer, printed versions on paper are not considered

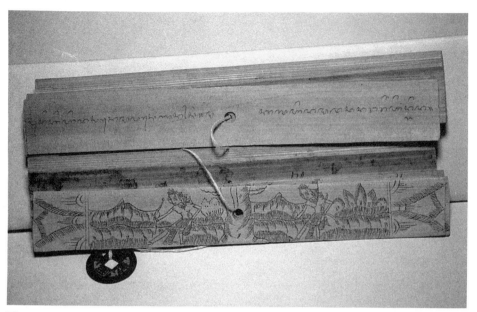

**Figure 10**  *Palm-leaf picture book with text and illustrations related to a segment of the* Ramayana; *purchased in Bali, 1969. Photo by Michael Gabrick and Chris Nickrant.*

an adequate substitute, even though they might be exact copies of palm-leaf manuscripts.[12]

Some story cloths used by *dakkalwars* in Maharashtra depict the Basawa version of *Purana* myths.[13] Certain *kalamkari* cloths of the Andhra region show scenes from the *Ramayana*, or sequences from the stories associated with such gods as Krishna and Ganesh (see figure 38).[14] The *par* are long horizontal cloths with scenes of epics related to deities and heroes. They are used as the center of performances by bards who recite in a chant, while dancing and accompanying themselves on a stringed instrument. Further aspects of these performances are mentioned in Chapter 2 and Chapter 12 because they can be considered bardic or folkloric in character, but there is an element of religious ritual to them as well. The cloths are handled as sacred objects.[15]

Victor Mair, in his search for the roots of Chinese picture storytelling, has examined much of the evidence related to scrolls, temple paintings and other early pictures in Asia that were associated with storytelling. He concludes that it was in India that such storytelling began, most likely as part of Hindu ritual. His book, *Painting and Performance*, reproduces a few examples from earlier centuries as well as some from recent times.

## Jain Storytelling

Jainism arose in approximately the same era as Buddhism. Jains believe that Gosāla Maṅkhaliputra (c. 500 B.C.E.), a leader of a related sect, was a *mankha*, or picture showman. *Mankha* were similar to the *yamapattaka* in that they also showed pictures of the delights of heaven and the sufferings of hell.[16] Victor Mair gives an extensive quotation from a Jain novel of 779 C.E., indicating the

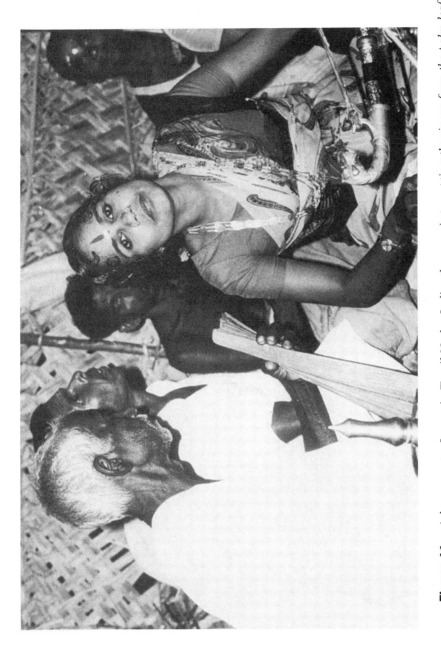

**Figure 11**    *A bow-song performer in Tamil Nadu, India; the guru is prompting the singer from the palm-leaf manuscript. Only the tip of the bow is visible.    Reproduced with permission from* Singing of Birth and Death *by Stuart H. Blackburn (Philadelphia: University of Pennsylvania Press, 1988).*

manner in which these picture scrolls were used for narration, as well as an example of one of the stories told.[17]

## Sikh Storytelling

Religious storytelling for the Sikh people occurs mostly on the great religious festivals commemorating the birth or death of one or another of the gurus honored by the Sikhs as their founders and early martyrs. On those days, it is customary to invite religious bards into the *gurdvara* (Sikh temple) to recite or chant the stories related to the lives of the gurus. Sometimes, religious meetings are organized to coordinate with the great cattle fairs, which bring many rural and village people into the towns. There is invariably a *dhadhi* (bard) performing one or another of the texts related to the gurus, or sermons by recognized religious leaders.[18]

## Buddhist Storytelling

Siddhartha Gautama, the founder of Buddhism, was born into a high Hindu caste, so it is likely that he was thoroughly familiar with Vedic ceremonials and the stories attached to them. Therefore, it is not surprising that the use of storytelling as a means of proselytizing would become a part of Buddhism as well. Furthermore, the very nature of certain beliefs in Hinduism and Buddhism, such as their emphasis on rebirths and former lives, seems to encourage narrative.

*Tathâgata* is another name for the Buddha, meaning "He who has come" in Sanskrit. In one of the sacred texts of Mahayana Buddhism, there is this passage:

> I am the *Tathâgata*, o ye gods and men! . . . and the *Tathâgata* who knows the difference as to the faculties and energy of those beings, produces various *Dharmaparyâyas*, tells many tales, amusing, agreeable, both instructive and pleasant, tales by means of which all beings not only become pleased with the law in this present life, but also after death will reach happy states. . . . Therefore, Kâsyapa, I will tell thee a parable, for men of good understanding will generally readily enough catch the meaning of what is taught under the shape of a parable.[19]

Several hundred years after the death of the Buddha, when Theravada Buddhism was well established, a treatise composed for the purpose of explaining further some of its beliefs and practices questioned rhetorically:

> Why do the brethren concern themselves with recitation of, with asking questions about the discourses, and the pieces in mixed prose and verse, and the expositions, and the poems and the outbursts of emotion, and the passages beginning "Thus he said," and the birth-stories, and the tales of wonder, and the extended treatises?[20]

The answer was, simply, because "recitation was a good thing." In many parts of Asia, these Buddhist stories are so intertwined with their Hindu antecedents that it is impossible to say which is stronger or richer in narrative tradition. It was Buddhism, though, that was the stronger medium of transmission.

In South and Southeast Asia, China, Korea, and Japan, Buddhism made a dramatic impact. The scholar Průšek, for example, translates a section of a Chinese work, dating from 1235 C.E., in this manner:

. . . those narrating scriptures, which means the unfolding and narrating of Buddhist books; those speaking of visits and invitations, which means things like guests and [their] patrons, meditation and enlightenment.[21]

In 1279 C.E., in almost the exact same words, another Chinese work describes the storytellers who tell in the same manner, and then goes on to speak of "narrators of funny or humorous scriptures."[22] Průšek does not come to any firm conclusion but does speculate that there were probably storytellers of at least two types in the early centuries of Buddhist penetration in China: one type that memorized and recited stories from existing Buddhist and Hindu scriptures and another type that created original works, based on some of the religious themes of Buddhist tales but heavily influenced by secular stories.[23]

A student of Průšek, Věna Hrdličková, delved further into this question. According to her conclusions, the gradual development of storytelling from sermons in the temple to stories in the marketplace occurred in the time from the later Han dynasty to the beginning of the T'ang (approximately 200–700 C.E.). Sutras with an entirely religious content would be recited in a sermon, using the translated texts that provided only the core words. There was a strict form for this. The monk-preacher took his place on a raised platform, paid respects to Buddha, and sang or chanted an introductory hymn. The recitation of the sutra followed, then another hymn, a closing obeisance to Buddha, and finally, with great dignity, the preacher descended the platform.[24]

Gradually these performances were enriched with descriptions and illustrations from daily life, in which the preachers used their own words. These changes probably occurred as a response to questions from the audience. This was, after all, a new religious system to most of the listeners.

Průšek and Hrdličková confined most of their discussions to the texts used by these storytellers, and they did not comment much on the pictures that accompanied the texts. Sometimes these sequences of pictures were on scrolls, palm-leaf books, or in folded-up manuscripts, and the texts were either on the back or at the side of the pictures; in other instances the pictures were completely separate from the texts; in still other cases, picture narratives were drawn directly on temple walls, and core words were sometimes scripted below or above them. Arthur Waley, a translator of many of the texts, was inclined to believe that the teller did not necessarily show the pictures to the audience during narration.[25]

This does not explain why many of these formats still exist today, in various parts of India, precisely for professional performers to use in the telling of stories from the Hindu epics. And the small wooden *kavads* (fig. 12), found in many devout Hindu homes, are likely to be used in an informal way to tell the portions of the *Ramayana* and other texts that pertain to the moral values the parents and grandparents wish to convey.

Victor Mair, as has been mentioned, has shown quite convincingly that the pictures were a natural adjunct to certain forms of Hindu storytelling in India, and Buddhism expanded the use of these forms and carried them through much of Asia.[26]

The general consensus among scholars is that both the art and the literature of virtually all areas of Asia were influenced in some way by Buddhism. Buddhist teaching through storytelling was directed at the masses, and this helped to bring about the use of vernacular literatures. The scholar Demiéville summarizes:

**Figure 12** *A wooden kavad from Rajasthan, India, depicting scenes from the Ramayana. The size when closed is approximately three inches wide by seven inches high. Photo courtesy of Ruth Stotter.*

> The earliest dated work of vernacular literature [in Chinese], in the middle of the 8th century, is a fictionalized amplification of a famous episode of the Buddhist legend, which lent itself to dramatic effects and also to figured representation.[27]

> Another specific feature of Indian literature which was to be adopted as a regular feature in the Chinese . . . was the mixture of prose and verse. The stories liberally included in their scriptures by the Indians, who are born storytellers, contributed to the development of literature in China.[28]

Demiéville is referring to the Chinese only, but the statements could fit equally well a number of other Asian countries influenced by Buddhism in much the same way.

In Japan the Buddhist inclination to use pictures as an adjunct of storytelling caused a revolutionary change in literature, especially performance literature, in the middle ages. This will be covered in further detail in Chapter 12. Here it is pertinent to refer only to the religious variants of this picture storytelling. The *etoki hoshi* or picture-telling priests emerged in the twelfth century, probably in emulation of their Chinese counterparts. *Hoshi* generally refers to a person of relatively low social rank who was attached to a temple or shrine and performed religious or semireligious ceremonies there.[29] *Etoki* refers to a process of "picture explaining," generally of a series of related pictures depicted in a mural or on a scroll. There was also a category of traveling missionary *etoki hoshi*, who went out to proselytize and raise funds for their home institution.[30]

The female counterpart of the missionary *etoki hoshi* were *Kumano bikuni*. Not much is known about these nuns who probably originally came from religious centers near the three sacred mountains near Kumano. Some were referred to as *uta bikuni* (singing nuns!) and others as *etoki bikuni* (picture-explaining nuns). Barbara Ruch, who has studied these performers in some detail, believes the figure shown in figure 13 presents a fairly accurate portrait of an early *etoki bikuni*. Note that the picture she is "telling" relates to heaven and hell, much like the Indian *yamapattaka*.[31]

It was the missionary *etoki*, especially the female ones, who did the most in preparing Japan for the commercialization of printing in the following period. They took their stories along in written form and distributed these texts as part of their missionary activity. Thus were spread a number of tales, in the form of booklets, making them a familiar part of everyday life. By the end of the Muromachi period most of these proselytizers had been deprived of their official religious functions. But in the eyes of their public, they still had a magico-religious aura. Ruch points out that "even when their function had become little more than entertainment, the very presence of a *Kumano bikuni* was believed to bring good fortune to a house where she visited."[32]

The secular counterparts of these storytellers are discussed in Chapter 2 and Chapter 12.

Today, one can still find *etoki* performances at temples in Japan. Color plate 6 in Mair's *Painting and Performance* shows a monk at the Dojoji Temple in Wakayama Prefecture in the process of unrolling the scroll as he tells its story.

Modern forms of Buddhism still use the oral story as a teaching and expository device, especially with children. The Jataka tales, relating to the adventures of the Buddha in his former existences, are narrated and read aloud in many printed versions. Since only a few sects of present-day Buddhism have separate, formal religious instruction schools for young children (of the Christian Sunday-

**Figure 13** *A* Kumano bikuni *and her assistant performing* etoki *at a roadside. Detail from a pair of folding screens, "A Festival at the Sumiyoshi Shrine," seventeenth or eighteenth century. Photo No. 00.26 courtesy of Smithsonian Institution, Freer Gallery of Art, Washington, D.C.*

school type or the Islamic Koranic-school type, for example), the use of stories in rituals at shrines and temples and elsewhere, is probably the method through which most Buddhist children first encounter the precepts and moral values of their religion. For those children who enter monasteries for a period of three months or more (generally when they are twelve years or older) the training is more in memorization of texts rather than in storytelling.

## Judaic Storytelling

As has been mentioned in Chapter 1 to this book, the Old Testament contains fragments of stories and legends, but only one description of a storytelling occasion. Gerhardsson is among the many scholars of the Old Testament who believed that once the Judaic texts became relatively fixed, either in oral or written transmissions, the religious authorities placed emphasis on memorization of the Torah and other scriptures. Talmudic literature makes many references to the fact that children were expected to learn to recite the scriptures by heart after reading or hearing them. When interpretive material was added, it was extremely conservative.[33]

A parallel can be drawn with the Greek reciters, known as *rhapsodes*. They were conscientious in their attempts to render Greek epic narratives in the exact words as written down, but they were not creative storytellers who allowed spontaneous changes. It is likely, then, that for orthodox Jewish purposes, storytelling did not serve too well. The nature of creative storytelling is such that it changes with each teller and each telling, and this left too much chance of misinterpretation, in the view of many orthodox religious leaders.

Still, a certain amount of storytelling was acceptable, especially in the reciting of the haggadic portions of the Talmud. As Gerhardsson and others point out, this haggadic material had an advantage over the halakic precisely because it is full of parables and narratives, which are easier to remember.[34] There was usually more leeway given to "free" transmission of such material, because word-for-word memorization was not always required.

In the middle ages of the Common Era, there is evidence that in preaching, some rabbis inserted stories if they fit the theme of the scripture being expounded upon. This was in addition to the stories appearing in the orthodox oral tradition and in the Talmud. Some medieval versions of such "stories within sermons" survive, and Moses Gaster assembled a representative collection in the 1920's. Here is an example, taken from his book:

> R. Akiba used to say, "Whatever God does is done for the best." Once when he was travelling he had with him a lamp, an ass and a cock. Coming to a place where he was refused shelter, he encamped a short distance from the town. The wind came and blew out his lamp but he said, "What God does is done for the best." Then a lion came and devoured his ass. A cat came and strangled the cock. He repeated: "What God does is done for the best." In the morning he came again to the town and found it completely devastated by robbers. He saw how mercifully he had been spared. The light of the lamp, the braying of the ass and the crowing of the cock would have attracted the attention of the robbers.[35]

There have probably been other uses of storytelling in an orthodox Jewish context. The difficulty has been to identify this material. One of Israel's leading folklorists, Dov Noy, pointed out that some Jewish scholars have opposed this type of research, because they believe that "any text or ritual that deviates from the Jewish norm is pagan, and hence does not belong to the domain of Jewish religion."[36] Since the proscriptions are sometimes strong even to the present day, it is likely that some forms of storytelling, even those practiced by recognized orthodox leaders of the Jewish religion in the past, have not been recorded.

In those areas where the Jewish people lived an almost completely oral life because the surrounding culture was also oral, there seems to have been greater use of freely adapted materials, in sermons and in other forms of teaching. Among the Kurdistani Jews, for example, not many were literate. They spoke a form of New-Aramaic, and passed on much of their religious literature in that language, rather than in Hebrew. Many of the homilies used in temples contained material from the Bible and Midrashic texts, but they also used "tales and legends of the life and deeds of the patriarchs, ancient kings and heroes, prophets and rabbis, mystics, and ordinary pious men and women, all carefully selected to fit their particular audience."[37] These were more often told rather than read.

The storytelling tradition of the Hasidic Jews has been well documented and recorded. For them, storytelling is very important. According to Mintz:

> Storytelling won an established place in the life of the earliest hasidim and it became part of the Shabbes ritual. . . . The Rebbes often wove their teachings into an extended metaphor or parable or told an illustrative tale. . . . The telling of tales can be a mystical expression on various levels. To tell tales of the tsaddikim is one means of glorifying the tsaddikim and of contacting their piety and power. . . . In this light, the hasidim believe that tales, like prayers, contain the potential to be active agents.[38]

The Hasidim consciously use storytelling as the best way of introducing their religion and its practices to the children of their communities. Many of the stories used date to the time of their founder, the Rabbi Baal Shem Tov (c. 1700–1760 C.E.), and some of these tales have him as their central character.

In the United States, certain Jewish congregations have used storytelling with organized groups of children. There have even been manuals, like that of Shafter, outlining special methods and sources for the Jewish storyteller.[39] These were generally for Reform Jewish congregations.

Recently, a Jewish Storytelling Center was begun in New York at the YM-YWHA under the leadership of Peninnah Schram.

## Christian Storytelling

Just as the Buddhist religion could and did draw on its rich heritage of Hindu lore, so did the Christian draw on the legends of Judaism. Added to this were the oral versions of the Old Testament and of the gospels.

Gerhardsson writes:

> We must take into account the fact that most of the gospel material is haggadic material and that haggadic material is often transmitted with a somewhat wider margin of variation in wording than halakic material.[40]

He was referring to the fact that many of Christ's teachings are expressed in parable form, rather than in explicit laws or rules to be remembered. Also, he believed, like many other New Testament scholars, that the gospel texts had been written down in much the same form they had come down orally. Werner Kelber, author of *The Oral and the Written Gospel*, disagrees with Gerhardsson to some extent. In his examination of the gospel of Mark, he paid particular attention to the clues that would indicate which portions had been composed and perfected orally and which had been composed by a writer. He believes that there were parts of the gospels based on oral narratives and parts that were composed in written form right from the beginning. His conclusion: "Both in form and content the written gospel constitutes a radical alternative to the oral gospel."[41]

Accumulating along with the stories of the Old and New Testament and other traditions were the orally transmitted stories and legends of early saints and the *exempla*. The *exemplum* is a classic fable or popular anecdote to which has been added a moral, in this case a Christian one. They were used in sermons, much as parables were used by Christ. The oldest known Christian examples occur in the homilies of Saint Gregory the First (c. 600). They probably developed in much the same way that the stories of the Buddhist monks and those of the Jewish rabbis evolved, becoming secular enough in their use of illustrative material that the masses could understand their meaning easily. In the thirteenth and fourteenth centuries, certain monks developed the narration of the *exempla* into an art that was very successful. This was in large measure due to the example set by the Dominicans and by prelates such as Jacques de Vitry, known to have compiled a number of collections of sermons with stories. Here is a typical *exemplum* from one of his sermon books:

> A poor man earned with his own hand a modest living and when day was done sang and rejoiced in his cabin with his wife and then slept happy and secure. His wealthy neighbors, on the contrary, were always immersed in care and anxiety, and never sang. They wondered at the joy of the poor man, and even complained that with his singing he would not let them sleep. One of them, a very rich man, said: "I will make him lose his desire to rejoice and sing." Then after he had concealed the others in a place from which they could see what happened, he threw a bag of money before the poor man's door while he was absent. On his return, the poor man found it and hid it. That night he began to be anxious and careworn, fearing lest the money should be stolen from him, or he should be accused of theft, and did not rejoice or sing with his wife as he was wont to do. After a time the rich man and his neighbors began to ask him what made him so thin and sad. The poor man did not dare, at first, to confess the truth, but after the rich man had told him he knew his secret, the poor man exclaimed: "Take back your money that I may rejoice and sing as I was accustomed to do." [42]

Such narration could compete with other performances to be found at marketplaces, on street corners and at fairs, where the monks collected their share of listeners.[43] However, it was not too long before these performances became totally secular, and incurred the wrath of the church authorities. From then on, they must be considered as folk storytelling rather than religious. However, some sermon books from the thirteenth through fourteenth centuries indicate that it was permissible to use *exempla* and even funny stories, to liven up the preaching. The *Forma Praedicandi* of Robert of Basevorn recommended the following:

According to Cicero, "joking at the proper moment" is to present something cheerful that will please when your audience gets bored, whether it be a jest to produce laughter or a fable or some strange event. This should be done especially when they begin to fall asleep. Now, when the Decretum forbids to use fables, it should be understood as referring to shameful fables, such as concern the sins of Jove and similar tales. This rhetorical ornament should be used sparingly, at the most three times in one sermon.

Trans. by Siegfried Wenzel[44]

It is truly a remarkable coincidence that there also exists for the Christian religion a type of religious picture storytelling that parallels that of Hindu and Buddhist telling in Asia. The format was not exactly like that of the Asian scrolls, because it was shown vertically rather than horizontally. These Christian picture scrolls are known as *exultet* rolls, because all of the twenty-two rolls known to exist carry the same text. It is a part of the Easter vigil service that begins with the word *exultet*, meaning "rejoice."[45] The rolls were used in the liturgy at the moment of the blessing of the new candle. Figure 14, reproduced from an *exultet* roll, shows the deacon chanting the text while showing the pictures to the congregation.

Although all the rolls were produced in Italy during the eleventh and twelfth centuries, they were not identical. A few of the artists chose to illustrate different points, expanding the text by visual means. Old Testament vignettes are particularly emphasized. Although the text is not a pure narrative, it becomes much more so by virtue of the narrative quality of the illustrations.

There seems to be no explanation as to why this particular segment of the liturgy was chosen for this purpose. Nor does there seem to have been any adaptation of this picture device into other uses related to storytelling and religious instruction; that is, there is no *known* connection to later forms of teaching religion through sequences of pictures that tell a story.

A case might be made for the possible transformation of the *exultet* roll into the early form of triptychs or trunk altars that may or may not have been the forerunners of religious picture sheets used by early *bänkelsänger*. However, it is just as likely that the inspiration for the picture sheets came from altar paintings or church murals or windows. At any rate, Leopold Schmidt was convinced that all readable picture stories of a sequential nature had their origins in religious art. It was religious promulgation of this art that made it (and the stories depicted in it) popular with the masses and opened the way for secular picture sheets, in which each scene occupies its own square.[46]

Brednich also believes that there was an early form of *bänkelsang* that was religious in character. The museum in Freiburg im Bresgau with which he was formerly associated has been attempting to assemble all the available pictorial evidence for the early history of *bänkelsang*. Brednich believes that the mezzotint by Jacob Gole, reproduced in figure 15, is one of the examples of the precursors of the religious street and market singers.[47] The singer here is performing indoors, but there is no question that he is chanting or reciting some religious narrative, for the pictures can just be made out. Later examples of such art from the eighteenth century show that there were outdoor market singers who told or sang religious stories. From their dress they do not appear to be members of religious orders, but there are not enough known examples to be conclusive.

The wandering type of Christian religious storytellers that survived the longest

**Figure 14** *Segment of an eleventh-century* exultet *roll. Reproduced from Add. ms. 30337 in the British Museum. Photo courtesy of the British Library.*

**Figure 15** *Jacob Gole*, Sänger mit Triptychon *(c. 1600). Photo courtesy of Deutsches Volksliedarchiv, Freiburg im Bresgau.*

were the *kalêki* in Russia. They date to the early years of Christianity in that country. Originally, they were a mixture of well-to-do pilgrims, lower orders of clergy, beggars, handicapped or maimed persons, runaway serfs, and many others with no permanent home. Later, they were almost exclusively from the ranks of the poor, the crippled, and the blind. They wandered from monastery to monastery, always assured of a place to sleep and a bite to eat. They also got their religious training in the monasteries.

The *kalêki* reached their zenith in the reign of Alexis, father of Peter the Great. At that time, the secular performers of *byliny* (oral epic poems), known as *skomorokhi*, were banned from performing publicly and the *kalêki* were not (see Chapter 2). While the *kalêki* usually performed oral narrative religious poems, known as *dukhovnie stikhi*, it was not uncommon for them to know some of the *byliny*. The Chadwicks speculate that the *kalêki* probably stepped into the gap left by the banished *skomorokhi* and learned to perform secular narratives too.[48]

The *kalêki* performed in churchyards, at church festivals, at funerals, and in the neighborhood of monasteries. There were both male and female groups, but they seemed to travel separately. The women had a distinctive form of dress that resembled that of the Carmelite nuns, except that they did not use a veil. The men wore rough peasant clothing. All carried a special type of knapsack that held their few possessions (see figure 16).[49]

Modern forms of Christian storytelling are those associated with the Sunday-school movement and with parochial schools. The Protestant Reformation had discouraged the telling of legends of the saints; even the use of *exempla* was frowned upon. Stories from the Old and New Testaments were considered quite appropriate, however. These did not have to be told word for word, but were not supposed to deviate from the basic text.

The increased use of storytelling in Protestant churches in the United States may well have come about because of the rise in number and influence of black and white preachers from the South, particularly among Methodist and Baptist congregations. Gradually, they evolved a more dramatic style than had been common in the Puritan-influenced areas of the United States and Canada. Both Reynolds and Rosenberg give excellent descriptions of the preachers who used (and still use) a storytelling style.[50]

By the late nineteenth century, virtually every village and town in the United States had a Sunday school, most of which had small libraries of storybooks with Biblical themes.[51] In the early years of this century, several manuals for Christian storytellers were published. The most influential was that of Edward Porter St. John. He advocated the use of selected folk and fairy tales, for he believed that they offered as good a sense of morality as did many Bible stories. He reported that in New York City there was even a special Sunday School Storyteller's League.[52] After his work was published, it became quite acceptable and common for Sunday Schools to use storytelling of a much broader and inclusive type, not exclusively based on biblical themes. In the following decades, many other manuals appeared, for the use of religious storytellers in a Christian context.

The Baptists were particularly strong in their promotion of storytelling. In the years from 1930 to 1940, they set formal guidelines for storytelling procedures in their formal religious education programs[53] and even began a quarterly magazine to help their Sunday-school teachers become better storytellers.[54]

Curiously, although there were many more stories and legends of saints cur-

**Figure 16** Kalêki, *wandering religious storytellers of Russia. Reproduced from A.P. Bessonov,* Kalêki Perekhozhie *(Moscow, 1861–1864). Photo courtesy of the Library of Congress.*

rent among Catholic groups, there does not appear to have been a conscious effort made by any authorities to guide teachers in a Catholic method of storytelling. The parochial schools did not seem to have organized storytelling of the kind found in Protestant Sunday schools. Religious instruction in parochial schools was usually catechism learned by rote and selected Bible stories read aloud or even used as the basis of reading lessons. Only in recent years has there been a tendency to absorb some of the Protestant Sunday school storytelling techniques in Catholic religious education of the young.

However, it is among theologians of all types of Christian persuasion that there has been the most extensive recent discussion of the uses of story, especially oral story, in Christian teaching. In 1976, Hans Küng questioned whether this new theological interest in storytelling and narrative was simply a contemporary trend that showed nostalgia for all forms of narrative.[55] Whether it is due to nostalgia or not, it continues. This writer found more than a dozen Christian theological studies related to storytelling issued during the past decade.

## Islamic Storytelling

Stories were not told in the time of the Prophet, according to Islamic belief. Only later did storytelling of an approved kind grow up, within the strict boundaries of prescribed, orthodox tradition. Of course, as in other religious movements, there were a number of persons who attempted to create new stories by embellishing accepted oral tradition.

Omidsalar translated a segment from the work of a historian, Abu al-Fadl-i Bayhaqi (995–1077 C.E.) who stated that one should listen only to accounts of the past or the Scriptures as read or told by someone "truthful and trustworthy." However, he noted:

> But the majority of the common people are such that they prefer impossible lies. Such things as stories about demons and fairies and ogres, and mountains and seas [which are narrated] when a fool begins an assembly and a bunch like himself gather around him and he says, "In such and such a sea I saw an island and 500 men landed somewhere and baked bread and set up pots, and when the fire got going and its heat penetrated the earth, the earth began to move." . . . [and] other such superstitious tales that lull people into sleep in the same way as the night. And the number of those who are considered wise and who seek true words to believe in is very small.[56]

Yet in a manuscript dating to approximately 1200 C.E., an Islamic scholar lauded the commendable character of storytelling:

> Storytelling is an innovation, but how wonderful is that innovation! How many a prayer is answered, request granted, companion won, and how great is the knowledge received, through it! . . . a jurist or reader of the Quran is not capable of bringing to God a hundredth of the people the [preacher] is capable of bringing. . . .[57]

At the same time he strictly admonished the believers to listen only to those who were trained in "special branches of learning and knowledge" and those who were commissioned by the imam to tell stories. True stories were those that followed orthodox thinking regarding the life of the Prophet.[58]

The Arabic word for tale, *hadith*, came to mean, in an Islamic context, sayings or parables associated with Mohammed. In the third century after his death, there was already a saying: "Woe to him who spreads false *hadiths* to entertain people, woe to him, woe." Goldziher cites this passage and many others from Arabic language sources in which the secular storyteller is made fun of or taunted. He used the term *qāss* or *qāssas* to denote the religious narrator:

> Only the holy subject of their tales differentiated them from the profane tellers of anecdotes who gathered audiences at street corners in order to recite piquant stories and yarns. . . .[59]

The term *qāss* gradually came to have a negative connotation in orthodox Islamic circles. But Goldziher pointed out that the Prophet himself used the alternate term, *qāssas*, to describe his message.

In orthodox Islamic families, boys were (and some still are) sent to Koranic school when they reached the age of four years, four months, and four days. This is usually interpreted more loosely now, especially in countries where birth dates are calculated differently, but children are still started on their Koranic memorizations when they are very young. In some cases, girls are sent to such schools. Most of the time is spent in having the children listen to simple verses and then repeat them after the teacher. However, there are some schools in North Africa, and in some sub-Saharan African countries, where there are other activities similar to those in a kindergarten, including the telling of stories with social and religious morals.[60]

## Sufi Storytelling

The Sufis are a sub-group of Islam. The Sufi movement dates to approximately the eighth century of the Common Era, and storytelling is an important part of the methods used to teach the principles it espouses. The initiate questions the Sufi teacher, who often responds with stories, preferably orally. The teacher believes these can illuminate the question in such a way that the listener is better able to answer the question by himself or herself. That is, one is supposed to listen to or read the "teaching stories" until understanding comes about.

In recent decades, Idries Shah had written down numerous examples of the process by which this is done. In one of his books he states:

> Sufism has perfected, among other techniques, a characteristic teaching method which is almost unknown outside the ranks of the initiates of the Way. This method, called Diagrammatic of Impression Tales, is contained in the special use made by Sufis of oral and other literature.
>
> Sufi stories, though they may seem on the surface to purvey a moral, or appear intended to entertain, are not literary forms as these things are commonly understood. They are literature incidentally, but teaching-materials primarily.[61]

## Other Religious Storytelling

It is far more difficult to discuss religious storytelling for those people whose moral code is based partly on animism and partly on a strict system of social ethics. Native American groups, for example, consider most of their storytelling as having at least some religious value. For the outsider, it is often impossible to perceive just what elements in the stories make them religious. Nevertheless, in case after case it is recorded that stories were and are looked on as "holy" or "sacred."

The Mandan-Hidatsa group had special words to distinguish stories that had to do with creation and the origin of things, called *māshī* or *hoge*; but in addition there were *māshī aruhopa* or *hohohopini'i*, stories explaining origins of ceremonies and of powers considered holy. The latter stories were considered extremely sacred.[62]

Interestingly, for the Winnebago, *waikan*, a sacred story with spirits or deities as heroes, ended happily; ordinary stories about human beings often ended tragically. The *waikan* had a high monetary value. They could be passed on through bequest, or they could be sold from one teller to another.[63]

Opler told of the Apache custom of painting the face with red ochre after a night of storytelling. The paint was supposed to stay on all day as an indication that the wearer had been influenced by the holiness of the stories.[64]

Peoples of the Pacific, such as the Polynesians, used storytelling for religious purposes in the past. The telling of these stories was usually accompanied by dance. The early forms of the hula were semireligious in nature.[65]

The Maori used storytelling in their *whare wananga*, or house of knowledge, where young people were trained in the sacred traditions of their clan. The stories were, for the most part, secret and unknown to all except the *tohunga*, the graduates of the houses of knowledge. Best concluded:

> A people like ourselves . . . who hold our sacred teaching so cheaply as to make our Bible as common as the daily newspaper, simply cannot conceive the feeling the old-time Maori had for knowledge of the above kind.[66]

Other Polynesian groups had the equivalent of the houses of knowledge. Because of their secret and sacred character, restrictions were put on observers, so it is impossible to give an objective description of just how storytelling was carried out and the impact it had, both for the *tohunga* and for the common people. An interesting device was used by the Marquesan *tuhuka* (equivalent of *tohunga*) to keep intact the sacred stories of their group (see figure 31).

African religions also use song and dance to express religious feeling. There are quite a number of citations referring to religious chants, but none that indicate that the prose narrative story was used for direct religious teaching.

Biebuyck and Mateene reported a situation in which the act of storytelling was looked on as a religious ritual by the teller but did not necessarily have such a meaning for the listeners:

> For the bard himself, the act of narrating the story has religious significance. He believes that Karisi, deified, wanted him to learn the epic; to perform the drama adequately makes the narrator "strong," protects him against disease and death.[67]

On the whole, though, most storytelling in modern Africa is intended to entertain and to teach general social and moral values rather than to promulgate specific religious beliefs.

# CHAPTER 4

# *Folk Storytelling*

In the first chapter of this book a number of quotations from ancient sources were cited to indicate that there is written evidence that storytelling took place in homes, during communal or group work, at religious and social gatherings, and in streets or marketplaces. The persons who told the stories to adults and children were generally not trained in that art, except through practice and imitation; they did not seem to be restricted to any particular educational level or social class. Folk storytelling, for purposes of this book, will be comprised of most of the qualities listed above.

Some early commentaries did seem to regard this kind of story with disdain, as though it were somehow less important than heroic literature or history. The Emperor Julian (C.E. 331–363), for example, wrote:

> But I am bound to say something in defense of those who originally invented myths; I think they wrote them for childish souls: and I liken them to nurses who hang leathern toys to the hands of children when they are irritated and teething . . .
> So those mythologists wrote for the feeble soul whose wings are just beginning to sprout, and who, though still incapable of being taught the truth, is yearning for further knowledge . . .
> *Orations* VII, 206 D., trans. by Wilmer C. Wright[1]

This is an attitude that is carried over, to a certain extent, to modern times. As recently as 1935, the eminent anthropologist Ruth Benedict could find great interest in myths as socio-religious expressions of a culture when they were performed or transmitted in a serious manner or in what we would call bardic form; but as soon as the stories served as children's amusements they were, in her view, not worth studying.[2] Delargy also slighted the stories told for and by women and children. In his opinion they were obviously not as worthy of merit as those told by men at their gatherings.[3]

This disposition on the part of some folklorists and anthropologists appears strange in view of the fact that numerous testimonies to the power of the folktale stress that it was those heard during childhood that seemed to have the most profound and lasting effect. They might well appear in retrospect to have little artistic or literary merit. And yet, writers, artists, inventors, scientists, politicians, and a host of others have testified in memoirs and autobiographies that it was the stories they heard when they were very young that most profoundly affected them. T. S. Eliot was speaking of written literature when he wrote:

> I incline to come to the alarming conclusion that it is just the literature that we read for "amusement." or "purely for pleasure" that may have the greatest and least suspected influence upon us.[4]

His conclusion might well have applied also to stories that were heard and seen, much like those referred to by Goethe (see page 179).

This will be one of the premises on which this chapter and parts of subsequent chapters are based: that the stories told to children or overheard by them by accident or through guile are indeed very important; and storytelling sessions involving children have as much cultural validity as those involving mostly adults.

## Storytelling in the Home

Linda Dégh is one folklorist who would agree to the importance of storytelling to children. In her opinion, it is the vital link that provides the means for transmission of the folktale tradition.

> It does not matter whether the children's stories are told well or badly or whether they are read. They constitute the first real encounter with the folktale, and it quite often happens that it is decided then and there who will become, sometimes after many decades, a good storyteller.[5]

This is what must be kept in mind when reading the accounts of folk storytelling in many parts of the world. Some of the sessions might appear to have very little to do with children. Yet it is likely that even those meant strictly and exclusively for adult audiences had their secret child listeners who were deeply moved by the things they heard, and remembered them all the better for having heard them illicitly.

Fortunately, children do not have to get all their exposure to stories by secretive means. Storytelling in the home is one of the most universal of human experiences. Here we shall discuss only those accounts that specifically mention the importance of this activity for children.

Among many African peoples, there is still a high priority assigned to family storytelling. Béart quotes this maxim from the Ivory Coast:

> "The *gouros* gods only give children to those who can tell at least a hundred tales."[6]

Children of the Ewe people of Ghana are simply not considered educated unless they have heard many times the *gliwo*, animal stories that are intended to teach basic lessons in obedience, kindness, courage, honesty, and other virtues through indirect example.[7]

According to Mbiti, children have to be present when a story is being told to the Akamba of Kenya. If one child has to go to another house to fetch something, the narrator will wait until he or she returns.[8] The Shinqiti of Mauritania have a cycle of folktales especially for children that consist of episodes in the life of an imaginary woman, each one of which implies a moral or a virtue that is supposed to be absorbed by the young in entertaining fashion.[9]

Some groups in Africa have special names to describe the storytelling events within the family circle. For the Edo of Benin, Nigeria, such a gathering is called an *ibota*. It includes the children, youths, wives, and the head of household in one compound. It usually takes place in the largest room and it can celebrate anything from the successful sale of a crop to the visit of a relative, or just being in a good mood. Anyone can tell stories or make riddles or sing songs at the ibota, except the head of the household who is always the listener.[10] The *okpobhie*, in contrast, is a storytelling event also held in the family compound, but performed only by professional storytellers who play the *akpata* or *asologun* (see figures 33 and 34).

For Xhosa and Zulu children it is assumed that an accepted part of their social life will be not only listening to narratives, but also learning to perform them adequately, so that when they in turn are parents and grandparents, they will be able to tell them regularly to their offspring. The performance of the *ntsomi* among the Xhosa and the *nganekwane* among the Zulu is almost exclusively a family compound affair (see figure 17). This does not prevent it from being an art form that achieves a high degree of aesthetic harmony. The children in such situations are often just as demanding an audience as the adults, because they have had training in listening and narrating beginning at an early age. They are well aware of those performances that reach a peak of perfection and those that don't. Often they will join in the calls for bringing to a close a poor performance.[11]

In the Bahamas, where folk stories are nominally directed toward children, it is usually they who begin the storytelling sessions, either by a direct appeal, or by referring to the "Cric-crac" opening.[12]

Native Americans also perceive the narration of stories to children as being of the greatest significance. "If my children hear the stories, they will grow up to be good people; if they don't hear them, they will turn out to be bad," opined Yellowman, a Navajo informant.[13] This is substantiated by the fact that virtually all collections of Native American tales that describe the storytelling occasions and audience mention the fact that children were present and were expected to listen carefully and attentively.

And yet, as Hymes points out, the stories were entertainment, too. "Scholars are sometimes the last to understand that these stories were told and told again, not simply to reflect or express or maintain social structure, interpersonal tensions, or something similar, but because they were great stories, great fun."[14]

Some families not only had sessions for education and fun, but needed and wanted to perform regularly the tales considered as the sacred property of the family. This is commonly reported in the Pacific and borders on religious storytelling. These stories were sometimes told in a special language and had to be told exactly, but their sacredness did not prevent them from being enjoyed as entertainment as well.[15]

The same situation is reported among the Australian aborigines. The telling of

**Figure 17**   *Mrs. Nongenile Masithathu Zenani, gifted* ntsomi *teller from South Africa. Photo courtesy of Harold Scheub.*

their myths was—and still is—"the most common form of aboriginal entertainment, one which included the women and children, so they, too, might learn some of the great stories."[16] A favorite style for many of the women to tell these myths is by accompanying their dramatic narrations with equally dramatic designs drawn in the sand (Chapter 12).

In some societies, wealthy homes had a man or woman among the servants whose special task was to tell stories for both the adults and children. Sometimes there was a different teller for each age group. This was frequently encountered in India and Russia in the nineteenth century and in the early years of the twentieth.

In the Hungarian community of the Szeklers, folk storytelling took place both within the family and at other social gatherings or occasions. The home-based telling was principally for the benefit of the children, but there does not seem to be any indication that the tales used were different ones, except that the average woman who did the home storytelling rarely used her creative talent consciously, as did the best storytellers (women and men) who told for the village at large. There were exceptions, like Zsuzsánna Palkó (see figure 46), who put the same feeling into the versions of tales she told her grandchildren at home that she did when narrating at a more special, public occasion.[17]

The Romansh tellers in Switzerland described by Uffer also told a great deal in the home.[18] One of them, Ursula Bisaz, reported a reaction common to children in many parts of the world, that is, their dislike of change once they find something they like. Bisaz, who was a gifted storyteller, would occasionally like to alter or change the words and even some of the events of the stories she told, but if she did, her grandchildren would invariably say with disappointment: "Granny, last time you didn't tell it that way."[19]

It must be mentioned that there are a few instances reported where recreational storytelling was not considered appropriate for children. For example, Ammar writes:

> There is hardly any adult . . . who admits he tells stories to his children. Stories . . .
> are considered to be demonic, and of no particular value.[20]

Nevertheless, children in the village in Egypt where this was noted managed to tell eleven tales, so they must have heard them somewhere. Furthermore, two folklorists working just a bit further south on the Nile were able to observe any number of occasions when grandmothers told to groups of children, generally from ages six to nine.[21]

The only reference to storytelling practices in Africa south of the Sahara that could be interpreted as restrictive for children in any way is the description Raum gives for the Chagga people of Tanzania. According to that account children are told a few very simple animal stories with a moral, for didactic purposes, but they are restricted in their permission to listen to the stories adults tell each other for entertainment.[22]

Gorer reported that the Lepchas of Sikkim also did not consider their tales, with the exception of one or two animal fables, as appropriate for children.[23] It is likely that had he asked some of the children to recount them, he would have heard at least the bare outlines of the stories told by the adults.

In an early study related to child life in what was called "primitive" society, Miller implied that children heard stories only for purely didactic reasons,[24] but this flies in the face of much evidence to the contrary.

The reason for the lack of storytelling opportunities for children is much more likely to be a lack of time or interest on the part of the parents, rather than a desire to protect children from hearing stories. This trend can be noticed dramatically in immigrant groups or in those that are changing swiftly from rural to industrialized societies. Bianco reported, for example, that almost all the informants among the Italian Americans she interviewed had heard stories from their parents. Those parents were in most cases born in Italy. But the younger age group, especially those under thirty, rarely told stories to their children or among themselves.[25]

Contrasted with this were the *veglia*, or storytelling evenings in homes in the Tuscan part of Italy. Falassi describes the manner in which the first part invariably concentrated on *märchen* and other types of folktales most appealing to the children. Following this was a period of "riddles, catches, lullabies and folk prayers." The children then went to bed, often protestingly, and there were then narratives and folk songs about courtship and marriage.[26]

Because there has been a lessening of such family telling, grandmothers or older storytellers will frequently voice complaints that the younger generation is too lazy or too preoccupied to carry it out. This is not a new complaint as is evident from the words of Anna Liberata de Souza, as reported by Mary Frere in 1881:

> When I was young, old people used to be very fond of telling stories; but instead of that, it seems to me that now the old people are fond of nothing but making money.[27]

The fact remains that there are parents and grandparents and other adults still telling stories to their children, and not only in so-called "traditional" societies, or among economically poor classes who have little access to other entertainment. To cite just two relatively recent examples: the children's book writer Jane Yolen has described in some detail the manner in which she writes and tells stories for children as a professional, and how she has done so for her own children in the privacy of her own home.[28] The late Nobel-Prize-winning scientist Richard Feynman, in a NOVA television interview, went on at some length about the different methods of storytelling he used with his son and his daughter, not because of their sex differences, but because of their different personalities.[29] The pages of past issues of *The National Storytelling Journal* (now *Storytelling Magazine*) are full of descriptions of current family storytelling of an informal nature.

## Seasons and Times for Storytelling

Some families have storytelling activities only for short, fixed periods of the year. In rural Korea, this is during the month of October, or harvest time. At this time, the myths that usually are only performed during rituals will often be recited in the family.[30]

Many African groups also selected the time just after the rice or millet or other main crop was ripe as the most appropriate for telling tales, and the sessions were invariably in the evenings, for it was believed that it was unlucky to tell in the daytime. This was probably because the tribal authorities wanted to be sure the necessary work in the fields was not delayed by the fun of storytelling. An Igbo proverb says: "A lazy person listens to tales in the morning."[31]

There is ample evidence that, even if supposedly prohibited, storytelling was and is done in the daytime in Africa. For example, children among the Masai knot grass as a kind of "crossing one's fingers" method to ward off any misfortune that might come to them when they feel they simply must tell stories in the daytime.[32] Obviously, some of these methods got carried by Africans to the Americas, because in Surinam, if a narrator absolutely must tell in the daytime, he or she plucks a hair from the eyelid before beginning.[33]

Among the Dinka of Sudan the session would last as long as there were people awake. The last storyteller was often the last person awake.[34] In Rwanda, the telling might take place during the day, if it were particularly dark and rainy and no work could go on.[35]

For Native American groups, telling was invariably done in the winter. Children were required to listen to the myths as part of their training, and sometimes, if they fell asleep, had to jump into an ice cold lake or river for a short swim.[36]

Cammann describes such a warm and intimate picture of the *"märchen* evening" in a West Prussian village home at the turn of the century that one can only envy the children and adults lucky enough to have been present.[37] The usual time for starting was on winter evenings at four o'clock in the afternoon. A favorite request of the children, then as now, was for something scary or creepy.

One woman, Anna Spurgarth, remembered eight straight winters, from 1900 to 1908, of frequent storytelling in her home, at which most of her school friends from the village were also present. Some adults were always on hand as well, for Anna's father was well known as a good and entertaining storyteller. Whoever fell asleep had to put a fifty-penny piece in a saucer on the table. Smaller children might be sent to bed when something of an adult nature, not considered appropriate for children, was being told. Most of the stories were told by Anna's father, Karl Restin, but other adults sometimes contributed a story. Birthdays, anniversaries, and other special days always called for a story evening.[38]

The Italian *veglia* in Tuscany was also held in the evenings, during the period after fall sowing and the beginning of Lent, generally on Thursday, Saturday, and Sunday.[39]

Peninnah Schram and James S. Goodman are two storytellers who point out that for many Jewish families, the Sabbath, especially in holiday time, is the most frequent time for shared stories that entertain and teach. For Schram, the stories she heard on such occasions in childhood "transmitted concrete as well as moral meanings, emotions, attitudes, and interpretations of Jewish values."[40]

## Community Sites for Folk Storytelling

In some countries, storytelling took place in a home, but not in the home of the narrator. Such occasions often had special names, and they cannot be treated as family storytelling because there were usually members of an entire village present. Typical of this kind of event is the Irish *céilidhe*. Delargy called a house where such an event took place a *toigh áirneáil*. The storytelling "season" usually opened near Halloween (October 31) and ended near St. Patrick's Day (March 17). The audience did not pay, but they were responsible for bringing in turf for the fire, and plenty of water for the home owner.[41] Carmichael's description of a *céilidh* in the Scottish Hebrides is a bit different, in that women and children seemed to be accepted members of the audience. He speaks of the women as knitting, sewing, spinning, carding, or embroidering in the background. The children squeeze in wherever they will fit, even in the rafters. "Occasionally a moment of excitement occurs when heat and sleep overpower a boy and he tumbles down among the people below, to be trounced out and sent home."[42]

The *céilidhe* has changed format only slightly in some communities, and can still be encountered if one has patience and spends time in certain villages in rural Ireland. Henry Glassie found that in Ballymenone, it is now called a *ceili*, and the tales told there can be historical, but more often now they are based on present-day events, serious or humorous. Everyone who lives there is aware of which homes are "*ceili* homes." Sometimes a gathering results only in pleasant talk and exchange of news, but other times it is lifted out of the ordinary into a performance.[43]

In a recent summary of how the folk traditions are living on and being recorded in Wales, Gwyndaf mentions the types of village centers that still operate for the Welsh equivalent of the *céilidhe*.[44]

There were and are other traditions of public gatherings for folk storytelling, not in homes, but in village "gathering houses" or in tea or coffee houses. The latter were often the setting for professional tellers to perform; such tellers are covered in Chapter 5. But there were some instances when groups of villagers gathered in a tea or coffee house to hear one of their members entertain them with stories. The setting was chosen because it was convenient and convivial and had the requisite amount of space. In Persian, such an occasion was called a *ma'rika* and is a custom dating back to at least the sixteenth century. Modern variations of it still take place in coffeehouses.[45] Both folk and bardic storytelling are practiced at such times.

This has a modern parallel in North America and parts of Europe as well—storytelling in the local bar or tavern. Many of Richard Dorson's informants were located in such locales.[46] Taggart also noted that Nahuat men frequently told stories while drinking in bars, as have any number of other modern folklorists searching for storytelling in the present day.[47]

And storytelling is as likely to take place in urban work and play environments of today as it is in small town or rural areas. Jan Brunvand, a folklorist who has made a specialty of collecting such tales, calls them "urban folklore."[48] Schwartzman found that spontaneous stories were extremely important in the daily work life of staff and patients at a community mental health center.[49]

Adams gives an excellent picture of a village folk storyteller who usually performed for groups of children in the candy shop she managed. Tsune Watanabe told chiefly *mukashi-banashi*, the equivalent of *märchen*. It was interesting to note that although Watanabe perceived her role of storyteller as having been greatly diminished in recent years, she was still held in esteem by the young people of the village. She claimed that the children and young people no longer had an interest in her stories, and yet it was a young man who led Adams to her, pointing out that she was the best storyteller around.[50]

During the winter months, the gathering place for families in northern Italy was the stable, because there was more warmth there from the animals. Clementina Todesco, who grew up in Faller, learned most of her stories from her next-door neighbor, an elderly man who spent most of his evenings with Clementina's family.[51]

Sherzer tells about the gathering house of the Kuna, of the San Blas Islands of Panama:

The "gathering house" is the nerve center of a Kuna village. It serves to bring people together on a regular basis. It is a place to see and be seen, to learn the latest news, often as it is happening. . . . [It is] a talking house, a performing house, a listening house. Here, through language and speech, the Kuna learn about proper ways of behaving, learn about the past and present world around them, solve their problems, joke, enjoy words, and relax.[52]

## Storytelling During Work

The tedium of work was often relieved by a background of tale telling. Sometimes the very rhythm of work became part of the rhythm of the story, or vice versa. Linda Dégh found that several members of the famous Hungarian Szekler storytelling family, the Zaiczes, told quite regularly in the fields of sugar beets. They were foremen and entertained the other workers as they hacked away. According to one worker: "everybody was glad to work under a foreman who could tell good stories."[53] Other work during which storytelling was practiced by this group of people included carting wood from the forest, fishing, and cobbling.[54]

Brinkmann mentioned that a favorite time for storytelling in a rural German village was during weeding or during harvesting of potatoes. He also observed it among a group of workers in a sand pit, and in a place where a building was going up.[55]

Gorer remarked that one of the occasions for storytelling for the Lepchas of Sikkim was while weeding. Often one skilled teller would be selected to tell short stories all day, while the others worked. That person would get special tidbits of food at the evening meal as a kind of pay.[56]

The work that seemed best suited for storytelling was that associated with cotton or wool. Persons sifting, carding, spinning, and weaving were so well suited to listening to stories, without breaking the concentration of their work, that this is reported wherever such work was done. East mentioned this as a favorite pastime of the spinners of cotton among the Tiv of northern Nigeria.

As soon as it was dark they lit a fire in the middle of the village, and the children, the older men and the women all gathered round it to spin cotton and tell hare-stories.[57]

A similar custom was noted among the Jula of Burkina Faso, formerly Upper Volta, where the women had to clean, card and spin the cotton grown each year.[58]

Hoogasian-Villa found among her older Armenian informants in Detroit quite a number who had learned stories while listening and sifting the seeds out of cotton, back in their Armenian childhood.[59]

Delargy mentioned that at the Irish airneán, a women's gathering to spin and card wool, storytelling was the expected accompaniment for at least a part of the working time.[60] Sometimes one of the women would tell, but at other times a shanachie would be invited in and even paid a bit to tell his tales. A gypsy teller in Romania mentioned to the folklorist Bela Gunda that he, too, had frequently been paid to come in and tell tales to women as they spun.[61]

The Szekler ethnic group from Hungary had a very strong tradition of telling tales in the spinning rooms of the village. This was true in the period when they lived in Bucovina, Romania, and also after they were repatriated to the area around Kakasd in southern Hungary. Spinning took place during part of the day, from Monday through Thursday, and on most winter evenings. For the day spinning, the women found tellers among themselves. In the evenings the men often gathered with their wives, and then some of the best tellers, usually men, would narrate, often until one or two in the morning.[62]

This writer remembers family storytelling in Polish-American families in Wisconsin that took place during the evenings of Advent and Lent, when goose feathers were stripped from their tiny quills. Also, women often told stories while quilting together at large frames. If the stories were a bit vulgar or bawdy, they were told in a Polish full of Kashubian expressions, so that the children could not understand.

The Nahuat of Mexico, who frequently come north as migrant laborers, sometimes use the brief time while resting in the evening for storytelling.[63]

Some folklorists report that after long working days it is rare to find a storytelling occasion because people are too tired. But a community work project, in which all have shared the tasks equally, usually resulted in the shared good feelings necessary for a communal storytelling atmosphere. Such an occasion was called a *mingaco* in Chile. It has apparently died out.[64]

## Other Occasions for Folk Storytelling

Personal celebrations and feasts on the occasion of a wedding or child naming are often the time to tell stories. Babalola reported that the *ijála* chanters of the Yoruba, who used to recite only for hunters' groups, now are commonly asked by other persons in the community to perform on those two occasions, regardless of whether they are members of the hunters' groups or not.[65] Cejpek mentioned that weddings and births were also times for storytelling in Iran.[66] The Lepchas had a long story lasting from two to three hours that was a part of every marriage ceremony.[67] The Suk, from the Sudan, also used the marriage feast as one of their favorite periods for a good long story session.[68]

Stories at wakes for the dead were common in Ireland and Europe and can also be found in India and some parts of Africa. For the Szeklers of Hungary, this kind of storytelling had tremendous social importance. The order of narration was an indispensable part of the ritual of the wakes, which lasted forty-eight hours. The wake served as the single most important social occasion for the married and the elderly. A beautifully arranged wake would be discussed for years after the event, and all who had been present would remember the stories told. The storytelling alternated with singing and the saying of prayers. The stories told were usually short anecdotes and long, involved *märchen.*[69]

Although the above are comparatively recent examples, the custom of storytelling at wakes is very ancient. As cited in Chapter 1, it is mentioned in a number of the *Rules of Vedic Domestic Ceremonies*, compiled about 200 B.C.E. in India. The sūtra already cited referred to the death of a guru. In a later sūtra there is another mention of storytelling at what might be called wakes for ordinary persons:

> Now the water libations [which are performed for deceased persons] . . .
> When they have come out [ of the water] and have sat down on a pure spot that is covered with grass, those who are versed in ancient tales should entertain them [by telling tales].
> *Páraskara-Grihya-Sūtra*, III Kanda, 10 Kândikâ, 1, 22, trans. by Hermann Oldenburg[70]

In some Catholic countries, storytelling followed after special services during Lent. A Canadian informant remarks:

> At this time, young boys and girls in the region would set out from home after the daily family prayer and gather at his house to hear one or two folktales each evening.[71]

Delargy mentioned that after the stations of the cross each week in Lent, it was customary to gather for a folktale session.[72]

Storytelling among soldiers has also been mentioned since ancient times. In Israel, a particular kind of storytelling session, called a *kumsitz*, developed among the Palmakhnik. This was a kind of paramilitary or underground group organized during the fight for independence and existence as a separate state. The men and women would usually get together for an evening of self-entertainment. The stories they told were known as *ha-chizbat*, derived from an Arabic word meaning "to lie." The stories could be fanciful, exaggerated, humorous, and even preposterous, but they had to be based on a kernel of truth. Sometimes the *kumsitz* was used as a device to recruit youths from the high schools.[73]

An intriguing use of persuasive storytelling for a better legal outcome occurred in medieval times in Europe. When a person who had been judged guilty of some crime applied for a pardon, he or she often told an account of the crime and the reasons for asking for the pardon in the form of a long story. Many of these "tales" were written down and at least one scholar has suggested that from the evidence, one can tell that the best storytellers were often the most successful in getting pardons.[74]

The folklorist Richard Bauman focused on another amusing and unusual occasion for storytelling, most often of the highly exaggerative type. He studied the tale telling and other verbal exchanges that go on in the small town of Canton, Texas, on the Sunday preceding the first Monday every month, when there is a session of coon dog trading or selling.[75]

Ed Bell, who has appeared at a number of storytelling festivals and can also be seen on videotape, originally began his storytelling at a bait camp for sport fishermen, in Indianola, Texas.[76]

Some persons have such an urge to share their tales, they need no special occasion in order to be persuaded to tell them. Delia Poirier, a storyteller of French Canada, baldly confessed:

> One winter, I visited in turn every house in the entire village to tell my tales. I went out three nights a week. I would have gone more often, but I didn't want people to think I was a gadabout.[77]

She was reported to be well liked in the community, so her "gadding about" obviously was not a nuisance.

## Street and Marketplace Storytellers

The most visible of folk storytellers have been the street and marketplace narrators of the past and present. India may well be the source and inspiration for many of them. As was discussed in greater detail in Chapter 3, the religious storytellers gradually absorbed a rather secular style and content. The "picture showmen," as the Indian scholar Coomaraswamy called them, took to the streets and public places. By the time this custom was spread by Buddhists to China,

Java, the other parts of western, eastern and southern Asia, it began to have more and more secular content and appeal. Traders probably carried the public manner of telling stories to Persia, Greece, and toward Europe and the Middle East. Whether or not they were influenced by these accounts from the East, minstrels and bards in Europe were undergoing much of the same process of change, from sacred and/or heroic performances to many that were secular and popular in appeal.

Unfortunately, there is as yet no complete history of storytelling in India, at least none readily available to the Western reader. From Sanskrit scriptures and other early works, it is evident that tales of an entertaining nature were told (see Chapter 1). How street storytelling could spring up from the traditions of family, religious and folk storytelling or from the courtly minstrel tradition in India is not totally clear, any more than it is in Europe. The only point on which scholars agree is that it is still impossible to entirely separate the folktales from the myths, the secular from the religious, the popular from the classical. They are inextricably intertwined in our old stories. Since this is so, one can turn to modern storytellers in an attempt to find out what they might have been like in the past. There is not likely to have been dramatic change in their storytelling style and content over the last few centuries.

In present-day India, in rural villages, small towns, and even some of the bigger towns and cities, one can still encounter itinerant storytellers. Those that perform in a more elaborate style, using large picture cloths and scrolls, have been mentioned in Chapter 2 as being of the bardic type, mostly because the content of their stories is heroic. It must be admitted that this is rather arbitrary, since the *Ramayana* and other epics can be perceived by the average Indian as heroic, homey and folklike, or religious, and sometimes all of that in the same performance.

Others that fall somewhere between bardic, folk, and religious in their style include the type that can be represented here by the *burrakatha* performers and the *Dasarulu*, both found in Andhra Pradesh. The former are believed to have developed from a type of storytelling that was done only by women, beginning in about the fifteenth century, C.E. Now, however, the majority of performers are male. They go about in groups of three, a teller and two musician-responders. One of the responders is expected to add or insert comments on contemporary social and political problems as they might fit into the story; the other responder-musician is expected to add comic relief whenever needed. They perform either in front of a building where they expect to attract attention, or in the courtyard of a home, if they are invited to perform there for a special gathering or occasion. There are full-time professional performers, as well as those who do it only part-time. Their repertoire consists of historical tales and myths, episodes from the *Ramayana* or *Mahabharata*, local folklore, and even stories borrowed from Christian scriptures.[78]

The *Dasarulu* sometimes make their appeals in the street, but they generally are invited into a home to perform. They go about in pairs, approach houses in the village likely to be able to pay in grain or cash for their entertainment, and sing samples of their work, accompanying themselves on lute and drum. They only perform during the off-season, when there is no planting or harvesting to be done. Their style is a lively and rapid prosimetric mixture, and their repertoires range from the Indian epics, to *puranas*, fairy tales, pilgrimage tales, historical events, local events and personal experience tales.[79]

In her study of the Thousand and One Nights as a genre, Gerhardt states that time-gaining frame stories are apparently of Indian origin, but they were adapted and taken over by Persians fairly early, probably in the late Sassanian period (224–651 C.E.). The Arabic versions appeared a bit later. Virtually all of these collections of stories, she finds, have "highly ingenious devices to introduce, to justify, to authenticate the telling of a story, to set it off, to make it serve a purpose. Stories are fitted one into the other like Chinese boxes."[80]

Boyce believed that the kernel for the *Thousand and One Nights* came from *Hazar Afsan*, an early Persian work, although many of the stories were obviously Indian in origin.[81]

These frame stories were probably performed orally at inns and in caravan-serai in a manner similar to that described by a nineteenth century traveler:

> . . . they had lighted a fire in front of their tent, and were squatting around it. . . .
> One of the camel-drivers was engaged in telling stories to a rapt audience. . . . With
> a clear, unhesitating voice, which he raised or lowered as occasion required, he
> pursued his tale, pausing only when he had made a point and expected the ap-
> plause of his hearers.[82]

After the Middle Ages, the time-gaining frame stories were written down in more and more versions. They could be found in manuscripts in Persian, Arabic, and a number of European languages.

However, public telling of these same stories survived in the marketplace and in the teahouses and coffeehouses in the Middle East and North Africa. It is really because of the colorful and dramatic presence of these narrators that we find the word "storyteller" began to be used to describe an oral teller of tales, rather than a person who told fibs. English travelers of the nineteenth century describing such public storytelling sessions were the first to use the term consistently in their written and printed accounts, as in the following example:

> In a Persian town they are to be met with in every street. In open sites, such as are
> often found near market-places, great sheds are erected, open on all sides and
> furnished with rows of steps capable of seating three to four hundred persons
> squatting on their heels. In front of the audience is a platform from whence a
> succession of storytellers repeat their stories to a succession of listeners from morn-
> ing to night [fig. 18].[83]

This might almost be considered theatrical storytelling, except that in most cases there was no fixed entrance fee for these performances.

One of the most colorful scenes still frequently encountered in present-day North African marketplaces is the animated storyteller, surrounded by a wide variety of listeners. The audience can be a mixture of young and old, in modern or traditional dress. This writer has seen a number of such performances in Morocco and Tunisia. In Tunisia this itinerant type of teller is called *fdawi*. His performance is geared to building suspense until the climax of the story. With the audience waiting with bated breath, he stops to collect whatever coins he can, and only then finishes his tale. An impressive aerial photographic view of one such teller and his large audience in Marrakech, Morocco can be seen in the *National Geographic* for March 1932.[84]

When the tales of India moved in the other direction, to China and Southeast Asia, it was Buddhism that carried along this richness of narrative. After becoming secularized, the tales were added to and narrated by all types of tellers.

**Figure 18**   *Kashgar market storyteller. Bettmann Archive.*

The professional performers who told in teahouses and in special theaters are described in Chapter 5. There were also amateur storytellers who went from town to town and village to village, presenting their tales at marketplaces and on street corners. A number of the picture-telling performers were itinerant tellers who told purely secular tales. Examples of these could be found recently among the *patua* of Bengal.[85]

Other street storytellers would try to attract attention by clapping together two small pieces of wood. Or they might play a two-stringed instrument. Some of them were blind or physically handicapped. Many of these latter were accompanied by other family members.[86]

Chinese marketplaces were often in temple courtyards. As recently as 1950–1954 the *T'ien-ch'iao*, Beijing's Heavenly Bridge, was a place where one could encounter outdoor performers of all types. The storyteller sat at a small table, and the listeners were on benches in a semi-circle around it. Fees were not fixed. Contributions were collected in the middle of the story or just before the climax, as in Persia and Turkey. The narrator had to hope for the best and tried his utmost to perform well. Although these street storytellers were usually very poor and of the lowest social classes, they had a certain pride that lent them dignity.[87]

Japan had street and itinerant storytellers in the past (fig. 19), but it is much more difficult to locate precise information on how and where they performed and what their social position was. There was, for example, a secular *etoki hoshi*, a man who recited stories to pictures, using a pheasant feather on a stick to point out the various scenes as he narrated. The stories may well have been bardic in character, rather than folkloric. The female equivalent, the *Kumano bikuni* (see figure 13) also became secular, itinerant performers, and Barbara Ruch speculates that many of the narratives they used were changed by their personal experiences. Essentially, however, they remained in the public consciousness as religious performers, regardless of how they changed.[88]

For the modern types of Japanese public storytellers, there is more documentation. One of the more extensively practiced forms was *kamishibai*. The term means "paper drama" or "theater of paper." It had its roots in earlier forms of picture storytelling, in *kabuki* theater, and in shadow-puppet plays. Satoshi Kako and Koji Kata have documented the gradual adaptation of earlier indoor theater forms into the outdoor form of storytelling with pictures known as *kamishibai*. Koji Kata was himself a *kamishibai* performer, and his autobiography was a best-seller in Japan when it came out in 1977.[89]

In its modern, most popular form, *kamishibai* began around 1930. This was a time of economic depression, and *kamishibai* was used by many unemployed workers as a means of making a little money. The performers were exclusively men, and they were looked down on by middle-class parents because they were identified with the racketeers who had dominated earlier groups of outdoor performers. Also, many of the stories they told were considered to be vulgar and in bad taste, and the candies they sold were believed by many mothers to be unsanitary.[90]

It was the children who began to enjoy the *kamishibai*, especially the children of the urban poor and working classes. There were performers in most of the major cities. They usually went about on bicycles for greater mobility. Each had a repertoire of three or four stories which he carried with him in the wooden frame that also served as a means of presenting the picture cards during the telling of the tales. For a further description and illustration of the frame, see Chapter 12.

**Figure 19**   *Outdoor market storyteller in Yokohama, Japan, late nineteenth century. Picture courtesy of The New York Public Library, Picture Collection.*

During the Second World War and immediately after, *kamishibai* was virtually the only entertainment regularly available to children. There were about 25,000 performers around 1950. Kako estimates as many as 7.5 million children could have seen a performance on any given day when they were all performing, since the performers usually repeated their programs about ten times in different places during each day and had an average audience of thirty children each time.[91]

Educators tried to prohibit *kamishibai*, but in vain. Later they attempted to adapt it to an educational format, with stories that were considered more "suitable" or proper. In this way, many of the favorite folk tales were eventually printed in *kamishibai* format (fig. 20).

A contemporary writer, Morio Kita, has given a memorable picture (semiautobiographical) of one child's reaction to the *kamishibai*.

> The fact was this. Lately Shuji, all by himself, went out more frequently than before and was absorbed in *kamishibai*, which visited the neighborhood at twilight time. In comparison to other children, he could be described as unhappy. The reason for this unhappiness was that he had not a single *sen*. At the beating of the clatters, a mass of children ran to the *kamishibai* player, each trying to be the first to give the tightly grasped one-*sen* piece to him. The player gave a candy, dyed red and white, in exchange for the one *sen*. Nibbling their candies, the children intently watched the illustrations painted on coarse papers, listening to the narrative given by the player in a husky voice. Shuji, however, had no capital to procure candies. Stationing himself, mostly by luck, in the front row, he was roughly thrust aside by the *kamishibai* player.
>
> "Those who don't buy candies go behind the others!"

**Figure 20** *Modern educational form of* kamishibai *being used in a kindgarten. Photo courtesy of the editors of* Kamishibai *magazine, Tokyo.*

Shuji, stealing occasional, envious glances at the candies possessed by the other children, stretched himself from behind to catch glimpses of a monstrous figure of a man with the mask of a skull, long ominous fingernails and a flying red cape.

"Here comes the man of justice! His name is no other than the Golden Bat!" At this point the player thundered a little drum.

After several such experiences, even the little head of Shuji began to realize the importance and necessity of money.

*Nireke no Hitobito* (*The Nine Families*), trans. by Kiyoko Toyama.[92]

In Europe, the street storytellers usually did not relate long, complex tales of the *märchen* type. Their stories were more likely to be based on news events of the most sensational type, often put into ballad form. Or they were short anecdotes strung together. Like the storytellers of India and China, some of them probably had their roots in the religious storytelling of wandering monks. Others were probably the remnants of organized troupes of bards and minstrels that had once been common in courts, and at all public gatherings of any size. Wherever they came from, they quickly seized on the medium of print as an adjunct to their oral talents rather than viewing it as a totally competitive medium.

According to Coupe, the publisher-vendors first appeared in the sixteenth century. At that time, the engraver, publisher, and printer was generally the same person. They went to all the fairs and sold their wares to anyone who would buy.[93] Hans Fehr, who has also written on the mass printing media of the sixteenth century, states that the printers directed three types of printed matter toward three kinds of readers. The book was aimed at the learned and scholarly; the *flugschrift* (chapbook or pamphlet), at the educated, that is, those who could read; and the *flugblatt* (picture sheet or broadsheet), at the mostly nonliterate folk.[94]

Booksellers, hawkers, peddlers, itinerant street singers, and others would buy the materials in quantity. The street singers were a motley crowd, looked down upon as the dregs of society. This contempt may well have been political or religious in origin because the authorities feared the growing awareness of the masses. And there was no question that the masses listened to the street singer with all of his or her gory details. They then often bought the cheap broadsheets or chapbooks in hopes of finding still more detail than had been given in the performance, or to be able to repeat part of it to their families or neighbors.[95]

The street performer was often called a *bänkelsänger* in German because he or she stood on a bench in order to be seen better. Some of the other names for this performer were: *krámařský zpěvák* (Czech); *liedjeszanger* (Flemish or Dutch); *chanteur en foire* or *crieur de journeaux* (French); *cantambanco* or *cantastorie* (Italian); *ploshchadnoi pevetz* (Russian); *cantor da feria* (Spanish); *pevci* (South Slavic); *marknadsångere* (Swedish).

The *bänkelsänger* usually had a long pointed stick, which was used to point to the pictures that showed all the lurid details of the most melodramatic events in the story (see figures 21 and 22, and see also figure 40). Most of the pictures were woodcut prints, painted in by illuminators. After the story had been sung, the singer, or members of the singer's family, passed through the crowd; they either collected coins outright for the performance, or they sold individual broadsheets or pamphlets that contained the story ballads or news events written up in exaggerated style. There is no concrete evidence for the prices at which the broadsheets were sold, nor is it known in what numbers they were issued, or how many the average performer might have sold.

**Figure 21** *Etching, dated 1740, by C. W. E. Dietrich, showing a* bänkelsänger *surrounded by his audience. Photo by Chris Nickrant.*

**Figure 22** *Market scene with* bänkelsänger *in foreground. Reproduced from* Münchener Bilderbogen, *No. 120, "Der Jahrmarkt" (originally published in Munich by Braun and Schneider, mid-nineteenth century). Picture courtesy of The New York Public Library, Picture Collection.*

The broadsheets of the seventeenth century were the most artistic of all. The printers used copperplate engravings and woodcuts. During this period, the picture story played an important part in the imaginative life of all classes. This was true for much of Europe, for the peddlers and performers penetrated into all parts of the continent.[96]

The quality of the picture sheets, the broadsheets, and the chapbooks began to decline in the eighteenth and nineteenth centuries, and with the exception of a few publishing efforts, such as the *Münchener Bilderbogen*, they were designed for the poor and non-literate masses only. The middle classes thought it proper to purchase regular books and newspapers. There are few contemporary descriptions of that time to tell us how the singer might have changed performance techniques or how extensive the individual repertoires were. The best one can do is to speculate, based on some of the statements of the few surviving performers of this kind, from the twentieth century. Dominik Rolsch was one who inherited from his father the profession of itinerant street singer. He remembered that his father had told him that shortly after his marriage he owned a wagon in which to live, two dozen new *schilder*, and a music wagon with a built-in organ.[97]

Curiously, in northeastern Brazil there is a surviving form of this tradition, the *literatura de cordel* (fig. 23). The name comes from the custom of hanging out *folhetos*, cheap publications with woodblock illustrations, on a clothesline type of string, from tree to tree, usually in an open marketplace. The poets there, for the most part, now sing or recite by reading aloud from their printed works in some public hall, or even on recordings or television or radio. However, there are those poets who still perform outdoors, extemporaneously, and from comments by some in the audience, it is apparent that they prefer this style. In her book examining this tradition Slater quotes one of the listeners:

> I grew up in the countryside, and we learned a lot of *folhetos* by heart just listening to them over and over again when there was nothing else to do. Those old stories remind me of all those long hot mornings with a deep blue sky above us, and so, I like to hear them because they remind me of where I was born.[98]

Itinerant street storytellers were obviously popular in parts of Africa, at least at the turn of the century and on into the 1950s. Because they used an unusual method of story selection, involving nets, strings, vines, and other objects, they will be described in Chapter 12.

**Figure 23**    *A poet reads from* literatura de cordel *in northeast Brazil. Photo courtesy of Regina Yolanda de Werneck.*

# CHAPTER 5

# *Theatrical Storytelling*

There are some parts of the world in which storytelling developed as a form of theatrical entertainment. The term "theatrical" will not be used here in a pejorative sense, to imply overly-dramatic or showy, exaggerated storytelling. Many of the forms of storytelling described in earlier and later chapters are as dramatic as the type of storytelling being considered in this chapter. What distinguishes this kind is the fact that it was or is performed in actual theater-like buildings, and the audience that goes to see and hear it pays entrance fees in much the same fashion as it would for entering a theater. In other words, this kind of storytelling is barely distinguishable from legitimate theater as it is commonly experienced.

## Chinese and Mongolian Theatrical Storytelling

The most elaborate and studied type of theatrical storytelling was common in China, Mongolia, and Japan for at least seven centuries and still is practiced, although in very restricted terms compared to previous centuries. The origins of Chinese theater storytelling are religious, as indicated in some detail in Chapter 3. In the later years of the Sung Dynasty (960–1279 C.E.)[1] and all during the Yuan Dynasty (1279–1368 C.E.) these storytellers increased in number and became almost completely secularized. They were organized in guilds through-out China.[2] So important was their work to the development of the written literature of China that it is almost impossible to separate their oral perfor-mances from the written versions of their tales. Scholars disagree about certain aspects of these storytellers. The most frequent point of contention relates to whether the surviving texts served as memory aids to the tellers, or whether they were handwritten or printed literary versions of the tales designed for reading.[3] The common term for these written and printed texts is *hua-pen*. Some of them, like the *pien-wen* texts, may have been intended to accompany the picture scrolls described in Chapter 3 and Chapter 12.

Průšek, a sinologist who has written extensively on the subject, believed the *hua-pen* was used as a kind of secret prompt book by the storyteller. In his view, printers later managed to acquire some of them, had accomplished writers polish and flesh them out, and then published them. After the writers heard and saw the stories recited again and again, they would perfect the printed editions.[4]

Hrdličková, on the other hand, believed that the *hua-pen* were not to be confused with the *tz'e-tze*, also called *ti-pen* or *chiao-pen*, handbooks of secrets handed by the master to each student on completion of the apprenticeship. In her opinion, the *hua-pen* were definitely written down and published for general reading, or for reading aloud in public.[5]

Yau-Woon Ma expressed the view that it is still too early to say whether the *hua-pen* and the *pien-wen* are related. The majority of these texts are relatively recent discoveries and there must still be much more study of both types before one can say how they influenced each other. But Ma did agree that, even though we may not know precisely what texts were used and how, "storytelling, presented in sophisticated forms, free from religious influence, organized and practiced on a professional basis, had already acquired some status and independence as an art form (and, needless to say, as a popular entertainment) as early as the eleventh century."[6]

There were many guilds, each specializing in teaching and performing certain genres or types of stories. It was the guild that negotiated the contracts for each of its members to perform, first in teahouses and then in the storytelling theaters.[7] They told their stories in an idiom approximating the vernacular, with lively coloring and long and inventive descriptions. The proof of their liveliness lies in the fact that virtually none of the works written in the literary language from the Sung and Yuan dynasties is considered above average, while quite a number of the works recorded from the oral storytellers of the period, in the vernacular, are still considered outstanding. The majority of the famous long novels of the Ming period (1368–1644 C.E.) were developed from the works of these storytellers.[8]

There is very little documentation for this kind of activity in present-day China. Hrdličková's research, conducted mostly in Beijing, Tientsin, and the small towns of northern China dates to the early 1950s. But according to her it was in Shanghai that the *shu-ch'ang*, or storytelling halls, were most popular, especially in the latter half of the nineteenth century and the early part of the twentieth.[9] Eberhard found a few storytellers of this type still practicing in the late 1960s in Taiwan, but no longer in special theaters. They generally told in a temple or in a teahouse.[10] The audience consisted only of old men, indicating that the tradition was much weakened.

More recently, Kate Stevens of Toronto, a specialist in drum song singers and "bamboo clapper" storytellers, has visited a number of sites in China where storytelling is still practiced in the traditional ways. In Beijing, she recorded Gao Fengshan and one of his students, at the Lao-She teahouse. Gao Fengshan can be considered a descendant of either the guild-type tellers or the street storytellers mentioned in Chapter 4 (see figure 32). Since he performed regularly for a fee, he can be included here. Many of the tellers who used bamboo-clappers as accompaniment told their stories in prosimetric style, but Gao Fengshan's tales are mostly in poetry. An example of his style, in the manner in which he passes it on to his students, is given in Chapter 10.

Kara's researches in Mongolia date to 1959–1960, but it is not entirely clear if the public storytelling halls, the *üliger kelekü tangkim*, that he encountered there are of the same tradition as the Chinese *shu-ch'ang*.[11] The epics that the Mongolian bard performs start with a rhythmic prose recitative. The body of the epic is in verse and is generally accompanied by a four-stringed instrument. Another performer in the halls is the *üligerčin*, the folk storyteller.[12] This would seem to indicate that the same varieties of storytelling styles are to be found in these Mongolian halls as were found in the Chinese *shu-ch'ang*, and are still found in the Japanese *yose*. There is an admission charged upon entry, and one is expected to take tea, just as in the *yose*.

## Japanese Theatrical Storytelling

With regard to these Japanese *yose*, there is a considerable body of descriptive documentation in English and German as well as in Japanese. In 1897, Brinkley recorded that there were 180 *yose* in Tokyo and many more in other parts of Japan. The storytellers were divided into schools, usually under the direction of a master, of whom there were ten at the time. Brinkley called the tellers *kōshaku-shi*.[13]

Adam, a French visitor to the *yose* in 1912, and Meissner, a German folklorist studying them in 1913, gave even more details.[14] Adam cited the number of *yose* as 243, but it was not clear if he was referring to all of Japan or only Tokyo. Each *yose* could seat 500 to 1,000, he claimed. He called the apprentices *zenza*, the storytellers *hanashi-ka*, and the master, *shin-uchi*. The most interesting aspect of his book is the illustrations. They include an exterior of a *yose* (fig. 24), an entryway, an interior, a stage setting, a typical audience, and numerous other fine details.

Meissner's count of the *yose* in Tokyo in 1913 came to 151, including all types, but he stated that each *yose* seated only 250–300 persons rather than the 500 to 1,000 suggested by Adam. The entrance fee was about ten *sen*, and another 15 *sen* usually had to be spent in ordering tea and for gratuities. Thus, this was an entertainment in reach of the middle and working classes.[15]

Meissner listed the ranks from apprentice, the *zenza*, up to *shin-uchi*, the master. He also described in some detail the various types of storytellers who performed in the *yose* at that time.[16] Both Meissner and Adam reported the oddity of a European performer who had become a master in one of the *yose*.[17]

A later study by another German folklorist, Barth, expanded the picture considerably. Barth concentrated on the tales and the tellers. There were the *kodan-shi*, who performed narratives of warriors (*samurai*), more or less historically based, and the *rakugo-ka*, who presented witty, humorous narratives of much shorter length. The *naniwabushi* told almost exactly the same historical *samurai* tales as the *kodan-shi*, but they accompanied themselves on the *shamisen* and, from time to time, would break their narrative with a song.[18]

Barth mentioned that all of these performers were turning to radio because people were not going to the *yose* as frequently as they had previously. Some of the performers were employed in a new profession, that of providing running

**Figure 24**   *Entrance to a* yose *in Tokyo. Reproduced from Jules Adam,* Japanese Storytellers *(Tokyo: T. Hasegawa, 1912). Photo courtesy of The New York Public Library.*

commentary and dialogue for the silent films! It was Barth's impression that the *yose* was an institution that was peculiarly Japanese, without any foreign influence.[19] However, Průšek and Hrdličková have shown in their research that the origin was almost certainly Chinese, with some aspects probably traceable back to India, especially in the period of Buddhist expansion. Barth did mention the *biwa-hoshi*, monks or persons in monks' clothing who went around playing the lute (*biwa*) and singing epic songs of wars and folk heroes. And most of the early *kodan-shi* were poor *samurai* or former monks.[20]

In 1815 a number of decrees were promulgated against the *rakugo-ka*, but there was such a public outcry that the authorities had to desist. They did, however, insist that the *rakugo-ka* begin performing stories that were more "truthful" and filled with good example. After that the stories changed somewhat, but not entirely.[21]

The modern updating of this picture can be found in the articles of Hrdličková.[22] By the time she began her research in the 1960s, there were only two schools or guilds of the *rakugo-ka* remaining. There was a total membership of 227. They performed in seven *yose* that still remained in Tokyo. There was only one hall left where the *kodan-shi* were performing. The twenty-two *kodan-shi* had only a few pupils. The *kodan-shi* still performed with a little table in front of them, where formerly they used to place the handbook of texts that was used as a memory aid.[23] This would seem to indicate that this kind of storytelling was influenced by the medieval Chinese tellers, whose use of promptbooks was apparently quite common, at least according to some scholars. For ordinary appearances, the tellers have a kimono embroidered with the family crest, but on festive occasions they wear much more ceremonial dress.

The storytelling performances are sometimes interspersed with other acts, such as jugglers, magicians, and singers, but the good tellers are always placed toward the end of the program, and they have no interruptions. The majority of the audience is now composed of older men, but family groups are still seen. When this author visited a *yose* in 1980, the audience consisted almost entirely of groups of office and blue collar workers on company-sponsored outings, with a sprinkling of extended families. The performances, which continued for a period of about seven hours, consisted almost entirely of storytellers, of greatly varying ability.

Some of the performers also appear on television and radio, and this has enchanced their reputations. Although definitely waning in numbers, the tradition of the *yose* seems to cling tenaciously to its position in the cultural and social life of ordinary Japanese.

The Far East seems to be the only part of the world where this particular type of storytelling flourished. There are no exact parallels in other cultures, especially not in terms of the strict training, the manner of payment, and the presentation in a formal theater type of building. The only storytelling that remotely resembles it are the occasional theatrical narrators performing in Europe and North America. But in no case were they or are they the product of a strict apprenticeship and of completely oral training. In most cases, they have learned the art through dramatic training and their stories come from written sources or they are composed out of personal experience.

## European Theatrical Storytelling

The Grimm Brothers' *märchen* were very popular as selections in dramatic theatrical storytelling. Rougemont recounts how thrilling it was to hear them told in a concert hall by Vilma Mönckeberg-Kollmar, back in the 1930s.[24] In fact, the performance so impressed her that she vowed to become a storyteller and later did just that.

Others based the drama of their presentations partly on the ability to describe a "picturesque" or "exotic" people that they might have visited, and from whom they purportedly gathered their tales. Such was the case with Elsa Sophia von Kamphoevener, who had spent many years living with a group of Turkish nomads.[25] She returned to Germany and began presenting evenings of oral narration of their tales in theaters throughout the country. There are many persons in present-day Germany who still remember these performances as being most impressive.

Currently, it is in France that one can find the most frequent presentations of storytelling in a theatrical setting. The Centre de Littérature Orale, usually known as CLIO, under the leadership of Bruno De La Salle has trained groups of tellers and musicians to recreate, in theatrical form, the oral narration of traditional texts related to King Arthur and the search for the Grail, the *Chanson de Roland*, The Thousand and One Nights, and the *Odyssey*.[26]

There is also a fairly large group of professional storytellers, more than forty in all, who present their programs principally in small theaters or recital halls. Admission is handled much like in other theaters. A short description of the style and background of about fifteen of this type of teller are given in Gorog's article on the subject.[27]

In Italy recently, a number of storytellers have attempted to reproduce in a theatrical setting the style and content of the repertoires of the *cantastorie*, or public marketplace storyteller.

## North American Theatrical Storytelling

In North America, the best known of such performers in the first three quarters of this century was probably Eva Le Gallienne, who had made a specialty of reciting the tales of Hans Christian Andersen. Such entertainments often started out as "readings" but soon developed into dramatic narrations with the book serving more as a stage prop than as a necessity. In the mid-1950s, Le Gallienne also opened the first seasons of storytelling at the Hans Christian Andersen monument in Central Park in New York City.[28]

Gudrun Thorne-Thomsen, Ruth Sawyer, and Marie Shedlock had all done this kind of storytelling, as well as the institutional type. All three used largely folk material or stories by writers such as Andersen, who wrote in folktale patterns. It was Miss Shedlock's manner and style of telling that most influenced the development of storytelling programs of the New York Public Library, and many other public libraries as well.[29]

Recently, there has been an increase in this kind of storytelling in the United States and Canada. The National Association for the Preservation and Perpetuation of Storytelling estimates that among its members are some twenty persons who could be called theatrical storytellers, because they perform on a regular basis in theaters. Carol Birch experimented with a series of performances at the Mark Taper Forum in Los Angeles in the early 1980s. Tellers such as Norman Dietz, David Holt, Jay O'Callahan, and Gamble Rogers often tell stories that are composed out of personal experience, rather than tales based on folklore or written material, and many of their performances are in theatrical settings.

Diane Wolkstein, on the other hand, has recently made a specialty of performing segments from Inanna, the Sumerian goddess myth, and picture storytelling
of the *Ramayana*, in the Indian tradition. Many of these epic performances are
in theaters, whereas her telling of folktales more often than not occurs in a
school or library setting. Connie Regan-Blake and Barbara Freeman, a duo who
perform under the name The Folktellers, have presented their tales in a theater
for the past few years, under the title *Mountain Sweet Talk*. A number of other
tellers perform as part of a group series, such as the "Storytellers in Concert"
series produced by Lee-Ellen Marvin in Cambridge, Massachusetts.

Some professional tellers, such as Garrison Keillor and Spalding Gray, evolved
their theatrical style over public radio or in film and television.

Many of the storytelling festivals now organized annually in the United States,
Europe, and other parts of the world present storytelling that could be called
theatrical, and the sites where the festivals are held are often theaters. These are
described in the last chapter.

## Russian Theatrical Storytelling

There are some examples of Russian folk storytellers who attempted to trans-
fer their art to the formal setting of the theater. Sokolov reported that a woman
had been honored by the state for her unusual storytelling gifts, and then went
to Voronezh and Moscow for the winter of 1935–1936. There she performed in
public halls and theaters the same stories she told in her village. She was paid
much like any other theatrical performer.[30]

## Indonesian Theatrical Storytelling

If it is extremely difficult to draw the line between storytelling and theater in
the Chinese *shu-ch'ang* and the Japanese *yose*, it is doubly so in the case of the
*dalang*, the narrator who is both storyteller and puppeteer in the *wayang kulit*, the
shadow-puppet play of Indonesia. Most accounts and studies seem to treat the
*wayang kulit* as theater, which it certainly is in its totality. Yet the *dalang* performs
alone, except for the members of the orchestra who accompany him. And his
narration comes out of a storytelling tradition, similar to the *wayang beber* and
other forms of picture storytelling (see Chapter 12). He could be and is considered by some to be a storyteller.[31]

> Even today, he never fails to burn incense and to pronounce the *kochap ing
> pagedongan* (invocation to the audience) at the opening of the stage. Then he sta-
> tions himself behind the screen which he will not leave during the whole perfor-
> mance, beginning after evening prayer and continuing until dawn.
>
> Thus, he must have, above all, physical endurance against all strains for he
> cannot allow the high tension of the play to fall for a single instant lest he could lose
> the attention of the spectators during the performance. In addition, he must pos-
> sess a prodigious memory in order to recite correctly the whole repertoire in verse;
> he must have a certain sense of humour, great deftness and range in his vocal
> chords (for he must make the puppets speak in different tones according to their
> sex), and a refined musical sense.[32]

Coomaraswamy found parallels between *dalang* and the early picture showmen
in India and those of Persia and China.[33] Mair elaborates on this speculation and

sees a continuum in Indian picture storytelling and the use of shadow puppets to accompany narration that is essentially storytelling. He also writes:

"... we have repeatedly seen how difficult it is to separate this particular genre of folk performance from a host of associated and oral performing arts. This is not surprising in light of the fact that a given group of performers often specialized in telling the same story or stories in several organically linked media."[34]

Of course, an element of storytelling is inherent in much of theater. But theater, in most of its definitions, requires a director whose role is different from that of the actors. The *dalang* needs no director and frequently improvises his narration, much as a storyteller does, rather than stringently following a script, as most actors do.

# CHAPTER 6

# *Library and Institutional Storytelling*

It is not quite clear just which public library in the United States first began to have regular story hours for children. Nor is it possible to state definitively which children's librarian first propounded the idea. Caroline Hewins, a pioneer in public library work, is known to have read aloud on Saturday mornings in the Hartford Public Library, from approximately 1880 on.[1] But this was definitely reading aloud, and no mention of oral narration or storytelling was made in her reports.

The Carnegie Library in Pittsburgh, which began regular story-hour programs in 1899, is usually credited as being among the first to have offered this activity as an accepted part of work with children in the public library.[2] This might well be true, but there is some evidence that other libraries began a regular story hour much earlier than 1899. For example, Mary Ella Dousman, writing in 1896 and describing the notices that were put up in Buffalo prior to the opening of the public library there, cites the text of the placards:

> BOYS AND GIRLS—Books for You to Read
> Pictures for You to Look At
> Maps for You to Put Together
> Magazines for Everybody
> Someone to Tell You Stories[3]

The new librarian is quoted as saying: "We shall have a regular hour for storytelling."[4]

There surely must have been further discussion among the pioneer children's librarians on this subject. Yet no other references to a regular story hour in public libraries could be located for the years prior to 1899. Nor do historical records or internal reports in any of the public libraries operating at that time indicate that they had such activities.

## Carnegie Library and Pratt Institute

The programs of the Carnegie Library in Pittsburgh and the Pratt Institute Free Library in Brooklyn seem to have sprung up spontaneously at about the same time. Their impact was great because they were the two most important centers at the turn of the century for the training of children's librarians. The graduates took positions in Brooklyn and Pittsburgh and also spread out all over the country. They took with them the experience of actually having seen story hours; perhaps they had even participated in one as part of their training.

Some of the early story hours, at least at Pratt Institute, seem to have been delightfully free of any pretensions. They probably were close to folk storytelling experiences, because as Anne Carroll Moore wrote, "the people who have told stories for us are volunteer visitors."[5] Here is how she described one of them:

> A most delightful improvised story was told about two children who were lost in a forest. . . . The sixty children in attendance ranged from three to twelve years and formed an ideal group.[6]

She mentions also that for a Christmas story hour, a librarian of German origin told simply and expressively of her childhood experiences during the Christmas season.

In Pittsburgh, the programs seemed a bit more formal and literary from the very beginning. The series that opened the formal storytelling programs in 1899 was of stories based on the plays of Shakespeare.[7] For the second year an outline of sixteen stories from the *Iliad* and the *Odyssey* was prepared; these programs were held simultaneously in the Central Library and in all of the branches.[8] The story hour in Pittsburgh was not meant to be a formidable experience or to approximate a literature class in school, however. On the contrary, as F. J. Olcutt pointed out:

> We have found that even our weekly storytelling lectures are seized on by the teachers as material for compositions and tests of memory, which, if not prevented, would defeat our main object in telling the stories. We aim to produce an unforced, natural love for the best in literature.[9]

The very fact that a flexible length was suggested, rather than a fixed one-hour session, implied that the storyteller was not expected to overdo it. The storyteller was supposed to watch out for "audience fatigue" and bring the story to a stop as soon as attention lagged.[10]

The cycles of stories told in Pittsburgh included the three already mentioned and the following: the Volsunga Saga, Robin Hood, *Beowulf*, Cuchulain, King Arthur and His Knights, and the *Chanson de Roland*. These were told in story hours for children aged ten and up.[11] In 1902 a story hour was organized for children nine years old and younger. For them the selections were fairy tales, fables, nature myths and Bible stories.[12]

Richard Alvey, in his dissertation on "The Historical Development of Organized Storytelling to Children in the United States," analyzed in great detail the early philosophical differences between Anne Carroll Moore and Frances Jenkins Olcutt. Moore, he felt, emphasized the story hour as a "sociocultural event" whereas Olcutt never deviated from her insistence on tying in the story hour to books, literature, and the specific goals of the library in promoting them.[13] Gradually, Moore came closer to Olcutt's position, perhaps because in her work as Head of Children's Services at The New York Public Library, she had to justify this storytelling work in relation to the collections. When this writer was trained in the work of storytelling at the New York Public Library in the mid-1950s, not long after Moore's retirement, the goals were very similar to those of Olcutt. However, the type of stories recommended for telling were modeled more on folklore than on the written literary classics that were promoted by Olcutt.

By 1900, at least five libraries were reporting regular story hours of the types recommended by Pittsburgh or Pratt staff or graduates.[14] They were usually held weekly during the months from November through April. This activity was soon to mushroom, not only because of the spreading out of Carnegie (Pittsburgh) and Pratt graduates, but also because of the first storytelling and lecture tour of Marie Shedlock.

## Marie Shedlock

Marie Shedlock, a teacher in a successful girls' school in London, abandoned teaching to become a public lecturer.[15] When, in 1900, she was brought by Charlotte Osgood Mason to lecture at Sherry's in New York in an ongoing afternoon lecture and concert series, she had one lecture in her repertoire. This was titled "The Fun and Philosophy of Hans Christian Andersen." In the course of her talk, she told seven Andersen tales. One of the persons who heard her was Mary Wright Plummer, then head of the Pratt Institute Library School. Plummer invited Shedlock to lecture at Pratt in 1902 and to tell stories in the Children's Room the following year.

Mary Wright Plummer and Anne Carroll Moore must have talked at length to their colleagues around the country about this excellent teller of Andersen tales. In the subsequent years of her first U. S. tour, from 1902 to 1907, Marie Shedlock performed in many public libraries,[16] whereas in her first two years of the tour she had lectured mostly in tearooms, small concert halls, kindergarten teacher training schools, and the like.

Shedlock's style was polished and skillful, yet very simple and with few gestures. It emphasized delight in the story. It was the antithesis of the style propounded by elocutionists of the day. She often wore gowns that suggested the costume of Mother Goose or a fairy godmother.[17] Over the years she increased her repertoire greatly, telling legends and folktales of many types. But she was always to remain closely identified with the interpretation of stories from Hans Christian Andersen.

## Gudrun Thorne-Thomsen

Another person who had a strong influence on organized storytelling in the United States was Gudrun Thorne-Thomsen. An immigrant from Norway while still in her teens, she became a teacher at the University of Chicago, lecturing in the school of education. Like Marie Shedlock, she was soon also giving lectures and demonstrations in other places, particularly in library training schools and teacher training schools. Her influence was greatest in the Midwest and the West, but the fact that she made several disc recordings that were distributed by the American Library Association also helped to spread her quietly inspiring style to all parts of the country.

May Hill Arbuthnot, author of the first editions of *Children and Books,* found in Gudrun Thorne-Thomsen "the greatest expression of the folk art of storytelling that this generation has known." She described her as "the quietest of all the storytellers and the least humorous. Sometimes in telling a saga she is almost austere, and her stories are apt to fall continuously into a minor key. Her art is the essence of dramatic simplicity—no embellishments, no exaggeration, but a complete integrity of words and spirit, and all so quiet, so still that you can hear the heart speaking."[18]

Thorne-Thomsen was also influential in the development of park and playground storytelling (see Chapter 7).

Many of the reports of storytelling in libraries over the next few decades revealed the influence of either the "Carnegie Library" or the "Marie Shedlock" style. If a library's printed program showed a series of story hours based on heroic epics or Shakespeare, there was almost sure to be a librarian on the staff who had attended the Pittsburgh school or who had gone there for a summer of observation and study. If the programs included more Andersen stories, short legends, and unusual and poetic folktales, chances are the person who planned them had studied at the library schools of either the Pratt Institute or the New York Public Library, and had probably heard Marie Shedlock lecture or demonstrate the telling of stories.

Gudrun Thorne-Thomsen's style was copied in some libraries, but it was more often encountered in teaching institutions.

## Storytelling in Schools

There had been earlier attempts by educators to stress the importance of storytelling. In fact, the Kindergarten Teachers' Group of the National Education Association had been very active in the promotion of storytelling, as had the kindergarten training schools. Kindergarten teachers were among the first to write extensively about storytelling to class groups of children, at least in the United States. They wrote so much on the subject that Alvey concluded:

> One could nearly summarize kindergartners' claims for the benefits of storytelling ... by stating that they suggested that almost every conceivable benefit or desirable non-physical need of the child could be realized through properly employed storytelling.[19]

One of the most enthusiastic storytellers from among the kindergarten teacher's group was Mary W. Cronin of Boston. She had been trained in Froebel methods, and was well-known as a storyteller in the Boston area by 1910.[20]

But in spite of the enthusiastic support for storytelling among such prominent educators as Friedrich Froebel, Maria Montessori, John Dewey, Johann Friedrich Herbart, and others, teachers did not take to storytelling as enthusiastically as did librarians. Of the four professional groups in the United States analyzed by Alvey—teachers, librarians, religious educators, and recreational directors—it was the educators who were the least involved in the actual practice of storytelling.[21]

The only educational group in the United States (above the kindergarten level) that accepted storytelling and even insisted on it as a necessary part of the school curriculum was the Ethical Culture Society. This group was founded in 1876 by Felix Adler, who expounded his beliefs on education and on the importance of storytelling in his book *Moral Instruction of Children*. Most of the schools operated by the society still include storytelling as a part of the regular curriculum.

The formal school systems had not achieved anything comparable to what the public libraries had succeeded in doing within a very short time, namely, to establish as part of their operative policy and philosophy the importance of scheduled story hour programs. These programs were administered in a number of cases by special staff, whose responsibilities included training storytellers, planning programs for the entire season, and arranging to have them printed in special bulletins or in regular library programs.

## Library Supervisors of Storytelling

Carnegie Library in Pittsburgh and the New York Public Library were the first to have full-time supervisors of storytelling. Edna Whiteman of Cleveland was appointed the first supervisor at Carnegie in Pittsburgh, in May 1912. One report discreetly mentions that "at first there was some opposition from librarians to this special supervision."[22] But this seemed to disappear as newer members of the staff were added. Apparently, some of the staff members with years of experience felt it was an intrusion to have someone observe and evaluate their storytelling.

The New York Public Library position was created earlier, in 1908. The first person to fill the post was Anna Cogswell Tyler, who as a student at Pratt had heard Marie Shedlock tell Andersen's "The Nightingale." She had decided then to become a children's librarian so that she could tell stories regularly.[23]

Another library that added a full-time supervisor of storytelling was the Enoch Pratt Free Library in Baltimore, c. 1925. Boston Public Library hired Mary Cronin on an expenses only basis in 1911, and on a more permanent basis in 1912. When the library managed to find additional funds, she was joined by her husband, John Cronin, and her sister, Mrs. Margaret Powers, soon after that.[24]

## Opposition to Storytelling

Not all public library administrators were completely in favor of storytelling. John Cotton Dana, a well-known librarian and lecturer in library schools, believed that the function of storytelling belonged in the public schools. "It is probable that the schoolmen know better when and how to include storytelling in their work with a given group of children than do the librarians," he wrote in 1908. He conceded that there were more librarians than teachers who were skilled in telling stories, or who *wanted* to do storytelling, which was also important. To satisfy these creative urges on the part of some children's librarians, he recommended the following:

> If, now, the library by chance has on its staff a few altruistic, emotional, dramatic, and irrepressible child-lovers who do not find library work gives sufficient oppor-

tunities for altruistic indulgence, and if the library can spare them from other work, let it set them at teaching the teachers the art of storytelling.[25]

Dana did not reckon with the wide appeal that storytelling had among public librarians. Nor did he take fully into account the fact that administrators generally like visible signs of library use. The lines of children waiting to get into the story hours were obviously impressive. Also, the number of books checked out on a day during which there was a program was invariably higher than on nonprogram days.

The most persuasive answer to Dana in 1908 was the fact that large numbers of children were not in school. The children that did go to the urban public schools were often of immigrant families and English was usually their second language. Many of these immigrant children were in crowded classrooms where the likelihood of sustained teaching, much less storytelling, was remote. The teacher was probably hard put to cover the basic skills of reading, writing and arithmetic on which her pupils were sure to be tested.

The public library took seriously its responsibility to serve these children. It was believed they were more accustomed to oral traditions than written ones, so the story hour was considered especially appropriate. There was also a hope that by introducing the children early to good literature, it would improve their English. The librarians believed this could be done more easily through informal reading aloud, story hours, and the use of books with simple texts and many pictures. A 1909 article on storytelling in the Cleveland Public Library mentioned that 76 percent of the children in the public schools of that city were of foreign parentage, and that many more were out of school. The article cited as one of the main goals of storytelling, "the presentation of stories which children have found difficult to read."[26] This referred not to reading difficulties per se, but rather to those encountered by non-English-reading children.

By 1927, there were regular storytelling programs in 79 percent of the public libraries of the United States.[27] Furthermore, in many urban areas, children's librarians were also providing storytelling services for park and recreation departments, for schools, for hospitals, and other institutions.[28] With the Great Depression, however, came a decline in the number of staff. The amount of time that could be given to storytelling was reduced. For the decade from 1930 to 1940, there are fewer articles on the subject in professional journals than for any other decade between 1900 and the present. The story hour programs were not by any means discontinued. In the libraries, they very much held their own, but librarians did cut back on the number of story hours in outside institutions. Radio and film were also beginning to make inroads on the attendance figures. Some libraries switched from the Saturday morning story hour to one held after school on a weekday afternoon.

## Preschool and Picture-Book Story Hours

The first picture-book story hours were begun in the decade from 1930 to 1940. Gross cites the Detroit Public Library as having the first preschool picture-book story hour, for three-to-five-year-olds.[29] Other early story hours for preschool children were in Maumee, Ohio (1939–1940)[30] and Milwaukee (c. 1940).[31] Many of these still used orally told stories, followed by a period in which the children looked at the pictures in the books (fig. 25). This was in

**Figure 25**    *The first Pre-school Story Hour at the Milwaukee Public Library, November 1941. The teller (unseen) was Norma E. Loos. Photo courtesy of Milwaukee Public Library.*

line with the recommendations of Marie Shedlock, the most widely followed model insofar as librarians were concerned (see the Picture Books segment in Chapter 12).

The public libraries were just beginning to come out from under the pall of the depression when World War II broke out. Once again there was a shortage of staff, and many children's librarians had to do more administrative work as well as work with the public. Some librarians, however, used the war as a special impetus to expand the storytelling program, contending that the children needed stories at such times more than in a time of peace.

Picture-book storytelling became more and more popular. In 1944, the Library Extension Division of New York State's Department of Education found it expedient to issue guidelines and instructions for carrying out picture-book programs.[32] After the war, and in the decade of the 1950s, there was a spate of articles dealing with the picture-book story hour, both for preschool children and for slightly older children. The impact of this on picture-book publishing is discussed in Chapter 12.

The traditional story hour received additional momentum in the 1940s, 1950s, and 1960s, partly through the inspiring articles and teaching of librarian-storytellers such as Elizabeth Nesbitt and Frances Clarke Sayers. Nesbitt, formerly supervisor of storytelling at the Carnegie Library in Pittsburgh, was later a lecturer in the library school there. Sayers had been coordinator of work with children at the New York Public Library before going on to teach at the University of California, Los Angeles. There were also numerous attempts to revitalize the training of library storytellers by having symposia, seminars, and festivals at which the less-experienced tellers could hear and observe those with many years of telling experience behind them.

Gudrun Thorne-Thomsen (until her death in 1956), Ruth Sawyer, author of one of the most popular manuals on storytelling, and Augusta Baker, storytelling specialist and later coordinator of children's work at the New York Public Library, were frequently asked to lecture about storytelling and then to demonstrate their skill in telling stories (fig. 26). In England, librarian Eileen Colwell took on this task. In Japan, Momoko Ishii did the same, passing on what she had learned during her stay at the Toronto Public Library.

Nevertheless, by the mid-1960s, the traditional story hour had declined in public libraries, and its place was being taken by the pre-school hour, or the picture-book story hour, or the combination film and story-hour program. Whether this was caused by the expanding influence of films, radio, and television, or by the lack of time and staff needed to prepare good story hours that would consistently attract children, is an aspect that has not yet been fully researched. Alice Kane of the Toronto Public Library was inclined to believe that it was a lack of enthusiasm on the part of librarians and an unwillingness to expend the extra effort needed to sustain a good story hour program.[33]

In the early 1970s, while doing field work for his dissertation, Alvey observed storytelling in school and public libraries of all sizes as well as in other institutions and organizations. It was his general conclusion that the professional librarians in the small libraries and in school libraries rarely had the time or the incentive to prepare and present a traditional story hour. Only in the larger library systems were such programs being sustained. However, there were still a large number of enthusiastic storytellers individually carrying out programs by dint of special, personal effort.[34] These observations can be confirmed by this writer's

**Figure 26**  *Augusta Baker conducting a storytelling hour at the Chatham Square branch of the New York Public Library. Photo courtesy of The New York Public Library, Public Relations Department.*

own experience in the same period, at numerous storytelling seminars and workshops in libraries throughout the United States and Canada.

It must be emphasized that the above refers to the story hour that involves orally told stories, unaccompanied by films, pictures, and other recording devices. Almost all libraries of all types and sizes were managing to carry out picture-book story hours for young children of preschool age or under eight years of age.

Ethna Sheehan and Martha Bentley of the Queensboro Public Library conducted a country-wide survey of storytelling in libraries in 1961.[35] Of the thirty-six library systems queried then, over 77 percent said they still had the traditional story hour as part of the library programs. Since only systems serving populations over 100,000 were included in the survey, this would seem to indicate that there had not been much change in the decade between the early 1960s and the early 1970s. It also adds weight to Alvey's conclusion that the traditional, organized story hour for children in the United States grew and matured to steadiness only in the libraries. The storytelling programs in school classrooms, in parks and playgrounds, and in religious education programs were lost to other forms of education through entertainment. They could be found in those institutions only sporadically during the decades from the 1930s through the 1970s.

It is interesting to speculate why this is so. Alvey believed it was because the personal presence of outstanding storytellers, such as Shedlock, Thorne-Thomsen, and Sawyer, had a positive and lasting effect on library staffs. The librarians, he believed, more than the other groups, saw to it that there were continual personal contacts and multiple personal storytelling performances for the beginner as well as for the more experienced practitioner to observe. He concluded:

This exposure, coupled with an adequate printed model for referral and continual training and practice emulating the expert, no doubt largely accounted for the success of librarian storytellers. On the other hand, lack of these—or most of them— or possibly the absence of the peculiar effect of the *combination* of all of them, perhaps largely accounted for the ineffectiveness of teacher storytellers.[36]

This would seem at first to be a good explanation. But the fact remains that certain groups of teachers had an equal amount of exposure to outstanding storytellers, had adequate printed models, and had access to further training. Yet they did not produce a cadre of exceptional storytellers.

It would seem just as logical to search for the answer in the conditions under which librarians and teachers have been telling stories. The greatest difference lay in the fact that, in most cases, when public librarians told stories to children in groups, those children knew that there was nothing in particular that "had to be" or "should be" learned. Whether in their home institution or outside, the public librarians offered storytelling without an element of a lesson to be remembered or some vague thought that in the future the child should be called upon to recount the story and its message. The very nature of pedagogy seems to demand this of the teacher's use of storytelling. Thus, a subtle change in the storyteller/audience relationship occurs.

It is likely that the conditions and expectations of the school classroom, as well as a lack of models to follow, were some of the reasons that prevented teacherstorytellers from realizing their full potential. Pedagogy generally exerts pressures for explanation, interpretation, rationalization, and justification. This is the antithesis of storytelling as practiced by the well-known tellers that librarians emulate.

Another reason for the paucity of storytelling in the classroom may well have been the extensive course requirements demanded by various public authorities. Teachers in training must take many courses that cover subject areas as well as teaching methods. There was not always time for specialized courses in storytelling. Nor were many such courses available in teacher training institutions. However, there have been and still are some schools of education that include courses in storytelling for teachers as an elective. A good example of such a school is the Bank Street College of Education in New York, where there has been a regular, elective storytelling course for many years. The courses in library schools are usually open to education students in the same university and can often be included in education credits. It is not unreasonable to assume that a small percentage of teachers who took those courses in the past managed to include the story hour in their classrooms on a regular basis, in spite of heavy demands created by required subjects and activities.

## Recent Patterns of Library and Institutional Storytelling

While it is still likely that only a small percentage of teachers schedule a story hour on a regular basis in their classrooms, storytelling has penetrated the schools in other ways. In the past two decades it has become common practice to enhance the curriculum by various methods, to make it more attractive to children. One of the methods has been the use of outside specialists or "artists" who are invited into a school to interact with the children for a day, a week, or even a semester. Many of these "artists" are funded through grants from state Councils or Endowments for the Arts and/or Humanities. Others are funded through special community grants from business organizations, parent groups and service organizations. Encompassed in the term "artists" are storytellers, as well as persons who include the telling of stories as part of their presentation. For example, in the 1987–1989 registered and approved lists of the "Artists in the Schools Program" for the state of Wisconsin, there are three artists calling themselves storytellers, and ten others who list the telling of stories as part of their presentation.[37] Of the approximately 300 tellers listed in the *1989 National Directory of Storytelling* almost 200 storytellers indicate that they perform in schools around the country.

While there are still few regular courses in storytelling in teacher training institutions, there are numerous short term courses or workshops offered by them on an occasional basis, usually in summer. Augusta Baker, for example, has returned to the University of Nevada School of Education for many summers in the 1970s and 1980s to give a short course on storytelling. Also, many school systems contract with storytellers to provide in-service workshops for teachers, showing them how to incorporate storytelling techniques into their regular teaching, and how to use storytelling as a means of getting children to be more effective in their oral speech.

Some schools have developed a curriculum for the teaching of storytelling to children. Examples are the Hillcrest School in Toronto, the schools in California using the "Word Weaving" technique, Sacramento schools in the "Pocket Story Program" directed by Mary Lynne McGrath, and schools in Kirkwood, Missouri where a federally funded "Project Tell" was in effect from 1979–1982, directed by Lynn Rubright.[38] Other school systems sponsor a contest or festival at which children learn to tell stories and then perform in their schools and in public sites in their cities. The New York City Board of Education began such a program in the academic year 1976–1977 and it still takes place each year.

Storytelling manuals, which used to be aimed mostly at public library storytellers, now often include guidelines for school storytelling. This might range from advice as to how to justify storytelling in the curriculum from the pedagogical point of view, to specific recommendations of story materials that suit the average public school curriculum, to general advice on telling stories to children in particular grade and age levels (see Part 2 of the Bibliography).

In short, it is now probable that a fair number of schools have storytelling of some kind going on in their confines at least once a year.

In public libraries, the trend toward a decreasing number of regular story hours by the staff seems to be continuing, but the number of libraries using guest (non-staff) storytellers has increased dramatically. Generally, these programs are for family groups of mixed ages, rather than exclusively for children. The demand for such programs, together with the demand expressed by school systems, has enabled an entire cadre of librarian or teacher storytellers to leave their regular professional work and become full time storytellers. They have been supplemented by professional storytellers coming out of other professions such as the theater, religious ministry, the health professions and others.

The story hours that have continued (and even increased) in public libraries are those aimed at the preschool age. In a report recently issued by the National Center for Education Statistics, 83 percent of the more than 800 libraries surveyed indicated they had programs for children from 3 to 5 years old, 29 percent had programs for children from infancy through 2 years of age, and 82 percent had programs for school-age children. The survey did not ask for a breakdown by age group and program type, but it is likely that many of these programs have at least a short component of storytelling, because 79 percent of these same libraries reported moderate to heavy attendance at story hour programs by children under 14.[39]

There has been a new emphasis in the education and in-service training of children's librarians on learning about the stages of early childhood, so that selection of materials and programs can focus on very specific needs.[40] It is not uncommon to find public library programs planned specifically for two-year-old children, another for three-year-olds, and still another for four-year-olds. There are manuals and professional pamphlets designed to give guidance in planning and carrying out these very specific age-oriented programs.[41]

Recently, the Association for Library Services to Children of the American Library Association published a list of recommended "Competencies for Librarians Serving Children in Public Libraries." Part V deals with "Programming Skills" and the first two points in that section are:

1. Designs, promotes, executes, and evaluates programs for children of all ages, based on their developmental needs and interests and the goals of the library.
2. Presents a variety of programs or brings in skilled resource people to present these programs, including storytelling, booktalking, book discussions, puppet programs, and other appropriate activities.

It is thus clear that storytelling is still considered part of the normal job description of the children's librarian.

## Museum Storytelling

Museums have again turned to storytelling as adjuncts to their public programs. This is not a new idea. Mr. and Mrs. Cronin, the well-known storytellers in Boston, had initiated a major series of story hours at the Boston Museum of Fine Arts in 1911. It was paid for by the Boston Social Union. Later, that same museum sponsored summer storytelling and art programs for groups of children who were brought in from summer playgrounds and settlement houses.[42]

In New York, the Metropolitan Museum of Art established a series of storytelling programs for children and adults in 1917. Anna Curtis Chandler pointed out that these were designed to "facilitate better understanding of art objects."[43]

There probably has always been a small element of storytelling in the presentations of docents, as they led groups through the museum exhibits. The recent trend, however, has been to locate experienced tellers who can bring alive a current exhibit or some aspect of the general collections, by a program of stories related in period, content and style to the exhibits. The storyteller Laura Simms has developed a number of programs for exhibits at the Brooklyn Museum, and has trained docents there in storytelling techniques. Other examples of special programs Simms developed include those at the Metropolitan Museum of Art in connection with a Maori exhibit, and at the American Museum of Natural History as an adjunct to an exhibit on the Great Silk Road. For the latter Museum she has traditionally given an annual Halloween "ghost story" program that involves a number of objects from the Museum's exhibits.

Diane Wolkstein, another New-York-based storyteller, has also given many programs in museums. Recently, she narrated the legend of Tristan and Iseult at the Cloisters branch of the Metropolitan Museum in New York. Her versions of the Sumerian myth of Inanna, the Greek myth of Osiris, and segments from the "Song of Songs" have been performed in numerous museums.

For two years, Carol Birch conducted a weekly storytelling session at the Craft and Folk Museum in Los Angeles. Recently, in France, Muriel Bloch has initiated storytelling programs in conjunction with the Louvre.

In addition, many museums that are for children, or have special departments for children, have regular monthly programs of storytelling, sometimes directly related to the exhibits and utilizing pictures or objects from them, and sometimes purely for entertainment. These are usually given by professional storytellers who are contracted for their services, rather than by museum staff. However, there is a trend toward developing the skills of some docents or education department staffs so that they can include story performances as a part of their work.

## Storytelling in Other Institutions

There have been other institutions, both public and private, using storytelling on a sporadic or regular basis, but not too much documentation is available for these programs. Occasional reports indicate there was and is storytelling at penal institutions, but the only documented experience of such kind, over a period of years, appears to be that of Ruth Sawyer. At the request of the Federal Department of Justice, she told stories one month for each of ten years in the period 1935–1945 at the Federal Reformatory for Women in Alderson, West Virginia.[44]

Corporations have used storytellers in various training sessions, but again, very little of the specifics of such storytelling has been described or documented in print. The national railroad corporation, Amtrak, sponsored a storyteller on its trains for two seasons, as an entertainment supplement.[45]

# CHAPTER 7

# Camp, Park, and Playground Storytelling

There have been four types of organized storytelling to children in groups in the United States and Canada according to the folklorist-librarian Richard Alvey. These types he called educational, religious, library, and recreational.[1] Only the last-named type had as its chief and only goal, right from the start, the pure fun of storytelling. For park and recreation leaders, for camp counselors, and for club or playground supervisors, the one aim has been to amuse the children, and comparatively little time has been spent in trying to justify the amusement with edifying reasons concerning the liberating social value of communal entertainment.

Recreational storytelling of the organized type had its beginnings in neighborhood and settlement houses of heavily populated urban areas, in municipal parks and playgrounds, in camps run by scouting groups or philanthropic agencies, and in boys' clubs. According to Harriet Long, in her history of library service to children, it was in the years between 1869 and 1875 that the first directed playground was established, the first settlement house was opened, and the first boys' club was founded.[2] In those early years, however, there is virtually no mention of storytelling.

Jacob Riis, social reformer and journalist who did much to further the cause of free parks and playgrounds, obviously favored storytelling, for in his autobiography he wrote:

> I hear of people nowadays who think it is not proper to tell children fairy stories.
> I am sorry for those children. I wonder what they will give them instead. Algebra
> perhaps. Nice lot of counting machines we shall have running the century that is to
> come![3]

But in the early articles and books he and other social reformers wrote, urging the establishment of municipal parks, playgrounds, and recreation centers, there is mostly an emphasis on the need for physical play space.

Neighborhood and settlement houses stressed the study of both practical matters and the sharing of intellectual, culturally uplifting ideas, all in an atmosphere of social conviviality. The value of storytelling became apparent in these places sooner than in playgrounds. Jane Addams, in her autobiographical book recalling the early years of work in Hull House in Chicago, mentions the use of storytelling almost from the start. One of the first residents was a "charming old lady" who read aloud tales from Hawthorne and interspersed them with her own tales of recollections about Hawthorne, whom she had known.[4]

Hull House was also the scene of some of the early boys' clubs meetings. Jane Addams reminisced:

> Another memory . . . is that of the young girl who organized our first really successful club of boys, holding their fascinated interest by the old chivalric tales, set forth so dramatically and vividly that checkers and jackstraws were abandoned by all the other clubs on Boys' Day, that their members might form a listening fringe to "The Young Heroes."[5]

Notice that no mention is made of the fact that one activity is "better" than the others. The implication is simply that when there is a talent and it is shared with pleasure, the group will take up the offer with alacrity. In these early efforts, there is a remarkable freedom from "do-goodism," at least in the efforts of such a remarkable leader as Jane Addams. Few of the other social workers of the day documented their early work as vividly and frankly as she did, so there are not many other accounts of the uses of storytelling in social agencies prior to 1900.

The decade after the turn of the century brought the greatest impetus to organized recreational storytelling. The Boy Scout movement began in England in 1907 and in the United States in 1910. Camp Fire Girls, Girl Scouts, and Girl Guides followed closely after. The custom of sending city children away to summer camps in the country for at least a week or two began to be more prevalent.

## Playground Storytelling

The Playground Association was established in 1906. The members of this professional group worked in the newly established parks and recreational centers maintained by municipalities. In some cities, their jobs lasted only over the summer months. In others they were year-round, full-time occupations. These workers began to be trained in the special techniques of directing or supervising group play of all types.

All of this activity brought about an expanded interest in anything that proved to be fun for children. Storytelling was a natural outlet, especially for those workers with a talent and bent for it. During the second annual congress of the Playground Association, a storytelling committee was established. The chairman was Maud Summers. In an early article she had written:

> In the municipal playgrounds which have been built in so many cities, large and small, there is always a house known as the Recreation Center. If the playground is in a noisy section of the city near railroads, elevated trains, or factories, the children

should be taken into one of the rooms of this neighborhood house for the story hour.[6]

Summers died before her committee could present its formal report and recommendations, and the children's librarian, Anne Carroll Moore, was named the chairman.

Summers believed that the parks and playgrounds should use outside professionals for such specialized programs. In her view, the training and talent needed was too exacting to be expected of the average playground worker.[7]

The committee presented its report in 1910.[8] Not too much came of it, except that for many cities the trend was established: the storytellers for the parks and playgrounds were provided either by the public library (fig. 27) or by some other group, such as the local chapter of the National Storytellers' League.

Gudrun Thorne-Thomsen, on the other hand, advocated the training of regular staff to carry on such programs in recreation departments. In her view, long-term follow-through on such programs was best assured by having them done by regular staff members. Thorne-Thomsen made all of her recommendations after a summer of experimentation in the parks and playgrounds of Chicago.[9] It is ironic, but her report probably did much more to develop reading rooms for children in the Chicago Public Library than it did for the development of continued storytelling programs to be maintained by the Parks and Recreation Department of Chicago.[10]

Some cities probably did pay attention to Thorne-Thomsen's suggestions. For example, a report mentions that "storytelling in the playgrounds of New York City is considered an important feature of the work of the playground assistant whenever the conditions are favorable to carrying it on."[11] This was in addition to the storytelling assistance provided by staff of the New York Public Library. The patterns remained the same for quite a number of years. During the period 1957–1966, when this writer was on the New York Public Library staff, children's librarians from the staff gave weekly story hours during the summer months in Central Park, at the Hans Christian Andersen Monument, as well as at special sites in most of the larger municipal parks. The Parks Department provided a storyteller for one of the two weekly sessions at the Andersen statue. For many years, Diane Wolkstein performed that function. At the present time, staff from both agencies still do storytelling each summer, with the key location still being the Andersen statue in Central Park, where storytelling sessions are still held each Wednesday and Saturday.

Mary Cronin and her husband John were both very active in settlement house and playground storytelling before they were hired to become storytellers for the Boston Public Library.[12] Another city that had a professional recreational storyteller very early was St. Louis. That person was responsible only for the story-hour programs and occasionally assisted in directing group games. The assistants also did some storytelling, as did a number of volunteers.[13] San Francisco was reported to have had a professional storyteller for its parks and playgrounds during the 1930s.[14] On the whole, though, the majority of recreational storytellers were itinerant professionals.

In some cities the playground storytellers were encouraged to use costumes. A favorite choice was that of a "gypsy." These were often more romantic than authentic, as evidenced by surviving descriptions and photographs.[15] A steady sprinkling of articles in the pages of the official journal of the professional

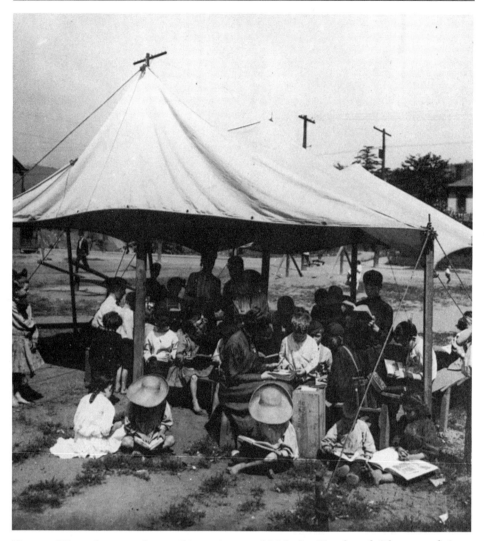

**Figure 27**  *Playground story hour, August 1910, in Hazelwood Playground (now Tecumseh), Pittsburgh. Unknown storyteller was from staff of Carnegie Library. Photo courtesy of Carnegie Library of Pittsburgh.*

recreation association indicate that some attention was paid to storytelling throughout the decades up to the 1970s. There is no question, however, that this activity, as well as many other organized park and playground activities, began to dwindle or change with the arrival of a much wider choice of free-time entertainment for urban children. Another reason was the cutbacks in municipal budgetary support, allowing for far fewer employees. And the element of safety has been added as a major factor in recent years, due to the drug related activities that have now usurped many spaces in municipal parks and playgrounds.

The Playground Association was eventually changed and absorbed into an organization that combined a wider group of professional interests, the National Park and Recreation Association. This organization has a number of divisions, and draws them all together during an annual conference. A number of park and playground members are still active members, but there is little or no indication how much storytelling they are doing, since the topic has not been covered in the conference for a number of years, nor has it been the subject of articles in the organization's journal and newsletters. There have also been no recent storytelling training seminars or workshops sponsored by the organization.[16]

However, it is known that quite a number of parks and nature centers, many of which have staff who are members of the National Park and Recreation Association, now offer regular storytelling events.[17] In Tucson, Arizona, this writer met a guide who told stories regularly to the persons taking rafting trips down the Colorado River. Jim Hamilton recently wrote of efforts to bring storytelling to Pennsylvania state parks, on a regular and consistent basis. The audience surveys they took after trial performances indicated there was great interest in and enjoyment of the programs.[18]

## Campfire Storytelling

Another reason, besides the financial one, for the decrease in planned summer activities in municipal parks and playgrounds was the rise in summer camping outside the city for children of all social classes. The scouting groups established many camping programs in the decades from 1910 to 1930, and social agencies followed after, arranging for children from even the poorest families to spend time away in a camp. In most of these camps it was traditional to end the day with stories told around the campfire. For the commercially or philanthropically run camps, such storytelling was likely to be an informal, spontaneous event rather than a consciously adopted program.

Among scouting groups it was more firmly established as policy, right from the first appearance of the *Handbook for Scoutmasters*. That book insisted that scouting was recreational and that the method to be used in all cases of teaching should be the story method, and not academic instruction.[19] The campfire was looked upon as a logical place for recreational storytelling. Once Franklin K. Mathiews became chief librarian for the Boy Scouts, the organization's literature made even more reference to the fact that storytelling around the campfire was a "must." Mathiews insisted that the stories be entertaining.[20]

Such campfire storytelling is the least organized and the most informal of all the types of organized storytelling to groups of children in the United States and Canada. In spite of a wide array of more modern and sophisticated forms of entertainment available to many camps, it remains persistently a recognized camping activity. This could provide the researcher with some interesting questions to investigate. Is there something intrinsic in the campfire that demands an almost instinctive response of narration on the part of those sitting around it? Does the child—even the sophisticated, urban child—suspend the usual expectations of entertainment while in a camping situation? Is the absence of television from most camps a factor?

A careful exploration of such questions might well lead to more conclusive evidence about the relative strength and appeal of oral, visual, and print media among children.

# CHAPTER 8

# *Hygienic and Therapeutic Storytelling*

Recently there has been a great increase of interest in the therapeutic uses of storytelling. However, there seems to be much confusion as to what "therapeutic" actually encompasses in this respect. In this book, the use of stories and storytelling for purposes of fostering and maintaining mental and physical equilibrium will be referred to as hygienic. This might seem a very medical term to use in referring to a process that is essentially a craft or artistry, but there is both historical and current evidence to indicate that storytelling has been used to keep a person healthy. It can therefore be termed hygienic.

Therapeutic will refer here to storytelling that is used to assist in healing or curing a person diagnosed as sick following standard procedures in the culture in question. This may mean diagnosis by a psychologist, a psychiatrist, or any medical doctor, or it may mean diagnosis by a practitioner of traditional healing and medicine. The illness may be mental, emotional or physical, or a combination thereof.

## Hygienic Storytelling

Many storytellers who claim to be practicing therapeutic storytelling are probably dealing with hygienic storytelling, which does not sound as interesting. Health or Hygiene, when taught as subjects in school, are often looked on as boring and probably unnecessary, if one uses common sense. Nevertheless, hygienic storytelling can be as important and challenging as therapeutic storytelling.

There is nothing new about such uses of storytelling. In many societies, it has been reported that storytelling was a part of wakes, or watches, to remember and pray for the dead. Some might think that this was principally for the purpose of giving honor to or remembering the deceased; however, an equally important reason is that it helps the surviving persons bring back into balanced calm the disequilibrium that has entered their lives because of the death. The quotation from the *Āsvalāyana-Grihya Sūtra*, cited in Chapter 1, makes clear that when one is trying to cope with such a misfortune, one of the best things to do is to tell "auspicious stories."

Perhaps the most explicit indications we have for early hygienic storytelling are those that date to the works of Ibn Butlan, a "Christian physician of the eleventh century who studied in Baghdad, practiced in Cairo, and eventually became a monk in Antioch."[1] He wrote an Arabic manual that was later translated into Latin in the thirteenth century, and which appeared in many manuscript versions, generally under the title *Tacuinum Sanitatis* (*Tables of Health*). The more complete versions of these manuscripts include advice related to health and storytelling. In the section where the importance of sleep is stressed, the *Tacuinum* recommended that "doctors advise people with cold hearts to have stories told to them that provoke anger, and those with hot hearts stories that entail pity, in order that their constitutions may be moderated."[2]

To achieve this state of equilibrium and maintain it, the *Tacuinum* advised each family to have a *confabulator*, literally, a person who converses. In some versions of the *Tacuinum*, however, the *confabulator* 's duties are described thus:

> A teller of stories should have good discernment in knowing the kinds of fictions in which the soul takes delight, should be able to shorten or extend his presentation of stories as he may choose, and to decorate, amplify, and arrange them as is fitting. He should not alter his appearance in conversation, nor should the purpose of the *confabulator* be interfered with by too much talking. A *confabulator* should be proper in manner and courtesy, be able to stay awake, be a good judge of discourses (not only histories of great princes but also delightful stories that provoke laughter), and be conscious of verses and rhymes, so that through these things a prince may gain an abundance of pleasures. For his digestion will improve because of them, and his *spiritus* and blood will be purified, and he will be freed from all sorts of troubling thoughts. . . .
>
> Trans. by Glending Olson[3]

Apparently, some medieval storytellers took this advice to heart, and even prefaced their telling of stories and fables with reminders of how healthy they were. A good example of this can be found in the introduction to the tale of *Aucassin et Nicolette*, a thirteenth century story in prosimetric form. This alternating verse and prose form is called *chantefable* in French. The sole surviving text was almost certainly written down from an oral performance. The introduction claims:

> There is no one so perplexed, so grief-stricken, miserable, or beset with illness, who upon hearing it [the story] will not be improved in health and cheered up through joy—it is that pleasant.[4]

The storytellers in Marguerite de Navarre's *Heptameron* have similar feelings about the power of story. In that work there are ten persons waiting for a bridge to be constructed. Some of them express the belief that they would fall ill or die if they did not have the diversions of hearing their companion travelers tell tales.[5]

The *Decameron* (c. 1350) of Boccaccio describes the withdrawal of a group of Florentine citizens to the country, to get away from the plague; there, they relax and amuse themselves in order to preserve their health. Pampinia, their leader, establishes a regimen of orderly pleasure. This includes a number of games and activities, but in the hottest part of the day she recommends the telling of stories. It is within this frame that the 100 stories are told. The contrast of plague-torn Florence and the beautiful and orderly gardens of the country estates to which the group withdraws to tell their tales has been seen by most critics and commentators of the *Decameron* as a literary device that Boccacio used to show dramatic contrast and give him a frame into which to fit the tales he wished to write. Glending Olson feels there was a more pragmatic reason for Boccaccio to structure the *Decameron* as he did. In his book *Literature as Recreation in the Later Middle Ages*, Olson cites many segments from medical advice books of the day to show that there was a psychological and medical basis for Boccaccio to use stories in this kind of setting, as a logical, medically acceptable method of avoiding the plague and staying healthy. Among the pertinent quotations he gives is one from Tommaso, a famous Florentine physician. Tommaso advocated retiring to a country home, surrounded by gardens with sweet-smelling plants and a few good friends (no "tipplers, loose women, gluttons, and drunkards"), and there making use of "songs and minstrelsy and other pleasurable tales without tiring yourselves out, and all the delightful things that bring anyone comfort."[6]

Over and over again, the medieval advice books on health stress moderation in all things. This included moderation in the kind and amount of stories one told or listened to, as well as moderation in all other forms of entertainment. But entertainment was definitely looked upon as a necessity to maintain good health. As in so many cases, people living at the time may have paid more attention to the fact that fun and pleasure was good for you, and less to the recommendation that it should not be excessive. The excesses were what caused religious authorities to rail repeatedly against certain forms of minstrelsy and public storytelling that was extremely bawdy and, in their view, often sacrilegious. Stories were to be told only if one could extract a moral or didactic message from them.[7] The power of these authorities was not strong enough to do away with storytelling of a purely recreational kind, but they did have a dampening influence, particularly in certain areas of Europe, and later in the colonies. The influence of the Puritans was especially strong in the United States. It affected in particular the children of many generations to come, because they were given stories, first orally and then in print, that were often overlaid with a thick blanket of didacticism. It is rare, even in the modern manuals of children's literature and storytelling, to find a recommendation that one should use stories with children because they are a form of mental recreation and such recreation is healthy for them.

This was perhaps the most novel aspect of Bruno Bettelheim's book, *The Uses of Enchantment*. It was praised highly and disputed roundly for its psychological interpretations of a number of the folk stories enjoyed by children during the past two centuries. In fact, there was really not much new about this aspect of *The Uses of Enchantment*. A number of earlier psychological studies had covered similar interpretations of these folk and fairy tales. However, in most of the reviews, scant attention was paid to the basic hygienic premise of the book, hinted at in the title: children *need* to hear psychologically complex, involving, and enchanting stories in order to grow up healthy in mind and psyche. The one area Bettelheim did not deal with was the difference in impact when these stories are told orally and when they are read.

## Therapeutic Storytelling

The advice in many of the medieval medical books recommending cures for various maladies of the body and spirit sounds remarkably similar to that propounded recently by Norman Cousins in *Anatomy of an Illness*, in which he recounts the healing he found in funny stories and in all types of materials that induced laughter. The difference was that Cousins heard and saw most of his stories by mechanically recorded means, whereas in the Middle Ages the storytelling would have been live.

An early account of storytelling used as a diagnostic tool occurs in two variants of a tale reported in the *Gesta Romanorum*, and in Sufi literature. In the former version, a knight calls upon a "cunning clerk" to determine why his wife is acting strangely. He suspects she has transferred her affections from himself to another. The clerk insists he must have time to speak to the wife, and is invited to dinner. After they have eaten, the clerk begins telling the wife many things, and puts his hand on her pulse. By bringing into the tale the name of the new beloved, the clerk is able to note the quickening of her pulse. When mentioning the name of her husband, the clerk notes that her pulse remains even and steady.

The Sufi version, translated by Idries Shah in his book *Caravan of Dreams*, tells of a princess who falls so ill, none of the usual doctors in the sultan's court can cure her. An elderly stranger arrives, insisting he can cure her. He tells her stories of other countries, other places, other peoples, all the while keeping his fingers on her pulse. He announces that the princess is sick with love for a man she met while on a trip to Bokhara. The sultan wishes to have the young man found and killed, but the stranger insists this will only make the princess more ill. He convinces the sultan to send for the young man, and the princess gets up from her bed. However, that is not the end of the "cure," for the old stranger (who is Shadrach) knows that the young man is a fortune hunter and will not, in the end, make the princess well. Shadrach gives the young man a special potion that makes him age prematurely, while he takes one to make himself younger. Day by day he keeps entertaining the princess with his tales, until at last she is cured of her fatal attraction for the young man (now aged), and falls in love with the wise Shadrach instead.[8]

One of the more extraordinary examples of curing by means of a kind of storytelling exists among the Kuna people of the San Blas Islands, off the eastern coast of Panama. Unlike many other Native American groups, the Kuna use no trance-inducing drugs or trickery in their curing.[9] They do use medicinal plants, but these are not believed to be effective without the accompanying use of *ikar*, an orally chanted text that uses a poetic language different from ordinary, everyday speech of the Kuna. Furthermore, there is also a use of wooden dolls, *suar nuchukana*, who represent good spirits.

There is an *ikar* for almost every possible situation: for relieving headaches, for enduring a difficult pregnancy, for passing through life stages such as puberty, to improve vision, against epilepsy, for calming mentally deranged persons, and many more. When a Kuna person falls sick, a *nele* (seer) decides if the cure requires medicine (usually plants gathered from the jungle by a specialist) and if the person also needs the performance of an *ikar*. The *ikar* is then performed by a person who knows the specific one called for. The *ikar* knower sits next to the sick person, who is usually in a hammock. The wooden dolls are at the side or under the hammock (fig. 28). There is also usually a pot of burning hot peppers. The performance typically lasts an hour or more, and is repeated several days in a row. The chant is addressed to the dolls, rather than to the patient. There are also *ikar* for preventive uses, such as warding off snakebite and strengthening children who seem prone to illness. And there are *ikar* to perform over newly gathered medicinal plants to make them effective.

The most complicated *ikar* is a mass curing *ikar*, which is extremely long and takes many years to learn. It lasts for eight evenings in a row, and uses very large dolls of balsa wood. These events are used to cure whole villages of epidemics or to rid an area that is perceived to be filled with disease, danger or evil.

The chants are memorized and recited not only in a curing or preventive situation, but for aesthetic enjoyment as well. This enables the *ikar* knower to remain proficient, even though the chant may be used only infrequently. However, in such cases they are chanted using a different voice quality. Here is a segment of the "*ikar* of the balsa wood," used in the mass curing ritual:

> The balsa wood spirit leaders are climbing
> They have all of their equipment.
> The balsa wood spirit leaders are climbing.
> They are at the mouth of the Opakki River.
> They fill the *inna* house (gathering house).
> They stuff the *inna* house.
> The spirits are ready to fight.
> The balsa wood spirit speaks.
> "You are going to the place of evil spirits . . ."
> The balsa wood spirit leaders are marching.
> Their golden hats are almost touching each other.
> Indeed their golden hats are almost touching each other.
> The balsa wood spirit leaders are marching.
> Their golden shoes are almost touching each other.
> Indeed their golden shoes are almost touching each other.[10]

In commenting on the reasons for the effectiveness of the curing process, Sherzer makes the point that the "repetitive, incantatory and euphonic" nature of the *ikar* performance is mentally and physically relaxing. When carried out by "a specialist in whom the patient has the utmost confidence and combined with the administration of actual medicine," they are most effective.[11]

There are other groups in Central America using similar curing rituals with dolls and chants, but few have been studied in such detail as those of the Kuna. In Mexico and Guatemala, this curing takes place mostly to heal persons suffering from "*susto*" or great psychological fright, principally children.[12] In the past decade, the small wooden dolls used for this purpose in Guatemala have been popularized and made into all-purpose "trouble" or "worry" dolls, commonly seen now in tourist and gift shops (fig. 29).

**Figure 28** *An ikar-knower performing a curing chant for a sick child among the Kuna of Panama. The chant is addressed to the wooden dolls. Photo by Joel Sherzer reproduced with permission from* **Kuna Ways of Speaking** *(Austin: University of Texas Press, c. 1983).*

**Figure 29**   *Guatemalan "trouble" dolls or "worry" dolls such as these, now commonly sold in gift shops, were originally devised for use by healers, to cure children of susto or psychological fright. Photo by Michael Gabrick and Chris Nickrant.*

## Storytelling in Modern Psychotherapy

Stories and storytelling are now used fairly frequently in psychotherapy, with both children and adults. Sometimes it is the therapist who is the teller, and in other cases the stories are elicited from the patient. The two persons who have developed the most structured storytelling procedures for children in psychotherapeutic treatment are Richard Gardner and Nathan Kritzberg.

Gardner called his technique the "mutual storytelling technique." The child patient is asked to tell a story with a beginning, a middle, an end, and a moral to it. The stories are composed by the child without pictorial stimulus and are recorded mechanically and then played back. The playing back is considered an important component. The therapist then recasts the story, using the same theme and same conflicts mentioned in the child's story, but concluding with a moral or lesson that seems more appropriate. This storytelling is only one of a number of techniques recommended in the therapy.[13]

Kritzberg, on the other hand, developed a complete method to use with children who were generally uncomfortable in a free-play situation, used frequently by therapists working with children. He designed two board games, TISKIT and TASKIT, to elicit stories from children, and to help them therapeutically process the contents of the stories, once they were told. TISKIT uses pictures to stimulate the flow of stories, and TASKIT uses words. There is a system of rewards given to the children at various stages of their story performance. The stories are recorded manually. The therapist in this method also recasts the story, but is not confined to using the themes of the child's story. Neither the child's nor the therapist's stories have to contain a lesson or moral.[14]

Since both of these models have been in use since the 1970s, there is now a fair amount of documented case experience, indicating how and when the models were used and with what success. Brandell gives a few brief excerpts from some of these documented cases.[15]

An unusual model of storytelling therapy combining elements of folk healing practice and modern psychotherapy was developed for use among Puerto Rican children in New York City. Giuseppe Constantino and his colleagues noted that among the families they were dealing with, there was still a strong reliance on certain aspects of traditional medicine. They decided to use *cuentos* (folktales) from the Puerto Rican oral tradition as the basis for a therapeutic modality they developed. The methodology and results of their seven year project were written up in *Cuento Therapy*.[16]

A number of children's hospitals and other institutions dealing with long-term care of children have appointed therapeutic storytellers as adjunct staff. Two who have written about their work in such situations are Elaine Wynne of the Children's Hospital in Minneapolis and Mark Freeman of Koret House, University of California San Francisco Medical Center.[17]

Recently, the child psychiatrist Robert Coles has written of his experiences in the use of stories and storytelling as an adjunct to psychotherapy. He described the dramatic moment when, as a new practitioner, he was advised by one of the senior psychoanalysts that "the people who come to see us bring us their stories" and he, as a doctor, should try to do his best to use the stories to "understand the truth of their lives."[18]

Storytelling psychotherapy with adults has been tried by a number of prominent therapists who have then written about their techniques or had others write about them. Among these therapists are James Hillman, Eric Berne, Ira Progoff, Carl Fellner, Robert Hobson, David Gordon, Milton Erickson and Nossrat Peseschkian.

Hillman, a depth psychologist, believed that to have story awareness, per se, was psychologically therapeutic. Berne, who devised the method known as transactional analysis, once stated: "People are born princes and princesses, until their parents turn them into frogs." Progoff's method involved the keeping of an intensive journal and writing down stories. Fellner developed the use of teaching stories for conjoint family therapy. He believed that if the stories were chosen well, each family member could use the message of the narrative in his or her own way; stories had to have many layers of meaning so they could have different levels of impact. Hobson recommended essentially a Jungian approach, believing the therapist should use culturally analagous stories to supply information new to the patient but relevant to the patient's problem. Gordon advocated the use of therapeutic metaphors, fanciful narratives that fit the specific situation of the patient; stories always had to be tailor-made for the patient.

Erickson's work is most extensively described. He, too, felt that storytelling was one of the most effective devices to use in therapy, especially if the stories were carefully developed. Rosen has written in some detail of Erickson's work.[19] Lee Wallas, another of Erickson's followers, designed a set of stories for use in treating very specific personality disorders and even developed a specific set of performance techniques that proved to be useful.[20]

Nossrat Peseschkian, a therapist who is Iranian by birth, but practices in Germany, where he was trained, uses principally stories from Baha'i sources to act as transcultural mediators between the therapist and patient. He wrote: "Especially when there are resistances to be dealt with, the stories have proved their value. Without attacking the patient or his concepts and value directly, we suggest a change of position, which at first has more the character of a game. This change of position finally allows the patient to see his one-sided concepts in relation to others, to reinterpret them and to extend them."[21]

# III

## The Format and Style of Storytelling

# CHAPTER 9

# *Opening of the Story Session*

Most theaters use the curtain to inform the audience that something is beginning or ending, and as a psychological device to suggest to viewers/listeners that they must suspend belief or time. So, too, do most storytellers use special opening and closing actions or phrases to prepare their listeners and themselves.

Delargy described how in Ireland the scene was set for storytelling by the man of the house, who passed a fresh pipe with tobacco, first to the most honored guest, then back to himself, and continuing to the rest of the company.[1] This was not unlike the preparations of a number of Native American groups prior to their storytelling. According to Beckwith, among the Mandan-Hidatsa Indians it was the custom to begin by opening the tobacco pouch, filling a pipe with tobacco, and offering a smoke to all. The smoking continued during the entire storytelling session.[2]

In folk storytelling in the village, sessions often didn't have a fixed beginning or end. In one of the tale cycles cited by Brinkmann, there are ten pages of conversation before one gets to the first complete telling of a folktale. This conversation is full of short anecdotes and hints from the audience, such as "How was that again with the—" or "How did that go again—?" Sometimes these hints are picked up by the storyteller, and he or she launches into the full tale. At other times the narrator passes them by, obviously not in the mood to tell that particular tale at the moment.[3] This is a common pattern in many parts of the world.

## West African and South Pacific Methods of Story Selection

A most unusual form of selection of a story for telling was recorded by Mary Kingsley in West Africa during the last years of the nineteenth century. In a number of places she had come upon traveling narrators, each carrying a net. Her description of these tellers carrying their unusual objects bubbles over with enthusiasm and admiration:

> I have seen one in Accra, one in Sierra Leone, two on board steamers, and one in Buana town, Cameroon. Briefly, these are minstrels who frequent market towns and for a fee sing stories. Each minstrel has a song-net—a strongly made net of fishing net sort. On to this net are tied all manner of things, pythons' backbones, tobacco pipes, bits of china, feathers, bits of hide, birds' heads, bones, etc., etc., and to every one of these objects hangs a tale. You see your minstrel's net, you select an object and say: how much that song. He names an exorbitant price; you haggle; no good. He won't be reasonable, say, over the python bone, so you price the tobacco pipe—more haggle; finally you settle on some object and its price and sit down on your heels and listen with rapt attention to the song, or, rather chant. You usually have another. . . . These song-nets, I may remark, are not of a regulation size. I have never seen on the West Coast anything like so superb a collection of stories as Mr. Swanzy has tied on that song-net of his. . . . The most impressive song-net that I saw was the one at Buana. Its owner I called Homer on the spot, because his works were a terrific two. Tied on to his small net were a human hand and a human jaw bone. They were his only songs. But they were fascinating things and the human hand one had a passage in it which caused the singer to crawl on his hands and knees, round and round, stealthily looking this side and that, giving the peculiar leopard-questing cough, and making the leopard mark on the earth with his doubled-up fist. Ah! that was something like a song.[4]

Two other persons recorded a custom similar to this. One was Rattray, writing in 1923:

> That evening I strolled down to see the chief to ask him about the next day's ceremony. I found him sitting in the court-yard of his "palace" listening to a story-teller. Somewhat like the late Miss Kingsley's "Homer" he was, for he derived his inspirations from his hat, round the entire rim of which were suspended articles that represented or reminded him of some proverb, story or riddle. You chose your little fancy, and he "was off."[5]

A modern folklorist, Verna Aardema, used this intriguing image of the "story hat" as the title for one of her collections of African tales for young readers.[6]

Carl Meinhof, a German scholar in search of different forms of script and recording devices, in 1911 recounted how he met with a missionary to Togo, Jacob Spieth, and one of his Ewe followers, Gottfried Antipatse. In Togo, they informed him, there were a number of persons who used "strings on which were strung all sorts of objects, such as feathers, stones, etc." Antipatse said they were for the telling of "proverbs" but Spieth said he was told by their owners that they were for telling "history."[7]

There are two more recent examples of similar objects denoting story repertoire. These are the story vines of the Lega, one of which is in the Smithsonian and the other in the American Museum of Natural History. Both were collected in the early 1950s in the area that is now Zaire, but not much documentation is available about the storytellers who used them. They each consist of a long

**Figure 30**   *Portion of the Lega story vine collected in Zaire in the 1950s and now exhibited at the American Museum of Natural History, Peoples of Africa Hall. Photo courtesy of the Museum.*

woven vine, on to which are attached numerous objects made of bone, plant fibers, or wood (see figure 30).

In the Marquesa Islands and the Cook Islands, there was a remarkably similar practice among some of the people living there in the earlier part of this century. The Polynesian Marquesans had various types of *toó*, knotted lengths of string that were used to keep accounts and to remember ancestral lineage. One particular *toó* was called a *moena tekao*, or story weaving, and had attached to it a woven sack, about the size of a child's head (fig. 31). In using it, the *tuhuka* (priest) asked the audience "Which story would you like to hear?" He then gazed intently into the sack (which was empty in a physical sense) and after a few moments of concentration would begin the stories. The sack, with its knotted string, was believed to contain all of the stories and songs that the priest knew.[8]

Another African variation in opening a storytelling session is reported by Junod and others. This is the custom of "riddling," that is, of making up riddles and guessing the answers to them. Among the Thonga of South Africa, for example, those not good enough at this back-and-forth word game had to pay a forfeit by being the first to tell stories.[9]

Seitel, in his ground-breaking book describing story performance among the Haya of Tanzania, also notes that riddling is a common prelude to stories. The questioner says: *Koi!* The audience responds *Lya!* The questioner then asks the riddle. The two words are purely formulaic and seem to have no meaning in this context. If the questioner does not get the response, he or she may not proceed. If the audience cannot answer the riddle, they acknowledge defeat and the questioner then demands a village as payment. The audience might suggest another village, but the questioner may hold out for a bigger village. This "exchange" of villages is, of course, purely imaginary.[10]

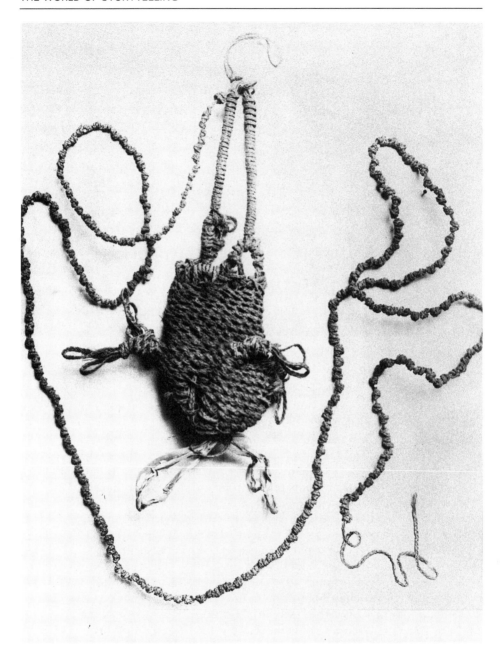

**Figure 31** Toó *with* moena tekao *or "story bag" attached, used by a* tuhuka *in the Marquesas as a symbolic container for sacred and historical tales; the* toó *contains roughly 245 knots, each with a meaning. Museum für Völkerkunde, Berlin, VI, 15966. Photo courtesy of Museum für Völkerkunde.*

## Other Methods of Storytelling Preparation

In preparing to perform the *penglipur lara* in Malaysia, the tellers frequently make a dish of offerings, burn incense and murmur invocations.[11] In the special Japanese storytelling halls or theaters called *yose*, apprentice storytellers prepare the stage for the master by bringing tea, arranging the cushions in the prescribed manner, and setting out any special items that are called for.[12] These formal, ritualistic preparations are echoed a bit in the ceremony of candlelighting that initiates the story hour in a number of public library systems in the United States and Canada.

By far the most common preparation for folk storytelling is the spontaneous gathering, often around a fire, of a group of persons whose past experience has led them to believe they can expect stories under such conditions, especially when there is a certain mood or atmosphere created by the cumulative events of the day or the seasonal weather. One Taos informant related how, during his childhood, an elder of the village would assemble up to twenty children for an evening's session:

> Each boy would bring with him two sticks of firewood. All would sit around the walls, and each in turn would tell a story.[13]

A Nez Perce informant mentioned two special winter lodges that were made: one for boys and one for girls. The best tellers were then invited in for long nights of storytelling.[14]

Among most North American Indian tribes, there was no storytelling allowed during the summer, spring, and early fall. Also, many believed that it was better to tell stories at night rather than during the day. The Zuni believe that you can hasten the coming of darkness by telling during the day. And if you tell in the time after the snakes have come out in spring and before they have gone underground in the fall, you must omit certain opening and closing lines and hold a flower in the hand, in order not to attract the snakes.[15]

Adamson mentions that among the Coast Salish it was the custom for people to prepare for stories by lying flat on their backs around a fire, so as not to get humps.[16]

Among the Kuna, the gathering house is the center for all forms of discourse, including storytelling. Every other evening, the people gather there. Persons who act as "policemen" file through the village, announcing the evening's event and urging the women to attend. Any chiefs that are present sit or recline in the middle of the house, on hammocks. Around them sit the spokesmen, and ritual specialists, on long benches. About 7:00 PM, the women start filing in, dressed in their best and carrying baskets in which they have the *molas* on which they are currently sewing, and a kerosene lamp to work by. Each woman chooses her spot on a bench, sets the lamp on a small table before her, places her children around her, and then talks to the women around her before beginning her sewing. Beyond the women, also sitting on benches, are the other men of the village, and around the edges are the "policemen," or caretakers of the village. The chief begins the "chanting." This may include news, public discussion of community projects, resolution of village problems such as arguments or thefts, and many other items needing discourse. And it may include storytelling, of all kinds. As Sherzer reports, the "smell of the pipes, cigarettes, and kerosene lamps . . . lend a special aura. . . . the symbolic seating arrangement in which the women are grouped together in a colorful array, dominated by the rich red of their *molas* and headkerchiefs in the misty darkness, and the overall impression is that of a dramatic chiaroscuro, all under the towering roof of the 'gathering house,' which forms an intricate pattern of bamboo and palm."[17]

In Australia, the Walbiri women who wish to tell stories must first prepare the sand by smoothing it out and clearing it of all rocks, twigs and other extraneous matter. As soon as they see someone doing this, the children around yell *"Djugurba!"* ("Dreamtime!") and sit down, prepared to listen to a story.[18]

In Africa there was and is a commonly reported proscription against telling stories during the day, especially during the planting and hoeing season. Vague, superstitious reasons were suggested for this. Some informants said that horns would grow on the storyteller if stories were told during the day or that the teller would grow bald.[19] Others predicted only that dire things would happen. Scheub is doubtful of these reasons, based on his observations among the Xhosa. In his opinion, the proscription was on economic grounds. If the work of the children lagged behind, especially during the hoeing season when everything grows by leaps and bounds in the tropics, it would be difficult to harvest a good crop later. So the threatening reasons for not being able to tell stories during the day were invented by the elders as a means of keeping all at their tasks.[20]

The only other folklorist or anthropologist who mentions this possible explanation is Michael Jackson. In his work with the Kuranko of Sierra Leone, he was frequently told that if one narrated stories during the day a parent would die. But one of his informants laughingly told him he was not afraid to tell in the day since both his parents were dead.[21] The explanation thus appears to be sound in view of the fact that few informants, whether African or Native American, were able to cite specific religious, historical, or social reasons for prohibiting stories during the planting, growing, and harvesting seasons. Scheub's reasoning seems logical since the forbidden times for storytelling are always during the productive hours of the day or year.

## Bardic Preparations and Openings

Most bardic storytelling did not differ greatly from folk storytelling in its preparations and openings. In ancient Greece, it consisted of a few strains on the cithara as a prelude, followed by a short address to Zeus or to another god or goddess, as the occasion demanded.[22] *Byliny* singers in Russia occasionally started with something striking and original, but the majority began with familiar or formulaic phrases to make the audience feel at home. A stock device was to open with a feast at which a wager was made.[23] Serbo-Croatian openings of this type were even shorter and more direct.[24]

The medieval Persian bardic storytellers opened by sitting on a chair, placed higher than the listeners, because the four legs of the chair symbolized knowledge, insight, patience and steadfastness, all qualities the teller was supposed to possess.[25]

The *bhopo* or *bhopi*, bardic performers of the *par* cloths, in Rajasthan and other parts of India, must make rather elaborate preparations: dressing up in a special shirt, skirt and turban; cleaning the ground; sprinkling it with water and touching it with gold to make it holy; erecting the picture scroll on its stands; setting up a small table in front on which to put a metal plate, a conch shell and a lighted lamp; tying bells around the ankles and the *jantar* around the neck; lighting the incense sticks; and finally, issuing the invocation to Ganesh, and other appropriate gods or goddesses, depending on the locality and the subject of the picture scroll.[26]

Another specific type of Indian bard, the performers of the Palnādu epic, must also dress in a very particular way: a white cotton lower garment is tied with a distinctive tie and knot; the left side of the chest is draped with a red and white sash; the right side of the chest is given a red and white mark, as is the forehead; a garland is strung around the neck; on the right leg is a jangling anklet; and wound around the head a turban with a crescent moon ornament; in the right hand goes a sabre and in the left a small brass shield.[27]

Performers of Arab epics like the *Sirat Bani Hilal* will, more often than not, open with an invocation to God, the Prophet and the collective Arab nation:

> The Merciful One did not create the likes of Muhammad
> The Prophet of Right Guidance came to us in all peace
> God bless you, O banner of Right Guidance
> O light of the eyes, O purity of the Merciful One . . .
> [continues on for 30 lines][28]

## Opening Words and Phrases

To actually begin the story, storytellers frequently call out or say slowly an opening word, phrase, or rhyme and then move right into the story. In English, we are all familiar with "Once upon a time—" or "There was once—." For those who wish to compare them in the original, here is a list of these well known opening phrases in some of the European languages:

| | | | |
|---|---|---|---|
| Albanian | *ishte njëherë* | Italian | c'era una volta |
| Czech | *kdysi za onoho času* | Polish | byl sobie raz or |
| | | | *pewnego razu* |
| Danish, Norwegian | *det var en gång* | Portuguese | era uma vez |
| Dutch | *er was er eens* | Romanian | era odata |
| Finnish | *olipa keran* | Russian | zhil byl |
| French | *il y avait une fois* | Serbo-Croatian | nekada |
| German | *es war einmal* | Spanish | érase una vez |
| Greek | *mià forà k'èva kairó* | Swedish | det var en gang |

Occasionally, the opening has a more stately variation that seems to warn the listener the story will be long and complex, and will probably have royalty as central characters:

> There was once, in old times and in old times it was, a king in Ireland.
>     W. B. Yeats, *Fairy and Folktales in Ireland*

> In a certain kingdom, in a certain land, in a little village, there lived . . .
>     A. Afanas'ev, *Russian Fairy Tales*

Peoples in other parts of the world who utilize the same or similar type of openings include:

Toucouleurs (Mali):    *Woneko wonodo* (There once was here)[29]
Sinhalese (Sri Lanka): *Eka mathaka rata* (In a country one recalls)[30]

| Japanese: | *Mukashi, mukashi* (Long, long ago) |
|---|---|
| | *Aro tokoro ni* (In a certain place)[31] |

The *tekerlemeler* of Turkey are rhymed introductions that usually have a non-sensical twist to them, but in essence they, too, put the setting of the story in the past:

> Once there was and once there was not, a long time ago, when God had many people but it was a sin to say so, when the camel was a town crier and the cock was a barber, when the sieve was in the straw and I was rocking my mother's cradle, tingir mingir . . .[32]

Native American opening phrases were also generally set in the past. Some of them were very terse, as, for example, the typical Clackamas introduction:

> He lived there.  *or*  She lived there.[33]

Others were closer to the European type of opening phrases, or at any rate, this is how they have been translated:

> White Mountain Apache: Long, long ago, they say . . .[34]
> Navajo: In the beginning, when the world was new . . .
> *or*
> At the time when men and animals were all the same and spoke the same language . . . [35]
> *or*
> There is a person, a real *milpero* (grower of corn) . . .[36]
> *or*
> Now we take it up.[37]

In Rwanda, the teller often begins with a repetitive refrain that may be translated thus:

> May I "sell" you a tale; may I make the tale penetrate you;
> May I rock you to sleep with a tale; may I wake you with a tale.[38]

The Dinka tellers of the Sudan usually open by saying "This is an ancient tale."[39]

But not all peoples begin their storytelling by putting their tales into the vaguely recent or distant past. Among the Xhosa of South Africa, as Harold Scheub reports, the folktale usually begins with: "Now for a *ntsomi*," or "A *ntsomi* goes like this." It is the action and singing during the story that help to build up atmosphere, not the preparation and setting of the scene.[40]

Other short introductory phrases are: "I can tell lies, too!"—a playful challenge by the Tiv storyteller of northern Nigeria;[41] "*a gbae se*," an untranslatable phrase, the closest equivalent of which is "Let's throw stories," from among the Bandi people of northwest Liberia.[42]

"And now listen to how the *dombra* tells about it," is a frequent device found among Kazakh storytellers. They use it to enter into the real story, after they have given a short synopsis or introduction.[43] This is similar to the "prelude" device used by some Russian storytellers, who follow it up with words to this effect:

> That's the flourish, just for fun;
> The real tale has not begun.[44]

## Call-and-Response Openings

In some parts of the world, the storyteller calls out a word or phrase, the audience replies, and the teller continues. This is most common in Africa, although it occurs in other parts of the world as well. In Cameroon, the exchange might go like this:

Narrator: Listen to a tale! Listen to a tale!
Audience: A tale for fun, for fun.
Your throat is a gong, your body a locust;
bring it here for me to roast!
Narrator: Children, listen to a tale,
a tale for fun, for fun.[45]

The Haya of Tanzania also have an extended exchange as an opening. The most common variant, as translated by Seitel, goes as follows:

Narrator: I give you a story.
Audience: I give you another.
Narrator: It's done.
Audience: The news of long ago.
Narrator: I came and I saw.
Audience: See so that we may see.
Narrator: I see . . . (here begins the story)[46]

The Wolof tellers of the Gambia region open this way:

Narrator: *Leb-on.* (There was a story.)
Audience: *Lup-on.* (Our legs are crossed, i. e. we are sitting.)
Narrator: *Am-on a fi.* (It happened here.)
Audience: *Da na am.* (It was so.)[47]

Among the Hausa of northern Nigeria the exchange that is heard most frequently is:

Narrator: *Ga ta, ga ta nan* (See it, see it here).
Audience: *Ta je ta komo.* (Let it go, let it come back)
*or*
*Ta zo, muji.* (Let it come, for us to hear.)[48]

Ben-Amos reports that in southwestern Nigeria, among the Edo-speaking peoples of the Benin area, "the storyteller opens his recitation with a string of proverbial phrases which include praise for the host, greetings to the audience, and wishes of blessing to everyone present." These are interspersed with responses from the audience or the storyteller's helper. Only after these have been completed does he actually begin his story, with a phrase such as:

*Umaranmwen sion sion sion.* (This is a nice story.)[49]

A similar custom is reported by Willis for the Fipa of East Africa. After the greetings, any person might begin storytelling and the opening exchange would go something like this:

Narrator:   There was a certain man.
Audience:   I was not there!
Narrator:   And a woman . . .
Audience:   I was not there![50]

Tedlock has given greater care to recording and deciphering in context the meaning of the opening and closing formulas of Zuni storytelling than many of his predecessors in anthropology and folklore. He points out that the present opening phrases have most likely been shortened. They can be translated roughly as: "Now we are taking it up" to which the audience responds "Yes, indeed!" following which the narrator continues: "Now it begins to be made long ago." The opening might be shortened, or the second part left out by the narrator, but if the audience does not give the "Yes, indeed" response, the telling will not be continued.[51]

Simpler and shorter call-and-response openings are the following:

Hungary and Central Europe[52]
Narrator:      {Bones, people}   or   {Bones}   or   {Bones }
Audience:      {Soup         }        {Meat }        {Bricks}

West Indies[53]
Narrator:   *Cric!*
Audience:   *Crac!*

Massignon does not say whether the *Cric-crac* opening found in France is a call-and-response type. One extended variant of this opening is given below, with its translation:

*Cric crac; cuiller a pot; marche aujourd'hui, marche demain; a force de marcher, on fait beaucoup de chemin.*

Cric crac; kitchen spoon; walk today, walk tomorrow; by walking and walking we cover a lot of ground . . .[54]

In the Bahamas and other West Indian islands, one or another of the following rhymes is used to start off the tale, often after the *Cric-crac* exchange between teller and listeners, or after the teller calls out "Bunday" or something similar:

Once upon a time, a very good time
Monkey chew tobacco and spit white lime . . .
                    *or*
Once upon a time, a very good time
Not my time, nor your time, old people's time . . .[55]

Similar rhymed verse beginnings are found in Chile:

To know and to tell
A lie does quite well.
I walked by a creek
Thrashing my stick.
I went through the corner
Stumbling along . . .[56]

Another place they are encountered is Romania:

Once upon a time when
Bears had tails as big as their head
And willows bore a fruit, juicy and red . . .
*or*
Once upon a time, a long, long time ago,
When mice ran after cats
And lions were chased by rats . . .[57]

These are probably related in source to the *tekerlemeler* of Turkey, mentioned above. However, they could also be representative of a spontaneous and playful period when, according to Huizinga, most speech of a special character, including laws, was in poetic form. This might explain why the practice is common to so many parts of the world.

Finally, it must be noted that there are places where there is virtually no "setting the stage" or creating of atmosphere by actions, words, phrases, or rhymes. For example, Mbiti reports that the Akamba in East Africa begin storytelling spontaneously by saying "The story of . . ."[58] Among Amapa storytellers in Mexico, it was recently noted that there was no particular preparation or opening and closing phrases.[59]

Perhaps the most unmarked or indistinct story session preparation of all can be found among the Yucatec Maya. In their language and custom, it is impossible to say "tell me a story." The only way to bring about a story is to initiate a discourse, to get someone to "converse" a story with you. This makes the dividing line between narrator and listener so thin it is almost invisible.[60]

# CHAPTER 10

# Style: Language, Voice, and Audience Response

According to John Ball, the storyteller's style includes "intonation, voice rhythm, continuity, speaking rate, pitch, voice intensity, pauses, facial expressions, gestures, pantomime or reenactment by the speaker, voice imitation (even of the opposite sex or of animals), and methods of reacting to audience response."[1] Such a specific listing of components should make for relatively easy definitions of the different types of storytellers, classified according to style. Nothing could be further from the truth.

While there are accounts of groups within which all storytellers seem to have the same or similar styles, there are many more reports and studies indicating the presence of diversity in the performances of any given group of tellers. This provides the listener with the delightful opportunity of discovering still another way of achieving effect, but it makes it more difficult for the scholar to report.

For the teacher of storytelling, whether working in a traditional setting or an institutional one, the task of describing and cultivating style is even more formidable. Most students or apprentices wish to know whether it is suitable or not to use voice change, to expend few or many gestures, to pantomime action, or to use subtle or exaggerated facial expressions, or none at all. It does not help much to be told that a world-wide survey would indicate that all of these elements can be present in good storytelling style. Most newcomers in the field are encouraged to observe and imitate the manner in which master storytellers approach each story, but there comes a moment when the new storyteller must decide whether to continue imitating or to begin innovating.

Putting the component parts of an oral style into written words presents difficulties that are often insurmountable. As Robert Georges and others have so clearly stated, every storytelling event is unique. One cannot even capture it on film.[2]

Dell Hymes and Dennis Tedlock have attempted to devise systems of describing the totality of storytelling style that include many of the points mentioned by Ball. In their view, most of the texts recorded by folklorists, anthropologists, and linguistics scholars focused too narrowly on the content of the language, treating oral narratives as though they were the equivalent of written short stories. They believe that it is necessary to describe the entire context of performance, and all linguistic and paralinguistic aspects of it, in order to come close to a general understanding of the meaning of the tale, and its specific meaning to the teller and audience as told in that recorded performance.[3]

This chapter can only suggest the barest outlines of that which comprises personal style in telling among many types of performers, as recorded by many observers and listeners. Some of these observers were probably more "in tune" with the storyteller than others. Their reports and comments are mentioned here as clues and guides to that which is visible and hearable in storytelling style. This might suggest to the present-day student of storytelling some of the things to look for when analyzing style at a live storytelling event.

The groups that have been the most extensively described, insofar as style is concerned, are Native Americans, certain African groups, Central European folk storytellers, Asian theatrical picture storytellers, North American institutional storytellers, and folk tellers among the Gaelic peoples. This does not mean that a composite style can be drawn up for each one, or that the descriptions are all accurate. Far from it. But the variety and extent of the reports on these groups does allow for better comparative study than is possible for other regions or peoples of the world.

## Native American Styles

Melville Jacobs was one of the first to write a book analyzing the oral style of a Native American group.[4] He examined the style and qualities oral storytelling has not only as literature, but also as a visible performance and as an expression of inner belief in a particular world view. His study concerned the Clackamas Chinook groups, but frequently referred to other related groups as well.

According to Jacobs, these Northwest raconteurs used a style that was "terse, staccato, or rapidly moving." Yet the terse delineation of characters and situations, he felt, was not conscious on the part of the storyteller.

> He was succinct because he had learned no other way of expressing himself. The few choices of things which could be expressed were items that had to be articulated with utmost brevity. Such a blanket characteristic of literary style must have been maintained during long eras because of several factors, including the exhaustive familiarity with actors, plots, and stylizations which adult villagers shared. Therefore story content was not repeated ad nauseam during formal recitals. Each person's acquaintanceship with literature because of formal recitals was heavily reinforced by year-round chitchat about and discussion of stories.
>
> These conversations were stimulated not only by psychological needs rooted in the cultural and social heritage but by challengingly different versions and treatments of plots given by in-laws, visitors, and alien peoples. The very manner of

performance and the limited time available during an evening encouraged compactness.[5]

Quite a few other folklorists, ethnologists or anthropologists who recorded tales from Native American groups mention this same succinctness or lack of descriptive matter. It was mistakenly believed by a number of those recording tale telling that the absence of emotion in the words of the story extended to the gestures and voice that the teller was allowed to use. This was probably because the recording sessions were not before a live audience, or because they were taken down in the summer season when informants were often uneasy about telling stories. Jacobs believed that even though the Clackamas storyteller never used words to convey the feelings of a character in a story, "voice, gesture and other devices for dramatic expression permitted a raconteur to act out the emotions of the characters."[6]

If one looks at the other transcriptions of tales told by Native American tellers, especially those made by anthropologists and folklorists trained in the methods of Franz Boas, one can find similar terseness and compactness, and lack of expressive emotion. However, Dennis Tedlock disputes the notion that the majority of Native American tellers had such a style. He finds that if narrators are observed and recorded as they tell in their own language during a natural uninterrupted storytelling situation, they will often use long sentences comprised of strings of clauses, full of parallelism.[7] Dell Hymes' work with oral narratives of the Chinook groups also supports the view that it was limited or faulty recording techniques that gave this incorrect impression of Native American style.

In describing the style of Andrew Peynetsa and Walter Sanchez, two of the Zuni tellers whom he observed and recorded in some detail, Tedlock mentions that they used ordinary language, but sometimes in a poetic or archaic way; they also used more onomatopoea than was common in everyday speech. Their voice manipulations included pitch changes, heavy or light stress, clear enunciation, stretching out of sounds, and higher, raspier tones for representing certain characters. Peynetsa preferred complexity or novelty of plot whereas Sanchez liked to emphasize detailed descriptions of persons, things and scenes.[8] In none of the stories recorded by Tedlock can one find the terseness or lack of drama common to many versions of the same or similar stories recorded in earlier decades.

There are a few hints in these earlier descriptions that indicate storytelling among Native Americans could be as dramatic and lively as anywhere in the world. Reichard mentions one teller among the Coeur d'Alenes who was so dramatic in his movements that he once "got up from his chair, went out the door, lay down on his stomach on the porch and worked his way in, crawling sneakingly as one would up to a tent in the dark." All during the pantomime he had been telling the tale and when that particular scene was finished, "he returned to his chair and quietly continued." [9]

A Kiowa woman storyteller observed by Parsons was found to be an excellent pantomimist, very dramatic in her performances.[10]

Barre Toelken's Navajo informant, Yellowman, also perceived the narration of tales as dramatic events. Without an audience, they were very dull, he explained.[11] Although Yellowman used a "pretty" or "older" language for telling stories, different from that used for everyday conversation, this does not appear to be a practice among all Native American groups. In some cases they used special language for different types of stories and in other cases everyday language was used for all types of stories. An unusual example of the use of a very special language (so special that ordinary listeners often cannot understand some of the specific vocabulary) is the "stick doll" language used by the Kuna of Panama for their curing or healing storytelling sessions.[12]

The listening style of the audience is often equally as important as the teller's style. Tedlock, for example, mentions that when recording his informants on tape, although there was invariably an audience, he could not get them to respond with the " ee——so" ("ye——s indeed") that he knew was common to such performances. Fortunately, he encountered storytelling in totally spontaneous situations, and was able to determine that this response does occur frequently during the telling of at least some tales. In fact, Tedlock noted that in all the cases where he observed storytellers in a natural storytelling situation (i.e. not one he had arranged specifically for recording), the narrators always brought members of the audience into the story in a direct way.[13]

A similar audience response, "E!," was common among the audiences among the Assiniboines, Crow, and Nez Perce. When this response was no longer given after every few sentences, the narrator brought the session to a close.[14]

The respondent in Yucatec Mayan storytelling is almost as important as the narrator. The respondent's speech might be a simple affirmative, like the "E" mentioned above, or it might consist of questions and comments to certain points in the story. Members of the regular audience at a story session may come and go as they wish, but the respondent must stay with the teller and be attentive to the end. Respondents are usually good storytellers in their own right. Often two tellers will alternate in the telling of stories at one session, with the second teller taking on the role of respondent for the first, and vice versa.[15]

Among most Native American groups, children were expected to be very attentive and not to interrupt the storyteller. Opler mentions that among the Jicarilla Apache, the older narrator would often stop if the children were misbehaving. It was probably to keep the children satisfied and interested that there evolved the custom of giving them kernels of corn to chew during the storytelling. But there is also a deeper meaning, related to the sacredness of corn as a symbol of life and the holiness of the stories. It was believed that the children would be helped by the eating to remember the content of the stories and their importance.[16] Others who noted that children and adults were expected to be quiet and almost unmoving during the storytelling were Beckwith, who recorded myths and ceremonies of the Mandan-Hidatsa, and Adamson, who wrote about the Coast Salish of western Washington.[17]

The patterns of Eskimo storytelling style appear to be similar, except that the audience could respond more freely. Hall reported that vocal and visual mannerisms were heavily used. "A very long pause accompanied by an almost imperceptible change of facial expression may turn the audience to bursts of laughter or expressions of pity, as the case may be." There was much mimicry and the tellers often tried "to talk like people from where the story took place."[18]

## African Folk Styles

The general consensus of both objective and subjective observers seems to be that African folk storytelling is ebullient, with much interaction between teller and audience. This is not as explicit in the writings of observers from the past century as it is in the commentaries of modern folklorists and ethnologists.

In the nineteenth century a number of travelers to Africa recorded their impressions of the storytelling sessions they had witnessed, or taken part in. The most widely read were those of Stanley. Scholars of today do not regard as very accurate the texts of the stories recorded in *My Dark Companions and Their Strange Stories*, because they were obviously only loosely translated at the time of performance and the language and action was romanticized and anglicized in Stanley's recasting of the tales. The descriptions of each of the tellers, and how they told, ring truer. A typical example is:

> Sabadu was unequalled in the art of storytelling; he was fluent and humorous, while his mimicry of the characters he described kept everybody's interest on the alert. To the Rabbit, of course, he gave a wee voice, to the Elephant he gave a deep bass, to the Buffalo a hollow mooing. When he attempted the Lion, the veins of his temple and neck were dreadfully distended as he made the effort; but when he mimicked the dog, one almost expected a little terrier-like dog to trot up to the fire, so perfect was his yaup-yaup. Everyone agreed as Sabadu began his story that his manner, even his style of sitting and smoothing his face, the pose of his head, betrayed a man of practice.[19]

This description and a number of others coincide with later and even some present-day descriptions of storytellers in action in the same region.

Other nineteenth-century writers who commented on the style of African narrators, rather than merely recording their tales, were Heli Chatelain, A. B. Ellis, and Edward W. Lane. Chatelain named and described in detail the various types of tales told in Angola. He placed "poetry and music" as separate types and stated that "not even a child finds difficulty, at any time, if excited, in producing extemporaneous song." He may well have been referring to poetic recitations, but he apparently did not understand that the poems and songs were often connective parts of tales; he could well have been referring to the singing interludes that make up a large part of Angolan folktales even today. This was probably because, as many of his notes indicate, he had his informants write down or dictate their stories to him. He seems to have had little opportunity to observe them told to local audiences, during natural occasions for storytelling.[20]

Ellis, in writing about the Yoruba professional storytellers of West Africa, mentioned the use of a drum to fill up pauses in the narrative and also implied there was much audience participation.[21]

Lane described the coffeehouse storytellers in Egypt who were, of course, following the style most commonly found in North Africa and the Middle East:

> The reciter generally seats himself upon a small stool on the *mastab'ah*, or raised seat, which is built against the front of the coffee-shop: some of his auditors occupy the rest of that seat, others arrange themselves upon the *mastab'ahs* of the houses on the opposite side of the narrow street, and the rest sit upon stools or benches made of palm sticks—most of them with pipe in hand, some sipping their coffee, and all highly amused, not only with the story but also with the lively and dramatic manner of the narrator.[22]

After the turn of the century, language study had become sufficiently advanced so that more accurate transcriptions of folktale texts appeared. Also, the folklorists began to take more and more interest in the individual informants and the circumstances of narration, and their notes began to reflect this. Torrend noted, for example, that the narrators in Northern Rhodesia (now Zambia) were free to borrow words and phrases from any language and were supposed to be able to understand and interpret the language of birds and animals, in order to imitate their sounds better. He compared a storytelling session there with the Latin rites of the Catholic church, in which the servers and congregation knew exactly when to break into chant, or what phrase to intone, often without being able to read or understand Latin, the language formerly used in Catholic ritual.[23]

Fortunately, bardic and folk storytelling are still practiced in many parts of Africa today, and a few scholars have recorded in writing, on tape and on film some of the styles of present-day tellers. One folklorist has even attempted to develop a kind of storyteller's sign language, using an outline of the human figure in different positions to annotate the different gestural parts of a story, along with its text.[24]

Among the most graphic short verbal descriptions is that of a storyteller observed by A. C. Jordan in South Africa:

> There began the most spontaneous cooperation I have ever seen in storytelling. No less than six of the audience went with the principal narrator. They began "fattening" the narrative with dialogue, mimicry, bird calls, graphic descriptions of the grass-warbler's stunts when left alone in the sky, etc., etc. What was most revealing was the attitude of the original narrator to all this. Far from feeling he was being interrupted, this man was the most delighted of all. He was obviously getting fresh ideas for future occasions of storytelling.[25]

It becomes clear, from this and other observations made by Jordan, that there is almost no distinct demarcation between tellers and listeners in this style of African storytelling. All are drawn into the tale and become involved in creating it as well as enjoying it.

This delight in interruptions that add to the story was obviously taken by some African peoples to the American continents. In Belize, for example, such interruptions are actually called "fatteners" and to add something to the story from the audience is called "fattening the tale."[26]

It was the inspiration and guidance of Jordan that led one of his students, Harold Scheub, to undertake an intensive study of the style of Xhosa storytellers, referred to earlier in Chapter 4. *The Xhosa Ntsomi* is invaluable for the person studying storytelling style, for it shows the great diversity that can occur within a relatively small geographical area and within the constraints of using one type of narrative.

The general style of the *ntsomi* tellers, if one can use that term to represent an amalgam of the styles of a large number of individuals, is a lively mixture of verbal and body language, often dramatic and exaggerated, using core-cliches, and interspersed with song and a great deal of audience participation. But as Scheub points out, the finest performer he encountered, Mrs. Nongenile Masithathu Zenani (see figure 17), seemed to perform in a manner contrary to the general style.

> She uses gestures sparingly, her face rarely betrays occurrences and emotions involved in the *ntsomi* she is creating, and her approach to her audience seems condescending.[27]

This apparent outer calm and indifference prove to be deceptive:

> A careful analysis of her style reveals that all of the usual technical and stylistic devices are utilized, but in highly subtle ways. Furthermore, so incisive and exacting are her words, and the actions they describe, that the experience is especially vivid and moving, one in which the audience, her petulant attitude towards its members notwithstanding, is eager to participate.[28]

Other performers Scheub singles out as exceptional are:

**Mrs. Macutsha Sidima**

[She] often drops to her hands and knees to give character and vividness to one of her creations. Her techniques are broad, her style approaching hilarious slapstick . . . episodes and details erupt with staccato rapidity from a deep and bellowing voice. Character development . . . is achieved through frenzied (but always controlled) action and a constant use of mime. Narration is uninterrupted, gestures are bold, and the world that she creates . . . is stormed by a humour that is direct and bombastic.

**Mrs. Martha Makhoba**

[She] performs with quiet skill, lacking the arrogance of Mrs. Zenani and the animated antics of Mrs. Sidima. Hers is instead a calm, assured competence often concealing by its very smoothness the complex strands that combine to create the illusion of a single textured production.

**Mrs. Mahlombe Nxesi**

Hers is a declamatory production. . . . When her *ntsomi* deals, for example, with diviners, it is in that part . . . that Mrs. Nxesi makes maximum use of her skills and demonstrates her total control over the audience. With exquisite timing and growing suspense which she knows so intimately that it has little difficulty becoming a part of her production. . . . Mrs. Nxesi artfully interrupts the rapid and rhythmic flow of her narrative with the audience-sequences; then, as the final response of the audience is still being uttered, she has again caught smoothly . . . the momentarily lapsed strand of the *ntsomi* plot, building to the next segment of the participation, so that there is a constant and pleasing overlapping of narrative and response. . . . It is a breath-taking exchange to witness. At the conclusion of such a performance she is quite exhausted.[29]

These were only a few from among the more than 2,000 performers observed and recorded by Scheub, with much more detail than can be quoted here. Reading about them, one can only comment that, had the opportunity allowed, one would have liked to follow Scheub in his miles of walking from village to village, as did the local children, so as to hear (and see and take part in) one *ntsomi* performance after another.

Scheub is not alone in expressing wonder at the liveliness, the variety and individuality of African folk storytelling. Evans-Pritchard, who as an anthropologist recorded tales in the Sudan many years ago in conjunction with other material, was later asked to edit and publish the tales. He found that even after the lapse of forty years he could still tell by the stylistic traits alone the name of the informant from whom he had taken down any particular story.[30]

Perhaps it was storytelling sessions similar to those described by Scheub and Evans-Pritchard that Béart refers to when he states that the atmosphere of storytelling was almost like a game in the French West African countries he studied.[31] Unfortunately, he gave no details, so we cannot compare them further.

Mbiti's introduction to the Akamba stories of Kenya depicts conditions of telling quite similar to those for the *ntsomi*, but he makes the pointed observation that grown-ups must refrain from interruptions. He does not make clear whether this means they cannot break in with the responses, or whether it only means that once the teller has begun, the adults must let him or her finish.[32]

On the other hand, among the Jula of Burkina Faso (formerly Upper Volta), there must be a respondent at all folktale telling events, similar in function to the respondent in bardic storytelling (see below). Every now and then the respondent says "That took place" or "That's true."[33]

The great majority of folk storytelling in Africa south of the Sahara has some musical or sung interludes or accompaniments, but there are instances when no song or music or body rhythm is present. Among the Bemba of Zambia, stories with songs are called *inshimi* and those without song are known as *imilumbe*.[34] Among the Mende in Sierra Leone, mythical stories of Kaso, the spider-trickster and Musa Wo, the trickster-hero, are simpler than the longer folk tales known as *domei*; the former are performed without songs while the latter invariably have songs and sometimes musical accompaniment.[35]

Ben-Amos presents a vivid picture of two storytelling styles in present-day Africa, one that is comparable to the *ntsomi*-telling sessions and one that is not.[36] The term *ibota* describes an event roughly equivalent in social make-up to the storytelling sessions observed by Scheub. It is usually the women of the household who are the most active participants. Just as in the *ntsomi*, the narratives are interspersed with songs, and there is much audience interaction. However, Ben-Amos chose to study in greater detail the *okpobhię*, an event at which professional tellers perform, in quite a different style than is evident at the *ibota*.

The professional tellers at an *okpobhię* are called either *ǫkp'akpata* or *ǫkp'asologun*, depending on which of the two musical instruments they use (see figures 33 and 34). The instruments are very different and will be discussed in Chapter 11. The styles used by the tellers, however, do not seem to differ measurably, regardless of which instrument they are using. In contrast to the *ibota*, at the *okpobhię* there is no general audience participation. The narrator usually brings with him a small choir of supporters, and it is they who give the responses whenever he signals them. According to Ben-Amos, they are usually persons whom the narrator knows well. The stories told are longer and more involved. "Once started, the telling can last all night long; till daybreak; often it will involve a single story."[37]

These stories usually treat of chiefs, magicians, and heroes outside of the court, and are full of precise details. Each character, however minor, is fully delineated, and the narrator makes certain that the exact relationships of all the characters, one to another, is clearly mentioned. This is in contrast to the folk narratives told at an *ibota*, and indeed to folktales in many parts of the world.[38]

In many ways these professional Benin storytellers resemble bardic tellers, but due to their "outsider" position in their society, they cannot be considered as bards.[39]

## African Bardic Style

Bardic style in Africa takes many forms but in general is more musical and dramatic than Native American style. Here we will consider again the two types, which for want of better names we have been referring to as chronicler-historian and praise singer. As mentioned before, the distinctions are not at all fine, and few scholars would agree as to just which types are to be considered as equivalents in each of the various languages of Africa.

The style of all of them is, more often than not, formal and precise, yet very lively and full of drama. Like the folktales, African bardic epics are full of onomatopoeia. They are a bit less formulaic in language than the Homeric epics. Calame-Griaule points out that, although both male and female bards of the Tuareg tell the epic stories with a lively and dramatic style, the women have certain restrictions on their gestures. They make fewer than the men, and avoid making gestures that are suggestive in any way, while the male bards often use them specifically to provoke laughter.[40]

Some of the earlier descriptions of chronicler-historians are to be found in Ellis[41] and Johnson.[42] They both wrote about persons in the Yoruba king's court called the *ologbo* or *arokin*. Ellis referred to the *ologbo* as the chief of the *arokin* and stated that they both narrated traditions. Johnson wrote that they "repeat daily in song the genealogy of the kings, events in their lives," and other narratives.[43]

Alagoa wrote that there were bards among the Ijo in the Niger delta, equivalent to the Yoruba *oriki*, who recited *kule* in a singsong fashion. *Kule* were praise songs of a bardic type.[44] This would seem to match the earlier descriptions of Ellis and Johnson, so that *oriki* may be the same word as *arokin*, or may come from the same root. Babalola, in his book on Yoruba chanting, mentioned the *oriki* only briefly:

> As the children do obeisance before their parents, first thing in the morning, the parents burst forth into *oriki* recitation in commemoration of their ancestors whose achievements their young descendants are to be inspired to emulate.[45]

The *kwadwumfu* in the Ashanti court were described by Rattray as minstrels who "drone like a hive of bees in the chief's ear."[46] Still another chronicler type is the bard found among the Nyanga and the Lega in Zaire, called *shékárisi* and *mugani wa lugano*, respectively. While singing and narrating, these bards take the role of the hero and often dance or mime the action. They also shake a calabash rattle and anklet bells at various times, for emphasis. Accompaniment is by percussion sticks played by apprentices. Members of the audience shout encouragement or clap their hands. The interesting point is that the entire epic would never be recited in sequence at one storytelling session.[47]

*Griots* of West Africa also have musical accompaniment, and they often have a respondant, usually one of the apprentices who is learning the epic. The respondant calls out "*Namu!*" ("I understand" or "I hear") at appropriate points, and the more skilled he is at this, the more he is appreciated and likely to advance. It is very rare for a Malinke bard to perform without a "*Namu*" responder.[48]

The Nigerian bards who sang the Ozidi saga, as recorded by John Pepper Clark, used words, mime and dance, along with music, to achieve the dramatic effects and emotions they wished to convey.[49]

In contrast with this, performances of the *hwenoho* in Dahomey, which include myths and clan chronicles, are narrated with little attempt at dramatization. Ordinary speech is used, and there is little or no audience participation.[50]

The praise-singer type of bard in Africa seems to use more or less the same style of performance, at least in terms of voice. It is generally high-pitched, often singsong, with a rapid, sometimes staccato, delivery. Occasionally, as with the *shékáriși* of the Nyanga people in Zaire, the *ebyevugo* of the Bahima in Uganda, and the *imbongi* of the Xhosa, there are short pauses to allow the audience a chance to participate by hums, murmurs or shouts of agreement.[51] The Bahima *ebyevugo* also snaps his finger and thumbs at the end of each verse.

Sometimes these bards are accompanied by drums, as in the case of the *oníjǎlá* among the Yoruba, or by rhythm and string instruments, as in the case of the Mande hunters' bards, called *donso-jeli*.[52] The *imbongi* of the Zulu usually walks up and down very fast while reciting, more or less to match the rhythm and tempo of the words. Occasionally the *imbongi* will even leap about and gesticulate.[53] As one listener put it, "their words jump and jab into the innards."[54]

Taken as a whole, all storytelling in Africa, whether folk, religious, or bardic, whether in prose or poetry, seems to be strongly influenced by music and rhythm. It is rare to find stories that do not have some rhythmical or musical interlude or accompaniment, using either the voice, body parts, or special instruments. Raum implies that the use of rhythm and music in conjunction with the story has a didactic or psychological purpose.

> The child quickly grasps that songs are a means of controlling the emotions. . . .
> The Chaga, like the American Indian, sings a song when in need of self-control.[55]

But the comments of other scholars imply that its function is much more for aesthetic or entertainment reasons. Okpewho, who has studied numerous epics as performed by bards in Africa believes that the performance character in general is stronger in Africa than elsewhere. He is of the opinion that this comes from the affective interest of the bard in his tale, whereas in the Sumerian, Homeric and European epic performances, the bard seems to stand more apart from the epic being performed.[56]

Another area in which the African bardic style differs is in its use of humor, which Okpewho finds is more common in African epics than in European. He is referring to humor that particularly appeals to and involves the audience, ranging from sexual to social to macabre humor.[57]

## European Bardic Style

Of the bardic manner of performing in pre-Christian and medieval Europe, we know practically nothing. There is not even much documentation about the performing style of those at the periphery of bardism, such as the *troubadours*, *trouvères*, and *minnesänger*. All that is known for sure is that the style was musical, similar to that of the ancient Greek *aoidoi* and *rhapsodes*. As to the use of gesture, voice change, pauses, and many other points, we are in the dark for most European bards.

The exceptions are the singers of heroic epic songs in the South Slavic areas (Serbo-Croatian region and Albania) and in Russia. Enough examples have been observed and recorded during the past two hundred years to conclude that their style has not changed much. The *byliny* singers in Russia, as reported by Sokolov, "performed leisurely, smoothly, with few changes of tempo. The long-drawn monotony of the melody not only does *not* draw the attention away from the content . . . it soothes the listeners, harmonizes exceedingly well with the tranquil measured accounts of distant times."[58] The creativeness of the narrators lay in how the formulaic phrases were used and in the way some details of language and content were changed to suit the particular performance. They did not rely on dramatics and voice change or gestures.

## European Folk Styles

The folk storytellers of modern Europe, on the other hand, rarely used song or musical accompaniment as part of their presentation, even though they had precedents to do so. The exceptions were some of the street performers.

Folk tellers of Germany, Scandinavia, Finland, Hungary, and Russia, whose styles have been recorded in great detail, used a wide variety of gestures, voice changes, and body movements, but these were not nearly as numerous or dramatic as that found in African tellers. Azadovsky was one of the first to record such storytelling style. The Russian narrators he described fell into three main types:

1. Tellers who used a disordered, episodic style; they often lost track of the story in all its detail and then had to find it again; long-winded.
2. The exact repeaters; desired to pass on the tradition just as it was received, with each detail intact; narrated slowly and calmly.
3. Tellers who were sparing of detail and uniform; used all the traditional formulae, but in poetic and inventive patterns; showed personality and character in telling; attempted to get across the psychology of the story and the characters.[59]

Sokolov, on the other hand, felt there were many more types than just those three:

> . . . we find tranquil, measured epic poets . . . also fantastic dreamers . . . moralists, searching after truth . . . realists specializing in the romantic tale dealing with everyday life . . . jokers, jesters, humorists without malice . . . bitter, sarcastic, satirical storytellers with exceedingly malicious and pointed social satire . . . storytellers who relate chiefly "shameful," that is, indecent, or even downright cynical erotic tales . . . storyteller-dramaturgists, for whom the center of interest and artistic invention lies in the manner of narration, in the skill and animation of the handling of the dialogue . . . bookish storytellers who had read plenty of cheap popular works or other novels of excitement and adventure, who were exceedingly avid for the "educated" bookish speech, and at times overly zealous in transmitting it . . . women who told stories for children. . . .[60]

Among the northern European types, Tillhagen gave us a good picture of the animation of the Swedish gypsy storyteller Johan Dimitri Taikon, who had wandered all over Europe. Taikon reminisced about how dramatic it was, narrating among a group of people in Russia, called the *Kölderascha*:

> Sometimes there were four, five persons who were telling stories. One was the wolf, one the prince, another the giant, caliph or whatever was wanted. That was real theater you understand. In the middle of work it would start. But only in the beginning. All the workers kept on working until after a while it got more and more tense, then they didn't give a hang and listened, waiting to take their turn as a character. Because the more the tale progressed, the more persons appeared. One, for example, was the judge and he sat down. He twirled his moustache, looked very serious, and then would start judging and giving wild opinions. There was the

guard, and the folk and God knows what all. Ah, what a trial; that was funny, so funny![61]

That is the closest any description of a European telling comes to the African situation described by A. C. Jordan, cited earlier.

Liestøl quoted the Norwegian folktale collector Jørgen Moe as he gave a vignette of an entertaining narrator whom he had heard:

> One cannot say he related his folktales, he played them: his whole person, from the top of his head to the withy thongs of his shoes was eloquent; and when he came to the place in the story where Askeladd had won the princess and all was joy and wedding bells, he danced the "snip! snap! snout! my tale is out" to an old rustic measure.[62]

Haiding made a special study of the gesture language of several Austrian storytellers, recording them in words and photos. A night watchman, Ernst Nemeth, "grabbed me on the shoulders, shook me strongly, then showed me how the ugly gypsy woman lighted her pipe and thereby turned her eyes upwards."[63] This occurred while Nemeth was telling the tale of "The White and Black Bride." There are very few European studies such as this that give the specific gestures used at specific moments in specific tales.

The German tellers in the village observed by Brinkmann used very different styles. Some underlined the meaning of various words and phrases by different forms of emphasis; others did not. Still others would use body movement, gestures, or a modulation of the voice to mysterious tones.[64] Trude Janz, an East Prussian teller who was recorded relatively recently (1960s and 1970s) preferred a style that was full of dialogue.[65] Flori Aloisi Zarn, a masterful Swiss storyteller recorded by Uffer, told in a very even style, smooth and flowing. "You have to tell such stories really well, with lots of beautiful words and with words the old people used," he is quoted as saying.[66]

The manner of delivery of two of the narrators that Linda Dégh observed in Hungary was outwardly quite different.

> Mrs. Palkó's strength is not in a dramatic performance of the tales . . . Her talent is, in the main, epic; and the narration is the important thing for her. She used few gestures or movements of her body. Her delivery could be called dramatic only insofar as she lived with the story as it went along, making reflex gestures in her identification with the hero. It was only in her anecdotes that her gestures became more vivacious. . . .[67]
>
> Andrásfalvi was a better performer than Mrs. Palkó. While he was telling a story he would rise and underline what he said by gestures and mimicry. . . . When he told a story, the listeners did not crowd in closely about him but left him a space open, because they were accustomed to his rising and moving about while telling a story.[68]

Yet in spite of Andrásfalvi's more animated performances, it was Mrs. Palkó who ranked as the finest all-around storyteller because the internal style of her *märchen* was so special (see figure 46). It had great richness of expression and was completely flexible, being lyrical and poetic, or hard and concise, or satirical and full of humor when the occasion demanded it. Her language was oftentimes "rhythmical, full of compact, expressive turns and idioms, of beautiful poetic images and alliterations."[69]

In addition to the narrators she observed and recorded, Dégh cites numerous other comments on Hungarian storytellers made by other folklorists. In general, she found that the Hungarian narrators preferred "epic width to dramatic conciseness."[70]

The Italian tellers at the *veglia*, or storytelling evening, in Tuscany used different styles, depending on the audience to which they were directing their telling. In the early part of the evening, when mostly traditional fairy tales were told, the style was that of the typical *märchen* teller: simple, full of wonder, yet not exaggerated. The stories and songs told for the young men and women of marriageable age were romantic and at the same time, sometimes a bit suggestive or containing a warning against unacceptable behaviour. The last part of the evening was generally for the older members of the family and invited neighbors, and the tales told then were full of the vicissitudes of marriage, often even tragic in their outcome.[71]

There are not a sufficient number of studies covering the style of storytellers in other countries to be able to make valid comparisons or draw conclusions that would apply to entire regions or peoples of Europe. Although there are many folktale collections, there seem to be no in-depth studies that discuss at length the style of other Italian, French, Spanish, and Portuguese folk storytellers. None could be located for either the nineteenth or twentieth centuries. Massignon briefly portrayed a few of the narrators she observed in France and Corsica in the middle of this century. From some of her comments, it might be safe to speculate that the delivery was full of emotion and gesture. About a Corsican storyteller, she wrote: "She used to take my hand and place it over my heart in order to link me with the parts of her tale which she thought most moving."[72]

This writer observed a Breton folk teller, Jude le Paboul, on several occasions in the 1980s. His style was lively in a linguistic sense, but there was very little use of gesture or body movement. Mostly it was his bright and sparkling eyes that changed focus for the different episodes and emotions represented in his tales.

Several persons have studied the repertoires and styles of Italian and other European folk tellers who settled in the United States. These must be considered as part of the ethnic folklore of that country, and will be mentioned later in the chapter.

## Gaelic Styles

The Irish storytellers would hardly be accused of being concise. We do not know how the *scélaige*, the medieval folk narrator, performed. But the style of his modern counterpart, the *seanchai*, more commonly known as the shanachie, has been sketched by Delargy, Carmichael, and many other observers of Gaelic storytelling in Ireland and Scotland.

> Obviously much affected by his narrative, he uses a great deal of gesticulation, and by the movement of his body, hands and head, tries to convey hate and anger, fear and humour, like an actor in a play. He raises his voice at certain passages, at other times it becomes almost a whisper. He speaks fairly fast, but his enunciation is at all times clear.[73]

The storytellers of the Highlands are as varied in their subjects as are the literary men and women elsewhere. One is a historian narrating events simply and concisely; another is a historian with a bias, colouring his narrative according to his leanings. One is an inventor, building fiction upon fact, mingling his materials, and investing his whole with the charm of novelty and the halo of romance. Another is a reciter of heroic poems and ballads, bringing the different characters before the mind as clearly as the sculptor brings the figure before the eye.[74]

Jackson implied that the Welsh Gaelic storyteller usually sat in a chair, as would be appropriate in a cottage by a peat fire. But he also remembered one teller who would jump up and stride about the room, swinging his arms and declaiming when he reached an exciting passage.[75]

More recent studies of Irish storytellers include those written by Millman and Glassie. Millman found it difficult to locate any really good storytellers of the types he had read and heard about.[76] Glassie, on the other hand, pointed out that one had to have endless patience, but the stories were there. The *ceili*, as it is called now, is still a functioning social event, at least in Ballymenone; but the tales and styles tend to be different from the past. He points out that the tales cannot be classified into the neat categories folklorists would like to study. For example, most collections of Irish folktales would not prepare one for the fact that the most frequently encountered type of story was the exaggerative "pant," a kind of tall tale based on a kernel of true experience.[77]

## Asian Bardic and Theatrical Styles

The Indian *bhopo* (male) and *bhopi* (female) must be excellent singers, dancers, musicians, and art interpreters. While singing the epics they perform in a kind of chant, they must incorporate certain dance steps and be aware of the appropriate picture on the *par*, the cloth that contains scenes of the particular epic they are performing. Only one *bhopo* or *bhopi* performs at a time, and he or she must play the *jantar*, a musical instrument, as self-accompaniment. An assistant holds up a lamp to shine light on the appropriate picture on the cloth, and sometimes joins in on parts of the chanting.[78]

The lead bow-song performers in Tamil Nadu in southern India have an assistant as well, and four or more musicians as accompanists. There is also a chorus of extra singers. The lead singer recites or sings the lines, sometimes repeating all or part of them, and the assistant then echoes a portion of it. At the end of a segment, the chorus echoes the lines. The narrated portions are delivered in a straightforward manner by the lead performer only. They are used to explain or advance the story. Occasionally, if the lead performer wishes to talk to the audience directly, he or she switches to an informal dialogue style, using local conversational idiom. In these parts of the performance one of the musicians or even a member of the audience can interject comments or questions. In between the prose sections and the sung poetry is a kind of recitative, chanted in a staccato pattern that builds up tension until the singer breaks into full-fledged song again. It is the skill of the lead singer in handling all these elements and moving the story onward that determines who is considered an outstanding performer.[79]

Very similar to the bow-song performances are the ritual performances of the Palnādu epic in the Telugu language in certain communities in the state of Andhra Pradesh. The narrative of the lead singer is punctuated by drumming and by vocal interjections of the drummer and cymbals player. There are similar divisions into prose, recitative, and sung poetry.[80]

Myths among the Ifugaos in the Philippines were recited in barked-out, terse phrases or sentences. The conciseness of language reminds one of the patterns common among some Native American groups.[81]

The Marandas indicated that in Melanesia, when epics are recited for entertainment or didactic purposes, they are told; when they are used for sacred purposes, they are sung. They gave no indications as to the use of gesture or voice change.[82]

The storytellers in the *yose* or *kodanseki*, public halls in Japan, use a style that is outwardly very simple. Only a few gestures are used, but they count for a great deal. Since the storytellers are seated, there is not much movement, but the little that is used is of great subtlety. There is extensive use of voice change, but not in overly exaggerated tones.[83] An amusing story in *Newsweek* in 1973 related how a young woman who began performing rather erotic stories in one of the *yose* in Tokyo used many more gestures and postures than the ones traditionally allowed. It was the posturing, more than the content of the stories, that caused a split in the Kodan Kyokai, the professional association of storytellers. The basis of the break was the disagreement between members who felt such a style was permissible, and those who did not.[84]

Other Asian groups whose style has been commented on at some length include the Turkish minstrels. Eberhard gives a general idea of the style of some twenty minstrels who performed the *halk hikayeleri* (minstrel epics) during the early 1950s. They varied from good performers to poor or mediocre ones who could tell only fragments of the epics, because the custom was beginning to die out. In all cases, a good voice was considered necessary, and the animated performers were more appreciated by the audiences than the passive ones.[85]

## Asian Folk Styles

It is a curious coincidence that the frequent and regular interruption of the storyteller by the audience is common to all parts of the Indian subcontinent, just as it is among those misnamed Indians, the Native Americans. As previously mentioned, the latter were supposed to say "E" or "eeso" or make some other sound signifying assent at the end of every few sentences of narration. In India, the sound was usually "Hum" or "Mmm," or something similar.[86] Not much else has been written or researched about the manner of narration in family storytelling situations in Asia.

A fairly recent picture of folk tellers from Turkey can be found in Barbara Walker's article in the *Horn Book*. They ranged from janitors to maids to prison inmates. One of them, Behçet Mahir, a janitor at Ataturk University, believed that he had to stand in order to perform well, so that "all two-hundred-and-fifty veins could be vibrating."[87]

Folk storytelling in the Pacific, to be successful, was supposed to put people to sleep, so the style was probably not particularly animated. Mitchell's study covers fairly recent observations of a Polynesian group, and, according to his account, a good storyteller chants or recites in such a manner that at the end the entire audience is asleep.[88] In Tonga, the very word for the most common type of folktale, *fananga*, means "stories that put to sleep."[89]

Gorer mentioned that although the Lepchas of Sikkim narrated their stories very vividly, there was almost no attempt at dramatization. Voice change and mimicry were observed only in a very few humorous stories. But all tales employed minute and specific details in the language.[90]

The Rawang of Burma have a very conservative style of narration. If the teller varies too much from what is considered to be the proper way of telling the story, the audience is sure to ask "Where did you hear it that way?" Myths especially must be remembered in word-perfect order. Any deviation is corrected.[91]

## Chinese Bamboo Clapper Style

A unique style is used by a group of Chinese tellers who might be classified as theatrical, bardic or folk. They tell stories taken from oral as well as written tradition. Quite a number of the stories are segments from the *Journey to the West*, in which the monk Tripitika, accompanied by his three disciples who have magic powers, is sent by the Emperor to fetch the Buddhist sutras from India. The tellers most often use a prosimetric style and accompany their stories with clever movements of bamboo clappers to suggest the sound of some action in the story or to give emphasis. Kate Stevens of Toronto has videotaped and recorded a number of such tellers in Beijing and Tiensin. Here is a sample of a text she recorded as told by a student of Gao Fengshan from Beijing (fig. 32). It is entirely in poetic style, rather than prosimetric. In this segment, Tripitaka's chief disciple, the Monkey King, must borrow a magic fan from a demon, the Lady Raksha, to put out the flames which burn over the Fiery Mountains and block their way. Lady Raksha does not want to lend the fan:

> "Sister, if that fan to me you'll lend,
> It'll save getting into an argument."
> Lady Raksha said "I won't agree—
> Let's see the worst you can do to me."

[Monkey decides it is time to pull out one of his magic devices:]

> . . . As he spoke into his ear he reached his hand—
> Took out Sea Queller, his staff with gold-tipped bands.
> And then called out one word: "Expand!"
> It grew thick as a bowl, with a six-foot span.

[Lady Raksha pulls out her twin swords.]

> There in the cave the two engaged—
>> One to, one fro,
>> One up, one down,
>> One left, one right,
>> Over and under,
>> Every place—

[Lady Raksha grows weary and drenched with sweat.]

> Eyeballs a-spin, she thought of a trick.
> Stretched out her hand for the magic fan—
> Reached out to meet him like a great arched span.
> Aiming right at Monkey she gave the fan a great swing—
>> My goodness me!
> On the spot she fanned away Great Sage Equal to Heaven, Dear Monkey

**Figure 32**  *Gao Fengshan, Chinese storyteller who uses traditional bamboo clappers while performing. Photo courtesy of Kate Stevens.*

Monkey felt the wind go past his ears in a whistling blast,
Floating and whirling he headed southwest.
Trans. by Kate Stevens[92]

One must see the videotape of this performance to appreciate the complexity of rhythms used by the teller as he manipulates the clappers throughout the telling, and changes his voice subtly to suit each character.

## North American Ethnic Styles

Storytelling style has been recorded for only a few among the many ethnic groups that came to the United States and Canada. The general consensus among folklorists probably would be that the characteristic styles were carried with the tales from the country of origin, and then changed a bit to suit the American situations. The Armenians of Detroit appear remarkably similar in their storytelling style to the Armenians of Turkey and the Armenian Soviet Socialist Republic.[93] Mathias and Raspa noted some difference in the tales of the Veneto region of Italy as compared with a woman teller who immigrated from there to the U. S. in the 1940s. When she first arrived, Clementina Todesco could tell long, involved folktales, in a fluid and poetic style. Gradually, she lost the ability to tell these narratives and concentrated on personal experience stories.[94] Bianco, too, found that there was a marked deterioration in the style of telling in the Italian-American community she studied.[95] Sklute noted much the same phenomenon in a Swedish-American community.[96]

The best overall view of a group of native and immigrant tellers in North America can be found in Dorson's "Oral Styles of American Folk Narrators." The Polish-American teller Joe Woods used fresh, colloquial, and idiomatic language in English even though it was his second language. He could handle dialogue with great ease. The Swedish-American Swan Olson had a gentle demeanor, but he told extremely violent stories. His neat, episodic shockers were based on personal experience and were all the more effective for the understated manner in which he told them. Burt Mayotte, a French Canadian, told with phrases that fell into a rhythmic beat.

Botkin was another folklorist who included brief descriptions of American storytelling style in some of his compilations. In the foreword to one of them, D. S. Freeman remarks:

What may be said of the style of storytelling in the South? . . . There were artists in narration but art no more was universal in this than in any other form of human endeavor. Herein is disappointment because in the rural South there was time enough for perfecting any embellishment the narrator devised . . . but the regrettable fact stands: storytelling was not as artful as it should have been. It was too long-winded, and it had too much of the echo of the political platform. Spontaneity was lost in the polishing of paragraphs.[97]

Marie Campbell and J. Frank Dobie have also given word pictures of the styles of a number of regional ethnic storytellers.[98]

## Religious Storytelling Style

Religious style generally was characterized by earnestness and a moral seriousness that was only occasionally lightened by slight exaggeration or humor. An exception to this appears in some of the tellings associated with the Jewish *Hasidim*, which sometimes permit religious laws to be parodied and the Rebbe turned into a comic figure.[99]

Among the Kurdistani Jews were tellers who were equally at home in telling religious tales and local folklore. Sabar describes one Yona Gabbay, who was known far and wide as the best teller of all types of stories. He could tell in Neo-Aramaic, Kurdish, or colloquial Arabic with equal ease, and used a style full of onomatopoeia, vocal effects, and humorous asides.[100]

Reynolds, in his excellent survey of the rise of pulpit storytelling in America, points out that it was the Southern black and white preachers who brought about the most dramatic shift in religious storytelling style in the United States. They used narratives in their sermons far more frequently than preachers in northern states, and developed their own patterns of call-and-response telling from the pulpit.[101] Rosenberg points out that such preaching still exists in many parts of the United States. He made a particular study of the preachers who use a chanted, spontaneous style of storytelling in their sermons, and pointed out how this style has affected political and other oratory in the United States.[102]

## Theatrical Styles

The recent trend in the United States, Canada, and France to present story-telling in a theatrical setting has brought about a change in some professional tellers. Previously, the few tellers who consistently told in theaters tended to use a style typical of the theatrical monologue. Now, there is a greater tendency toward dramatic movement on the part of the tellers, and a much broader range of voice manipulation. Some use musical accompaniment. There are even those who wear costume, either of a distinctive character or of a type to suggest a given place and period.

Some tellers who use material based partly on personal experience tend to try for a typical raconteur's style: offhand, folksy, and seemingly spontaneous. However, much of this is achieved by careful prior preparation. There are also those who imitate the specific telling styles of different cultures and peoples.

There is no survey covering the entire range of current professional storytellers in North America, but the thumb-nail sketches describing each teller in the various editions of the NAPPS annual directories can give some idea of what that range might be.

## Library and Institutional Styles

Library storytelling style generally tended to imitate that of bardic and European folk storytellers. In the early days of library story hours, from approximately 1900 to 1920, there was a concentration on telling hero tales, long myths and legends, and prose versions of some of the epics. In such cases it was usually recommended that the children's librarian use a formal, rather serious style. The early reports of the Carnegie Library in Pittsburgh indicate the purpose of storytelling was introducing the classics to children who otherwise might not get to know them. The storyteller-librarians were "given a series of seven lectures on Homer for the purpose of arousing literary interest in the epics and serving as an inspiration."[103]

Most of the storytelling manuals and the courses in library schools recommended a natural style, one in which the teller felt at ease with the material. On the whole, dramatic gestures, excessive voice change, and histrionics were frowned upon. Stories that were from literary sources, such as Andersen, Kipling, Carl Sandburg, and Eleanor Farjeon, were to be memorized word for word and were considered far too complicated for the beginning storyteller.

In recent years there has been a loosening up of these strict rules. Strict standards of performance are no longer being demanded of the children's librarians, chiefly because they require too much staff preparation time for the library to absorb. Many librarians have used folk storytellers from the community, and others who have designated themselves as professional storytellers, to give programs in their libraries on a regular basis. This allows the public to see and hear a variety of styles in the library. The range of styles that one can encounter in present-day libraries and schools is very broad.

## Changing Styles of the Storyteller

Parry and Lord both insisted that the Serbo-Croatian singer-storytellers they studied assumed a totally different style once they could study and memorize "book" versions of the epics they were narrating in song. They believed that the only true singers of tales were those who spontaneously composed as they performed. They kept alive the old themes and formulas by combining them in ever new ways.[104]

Folklorists who have attempted to record the same story as told by the same teller, but over a span of some time, have reported that there is considerable change in the language and manner of telling, even for those tellers who insist they have "memorized" their stories. Dournes, for example, had a number of Vietnamese tellers repeat the same stories they had given him ten years earlier. They insisted the stories were exactly as they had learned them from master tellers, but there was, in fact, a great deal of variation in the versions separated by a decade.[105]

The folk storyteller Ed Bell, who began as a raconteur at a Texas bait camp for sport fishermen, has knowingly changed his style for performances at folk festivals and civic luncheons. His stories tend to be longer and he mischievously tries to play up his identity as a "pretty rough old man" when telling to women's clubs; for businessmen's luncheons he chooses his most humorous stories and styles. For larger audiences, he has learned how to play to the crowd. As Mullen concludes:

> Ed Bell's ability as a storyteller developed over forty years. . . . When the opportunity arose to tell stories in new contexts he was able to use the same narrative skills and awareness of this audience as a basis for expanding and adjusting his repertoire to fit the new situations.[106]

This could probably be said about most of the successful storytellers throughout the ages. They were able to change and adapt their styles to fit the times and the expectations of new audiences, and thereby kept storytelling alive.

# CHAPTER 11

# *Musical Accompaniment*

Many of the previous chapters have mentioned various kinds of storytelling that were accompanied by some form of musical instrument, or that used the voice or a part of the body as an instrument. This chapter will concentrate on the instruments themselves. Insofar as possible, any instrument known to accompany storytelling will be described in such a manner that the reader should be able to recognize each one when encountering it in a museum, in its place of origin, or in any other place. The instruments will be treated here in the commonly accepted groups of chordophones, idiophones, membranophones, and aerophones.

## Chordophones

Chordophones include all stringed instruments that are plucked, struck, or bowed. Those that were used earliest for storytelling appear to be the plucked types, including the musical bow, the lyre, the harp, and the lute.

The musical bow is one of the oldest known examples of stringed instruments. It can be seen in prehistoric rock and cave paintings in North Africa that date back many thousands of years. The musical bow consists of a curved stick of wood, with a cord of string, leather, gut, fibre, or the like. One end usually rests on the ground during playing. Often a hollow gourd or calabash is attached and used as a resonator.

The Tamils of South India use a bow (*vil*) to accompany ritual story performance (see figure 11). This bow is anywhere from ten to fourteen feet in length and curved like a hunting bow. For performance, it is wrapped in colorful paper or cloth and fitted with brass or bronze animal figures at each end. Cow bells of various pitches hang from the frame. During performance, instead of having one end resting on the ground, the middle is held in place by lashing it to the *kutam* (pot), the instrument that is used to give the main rhythm to the performance. The lead singer-narrator plays the bow by striking it with a pair of wooden sticks to which are attached pairs of concave discs inside of which are tiny balls. When the string is struck, the balls jingle and the cow bells ring.[1]

The musical bow is used in parts of Africa to accompany certain types of narrative poetry. Norris mentions that in Mauritania it is popular with children for practicing narrative singing as well as for performing.[2] A more complex type of African musical bow survives in Brazil, where it is called a *berimbau* or *berimbao*. It is used mostly to accompany a specific type of acrobatic, martial-arts kind of dance, but there is also a historical narrative quality to many of the songs that are performed with it.[3]

The bow-lute, also called the *pluriarc*, is actually a multiple musical bow, since it consists of a series of curved bows, each with its own string. They are attached to one sound box. The *akpata* used by professional narrators of Benin is a seven-stringed bow-lute. The *akpata* is quite old, for it appears in at least three Benin bronzes from the seventeenth century (for one example, see figure 2). It has rattlers or bells made from split palm seeds, discarded caps of bottles, or other bits of metal at the top of each bow (see figure 33). From these depictions it would appear that the *akpata* had a ceremonial use, but that is not the case in modern times. In fact, the use of the *akpata* has rather somber symbolic overtones. There is a superstition that an *akpata* player who appears before the king to tell stories will die unless he breaks his instrument. The origin myths associated with the *akpata* are also rather doleful.[4]

Two ancient stringed instruments that are plucked are the harp and the lyre. The harp is generally distinguished from the lyre by the position of the strings. In a harp the strings are on a plane perpendicular to the sound box, attached to it and also to a curved or straight neck. In a lyre, the strings are stretched from the sound box, and parallel to it, to a straight crosspiece held in place by two "arms" extending upward on either side of the lyre. Both kinds of instruments appear to have been used to accompany narrative singing and reciting from ancient times onward.

## Lyres

A Sumerian lyre of Ur, dating back about 5,000 years, shows animals playing the lyre, eating, dancing, making merry, and behaving, in general, like humans (see figure 1). There are other similar scenes found in the art and artifacts of Ur. Frankfort theorizes that these scenes could have a bearing on some of the Sumerian and Greek fables and myths.[5] It is tantalizing to speculate whether this same lyre, now located in the University Museum, Philadelphia, was once used to accompany a singer who recounted animal tales similar to those in Aesop's fables.

The *kitharis* or *phorminx* mentioned so frequently in Homer is an early form of lyre. It is not definitely known if either or both of these were of the *lyra* type (bowl lyre) or the *kithara* type (box lyre, similar to those found in Ur). In Homer, the *kitharis* and *phorminx* are both associated with the *aoidos*, the poet-bard. He

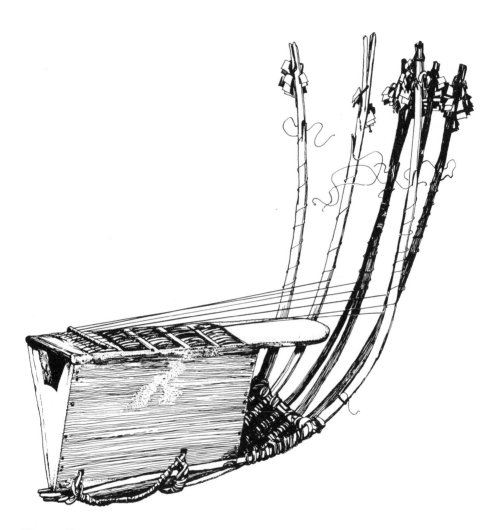

**Figure 33** *An* akpata *from the Benin region of Nigeria. The names of the strings are (from left to right):* ẹkhue, *"beginning" (uncertain),* ayere, *"memory,"* akugbe, *"unity,"* iye ema, *"mother drum,"* ẹkhue, *"beginning,"* ozi, *"strong wind,"* uke, *"small drum that men use." There are variations on this naming system. Reproduced with permission from Dan Ben-Amos,* Sweet Words *(Philadelphia: Institute for the Study of Human Issues, 1975).*

used the instrument to accompany his sung or chanted narrations that were recomposed spontaneously at each performance. Kirk expressed the belief that the natural accents in each Homeric hexameter line were further accented by a plucked note or chord on the *kitharis*. This was used to cover up any hesitation on the part of the composer-performer. Kirk concluded that it was precisely because the *rhapsode* did not change much of the text spontaneously, but instead recited it, that the need for musical accompaniment was lost. Therefore, the *rhapsode* used a staff for emphasis (see figure 3) instead of a *kitharis* or other musical instrument.[6]

Thus, the musical instrument is very functional in the case of the poet-storyteller. It helps to fill the gaps and cover hesitations, and allows the performer time to think of the next phrase. For the declaimer or reciter of already existing oral epic poems with relatively fixed texts, such accompaniment would have been a hindrance; it would have slowed down the performance and taken away the use of the hands so that no gestures would be possible. Other scholars have suggested that the reason the musical accompaniment was dropped by the reciter-storytellers (such as *rhapsodes* in Greece) was because it could not be heard by large audiences.[7]

The only place in Europe where the lyre seems to have survived up to modern times as an accompaniment to storytelling was among the *kalêki* in Russia. They were wandering groups of performers of religious narrative poems (see Chapter 3 and figure 16). In the south and west of Russia, one member of each group generally carried a lyre to accompany its performance.[8]

## Harps

The harp is one of the instruments most closely associated in the popular mind with storytelling. There are probably many cases where the term "harp" was used incorrectly, to describe lyres or lutes; just as there is reason to believe that the terms "lyre" or "lute" were used when a harp was clearly the instrument in question. There is enough pictorial evidence to indicate that the harp was a favorite of narrators from ancient Egyptian times to the nineteenth century. These instruments seemed to be equally at home in the drawing room or the inn, the castle or the more humble hearth.

Teutonic, Anglo-Saxon, Norse and Icelandic poets were known to have used musical instruments to accompany their narrative poetry. In *Beowulf*, for example, the instrument is called *gamenwudu* (playwood) or *gleobeam* (mirth-tree), as well as *hearpe*.[9] It is usually mentioned in connection with the performance of the *scop* or *gleoman*. All these terms are invariably translated as "harp" in modern English versions of *Beowulf*. However, the term *harpa* generally meant a type of bowed lyre when used in Northern countries, so there is some question as to whether *hearpe* refers to a harp or a lyre.

The first definite evidence of harps in Ireland dates to a period somewhere between the ninth and eleventh centuries. Carvings on stone crosses of that era show instruments that once were thought to be lyres but are now generally conceded to be harps because of the way they are shown being held and played. From the eleventh century on, there are more pictorial examples, usually showing harps with an outward curve of the pillar. They had metal strings. The player rested the body of the harp against the left shoulder (see figure 4). The left hand plucked the upper register and the right hand the lower. Usually the player had long fingernails used for the plucking. Most types of Irish bards probably used this kind of instrument in their performances.

The *telyn*, or Welsh harp, had horsehair or gut strings and more often a straight pillar rather than the curved, Irish type. But the harp served the same functions among the Welsh bards that it did among the Irish.

Harps are used in modern Africa as well as having been found there in ancient times. The *ardin* is played only by females of Mauritania, of the bardic caste. This instrument is a harp with resonator made of half a calabash, covered with animal skin, and having ten to thirteen strings of gut, spaced out on the long, straight arm. In performance, the harp sound box is placed on the ground against the right leg, which is pressed close to the body. The handle rests against the left shoulder, and the left hand grasps it, while the right hand plucks the strings. Sometimes the *tīggiwīt* has partners who assist her by tapping on the skin of the sound box, so that there is percussion accompaniment as well. The narrators frequently do not do their own accompaniment, but perform facing the musicians. Norris has a very clear diagram of this unique type of harp.[10]

## Lutes

Lutes, like lyres, have their strings parallel to the sound box. These strings pass along a neck, against which they are pressed by the player's one hand (to raise the pitch) while the other hand plucks, strikes, or bows (rubs) them over a sound box. There are short-necked lutes and long-necked lutes.

There is also a harp-lute, with strings at right angles to the sound box. It is found only in West Africa. Among the Mande hunters' bards, it is called a *donso-nkoni*. This version has six strings and a calabash sound box. It takes the bard ten to fifteen years of apprenticeship to become a master of the *donso-nkoni* and of the narratives that are sung to it.[11] A six-stringed harp-lute is also used by the *griot* narrators of the Kambili epic in West Africa.[12]

Plucked lutes used for the enhancement of narration include the *tīdinīt*, played only by male Mauritanians of the *Īggāwen* caste. The poet-narrator usually faces the musicians, who may include both male *tīdinīt* players and female *ardin* players, as well as other instrumentalists. There are no objections to men and women participating in the same performance.[13]

The Japaness *shamisen* is a form of lute. It was used by classical types of storytellers and later by *naniwabushi*, narrators of historical tales, who performed in public theaters.[14] An earlier form of Japanese lute was the *biwa*, a flat, short-necked lute used from the tenth to the fifteenth century by the *biwa-hoshi*. These were monks or secular men who wandered about singing songs or telling tales of war and folk heroes. The predecessor of the *biwa* was the Chinese *p'i p'a*, used by similar narrators in China.[15]

A single-stringed bowed lute is used by the Dagbon in Ghana. The body is made of calabash covered with taut animal skin, and the string is horsehair.[16] Chapter 14 summarizes the arduous training of these musicians and how they perform in connection with oral narration.

A lute-like instrument resembling a guitar, called the *bandura*, was sometimes used by the *kalêki* of Russia. This instrument differed from the lyre already mentioned as being used by this itinerant type of religious narrator.[17]

## Other Chordophones

Other chordophones used in different parts of the world as part of oral narrative sessions are the *dombra* and *balalaika*, the *saz*, the *gusle* and *gusli*, the *quyur*, the *rabab* and *amzad*, and various types of zithers and guitars.

The *dombra* was the forerunner of the *balalaika*, and the modern version looks somewhat like the latter instrument. It was and is used in Russia and by the Kazakhs. Kazakh bards and ordinary persons use it to accentuate certain types of storytelling, especially to reproduce sounds of animals or nature that occur in the course of a story.[18]

The *balalaika* (as well as other stringed instruments) was used by some *byliny* singers in Russia, but not by those in Olonets, where the largest group of *byliny* singers was recorded and studied.

Kazakh bards also use a *qobyz*, a two-stringed, bowed instrument with an alto pitch. The fingerboard curves upward, and thus the strings cannot be depressed to touch it. It is often adorned with bells and bits of metal that give off a tinkling sound during performances.[19]

The *saz* is a plucked, four-stringed instrument with a small body shaped rather like a pear and with a long neck. It is commonly played by minstrels in Turkey.[20] The *gusle* of Yugoslavia and the *gusli* of Russia are both used by narrators but are very different instruments. The *gusle* is a one-stringed-instrument shaped somewhat like a ladle and played with a bow. It is the chief instrument of the Serbo-Croatian bards who compose and perform oral epic narrative poems and can be likened in function to the *kitharis* of the Greek *aoidos*. However, Kirk believed that because the *gusle* is played by bowing this provides a continuous line of musical accompaniment, in contrast to the accompaniment of the plucked *kitharis*. In his view, this resulted in a formulaic structure in the Serbo-Croatian oral epics that is looser than that in the Homeric epics.[21] The *gusle* is called *lahuta* in Albanian.

The *gusli*, on the other hand, was a recumbent harp or psaltery, played on the lap. It once was used to accompany the singing of *byliny*, but in that form it became extinct some time ago. The modern folk version is different and not really related in function or form to the old *gusli*.[22]

The bowed chordophone used by Mongolian bards is called *quyur* or *quur*, or in Jarut, *hōr*. It is four-stringed. Its function appears to be similar to the *gusle*, since the Mongolian epics are also sung in a kind of rhythmic recitative, newly improvised with formulaic language at each performance.[23] This instrument is also called a horse-head fiddle, because the carved wooden headpiece often takes the form of a horse's head. One of the stories sung by Mongolian bards tells of the legend explaining why the instrument takes this shape, and the reason it is used for storytelling.[24]

Spike fiddles are bowed instruments in which the arm or handle pierces the body of the sound box and comes out the other side in a spike-like protuberance. Two types that are used to accompany storytelling are the *rabab* and the *amzad*. The *rabab* generally has two horsehair or metal strings: the first is called *qawwal* or speaker; the second is the *raddad* or answerer. The neck is made of wood, or sometimes ebony. The pegs are fitted into a notch on the upper end, and this end is often carved with an ornament or decoration. The soundbox is usually a perforated coconut shell covered with fish or gazelle or rabbit skin. The cane bow is stretched with horsehair.[25] Whereas the epic performers Connelly observed and recorded all used the *rabab*, and obviously with pride, the performer studied by Slyomovics had only disdain for the "frivolous" *rabab*, and preferred the drum.[26]

The *rabab* is also among the instruments used by *penglipur lara* performers in Malaysia. These are oral folk romances usually known by the name of the hero or heroine who is the central character. Some performers in parts of Malaysia are so skilled and talented that they can make their living by these performances. Others perform them only part-time or sporadically, like the performers of Egypt.[27]

The *amzad* is a one-stringed instrument, with a soundbox made of calabash over which is stretched skin of some kind. It is especially popular among the Tuareg, where it is most often played by women. The most frequent occasion for performance is at an *ahal*, a communal celebration of singing, oral recitation, and narration of various types. Generally, only unmarried men and women take part in an *ahal*.

The *leqso*, used by the *azmaris* of Ethiopia in the past, appears to have been similar to the spike fiddle. These professional poets and minstrels used instruments not only to accompany narration, but also for all types of entertainment.[28]

The *jantar*, used by the *bhopo* to accompany his picture recitation in Rajasthan and other parts of India, can also be classed as a one-stringed spike fiddle. Sometimes the *bhopo* uses a stick zither.[29]

The stick zither is a simple, straight stick to which is attached at either end a string, or possibly two. It usually has a gourd or calabash attached as a resonator. The *dakkalwars* of Maharashtra in west central India usually accompany their chanted myths with the *kingri*, a type of stick zither. During their recitation, they show the picture cloths on which are depicted episodes from their epics and myths.[30] The *mirasis*, a Moslem caste of minstrels from the central part of India, also use the *kingri* when performing.[31]

Some modern professional storytellers use the guitar as an accompaniment for ballad storytelling, or for added emphasis in folktales in which there are sung refrains.

## Idiophones

An idiophone is any instrument that is made of material that vibrates and does not need a membrane, string or reed to make it produce sound vibrations. Idiophones can be plucked, struck, shaken, scraped or rubbed. There are relatively few idiophones used to accompany storytelling, except for one type, common to much of Africa.

Plucked idiophones are called linguaphones, and the type that is uniquely African, and was taken by Africans to the Americas, is the instrument commonly known in English as the thumb-piano. This name is deceptive because the instrument is not of the same family as the piano, which is a chordophone. It has almost as many names as there are languages in Africa, and each type has some variation.[32] Not all types are used with oral narration.

One important type that is used by professional narrators is the *asologun* of the Benin region of Nigeria. It generally has nine lamellae or strips made of metal or cane. Each lamella is tuned in a particular way and has a special name (fig. 34). The *asologun* is used to accompany oral narratives at an *okpobhie*, a communicative event to celebrate a rite of passage, a new social position or job,

**Figure 34**   *An* asologun.*The names of the metal strips are (from left to right): 1 and 9,* ovbieho, *"a small voice, like that of a girl," 2–3 and 7–8,* enwanie, *"reply," 4–6,* ozi, *"strong wind." There are variations on this naming system. Reproduced with permission from Dan Ben-Amos,* Sweet Words.

passing successfully through some danger, and similar events. One might assume that the *asologun* and its player thus had only a happy connotation, but this is not the case. The professional storytellers in Benin society have a socially marginal position and are merely tolerated, rather than having a distinct and honored position in their society. The storytellers themselves consider their performances as psychosocial therapy, bringing release from unhappy and troublesome thoughts. Both the *akpata* (see the earlier part of this chapter) and the *asologun* are associated with evil spirits, so much so that they are banned in some parts of Benin.[33]

Central African groups seem to have happier associations with this instrument. In Zambia, where it is used by boys and girls of the Tonga and Ila groups to assist in composing and performing praise and story songs, there are two types. The larger one is called *kankobela* and the smaller one the *ndandi*.[34]

The term *sansa, sanza,* or *sansi* is used for the instrument generically by a number of peoples in Angola, Cameroon, the Congo Republic, Zaire and other places. It is called an *mbira* by groups in Zimbabwe, South Africa and Mozambique. In fact, in Mozambique alone it has at least fifteen names, among them *kalimba* and *chitata*, also commonly used in a generic way.[35]

When used to accompany storytelling, this idiophone is generally played by the narrator while singing the musical interludes, and the rhythm and melody are in counterpoint to that of the sung responses of the audience (fig. 35). Hugh Tracey included several excellent transcriptions of such story songs in his book *The Lion on the Path and Other Stories*.[36] Recently, a Zimbabwean storyteller, Ephat Mujuru, has made a career of demonstrating such *mbira* storytelling in North America and elsewhere.

Idiophones of the shaken type are most often gourds or bells. The Mende of

**Figure 35** *Garage Nyamuswa,* mbira *player and storyteller; to his left, in the white hat, is Saini Murira, doyen of* mbira *players in Mutoko area, northeast Zimbabwe. Photo courtesy of Andrew Tracey.*

Sierra Leone often accompany their singing by clapping or by shaking a *segbula*, a beaded gourd rattle.[37]

The Mwindo epic of Zaire that is performed by bards for the Nyanga-speaking peoples has a number of musical instruments to accompany it. The bard himself usually wears ankle bells and shakes a rattle made from a gourd filled with dried seeds. During the performances, there are sometimes young men who act as musician assistants, using drumsticks to strike a kind of percussion stick resting on other sticks.[38]

Another form of struck idiophone is the *batil*, a brass bowl struck with the fingers and palms much like a drum. Some *penglipur lara* performers of Malaysia use this instrument to accent their storytelling.[39] This is similar in shape and use to the *kutam* used by bow song performers in Tamil Nadu, except that the *kutam* is made of clay reinforced with iron filings.[40]

A scraped idiophone is found among a number of West African *griot* groups, and among the Mande hunters' bards. The latter call it a *narinyo*; it is a ridged metal pipe scraped with a metal bar to provide basic accompaniment and background rhythm at an oral performance. The apprentice bards are the ones who must first master the use of the *narinyo* before going on to the *donso-nkoni*, described in the section on lutes.[41]

Cymbals and bells are used by a number of oral performing groups in India, all mentioned earlier: those who perform the Palnādu epic in Telugu; the bow-song singers of Tamil Nadu; the *mirasis* of central India; and the *bhopos* of Rajasthan.

## Membranophones

Membranophones are instruments in which sound is produced by striking, rubbing or causing sound waves to hit a membrane or membrane-like material stretched over a frame or sound box. Three common types of membranophones are the tambourine, the drum, and the kazoo.

The drum is used extensively to accent or provide the rhythm of a performance of oral narrative, usually of the ceremonial type. Only a few examples can be mentioned here.

In the Dagbon area of Ghana, the court musicians and chroniclers use a closed drum of the hourglass shape, carved of wood and with skin covering both ends. For a description of the training involved in learning to play and perform with this instrument, see Chapter 14.

In chanting *ijála*, the Yoruba of Nigeria like to have drum accompaniment provided by other musicians, not by the chanter. The accompaniment is not necessary, however. Appropriate drums include the *dùndún*, a large hourglass drum, and many other types.[42]

The Kuranko people of Sierra Leone use drumming that closely resembles verbal speech in many of their story performances.[43]

*Burrakatha* performers in Andhra Pradesh are usually accompanied by two performers who use small earthen or metal drums called *dakki*.[44]

Other groups, all mentioned previously, who also use the drum to accompany storytelling include: the Mende of Sierra Leone, who use a *kili*, a slit drum; Malinke *griots*, who use the *tamani* drum; the *mirasis* of India who use the *dholak*, a small double-ended drum; the Palnādu epic singers whose accompaniment includes a pair of double-ended brass drums called *pambas*; the *chakkiyars* of Cochin who use a copper drum called *mizhavu*.

A few of the *penglipur lara* performers in Malaysia use a *rebana*, a frame drum shaped like a basin.[45] The wandering *areoi* performers of Tahiti used drum accompaniment of various kinds.[46]

An unusual storytelling drum was once a common household object among the Sami or Samer people, who are often incorrectly referred to as Lapps. The drum was made of wood from a tree that had grown with a clockwise twist. Reindeer skin was stretched over the sound box and decorated with magical patterns. The drum was played with a beater made of reindeer bone, with a smaller bone attached, used partly as a divination device.[47]

## Aerophones

Aerophones are instruments that produce sound by means of columns of air vibrations, such as trumpets, horns, flutes, etc. Not too many of these instruments have been used regularly with storytelling. The Tahitian *areoi* mentioned above did use flutes as well as drums, but this was mostly for their danced narratives. Winner mentioned that the Kazakh bards of the past sometimes used a *čybyzga*. This was a primitive aerophone made of wood and leather.[48]

A form of bagpipe made of a complete goatskin is used by one of the accompanists to the Palnādu epic performers in Andhra Pradesh, India.[49] The *maroki*, praise-singing bards of the Hausa in northern Nigeria were known to have been accompanied at times by trumpets and horns as well as drums.[50]

This chapter has probably not covered all instruments associated in some way with storytelling. It was impossible to survey all of the materials related to music that might have included mention of storytelling use. This review has concentrated on those instruments mentioned specifically by folklorists, ethnographers, and oral literature scholars in their descriptions of storytelling events.

# CHAPTER 12

# *Pictures and Objects Used with Storytelling*

While the majority of storytelling among the folk was and is accomplished without objects (other than musical instruments), there were and are important exceptions. This is especially true in the use of pictures to enhance the story or to sustain the audience's interest for at least a part of it. The reports of some early experiments in North American schools and libraries with "picture" storytelling are often filled with the naive belief that they were trying something totally new. This was perhaps justified in view of the paucity of folkloristic or ethnographic research at that time, especially research concerning street storytelling in Europe and Asia, and information about the picture storytelling found in various groups in Alaska, Australia and other places.

An article in *Publishers Weekly* in 1934, for example, describes the "new" technique of story hours with lantern slides devised by Julia Wagner and Ruth Koch after nine years of experimentation.[1] The method of projection may indeed have been new, but, in fact, Wagner and Koch were taking their places in a long line of picture storytellers, dating back to a period before the Common Era.

Another type of picture projection used with storytelling in the early decades of this century was the balopticon (fig. 36). A method used in the nineteenth and early twentieth was the panorama. This latter device was a series of pictures on muslin or canvas, from a few hundred feet to fifteen hundred yards in length, that was shown by hand cranking of the cylinders on which the cloths were wound. When they were shown, there was usually a recitation by a performer, that lasted from fifteen minutes to three hours. Most of these were declaimed from printed texts, but there were occasions when storytelling was used with them. Hedgbeth, in his doctoral dissertation on panoramas, quoted a letter in

**Figure 36** *A storytelling hour at the Wylie Avenue branch of the Carnegie Library, Pittsburgh (1933), showing use of a balopticon. Photo courtesy of Carnegie Library of Pittsburgh.*

which a friend writes to Frederick Catherwood, exhibitor of the Jerusalem panorama:

> . . . don't forget to tell them Woolf's story of the crocodiles and crabs . . . as it's something uncommonly in their way and would tickle a youthful audience who were not overnice.[2]

## Picture Storytelling in India and Other Parts of Asia Before 1500

For the origins of picture storytelling, we must go well beyond a century or two back in time. The beginnings are likely to have been in India, perhaps as early as the sixth century B.C.E. Fortunately, we now have an excellent review of this early evidence in the book written by Victor Mair, *Painting and Performance*. Much of what is covered in this section is culled from the text and illustrations in that book, and from items listed in his bibliography. For anyone interested in storytelling in general, and picture storytelling in particular, *Painting and Performance* makes fascinating reading.

A very early mention of the public exhibition of pictures, combined with the recitation of a narrative, appears to be in a work called *Mahabhasya* (c. 140 B.C.E.) by Patanjali. In it, he refers to dramatic representations of the Krishna legend in pictures, pantomime, and words, as performed by *granthikas* (reciters) and *śaubhikas*. There is quite a bit of disagreement still as to whether these *śaubhikas* were picture reciters or shadow play narrators or puppeteers, or even some other kind of performer such as a magician or illusionist. Coomaraswamy believed they were picture reciters[3] and Mair tends to agree with this. Lüders classifies them as actors and considers them as part of the history and tradition of the theater in India. He ties them in with the later custom of shadow-puppet plays, especially those of the *Ramayana*, that spread far and wide over much of Asia.[4]

Other early references describe the *yamapattaka*, the picture showman of scrolls or sheets on which were depicted the underworld and all the likely punishments or rewards each soul was to get for all the good or bad actions carried out in life (see the section in Chapter 3 on Hindu Storytelling). Still other references tell of picture storytellers who use the novelty of their profession to distract not only the audience but the surrounding merchants in the marketplace. Mair translates from a tenth-century collection of Kannada stories an amusing description of a teller who steals rice while narrating three stories with picture accompaniments. The folktale-like texts of the three stories are given as well, and they are full of details that one can easily imagine as colorful and dramatic illustrations.[5]

In the Mittal Museum in Hyderabad is a large painted cotton scroll, dating to the seventeenth century, that depicts the life of the sage Bhavana. It is known that the scroll belonged to a family of itinerant minstrels. They put on performances that lasted seven evenings.

> Performances by the storytellers always opened with prayers to Ganesha, the elephant-headed Hindu deity who is invoked before any undertaking. Ganesha's large image appears on the first panel of the scroll. Speaking in the vernacular Telugu, the narrator then began to tell the story. Three or four other members of the family played instruments or occasionally joined in the singing. As the drama unfolded, the scroll, suspended from poles affixed to a wall, was slowly unrolled, event by event.[6]

**171**

This same type of storytelling begins to be mentioned in historical texts related to other Asian countries beginning with approximately the seventh century of the Common Era. As was discussed in Chapter 3, the Buddhists were the main carriers of this tradition. In China, there emerged a form of telling called *chuan-pien*, or "turning transformation [picture scrolls]," and later came a related form, using *pien-wen* texts and pictures.

*Pien-wen* are story texts in alternating prose and poetry, most of them dating to the T'ang period (618–906 C.E.). *Pien-wen* are the first known examples of Chinese vernacular narratives. That the reciters or performers of these texts used pictures in some way is suggested by the appearance of the poetic (sung) text on the back of the only surviving picture scroll, now located in the Bibliotheque Nationale in Paris. Victor Mair has studied the history and development of *pien-wen*, and in his book *T'ang Transformation Texts* he cites numerous documents that show picture storytelling of this type was a widespread and flourishing tradition in China in the T'ang period.

This same period also coincided with the expansion of the Great Silk Road, which carried physical objects of trade and culture, as well as language and customs, back and forth. The Sogdians were a people prominently involved in this. They, too, developed a form of narrative art that was "a continuous sequence of individual scenes of secular and epic interest, in which identical persons appear in episodes or events separated by time."[7] Victor Mair concludes that this is the same technique used in virtually all other Asian picture storytelling art.[8]

Storytelling using alternating prose and poetry, and accompanied by pictures was, as Mair puts it, Indian by birth, fostered by Buddhicized Iranian uncles and Turkish aunts, and adopted by Chinese parents.[9]

We know that such picture storytelling reached even into Malaysia, and lasted there for a long time. A Dutch visitor to the area wrote in 1880:

> There is a sort of men who paint on paper men, birds, animals, insects and so on; the paper is like a scroll and is fixed between two wooden rollers three feet high; at one side these rollers are level with the paper, while they protrude at the other side. The man squats down on the ground and places the picture before him, unrolling one part after the other and turning it towards the spectators, whilst in the native language and in a loud voice he gives an explanation of every part; the spectators sit around him and listen, laughing or crying according to what he tells them.[10]

## Picture Storytelling in Modern Asia

In India today there are narrators who use pictures just as their ancient predecessors did. Indian tellers use pictures on cloth or paper scrolls that roll up, on cloth or paper or canvas that folds, on palm-leaf books, on wooden unfolding altar-like constructions, on temple walls.

Among the types of storytelling cloths to be found today are: *kalamkari* bard cloths of Madras and Andhra Pradesh (fig. 37); *par* cloths depicting stories of deified heroes from Rajasthan (fig. 38) and occasionally from other states as well; Saurashtra temple cloths from Gujarat; *pat* cloth (or paper on cloth) scrolls used by *patua* in Bengal and other parts of India; cloth or paper scrolls called *tipanu* used by Garoda picture showmen in Gujarat and Rajasthan; and *badd* cloths used by the *dakkalwars* of Maharashtra.

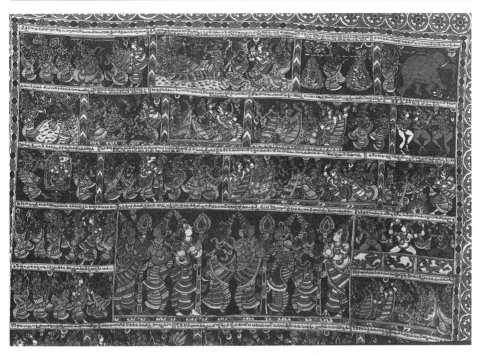

**Figure 37**  *A* kalamkari *cloth from Andhra Pradesh, depicting scenes from the* Ramayana, *and used to accompany storytelling. Photo by Chris Nickrant.*

The symbolism of textiles is ancient in India. The *Rig Veda* describes the universe as a fabric woven by the gods. Therefore, it is important that cloths used for telling a story, especially a sacred one, should be woven of one piece.[11] *Kalamkaris* are large pieces of cloth on which are depicted designs and scenes. The name *kalamkari* implies that the design is created by pen, but the process is really more complex than simple sketching on cloth. The Fergusons, who have observed the entire process in Andhra Pradesh in South India, describe it thus:

> Essentially, the design is created by a master of the art who draws it on handspun-handloomed cotton cloth which has been bleached. Some of his design may be printed with clumsy-looking wooden printing blocks, and this is usually the case these days with the border designs. The details of the process are complex. Suffice it to say that the students of the master are responsible for filling his design with color. . . . But the heart of the *kalamkari* is the fresh design on each. . . . Thus, while to the untrained eye *kalamkaris* may seem to be alike, a few moments of study will show the individuality of each piece done by a single artist and his school. Different artists and schools create substantially different pieces. Yet all the themes and symbols are stylized and . . . the stories depicted are limited in number and quite familiar to all.[12]

The *par* are made by a completely different technique. Om Prakash Joshi, in his book *Painted Folklore and Folklore Painters* of India, gives an excellent description of all the different types of *par* cloths and performers. *Par* means cloth scroll. They are generally about one or one and a half meters high and from two to five meters in length. Traditional painters from Rajasthan, in the northwestern part of India, paint the pictures on canvas, using locally made colors, usually

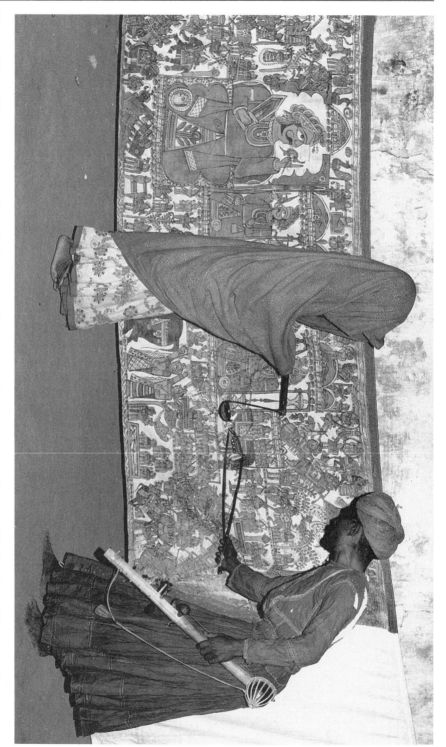

**Figure 38**  *A bhopo on the outskirts of Ahmedabad, Gujarat pointing to a scene on his par while it is being illuminated by the bhopi.*
*Photo courtesy of Joseph C. Miller, Jr.*

five. They depict episodes of the birth of a local god-hero, his adventures, his marriage, his fight with the enemy, and his death, together with the death by self-immolation of his wife.[13]

The performers are usually called *bhopo*. *Bhopo* means "priest for a folk-god" and this describes the folk religious aspects of their performances.[14] The *Pabuji par* (see figure 38) is concerned with the deified hero of that name, and is generally performed by a husband and wife team, *bhopo* and *bhopi*. As soon as the performers arrive in a village, the people begin to gather excitedly. The *bhopo* then purifies the ground and arranges the *par* on its stand, either in a central place, or in front of the patron's house, or near a temple or shrine. The performance starts in the evening, after dinner, and will go on all night long. The main performer narrates the story, and an assistant shines a lamp on the appropriate picture on the *par*.

> The bard jaunts back and forth in front of the *par*, often spinning, sometimes chasing his assistant, which excites the children, who sit right up front so that they can see and hear everything. . . . the bard may bend over and point out a particular scene which illustrates the episode he is reciting. At other times songs and recitations stop altogether. Then a spectator will offer a rupee to the deity. For this the bard or his assistant blows the conch shell in the name of the donor. . . . They continue all night. The next morning before the sun rises, they close the performance.[15]

Both Joshi and Mair reproduce numerous photographs of the cloths and of tellers performing in front of the cloths.

The *pat* tradition in Bengal, which is estimated to be at least five hundred years old, still survives in very rural areas. In contrast to the *par*, these scrolls are unrolled in a vertical fashion, since they are about a half meter wide and anywhere from three to fifteen meters long. They utilize brilliant colors and are most often made by the families of the storytellers themselves, rather than by professional painters. They used to be mostly of cloth, but are now more often on paper. As in the case of the *par*, when the cloth or paper wears out from use, they are copied and the old versions are ceremonially burned.

The itinerant professionals who show these cloth scrolls are called *patua*. They perform at market crossroads or in village centers, or for any individual or group willing to pay for the performance. Although the traditional content is the *Ramayana*, or episodes from the life of gods and goddesses, of late they have added new themes, such as accounts of famous robberies or murders, to attract a larger audience. They do not use promptbooks or any other textual material. It is strictly an oral and visual performance, sometimes accompanied by musical instruments.[16]

The *mata ni pachedi*, already mentioned in the chapter on religious storytelling, comes from Saurashtra, a region of the state of Gujarat in western India. Just the preparation of the cloth for printing takes days, for it is boiled twice, buried once, soaked and rinsed many times, and dried in the sun. When it is finally received by the printer, it is a pale yellow. The printer applies the design by hand, using carved wooden blocks and a thick black ink. The sons or apprentices then fill in with various compounds the areas that will be red or black. After boiling, rinsing, blueing, and bleaching in the sun, the cloth is ready to be used. There are two standard sizes: a two-meter square cloth used for the canopy over a small temple or shrine; and a rectangular cloth one to one and a half meters high and two meters long. The finished cloths are all red, black, and white.[17]

No example of a *badd* cloth seems to be reproduced in current literature, but from the brief written description available, they would appear to be similar to the *pat* or *kalamkari*.[18] It may be that *badd* is another form of *pat*, since the pronunciation of these terms is very similar, even though the romanization appears to be so different.

Paithan picture sets, from the town of the same name in Maharashtra, are painted on paper in sets called *pothi* containing anywhere from thirty to seventy scenes. An individual *chitrakathi* (picture teller) would grasp them at the top and show them to the audience while telling the narrative depicted. These were almost always stories from the *Ramayana* or *Mahabharata* or myths from the *Puranas*.[19]

The *kavad* is a wooden, altar-like construction with panels that open out (see figure 12). On each panel are one or more scenes, usually from the *Ramayana* or the *Mahabharata*, painted in glowing colors. They range in size from portable versions to large stationary versions.

In Japan, the picture storytellers were most often affiliated with temples, but they were not necessarily religious in their orientation. One female type was actually called a "singing nun" but they were that in name only. As Barbara Ruch states in her excellent survey of this kind of storytelling, these women combined an older profession with that of itinerant picture storyteller (see figure 13). The *etoki* style of picture reciting can still be found in some temples in Japan (see Chapter 3).

## Kamishibai Picture Cards

The *kamishibai* of Japan, described earlier in the chapter on folk storytelling, utilized pictures as a come-on. The tellers sold candies or, in rare cases, books or medals showing popular heroes. The children who bought something were allowed to stay and listen to the story or stories and watch the pictures.[20]

The wooden holder for the *kamishibai* picture sheets was generally about one foot high and about eighteen inches wide. On the top was a handle for carrying (see figure 20). The front had flaps that opened out like a triptych or miniature stage. These wooden frames were produced by carpenters who specialized in building temples or altars, and each player bought his own, sometimes after arranging for a special design or adaptation.[21]

The picture cards were usually printed in color and contained the highlights of scenes from the stories. Some sets of hand-painted pictures can be found, but most were printed and sold for the express use of the *kamishibai*. In 1937 there were some sixteen publishers in Tokyo, and most of them reinstated their wares after the war.[22]

There were usually from six to twenty cards in a set, fitted into a slot on the side of the wooden carrier (fig. 39). The teller could see the text relating to the picture being shown, because it was printed on the back of the card preceding it. In other words, when the first picture card, which was usually a title card, was pulled out from the front position and slid into the back position, the text shown on the back of it related to the second picture card. In this aspect, it resembles closely some of the palm-leaf picture books produced in India, Indonesia, Thailand and other Asian countries, for the public presentation of Indic and Buddhist stories.

**Figure 39**   *Illustration from a pamphlet showing how to use the* kamishibai. *Reproduced with permission of the editors of* Kamishibai, *Tokyo.*

Considering the impact that the *kamishibai* had on the public at large, and the fact that the same publishers who produced the cards were also later producing children's books, it is no wonder that one of the most popular formats for children's picture books in Japan is the horizontal style reminiscent of the *kamishibai*.

## Hmong Picture Cloths

Recently, beginning sometime in the 1970s, a kind of picture story cloth has appeared among the Hmong refugee groups in Thailand, the United States, and other countries. Traditionally, these people had always made *paj ntaub* (flower cloths) as a means of identifying their clan and region. However, after their dislocation as a result of the Vietnam War, they began to depict narratives showing episodes in the war, experiences from their past, or scenes from traditional folktales. These cloths began to be sold and now provide a considerable income for those most skillful in making them.[23] Recently, this author has seen the cloths used as storytelling devices in American schools where Hmong children are among the pupils.

## European Picture Scrolls and Sheets

In Europe the first evidence of narration accompanied by pictures appears to be in one of the *exultet* rolls, mentioned earlier in the chapter on religious storytelling (see figure 14). As was pointed out, although the text was usually the same, the various artists who illustrated the parchment rolls each selected different scenes to be emphasized and depicted. The roll illuminated in the eleventh century at the Abbey of Monte Cassino, and now in the British Museum, has fourteen illustrations, each about a foot square. It begins with a figure of Christ, continues with two angels, and then shows a female figure personifying "Mother Church." Following this is a vivid portrayal of "Mother Earth" teeming with animal and vegetable life, and then scenes from episodes in the Old and New Testaments.

In his introduction to a set of plates reproducing the illustrations, Gilson writes: "The subdued tones of olive-green and brown tints, and the dull pale gold, against which the blue and red of the principal figures stands out well, give a pleasing effect."[24]

Surely this must have provided fuel to fire the imaginations of many in the congregation, who probably had limited exposure to sequential visual story materials of such beauty and drama. For those children standing or seated close to the pulpit, it must have been an experience at least faintly resembling the picture-story hour of today, with its sequence of pictures on page or filmstrip, accompanied by the voice of the reader/narrator. It should be obvious that this experience would be different from the passive, introspective study of statues, altarpieces, mosaics, frescoes or windows on view in the church, in which case the story would be partly provided by the artist and partly by the viewer, much the way a book stimulates a story only partly conceived by the writer and then completed by the reader.

It is just possible that these *exultet* rolls were the inspiration for the religious marketplace singers that Brednich[25] and Schmidt,[26] among others, believe to have been the forerunners of the secular performers of the same type (see figure 15). For simplification, they will all be referred to here as *bänkelsänger*, the German term, but as mentioned in Chapter 4, they were common throughout much of Europe and each language had its own terms to describe them. Many scholars have shown pictorial documentation for the sixteenth and seventeenth centuries that includes examples of religious and secular picture canvases separated into squares or rectangles so as to create a story by depicting a series of actions. The terms sometimes used for this are tessellated or tessellation.

Whether or not the *bänkelsänger* and his picture canvas stemmed directly from the earlier religious forms of picture storytelling, they probably were influenced by bardic or epic forms of narration, because the method of presentation was through song or chant. It must be remembered, however, that the *bänkelsänger* never achieved the status of bard and often had to scrounge for a living by trying to collect coins for the performance itself, as well as through the sale of the cheap, printed versions of the ballads and stories they were singing.

Some of the *bänkelsänger* were regular employees of the printing companies whose wares were being sold. Others, perhaps the majority, were itinerants who had obviously developed some talent in presenting the stories in song, bought up supplies from various printers, made their own picture sheets (or possibly got a talented folk artist to do so), and then went on the road, stopping at towns on market days, when the crowds would be the largest.

The German technical term for these picture sheets is *schilder*. These picture sheets are now rare but we can see a wide range of them depicted in paintings or etchings of the seventeenth through the nineteenth centuries. They appear to be either wood-block prints, copper engravings, or oil on canvas. In more modern times some of them were painted or printed on paper. The inexpensive ballad sheets, called broadsides in English and *flugblätter* in German, were printed in the hundreds of thousands, but they, too, are difficult to find today. It is no wonder, then, that the *schilder*, made in very few copies or in unique examples, are to be found in very few museums or in the hands of private collectors.

Examples of late nineteenth-century *schilder*, some printed and hand-colored and others individually drawn and colored, are more common than those from earlier times (fig. 40).

The picture sheets were large enough to be seen by a small crowd standing around and generally contained up to a dozen or so of the most dramatic scenes from the ballads or songs. A common size was roughly one and one half meters wide by two meters high. The example shown in figure 40 depicts six scenes from the *moritatenlied* titled *"Verstossen, oder der Tod auf den Schienen"* ("Disowned, or Death on the Rails"). The text of this ballad is not extant but it obviously dealt with the love affair of a young girl, followed by her parents' rejection of this fact, their disowning of her, and her subsequent despair and suicide. The original is in color and measures about one meter by one and one-half meters.[27]

Brednich points out that publishers were not the first to use large pictures and sticks or pointers for advertising their wares. Two examples from among the many that he cites are Hogarth's view of Southwark Fair and the church-fair scene of the Flemish Imagerie Populaire, both of which show the use of large picture sheets advertising various services or goods.[28] But it was in the *schilder* depicting story ballads that the specially displayed picture advertising sheet was most effective and long lasting.

That they had a powerful influence on the audience is attested to by many writers, among them Goethe. In his *Wilhelm Meister's Theatralische Sendung* he writes:

> The folk will be most strongly moved above all by that which is brought under their eyes. A daub of a painting or a childish woodcut will pull the attention of the unenlightened person much more than a detailed written description. And how many thousands are there who perceive only the fairy tale elements in the most splendid picture. The large pictures of the *bänkelsänger* impress themselves much deeper on the memory than their songs—although these also captivate the power of the imagination.[29]

Their impact lasted until well into the twentieth century, as the text and photographs of Janda and Nötzoldt's *Die Moritat vom Bänkelsang* so clearly demonstrate.[30] Visitors to the Munich *Oktoberfest* and to other similar yearly markets or festivals could still listen and watch as the singer pointed his stick from picture to picture and intoned the many verses of his ballad. But they were not able to compete with films, and later radio. With the spread of these two forms of mass media into all parts of Europe, the picture sheets of the *bänkelsänger* disappeared from view.

Curiously, however, they survive in a slightly different format in northeastern Brazil, as part of the *literatura de cordel* tradition. Poet-performers still hang up their cheaply printed texts (often with cover illustrations) on a string, much like hanging clothes on a line, and then orally recite or read them to anyone who will listen (see figure 23). These folk poets have become so much the rage that they now appear on television, in public theaters in some of the larger cities, and even in literature seminars in universities. It appears as though most of the performances are now "readings" rather than storytelling. However, many people still seem to prefer the freely told versions.[31]

**Figure 40** *A picture sheet* (schild) *used by a German* bänkelsänger. *Photo courtesy of Fritz Notzoldt.*

## Picture Books

The picture-book story hour in libraries probably began soon after the regular story hours, at least in a few libraries. Yet there is little evidence that it was scheduled regularly prior to the Second World War. Professional journals make no mention of a "Picture Book Story Hour" before 1949. There are a few articles on the preschool story hour in the 1940's, but they still refer essentially to orally narrated stories unaccompanied by pictures. In one of them the librarian specifically mentioned that showing the pictures while telling the story was attempted but proved unsatisfactory, and she concluded: "We have found it better to show the pictures after the story has been told."[32] This was probably an echo of the advice given in the most widely used storytelling manual of the time, *The Art of the Storyteller* by Marie Shedlock. In her first chapter, "The Difficulties of the Story," she states most clearly in Point 6:

> After long experience, and after considering the effect produced on children when pictures are shown to them during narration, I have come to the conclusion that the appeal to the eye and the ear at the same time is of doubtful value, and has, generally speaking, a distracting effect. . . .[33]

However, internal reports in the New York Public Library indicated that in 1910 "there were 1,133 story hours including the extra story hours, *informal picture book hours*, [my italics], and story hour sessions held in conjunction with the playground association."[34] But it was not until Eulalie Steinmetz became supervisor of storytelling (1945–1953) that the story-hour sessions were formally divided into two distinct types:

1. Story Hour for boys and girls third grade and above
2. Picture-Book Hour for those below third grade[35]

The earliest article describing actual picture books and how they were used in a story hour appears in *Library Journal* and was written by Florence Sanborn. In it she suggests the use of picture books as a "vehicle for the hesitant, new storyteller to gain confidence." Since she gives explicit instructions on how to hold the book, turn the pages, and so forth, it would appear that she was writing about a new approach to library storytelling. Nowhere in the article does she suggest, though, that an entire story hour could be made up of picture storybooks; also the emphasis was still on oral narration rather than reading aloud. Having the text there was more like a promptbook.[36]

The first time that a librarian does suggest an entire story hour of picture book narration occurs in a little pamphlet written by F. Marie Foster and published by the Division of Adult Education and Library Extension of the New York State Education Department, some time in the mid-1940's. Foster recommended a short "picture book program" of from 20 to 25 minutes in length, and actually described (in text and photos) the kind of physical location needed, the manner of holding the picture book, the arrangement of the chairs for the child audience, and many other factors. One of the main reasons she cites for recommending such a program is that it "gives the librarian a real opportunity to see children's reactions to the books so carefully selected" for the public library children's room.[37]

In an article some years later, Adeline Corrigan implies by her title, "The Next Step—the Picture Book Hour," that this was not yet a widely scheduled practice in the public library. She does refer to the fact that children have enjoyed stories through pictures for hundreds of years. But she states that it is because of the recent increase in large picture books, clearly visible and understandable when shown to a group, that one can now have a picture book hour as a regular storytelling session for groups of children.[38]

Obviously the publishers were listening and reading such reports. There was a dramatic increase in the number of picture storybooks with illustrations selected not for family or individual reading but for their ability to stand out and be seen when held up in front of a group. The lavishly illustrated book had become too expensive for the individual buyers. In the institutional buyer, the publisher had a much steadier market for well-produced picture books. While this has changed a bit in recent years, due to improvement in color-printing techniques, a substantial number of picture storybooks are still produced with group use in libraries in mind.

Librarians adopted this new type of story hour very quickly once they discovered it and saw a steady stream of books being published to suit the programs. Also, they became much more adept at reviewing and criticizing the new picture books, not necessarily from an artistic point of view, but rather from the point of view of the library picture-book storyteller. To work well and hold the attention of a group of children already stimulated by films and television, the stories had to be very strong, with no unnecessary text. The pictures needed to strike a balance between showing too much and too little, and most successful illustrators were clever in building up suspense and surprise, just as the texts did.

The more librarians used picture books successfully in the story hour, the more they realized how much easier this kind of program was, in relation to the long and difficult-to-learn tales they were expected to prepare for the regular story hour. The more the story hour came to be associated with picture books, the more the older children stayed away, believing such things were for "babies." By the mid-1960's, a familiar lament was voiced, exemplified by this statement by a children's librarian of the Toronto Public Library:

> Almost all the librarians I have talked to report the same thing. Some of the enthusiasm has gone and what is more the older boys and girls have gone. Imperceptibly, week by week, their numbers dwindle until the librarian faces, on a Saturday morning, a sea of very young faces: Little children who want *The Three Bears*, not the *Three Men of Power* and who thrill to the exploits of Mike Mulligan rather than Grettir the Strong.[39]

Beginning in the 1950s one can find in the professional reviews of children's picture books more and more frequent comments about the usefulness of the illustrations in story hours, or, conversely, negative remarks about how difficult the pictures will be to see or how unnecessarily long the text is, making its use in the picture-book story hour limited. The reviewers were, for the most part, children's librarians who were reflecting their storytelling needs. It was not surprising, therefore, that in response to these reviews, an increasing number of trade picture books were published in the United States after World War II of the type suited to presentation in a group situation. They can almost invariably be differentiated from the European picture books of the same period, most of which have much greater detail in both text and illustration, and were designed for individual use.

In the past decade, these programs in North American public libraries have been geared to younger and younger groups of children. Many libraries now offer them for two- and three-year-old children. Interestingly, there is a movement back to the use of purely oral narration of rhymes and short stories, inserted between stories told with accompanying illustrations from picture books. There are now even manuals describing story hours for these age groups.

The picture-book story hour is now an established routine in most public libraries in the United States, Canada, Great Britain, Australia, New Zealand, the Nordic countries, Germany, and France. Even other European libraries, slower in their development of work with children, now have this activity in place. Public library systems in such places as Singapore, Japan, Venezuela, Greece, Ghana, and Kenya also offer the picture-book story hour as a regular program.

## Sand Storytelling

Certain groups of the indigenous peoples in Australia, among them the Walbiri, the Aranda, and the Pitjantjatjara, tell stories accompanied by the sketching of pictures in sand. Nancy Munn, who has written a detailed account of this procedure, states that "to talk" in the Walbiri sense means to speak and draw markings in the sand at the same time. She continues:

> Both men and women draw similar graphic elements on the ground during general discourse, but women formalize this narrative usage in a distinctive genre that I shall call a *sand story*. A space of about one to two feet in diameter is smoothed in the sand; the stubble is removed and small stones plucked out. The process of narration consists of the rhythmic interplay of a continuous running graphic notation with gesture signs and a singsong verbal patter.[40]

As can be seen in figure 41, the drawings are fairly large and dramatic.

Strehlow reported that among the Aranda, both male and female children used the technique to tell tales closely parallel to European nursery tales. His description of a child drawing and telling a story of an evil, witch-like creature who had chased, killed, and eaten a boy, is very graphic and dramatic. He indicated that among that group, young men had become so accustomed to this method of telling stories, they used it even when passing on sacred myths to the uninitiated, but they used a boomerang to draw the designs in the sand.[41]

## Storyknifing

It is curious that among the girls and women of certain groups living at the edge of the northern Pacific region, there should be a storytelling technique so similar to the sand storytelling of people at the southernmost tip of the Pacific.[42] For at least two hundred years, it has been the custom for the Yuk and other Eskimo groups in southwestern Alaska to fashion special knives of bone or ivory, and give them to the children for the express purpose of drawing pictures in the snow as they recited stories. This process is called storyknifing. It is still practiced by a number of groups in Alaska, generally among females from ages six to twenty-six, but now, more often than not, they use ordinary metal table knives (see figure 42).[43]

The designs invariably show swiftly drawn scenes of house interiors and outdoor natural landmarks, as well as stylized human and animal figures. For example, among one group, the following designs might be used:[44]

**Figure 41**  *A Walbiri woman of central Australia makes pictures in the sand as she narrates a story. Reproduced with permission from* Walbiri Iconography *by Nancy Munn (University of Chicago Press, 1986).*

CHILD      ADULT      OLDER PERSON

Each time, before a character speaks, a V-like design is drawn as a face:

Then, eyes, nose, and mouth are added:

When a character speaks again in the story, a stroke or two quotation marks are often added above the figure representing that character:

**Figure 42**  *Yupik children storyknifing in mud in southwestern Alaska. In winter, this is done in the snow. Photo courtesy and copyright of Lynn Price Ager.*

## Other Picture-drawing Storytelling

Among the Yukagir in Siberia, in the nineteenth and twentieth centuries it was noted that the women sometimes scratched narrative designs on bark, as they told of events in their lives. This custom was occasionally looked on as a form of picture writing. One of the most frequently reproduced examples is often referred to as a "Yukagir love letter."[45] However, if one goes back to the descriptions as to how these drawings were composed, it seems likely that this was simply another form of picture storytelling, comparable to the storyknifing of Yuk girls in Alaska.

In North America and Europe, there is evidence that certain short tales were developed that depended for their punch-line on a series of sketches that in the end completed a drawing related to the story. One type in particular, culminating in the drawing of a strange bird, has been shown to have been told orally in the United States, Europe, and Mongolia. Another, commonly known as "The Black Cat," was made popular by Charles Lutwidge Dodgson, author of *Alice in Wonderland*, in his version, "Mr. T and Mr. C."[46]

Japanese children pass on, generation after generation, a series of drawing chants that are little narratives of humor and surprise. These have been studied and collected by folklorists, and a few have been translated into English.[47] Motifs that are very popular in these tales are the appearance of the triangular ruler, flowers, the monkey, and a host of other animals. Many of them have phonetic shapes or numbers as part of the design, so they were looked on partly as a teaching device as well. Here are two short examples:

1. *tsu*
2. *ru*
3. *ni*
4. *wa*
5. *maru maru*
6. *mu*
7. *shi*

1. My big brother
2. Is eating beans;
3. He has a long mouth.
4. And there he turns into a duck.[48]

## Story Boards

In some Pacific island areas, especially in Papua New Guinea, one can still find story boards carved of wood that depict scenes from ancestral, historical tales or mythic events (see figure 43). These are probably updated versions of the boards generally called *gope* by many of the tribes. The *gope* were used as splashboards on outrigger canoes, as ancestral tablets, as secret and sacred objects of the clan. Their use and naming seemed to be very different among the many groups in Papua New Guinea. They were almost always oval, and contained human and animal figures, sometimes in important historic scenes. The crocodile was an

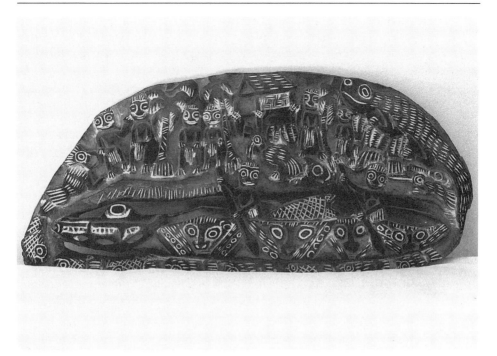

**Figure 43**    *Story board given to the author by students and staff at Administrative College of Papua New Guinea, 1983. Photo by Chris Nickrant.*

**Figure 44**    *Two Easter Island* rongo-rongo *boards, once probably used as a mnemonic device for storytelling. National Museum of Natural History, Cat. No. 151490. Photo courtesy of Smithsonian Institution.*

important totemic figure for many. They were more often used in ritual chanting of ancestral events than in what might be called folk storytelling. Some that were kept in secret or hidden places were revealed to children during initiation ceremonies, and the appropriate historical or totemic story would then be chanted. Nowadays, their use is much more informal.[49]

An intriguing script or mnemonic device used by the Easter Islanders was the *rongo-rongo*, often called a story board in English (see figure 44). A number of these boards were collected by various missionaries and visitors to the islands in the nineteenth century. Eyraud, one of the earliest Europeans to spend time there, noticed such boards in every house. A missionary who arrived two years later noted:

> They have songs accompanied by rhythmic motions, very monotonous and very indecent. They pretend to have had a certain script, by means of which they let pass to posterity the important facts of their country. I have seen this script imprinted on a piece of polished wood which was more or less long; it resembles very much the Egyptian heiroglyphics. Personally I do not believe that they have ever got any sense out of these characters. The few Indians who pretended to understand them, when put to the test, recited nothing but ridiculous and unintelligible tales.[50]

This disrespectful attitude toward their obviously sacred (and probably secret) stories was noticed immediately by the Easter Islanders, who promptly hid most of the tablets. Just a few years later, those who came to study the Island and its inhabitants were able to find only a few examples. However, it was discovered, fairly recently in the twentieth century, that certain families had kept alive this form of writing, and some of the narratives that went with it. The *rongo-rongo* boards that are extant in museums and private collections have never been satisfactorily deciphered, nor is there convincing evidence to indicate that this was a full script. Most scholars speculate it was a mnemonic device for assisting the professional reciters of the history of each clan, or for the ritual recitation of sacred myths. There were obviously a number of versions developed, probably by the members of individual families who were responsible for handing down these traditions.

The *lukasa*, a memory device found among the Luba of Zaire, is similar in function to the *rongo-rongo*, but not in appearance. Its most common use was to serve as a memory aid for the retention and recitation of the origin myths of the Luba. The *lukasa* are generally made of rectangles of wood and the designs on them have been described in some detail by T. Q. Reefe:

> A row of carved mounds called *lukala* invariably runs across the concave surface of the *lukasa*, dividing it in half. Beads and shells are attached to the board by small slivers of wood or hand-made iron wedges driven through their centers, and cowrie shells are frequently attached to the top and bottom. Beads are arranged in three ways: a large bead surrounded by smaller beads, a line of beads, and one isolated bead. Each configuration lends itself to the transmission of certain kinds of information. Board surfaces also have holes and lines cut into them.[51]

Because they were a part of the secret society of the Luba, they have never been able to be studied carefully and deciphered.

## Story Vines and String Figures

Figured drawings or art in a sequence are not the only ways to picture the main characters and events in a story. The objects on story nets and vines were fairly abstract, yet they represented key elements in the stories told by West African tellers (see Chapter 9). Even more abstract are the sequential sets of string figures commonly found in parts of Asia, the Pacific, and Africa.

Hornell discovered that a large number of the Fijian string games were originally meant to be worked out to the accompaniment of a chant. A year later Dickey recorded his researches in Hawaii and also found so many of the figures accompanied by chants that he suggested they might all originally have been devised as *aides memoires* to help keep alive the oral traditions of the people. His surmises were based on the fact that the allusions in the chants were to legend and myth and to well-known stories. "Some of them," he stated, "are short extracts, many of them changed, from long, famous chants."

In the December 1949 issue of *National Geographic*, an Australian aborigine, Narau, is shown in a photograph, composing string figures. The caption indicates that he "can tell 200 legends with a single strand of string."

Lindblom found the same type of suggestive evidence in Africa that Dickey found in Hawaii, namely that phrases with allusions to myths or tales were often said or sung during the formation of the figures.[52] The Leakeys, archeologists, while on a trip to Angola, were intrigued by the great number of string figures there. They wrote:

> One of the most interesting features of our brief study was that in a number of cases the Tuchokwe natives of N.E. Angola have "serial" figures in which the successive stages seem to represent the illustrations of a story.[53]

## Handkerchief and Napkin Stories

In the course of giving storytelling demonstrations to audiences of ordinary people, mostly in public libraries, this author was frequently asked about handkerchief stories. Many persons, whose ancestors had come from Europe in the nineteenth and early twentieth century, would remember a grandparent or other older relative or friend who had entertained them as children by forming figures with a handkerchief or napkin, and telling short stories. Only one of the numerous histories of the handkerchief alludes to this use, which probably began when the handkerchief moved from court and theater use to use among the bourgeoisie, and then among the common folk.

The figures for the mouse, the rabbit, the professor, and babies in the cradle seem to have been the ones most widely used. These figures, as made by a Dutch family, can be found in *The Family Storytelling Handbook*, along with the stories and rhymes that they told while making them.[54]

## Dolls

As was mentioned in Chapter 8, dolls are now frequently used in the actual narration of stories to children in therapy, or they are used to elicit stories that can be useful in therapy. There is some indication that dolls were used in storytelling during early times in India and other parts of Asia.[55] That these were the forerunners of shadow puppets or other types of puppets and marionettes is only speculation. The *etoki* performers in Japan are known to use dolls or figurines to graphically explain the story they are telling.[56]

The wooden dolls made by the Kuna in Panama, and other peoples of Central America, are symbols of spirits in the different types of wood. They are used in storytelling "curing rites" and can range from very tiny to quite large. In recent years, one type, previously used only in such a therapeutic fashion, have come to be made as touristic objects, and are sold as "trouble" or "worry" dolls (see figure 29). Since these have now been picked up for storytelling use with children in other countries, they have a second, invented storytelling tradition attached to them.[57]

Nesting dolls, also called *matrioska* or *babushka* dolls, have been used for storytelling, but it is likely this developed in institutions, rather than among the folk. It is known that the dolls were inspired by Japanese sets of boxes within boxes, from large down to very tiny. They were introduced by the toy makers and distributors of Nürnberg in the nineteenth century, but had no commercial success. Gradually, they began to be made as folk toys in certain villages in central and eastern Europe. With their use as the central motif of many pavilions in the Brussels World Fair in 1959, they were thrust into the public eye again, and began to be sold again commercially on an extensive basis, but they were still being made in villages that followed old folk patterns (fig. 45). In fact, some types are still made exclusively as folk toys. The only instances of actual storytelling use that the author has seen in Central Europe was in kindergartens in Poland and the Soviet Union.[58]

## Other Objects

The Japanese storytellers of the *yose* (described in detail in Chapter 5) used a fan, called either *hakusen* (ringworm) or *kaze* (wind) in their jargon because of the sounds or actions it could simulate. A good storyteller is known for the distinctive ways in which he uses the fan, achieving sounds of great subtlety and effectiveness.[59]

This fan is one of the remaining symbolic props that were used in traditional storytelling. It was believed that the souls of deities or ancestors descended through these objects during the narration. The other props commonly used were the branch of a *Sakaki* tree, a bow, a clay doll, and *gohei* (religious artifacts).[60]

The Chinese storyteller in the *shu-ch'ang*, the equivalent of the *yose*, similarly used a prop, a block of wood called *hsing-mu*. It, too, was introduced with great finesse, and when hit against a table properly, each time produced a different sound. A number of tea house storytellers of China, as observed by Kate Stevens in modern China, still use the bamboo clappers that were commonly used not only by professional tellers, but by amateurs as well (see figure 32). They could often be purchased in specialty stores. Two sets are usually used, a large one and the smaller one. The larger set is used only at the beginning, to draw attention, and occasionally at very dramatic moments in the tale. The smaller set is used in different rhythms to keep an almost constant accompaniment to the narrated portions of the story.[61]

For the Lepchas of Sikkim, everything in a story should be described minutely and precisely. They like to make their stories and descriptions clearer and more

**Figure 45**   *Nesting dolls purchased by the author in Poland in 1960.*

concrete by employing twigs and pebbles to represent the peoples and things being described.[62]

Crowley mentions this same characteristic as being prevalent among Bahamian tellers. He noticed that quite a number reached out and spontaneously used props from their immediate environment (such as a pen, a shirt, a cockroach, and other objects) to represent human or animal characters, or some object important to their stories.[63]

The Russian *skomorokhi* of the seventeenth century were described by a number of contemporaneous writers as wearing masks.[64] There does not seem to be any other reference to this custom among storytellers in other parts of the world, with the possible exception of *penglipur lara* performers in Malaysia.[65] The mask was generally used more as a theatrical device than as an aid to oral narration. The *skomorokhi* were definitely storytellers and not actors. There are no specific descriptions as to exactly the manner in which they used the masks in storytelling, or whether they used them only to disguise themselves as they went from place to place. They were the favorite targets of imitation. A number of *byliny* depict how one famous hero or another, disguised as a *skomorokh*, goes to a party or visits a court.

Although the *skomorokhi* can be classed as bardic storytellers as the term is defined in this book, on the whole the bardic form of storytelling is much more formal than their style encompassed. The *shékárịsị* of the Congo region are much more representative of the bardic style in their use of objects. They consider it appropriate to occasionally hold a representation of one of the favorite symbols of the heroes of the epics they recount. During the Mwindo epic, this might be a conga scepter, since that is the magical device that the hero uses in the epic.[66] For the bards of the ancient kingdom of Abomey, it was a spear, a baton, or a fly whisk that was used during the narration of the chronicles and epics.[67] The baton is also used by some *griots*.[68] The *omwevugi*, or bard, of the Bahima of Ankole (Uganda) used a spear while reciting. It was held horizontally or planted in the ground.[69] The Xhosa and Zulu *imbongi*, who sings spontaneous praise poetry of a narrative sort, most often carries crossed spears or a scepter-like club, which he uses to give emphasis and drama to the performance. Some anthropologists see the holding of these symbols as a purely ritualistic function, but Okpewho believes such objects help the bard recreate the hero convincingly.[70]

All of the above reinforce the notion that the use of the scepter conferred authority, even in very ancient times. The Greek *rhapsode*, however, used a staff, called a *rhabdos*, that more likely was originally a traveler's walking stick. It probably became associated in the public mind with this type of performer and thus began to be used as one of his symbols and prerogatives (see figure 3).

# CHAPTER 13

# *Closing of the Story Session*

The closings to storytelling are, more often than not, determined by the type of story told. For *märchen*, we are most familiar with the satisfying "they lived happily ever after." This has many variations and expansions. Sometimes, it may be in rhyme:

And soon was given to him a son and heir
And they lived happily without a care.
  Luigi Capuana, *C'era una volta,*
  trans. from the Italian by Anne MacDonnell

They had their wish fulfilled
Let's go up and sit in their seats.
  Barbara K. Walker, "Folktales in Turkey"[1]

Sometimes it describes the wedding of the protagonists in highly exaggerated terms:

The marriage lasted nine days and nine nights. There were nine hundred fiddlers, nine hundred fluters, and nine hundred pipers, and the last day and night of the wedding were better than the rest.
  Seumas MacManus, *Donegal Fairy Book*

I was there too, but no one had time to think of me. All I got was a slice of cake with butter on it. I put it on the stove
And the cake did burn
And the butter did run

And I got back
Not a single crumb.
   Reidar Th. Christiansen, *Folktales of Norway*

So they looked for priest and bishop
Fresh potatoes, corn and peas.
Those who didn't come by wagon,
Made the trip in burlap bags.
   Yolando Pino-Saavedra, *Folktales of Chile*

## Call-and-Response Endings

Just as some tales open with the audience responding to a potential teller, there are places where the ending involves an exchange of teller and listener. The most extended type of such an ending occurs among the Yucatec Maya. Such an epilogue was recorded by Burns, between Don Pas, a storyteller, and Don Felipe, his listener/interlocutor:

Pas: Let's hunt.
Felipe: My rifle's broken.
Pas: Where are the parts?
Felipe: I burned them.
Pas: Where are the ashes?
Felipe: Eaten by a falcon.
Pas: Where's the falcon?
Felipe: Went to the sky.
Pas: Where in the sky?
Felipe: Fell.
Pas: Then where did it fall?
Felipe: Went in a well.
Pas: Where's the well?
Felipe: Disappeared.
Pas: Where'd it disappear?
Felipe: Into your belly button.
Pas: True.[2]

Humorous folktales often end with a catchy rhyme, as in these six examples, used in different parts of the world:

They lived in peace, they died in peace
And they were buried in a pot of candle grease.

E lo ben
My story is end.

Billy ben
My story end.
   E. C. Parsons, *Folktales of Andros Island, Bahamas*

I step on a thing, the thing bend,
My story is end.
   E. C. Parsons, *Folklore of the Sea Islands, South Carolina*

I passed through a mouse hole
And my story is whole.
  G. Massignon, *Folktales of France*

And then I leapt into a saddle and rode high and low
To tell others this story of wonder and woe.
  *Fairy Tales and Legends from Romania*, trans. by I. Sturdza

Among some peoples, stories end with a rhyme or phrase that is not necessarily nonsense and yet does not have any particular meaning, although it may have had at one time. An example from the Thonga of South Africa goes like this:

*Tju-tju; famba ka Gwamba ni Dzabana*
(Run away; go to Gwamba and Dzabana) [This may refer to first man and first woman, but this is speculative.]
  H. A. Junod, *The Life of a South African Tribe*

The Wolof ending rhyme can be any of the following:

Here's where the story walks into the sea;
The first nose to sniff it out will go to heaven.
  *or*
The tale passed by here and went to heaven;
Whoever understands it first, will go to heaven.
  *or*
[The first line only of each of the above couplets.][3]

Or the ending may be one terse word or phrase, a dramatic way of indicating that "this is the end."

*Kungurus kan kusu.* (The rat's head is off.)
  F. Edgar, *Hausa Tales and Traditions*

*Dondo harai.* (With this, it's sold out.)
  K. Seki, *Folktales of Japan*

*Mahezu.* (Finished.)
  H. Chatelain, *Folktales of Angola*

*Le coq chanta et le conte fut fini.* (The cock crowed and the tale was ended.)
  G. Massignon, *Folktales of France*

*Kiruskidits.* (Untranslatable. The word is also used for the action of drawing up the strings of a tobacco pouch.)
  M. W. Beckwith, *Mandan-Hidatsa Myths and Ceremonies*

Among the Clackamas, as both Jacobs and Hymes report, many stories closed with a short epilogue that described the metamorphosis of the main story character into an animal, fish, or bird, or told what else might have happened to him or her; but a final brief phrase that ended the performance was usually given, and meant "Myth, myth" or "Story, story."[4]

Among the longer endings are the "runs" common among Gaelic storytellers:

It was long ago, and a long time ago it was.
If I were alive then, I wouldn't be alive now.

If I were, I would have a new story
or an old one, or I mightn't have any story!
Or I might have lost only my back teeth
or my front teeth or the furthest back tooth in my mouth.
    S. O'Sullivan, *The Folklore of Ireland*

Sometimes these longer endings are almost stories in their own right, as in the following examples:

Thus my story ends,
The Natiya-thorn withers.
"Why, O Natiya-thorn, do you wither?"
"Why does the cow on me browse?"
"Why, O cow, do you browse?"
"Why does the shepherd not tend me?"
"Why, O shepherd, do you not tend the cow?"
"Why does the daughter-in-law not give me rice?"
"Why, O daughter-in-law, do you not give rice?"
"Why does my child cry?"
"Why, O child, do you cry?"
"Why does the ant bite me?"
"Why, O ant, do you bite?"
Koot! Koot! Koot!
    Lal Behari Day, *Folk-tales of Bengal*

I was there but they kicked me out, so I went to the stables and chose a steed with a golden saddle. His body was of steel, the legs of wax, the tail of tow, the head was a cabbage and the eyes two corn cockle seeds. I rode up a silex hill and the horse's tail began to melt, the tail to break and the eyes to pop. I rode astride a big blue fly and told you all a clever lie. I rode astride a ringing bell and told you all I had to tell.
    *Fairy Tales and Legends from Romania*, trans. by I. Sturdza

Were it not on account of the spider
I should have greatly lied.
As it is I have told an untruth.
This lie is lucky for
Tomorrow morning when I arise from sleep,
I will obtain a money-bag full of money
behind my hut.
A pile of silver
the spider has placed there.
If I do not get a money-bag
I shall at least get a bitter gourd.
    A. J. N. Tremearne, *Hausa Superstitions and Customs*

Tremearne does not say so, but one wonders if the storyteller did not use this as a device to hint that payment by the audience was a hoped-for response.

## Payment for Stories

Such a hint at recompense of money, wine, meat, or other things can be found in quite a number of tale conclusions:

There's my story, it isn't very long.
If it isn't worth a penny, it's maybe worth a song.
  A. MacDonnell, *The Italian Fairy Book*

It's not to drink beer! It's not to brew wine!
They were wedded and whirled away to love.
Daily they lived and richer grew.
I dropped in to visit, right welcome they made me.
Wine runs on my lips, nary a drop in my mouth!.
  Y. M. Sokolov, *Russian Folklore*

I came here and saw men quarreling and as I went to calm them one of them came
for me at once and hit me hard, and as I cried out he took a bit of meat and put it
in my hand, and I brought it and placed it on top of the doorway here; child, go and
fetch it.
  E. E. Evans-Pritchard, *The Zande Trickster*

This is meant to be a joke or trick, of course, and often if a child in the audience
does not catch on, he or she may go to fetch it. It was simply a device for closing
the tale and session decisively; however, there could be some hint of payment of
food implied in the ending.

In India, public performances by bards and folk tellers alike, especially those
accompanied by music and picture scrolls, cloths or sheets, is virtually always
recompensed as part of the storytelling ritual. For example, the *bhopo* who performs in Rajasthan, chanting the story, playing the musical instrument known as
a *jantar*, and showing the pictures on his *par* (cloth or paper scroll), is given
money in the name of the deity for whom he performs. At the end of each major
segment of the epic, a donor comes up and presents money to the deity, the
assistant to the bard blows on a conch shell in recognition of the donation, and
this continues until all have given who wish to give.[5]

Other bardic groups in India, such as the bow-song epic singers in Tamil
Nadu, are treated more as professionals and receive a fee from their patron that
is more or less fixed for certain types of performances. However, they often, in
addition, receive individual donations during or after the performance, from
members of the audience.[6]

Among the Armenians in their homeland, there was an ending, used for
virtually all tales, that implied metaphysical as well as physical payment:

Three apples fell from heaven: one for the storyteller, one for he who listens, and
one for he who understands.
  L. Surmelian, *Apples of Immortality*

It is interesting to note that this ending changed somewhat when the Armenians
emigrated to the United States. Among the Detroit community of Armenian-
Americans, the commonly heard ending was:

From the sky fell three apples: one to me, one to the storyteller and one to the
person who has entertained you.
  S. Hoogasian-Villa, *100 Armenian Tales*

## Endings Indicating Whether Story Is True or False

In certain parts of the world, it is customary for the storyteller to add a kind
of mock-serious disclaimer for the "lies" or exaggerations that have appeared

in the tale. For example, Delargy reported that many Gaelic stories ended thus:

> That is my story! If there be a lie in it, be it so! It is not I who made or invented it.[7]

Megas reports the following as an occasional ending for Greek folklore in the past:

> Neither was I there, nor need you believe it.[8]

From the Bahamas comes this blithe acknowledgment of untruth:

> Chase the rooster and catch the hen
> I'll never tell a lie like that again.[9]

In Polynesia, the exaggeration is eliminated or softened, and the disclaimer might be:

> Just a tale that people tell.[10]

In Japan, the teller tries to convince the audience that it is not necessarily his telling of the tale that makes it true or untrue by ending thus:

> No matter whether it is told or not, that is the way it happened.[11]

In East Africa, the Haya method of closing implies that the teller has told at least a symbolic truth, for the story often concludes with words like "And when I saw these things, I came to tell you about them." Sometimes the narrator even states directly the lesson or moral of the tale, as the narrator interprets it. This statement is referred to by the same term one uses to decant a liquid so as to remove the sediment. "Stating the lesson directly might be seen as separating the cultural values expressed in a tale from the dramatic action that embodies them."[12]

A similar process takes place among the Mende in Sierra Leone. They say either "That is what I heard long ago" or "That is what I observed long ago." They, too, sometimes verbalize a moral or message statement.[13]

## Passing of Turn To Another Teller

Occasionally, a final rhyme, phrase, or sentence will suggest that the storyteller has finished and now passes on the turn for telling to another:

> *Y entro por un cano roto y salgo por otro*
> *y quiero que me cuentes otro.*
> I enter through a broken pipe and leave through another
> And now I want *you* to tell me another.
>    H. T. Wheeler, *Tales from Jalisco Mexico*

> *Fola foletta, dite a vostra;*
> *a mea e detta.*
> Fable, little fable, tell yours;
> mine is told.
>    G. Massignon, *Folktales of France* (Corsican)

> This story will have to do,
> For it went through a broken shoe,
> And came out in a little bean stalk
> So _____ can take up the talk.
>    Y. Pino-Saavedra, *Folktales of Chile*

In West Africa it might be passed on by saying something like: "now the tale jumps and lands on _____."[14]

According to Parsons, in the past the Taos Indians had a much more physical way of indicating whose turn it was next to tell a tale.

> As it grew toward daybreak if somebody was in the middle of a story, any one present who knew how would say, "Let's make him a *lamopolu'na*." Then they spread a blanket on the floor, put him in it and bundled him up, tying him in. Four or five would carry him out to the refuse heap, the heap of the dead, and roll him down. If he could free himself and catch somebody, that one in turn would be bundled down a slope, and the others would all run back to the house. While taking the "bundle" out from the house they had a song to sing which they kept up until they got to the refuse heap. [The song translates roughly as] "Deer hair bundle, pumpkin seed carving." [The concluding word is always] "*koiw'ekima*" (You have a tail) or "*Tenkkoiwe'ekim*" (So then, you have a tail).[15]

This was directed to the one whose turn was next and meant that he must tell a story to take the tail off, so it wouldn't freeze. The humor resulting from the homonym tail-tale in the English translation probably fits right into the spirit of the occasion!

Sometimes the audience decides when it is time for another teller to take over. In many places in Africa it is common for the audience to cut short a poor teller, and urge a better teller to take over. In Surinam, too, if the telling seems to be getting boring and meandering, two or more members of the audience might begin a song that is not connected to the story. Such a song is called a "cutting song" and indicates that it is time for the teller to cut the story short.[16]

## Endings Showing Punishment or Retribution

If there has been a truly evil person or character in the folktale, sometimes the happy end is followed by the meting out of punishments:

> They were tied to the tails of wild jackasses who were whipped and driven over mountainous trails: the largest piece they found later was only an ear.
> S. Hoogasian-Villa, *100 Armenian Tales*

> At once her brothers and her friends drew their swords and cut Mr. Fox into a thousand pieces.
> J. Jacobs, *English Folk and Fairy Tales*

> "Now what doom does such an one deserve?"
> "No better than this," answered the false bride, "that she be put naked into a cask, studded inside with sharp nails, and be dragged along in it by two white horses from street to street, until she be dead."
> "Thou hast spoken thy own doom," said the old King; "as thou hast said, so shall it be done."
> J. and W. Grimm, *Household Stories*, trans. by Lucy Crane

> Let it not be my end, but the end of the tale and of _____ and _____. (evil or negative characters in the tale).
> P. Smith, *Le récit Populaire au Rwanda*[17]

Among the Fon people of Dahomey, the fairly standard endings for the folk-tale have a mysterious air of half threat, half joke:

> The words I told, which you have now heard, tomorrow you will hear a bird tell them to you.
>
>    *or*
>
> Tomorrow morning you will hear the same story told you by a bird, but you had better not listen. If you hear it told by a bird, you will die.
>
>    M. J. and F. S. Herskovits, *Dahomean Narrative*[18]

## Other Closing Devices

After the last story was completed, most sessions came to an end. Sometimes this happened when all of the listeners had gone to sleep and no longer responded with their periodic expressions of assent and approval. In such cases the narrator, too, usually turned over and went to sleep. This custom is reported on the Indian subcontinent, among Native American groups, and in the Pacific Islands.[19]

Other sessions required a ceremony after storytelling. The Cowlitz, Native Americans of the western Washington region, often made their children take a swim after storytelling.[20] The Jicarilla Apache had different customs. After a night of storytelling they would all paint their faces (even those of the children) with red ochre, and then leave this on as a sign that they had participated in the wisdom of the tribe. Sometimes the storyteller was required to give gifts to the listeners on the principle that the night had been "stolen" from them.[21]

The ceremonial ending for story hours in many public libraries is blowing out the candle that was lighted at the start. Some storytellers use a rhyme in which all the children are told to make a wish. Others simply have one child blow out the candle, to indicate it is time to file out of the story-hour room.

# IV

# *The Training of Storytellers*

# CHAPTER 14

# A Brief History and Survey of Training Methods

Storytellers in the past and in the present have received their training in one of five ways:

1. Through inherited function or office.
2. Through apprenticeship arranged by a guild or professional group.2.
3. Through apprenticeship arranged on an individual basis.
4. At a school, university, or other formal institutional course.
5. By means of informal imitative learning from other narrators at home, in the community, or through books, films, and videotapes.

Storytelling is dependent on personality as well as on intelligence and experience. It is rare to find cultures where all members are trained in it to the extent they become expert tellers. Strabo, writing of the Parthians in approximately the opening years of the Common Era, indicated that this was expected of all young members of the society:

> [For the children] from five years of age to twenty-four they . . . use as teachers of science their wisest men, who also interweave their teachings with the mythical element, thus reducing that element to a useful purpose, and [they] rehearse both with song and without song the deeds both of gods and of the noblest men.
> *Geography*, xv, 3, 18, trans. by H. L. Jones[1]

The memory, spontaneity, and personality needed for a good performance would seem to make storytelling a profession that is not too well suited to being passed on through inheritance. The storytellers whose positions tended to be rigorously limited to offspring or close relatives were those who were noted as bardic reciters of oral narratives that were not supposed to be changed very much. In other words, they were as much historians as they were storytellers.

## Inherited Positions

The earliest mentions of inherited positions in storytelling are in Chinese, Irish, and Welsh. In Chinese, the first record of storytelling schools appears in 1235 C.E. The tellers were called *chuan*, and invariably if the sons or daughters showed any talent or inclination toward the profession, they began their apprenticeship while still very young. One little girl of six, the granddaughter of a master storyteller, was entered formally into training at that age because "she was of a lively temperament, had large and expressive eyes, a strong voice and clear enunciation."[2]

The guilds were responsible for the entire training process, which could last several years. It consisted of stages very similar to the modern storytelling schools in the Japanese *yose*, to be mentioned later. Suffice it to say that in the end, the social standing of the professional storyteller in medieval China was somewhat higher than that of the actor.

For the Irish and Welsh, the bards that we know most about are the *fili, ollam*, and *pencerdd*. The Chadwicks cited sources that seem to indicate there was a tendency for these professions to become hereditary.[3] Corkery agreed with this. It was, he wrote, "a profession that was hereditary, a rich, strongly-organised caste, an over-elaborated catechism of art." His description of the bardic schools did not cite any contemporaneous sources, but it agreed with those found in Toland and other writers:

> It is not probable that we shall ever discover the origins of the bardic schools. . . .
> They were ancient when St. Patrick came amongst us. . . When the schools did at
> last become Christian they did not become monastic; and they are not to be con-
> fused with the famous monastic schools. The Bardic Schools were lay, officered by
> laymen. . . . The Studies of the students were chiefly: history, law, language,
> literature.[4]

In the second tract on poetry in the *Book of Ballymote*, dating to the eighth or ninth century, there are a number of passages relating to the training of bards, *filid*, and *ollam*. Depending on the rank or grade, training lasted seven, ten, or twelve years and consisted of learning many sagas, the composition and recitation of all types of poetry, and oral lore of all kinds.[5] Obviously, when their ranks began to be filled entirely through inheritance, the bardic schools began to produce those who could write academic poetry; such persons were probably more interested in maintaining their rank and privileges in society than in perfecting their spontaneous art. This was bound to cause a decline in the quality of performance, for as Corkery remarked, "in art who does not fear privilege and organisation?"[6] The hereditary bard in Ireland and Wales died out, and the folk storyteller flourished.

There are still hereditary bards in Africa today. They are known under such terms as *diaré, gawlo, gêwel, griot, īggīw, lunga, mugani wa lugano, shékárịsị*, and *tīggiwīt*. The blood relationship is sometimes strictly insisted upon; in other cases it is loosely interpreted.

One of the groups practicing strict hereditary bardship is the Dagbon of northeastern Ghana. In the book *Growing Up in Dagbon*, Oppong translated the term *lunga (lunsi)* as drummer(s), as indeed they are. But they are also chroniclers of the past and recorders/narrators of the present. "They play an important part in all rituals involving royals including those performed at installation, naming and funeral ceremonies. The unbroken historical narrative, and royal genealogy which they remember and recite is the charter of the political structure of the kingdom, and the story of the origins of the people."[7] In short, they are bards as we are defining the term in this book.

The social and cultural constraints requiring the Dagbon child whose father is a drummer to be, in turn, a drummer are very great:

> He is compelled to assume the role at least in the nominal sense, while drummers' daughters, since they are not eligible to assume the role themselves, must give at least one of their offspring to replace them in the next generation. On the other hand strong sanctions also operate to prevent those unrelated to drummers from playing. Thus a drummer's sons stay at home to be taught by their father or are taught by a brother or father's brother. It is considered unthinkable for a drummer's son to stay in his father's house and not learn to play. Should he object very violently to learning his father's profession, however, then he may go to live elsewhere, escape by running away, and no evil should befall him so long as he always keeps his drum and plays it symbolically on Mondays and Fridays. But if a son learns when small and later goes south without taking his drum then it is said misfortune and even death will pursue him. Difficult as it is for drummers' sons to escape becoming drummers when they grow up, it is still more difficult for a daughter's son to escape learning, for he must replace his mother. The particular child who is to represent his mother and siblings with his maternal kin is chosen by divination and then 'adopted' by his mother's brother or maternal grandfather. . . . Even on the day that a drummer's daughter is married her husband is told that one day one of their offspring will be claimed for this purpose. It is usually after a daughter has born one or two children that one is taken at the age of four or five. . . . Should a drummer's daughter only bear female children then she must send a daughter who will later be given in marriage to a drummer, or to another man on the understanding that one of her sons will be given to learn to play. Thus it is a strongly sanctioned rule that any drummer's daughter, wherever she is, must send a child back to her natal family, otherwise illness and death . . . will visit her children, in the form of insanity, leprosy or other misfortune.[8]

To learn the massive body of oral material is an arduous and painstaking task. The young pupils learn to drum and to recite narratives and genealogies. The length of time it takes to become a good performer depends on the ability of the individual child.

> Learning is thought to be a very difficult process. . . . A typical teaching situation is for the teacher to recline in his entrance hall after supper in the evening, while the children gather round him, sitting and kneeling upon the floor. On one occasion witnessed, the teacher was rhythmically massaged by his eight pupils. While they sang songs they rocked back and forth rubbing their teacher's legs and back as they sang. . . . The senior and most competent pupil sang the leading phrases which were repeated in unison by the rest, without drum accompaniment.[9]

Oppong also described the training of children who become "fiddlers." That is, they play a single-stranded bow-lute, made of calabash covered with a taut skin, and at the same time they sing praises for their patrons:

> A child can begin to learn to play the fiddle when he is quite small, about five or six years old. The first step is simply to learn to move the bow up and down while

sitting next to the father or other teacher, who performs the finger movements with his left hand. Words and music are always learnt simultaneously, so that if the player does not sing aloud while he plays he tends unconsciously to mouth the words at the same time. As in the case of drummers, talents differ so that while one has a good memory for songs and praises, another has a sweet voice and a third may be a skillful player. Some boys born into fiddlers' families are said to be able to play in a matter of months, while another takes years to become a mediocre performer. For example one boy, Abu, was sent to his mother's older brother for training at about twelve, because he was misbehaving at home and had refused to stay with his father. He learnt to play with considerable competence in a mere five months, his performance being better than that of many pupils after three years' training. A boy practices playing at any time when he is free and if his father or teacher is at hand and hears him playing badly he will call him and demonstrate the correct way. By the age of nine or ten a boy with aptitude may be quite a competent player and be called by neighboring musicians to accompany them to play at celebrations in neighboring villages, as well as going to play with his father or teacher.[10]

This position of fiddler is also hereditary, but it does not carry with it the extreme obligatory force that the drummer's position has. Most sons do learn to play, and daughters are expected to learn to play rattle accompaniments. As in the case of drummers, one of the daughter's sons is expected to learn the art, but it is much easier for the boy who does not wish to play to escape his responsibility without retribution.

The bard commonly known by the term *griot* is also trained by inheritance. Some of the names for these bards in different parts of West Africa where the Mande language group is predominant are: *gêwel* in Wolof (Senegal), *diaré* in Soninke (Senegal), *jali* or *jeli* in Malinke (Mali and neighboring countries), *gawlo* in Toucouleur (Mauritania), and *īggīw* (male) or *tīggiwīt* (female) in Shinqiti (Mauritania). In his book *Gens de la Parole*, Sory Camara included excellent discussions of the social and religious aspects of the lives of this type of bard, from birth to death, but he mentioned little regarding their training. Norris described it sketchily and only insofar as their musical training was concerned:

> The art of playing these instruments requires years of training and instruction, and it is not uncommon to find miniature models of both instruments in the houses and tents of the *īggāwen*. Their sole purpose is to instruct children in the technique of the instruments they are learning to play.[11]

Since most of the Mauritanian families never marry outside their class, they have been able to maintain their musical and oral traditions for generations. Many of the families can trace their ancestry back for several centuries. Thus it is only natural that a child growing up in such a family would learn these arts as automatically as he or she might learn to talk and walk.[12]

In India, a number of bardic castes pass on their narrative and performing ability only to family members or to those families in the caste traditionally viewed as having these rights. For example, the performers of the Palnādu epic in Andhra Pradesh each have their traditional hereditary stories to perform in the ritual, passed on for generations. They even had temple lands allotted to them as payment in the past, although many have lost or sold the lands by now.

Most other Indian bardic groups have inherited positions by caste, and not by individual family. Typical of this would be the *bhopo* and *bhopi* of Rajasthan.

They might train sons or daughters, but in many cases a young boy from an unrelated family of the caste is sent to live with them and be trained. The training is under a strict apprenticeship system, in which the *chela* (student) gradually learns all the different parts: the sung narration, the playing of the *jantar*, the dancing steps. The process might take years. When deemed competent, the *chela* receives a copper ring, and can then take a major part in the performance, or even get a picture scroll and perform independently.[13]

There are a few cases of strict training by inheritance that are not exactly bardic forms of storytelling. In some cultures, family stories can be passed on only to descendants. But this usually means that all in the culture are oral-tradition carriers. Such would have been the case with a number of Polynesian groups. Handy described how children in the Marquesa Islands were trained. Their father built a special house for this purpose, called *oho au*, and then hired a *tuhuna* (shaman/bard) to instruct them. Usually, around thirty men and women from the same family group would also participate in the teaching, which lasted for one month. All other work was suspended during the period of learning. After it was over, the house was destroyed.[14]

The Maori equivalent of such a house was called *whare wananga*; the bard was called a *tohunga*. Seemingly, not all youngsters were chosen to participate, but only those of noble birth. Such persons would not necessarily become bards or storytellers, except that they would have to narrate the traditions a certain number of times so as to keep them fresh in their memory. Some would later become *tohuna* or *tohunga*.[15]

There is also the individual inheritance of certain stories, respected as a sign of the artistry of one individual who was able to tell them particularly well or because each story was considered as property to be bequeathed or sold. The latter occurs with the *waikan*, a type of sacred story among the Winnebago.[16] To a certain degree it was also practiced among the *byliny* performers in Russia.[17] Malinowski wrote of a Trobriand Islands chief who gave food and other goods to the descendants of a certain person in exchange for a dance, a song, and a story owned by them.[18] But this kind of situation does not describe the inherited "position" or "caste" of the storyteller, with all of its ramifications relating to lack of choice and duty.

Among the many brief descriptions available of ancient Greek bards, there is none indicating that they held hereditary posts, although the likelihood is certainly there. Nor do we know much about their training. We know a great deal about the performance and position in society of the Anglo-Saxon *scop* or *gleoman*, but we know nothing about his training and whether he passed on his position to his children, regardless of their talent. The same is true of the positions of the *cuicapicque* and the *amauta* among the Aztecs and Incas, respectively, although we do know that the latter were carefully trained in special schools.[19]

## Formal Apprenticeship

Apprenticeship that is not hereditary is the more usual kind of training given to bardic storytellers and to a few other kinds of storytellers too. The term "formal apprenticeship" means here a prescribed course chosen by the student and generally paid for in some monetary way, during which the apprentice usually lives for a time with the master and performs other duties as well as learning. In some cases the course has a prescribed length of time, and in other cases it can be cut short or expanded, depending on the individual abilities of the students.

The most formal training of this type today is probably that of the *zenza*, who are preparing to become master storytellers in the *yose*, public halls in Japan. By virtue of their style, they could be classed as bardic storytellers but they generally narrate stories of the longer folktale type. Hrdličková gives an excellent account of their training, and the following summary is taken from her two articles on the subject.[20]

The training of the *zenza* is essentially the same as it was in feudal times, except that it has been shortened somewhat, and the apprentices now join the master while still in their early teens. This change occurred at the end of the eighteenth century or the beginning of the nineteenth, when formal schools for carrying out the apprenticeship were established. Prior to that, the students had worked individually with masters, starting when they were somewhat older.

The act of "entering the gate of apprenticeship" is called *nyūmon*; as soon as this happens the master gives the apprentice his artistic name. (There are a few female apprentices, but they are very rare; the *zenza* will be referred to as male here.) The first period of apprenticeship now lasts from six to twelve months, and during this time, the young student is called *minarai*. Student time is spent observing and also performing menial chores.

The second part of the apprenticeship lasts two to three years, and the apprentice is now called a *zenza*. During the teaching period, the *zenza* must kneel in front of the master. He is orally given stories with "jaw-breaking passages" to learn. He may not write anything down and is usually required to repeat exactly what the master has recited until he has learned the "secret" of the story. At the same time, he usually must learn to play some traditional musical instrument, such as the drum.

Once he has mastered a few stories and is considered good enough to begin interpreting them in his own way, the *zenza* is occasionally allowed to perform. He even earns a small salary. But most of his time is spent in service to the master storyteller, preparing the stage and keeping the record books up to date. These are kept in the dressing room, and it is here that the *zenza* records the date, the stories told, and by whom, because the printed program gives only the storytellers' names, not the titles of their stories. After three or four years, the *zenza* in turn becomes a master storyteller.

There were public halls similar to the *yose* in parts of China and Mongolia. Virtually all of the storytellers who performed in these halls received training similar to that offered in Japan. There do not appear to be any such schools in present-day China or Mongolia. The main differences between the Chinese schools of the past and the Japanese schools of past times seem to be that the Chinese were more strongly hereditary than those of Japan and each school seemed to specialize in teaching only one type of story performance.[21]

There were such schools in old Persia as well, but they no longer exist. Mahmoud Omidsalar has translated the portions of *The Royal Book of Futuwwa* by Mulla Husayn i Kashifi (c. 1500 C.E.) that pertain to the training of storytellers.

How many are the rules of the storyteller? Eight. [The storyteller] must have studied the tale he wants to tell with a master . . . he must have repeated it enough times so that he may not get stuck. Second, he must start to speak eloquently and excitingly and he must not be plain and boring. Third, he must know what kind of narration is fitting for every assembly, when to stop and the like. He must mostly narrate things that people like. Fourth, he should occasionally embellish his narration with verses, but not in a manner that may cause boredom. . . . Fifth, he should not make impossible or hyperbolic statements lest he lose face among the people. Sixth, he may not make sarcastic or critical remarks lest he become an object of dislike. Seventh, he should not forcefully demand payment and should not pester the people. Eighth, he must not stop too soon or go on too late but must always keep to the path of moderation.[22]

Those who were "singers of poetry," that is, epic singers, had slightly different rules, but in both cases, there was limited extemporaneous material added by the teller. Most of it was memorized. Omidsalar found no evidence that the guild tellers used written texts, but Cejpek described the *kitabcha* as prompt books used by these professional tellers. In more recent times in Iran, they were replaced by cheap lithographic folk prints that the narrators used as memory aids.[23]

Another type of long apprenticeship is that served by the hunters' bard among the Mande language groups of West Africa. This training lasts from ten to fifteen years, but on a part-time basis. The young apprentice must first master the *narinyo*, a rhythm instrument, until he becomes a *nara*, or master-singer. Then he must learn to play the *donso-nkoni*, a six-stringed harp-lute. Once he can perform well on this, and learns to sing the traditional narratives, he can call himself a *donso-jeli*, or hunters' bard.[24]

Those who wish to chant the *ikar* among the Kuna of Panama's San Blas Islands, must remain for a long period of apprenticeship with a master. They learn the texts by strict memorization. The longer texts take years of study. When the master *ikar*-knower decides the student has learned enough to become an *ikar* performer, he announces this in the official "gathering house" of the village. If a student has been apprenticed away from his community, he brings a letter back from his teacher, describing what he has learned. This is read aloud in his home village "gathering house." He also usually gives a personal account of what he has learned, his travels, and his relationship with his teacher.[25]

## Informal Apprenticeship

The *oníjǎlá*, who performs in Yoruba in Nigeria and in neighboring countries, is also a hunters' bard. He begins chanting *ijála* under a master during late childhood or early adolescence. Some men are married before they start their apprenticeships. All the *ijála* chanters interviewed by Babalola gave as their main reason for going to a master "that they wanted to do it beautifully."[26]

In the first stage, the apprentice to the *oníjǎlá* listens as the teacher performs in his own house or at social gatherings where he has been invited to entertain. During the second stage, the pupil imitates the teacher word for word, repeating the narratives privately. He is also permitted to go along to public performances where he repeats the master's words simultaneously. If there are two or more such apprentices practicing in this way, it often makes the *ijála* performance sound like a group chant, but this is only due to the teaching method. The master is definitely considered the storyteller.

The third stage occurs when the master gives the pupil a chance to perform on his own. On the average, the whole process takes about ten years. There is no final test, and the apprentice leaves his master's service either without notice (if he fears the teacher will not approve of his departure) or with the blessings of his master, because the student has now been recognized as a performer in his own right.

In a number of places the apprenticeship is carried out even more informally. The Nyanga of Zaire call their bard *shékárịsị*. According to Biebuyck and Mateene, young men who are relatives or friends of the bard accompany him as he performs and thus learn the epic and how to present it orally.

> They are usually three in number, but now all these young men will ultimately be expert in narrating the epic. It is likely that only one of them—the more energetic, intelligent, assiduous, better-liked one—will be fully instructed by the bard in the performance in all its complexity.[27]

During the performance, the tasks of these young men are to beat the percussion instruments and to lead the refrains of the songs, in which the audience joins.

If one of these young apprentices falls sick or has other things go wrong in his personal life, this is usually interpreted as a sign that the spirits are angry at the slow and negligent way he has been learning the epic. In order to set this right, he must speed up his learning and make ceremonial offerings of banana beer.[28]

Ben-Amos describes the training of two professional storytelling groups in Benin and points out that this can be accomplished by formal or informal apprenticeship. Of the nineteen storytellers he interviewed, eight had learned informally from their fathers, uncles, or older brothers; four were instructed by friends; and six had been apprenticed to professional players outside their immediate family. In all cases, the instruction was direct and indirect. The student was given special musical patterns to practice, sometimes for hours, and the teacher corrected his mistakes. The verbal parts were usually listened to several times, and then the student, after asking the teacher to repeat a number of details, felt ready to assist in performing in public. Just as in the case of the *shékárịsị* of Zaire, the Benin tellers have a group of three or four apprentices, called *igbesa* in Edo, who support the teller in his performance. They learn to watch for the special signals that tell them when to join in the singing or when to stop.

The period of learning lasts from one to three years, during which time the apprentice may visit his teacher once or twice a week. The master also teaches the student how to make his own musical instrument before he graduates and makes his first professional appearance at a coming-out party.[29]

The training of the oral epic singers in Egypt is often an informal apprenticeship to a parent or older relative. Shamandi, one of the performers recorded by Connelly, recalled:

> My father . . . when we were sitting at home, taught me how to play. He did not send us either to the Kuttab (Koranic school) or to school. He said, "Hold the *rabab*!" So I held it. He said "Put your fingers here and do that and that." This is how I learned. Slowly, slowly I learned. He would hit me. I liked it though, so I learned. My father when he went to places to play . . . used to take me with him. . . . I was about seven or eight years old. He would make me sit next to him. . . . So I heard the poem from him while he recited it, while he played. So I took it from him.[30]

The training of the young *ntsomi* teller appears outwardly to be very informal indeed. Scheub was fortunate to be able to observe and listen to fairly young performers who were in the initial stages of learning, as well as to slightly older and more experienced *ntsomi* tellers and to accomplished artists. This enabled him to conclude:

> The "apprenticeship" of the young performer is quite casual, but this should in no way suggest that no period of apprenticeship is involved. . . . Nor does that apprenticeship lack rigorous standards. . . . She may receive some coaching in the very early stages from her parents and other sympathetic members of the family. . . . She learns, watches, listens, experiments, adopts, and adapts. She toys with new ideas, with nuances, idioms, songs, gestures, movements. . . . She begins with episodes and isolated details, with a few gestures, some cliches. She memorizes nothing, she remembers many things.[31]

The good *ntsomi* teller must show originality and contemporaneity, even within the framework of core plots that often stay the same. Scheub reports that it is not uncommon to hear the youngest children, just learning to talk, consciously using ideophones for animal sounds and actions, with great flair and originality.[32]

The bow-song epic singers in Tamil Nadu (male and female) also have very informal apprenticeships. Mostly, they first get their interest and learn the first stages by being present at the performances and liking the songs. However, there is some financial incentive to become a lead singer, and to do that well, generally the singer takes some instruction from one of the experienced and older lead singers.[33]

With regard to Serbo-Croation tellers, Lord distinguishes between the mere performers who carefully learn to present old, memorized versions in an authentic manner, and the real poet-singers, who create new versions each time they perform. The latter generally began to learn their art starting at the age of fourteen or fifteen. The young boy started by listening carefully to one or more singers of note whose style appealed to him. Some times he went off by himself to practice the songs, trying to remember them word for word. After he had built up enough confidence and learned the basic fingering of chords on the *gusle*, he performed for his companions. The more his competence increased, the more he realized he must use the formulaic phrases in his own manner, and the more confidence he would then have in adding his own variations. He would build up his own repertoire of favorite songs, but in each performance would try for a smoother delivery, better organization of the themes, and complete mastery of formulaic expressions. Some singers never reached that stage no matter how hard they tried.[34]

Another type of informal apprenticeship was that of the *aqyn*, or Kazakh bard. It was only after competing successfully at several *ajtys* (singing competitions) that the *aqyn* could finally claim to have become a professional. There were usually two "opponents" in the *ajtys*, and after the first had spontaneously composed a verse to one of the basic melodies used, the second had to reply, using the same type of formula. In most cases there were no fixed rules, but there was general agreement among listeners and "duelists" as to who had won.[35]

In North America today, numerous local storytelling clubs, centers, guilds, and groups can be said to give informal apprenticeship to new storytellers, mostly of the institutional type. Many of these groups are so constituted that their founders or leaders are the best-known and most experienced storytellers in an area. By meeting on a regular basis to demonstrate their skills, and by allowing persons new to storytelling to listen in and then try their first attempts at storytelling, they often give an informal "course" lasting several years. This writer observed that happening at the New York City Storytelling Center.

The Toronto Storytelling School, which now operates on a more structured basis, began essentially as an extension of the regular meetings of a group of storytellers there.

## Library School Courses

The modern substitute for the formal system of apprenticeship in many fields is the trade, technical, or professional school. As was pointed out in Chapter 6, the public library perceived one of its functions to be that of purveyor of oral literature for children. It is not surprising then that the early library schools, many of them operated by library systems and not by universities, included course work in storytelling. The first to do so were the Carnegie Library Training School for Children's Librarians in Pittsburgh, which opened in 1900, and the Pratt Institute, which began a specialist course in children's library work in the fall of 1899.[36] The training offered in Pittsburgh was two years in length and included courses in "Storytelling and Reading Aloud" both years.[37] At Pratt Institute, there was no special course, but one of the theses assigned to all students in the children's specialist program was "Storytelling and Reading Aloud in the Children's Library."[38]

Some of the other library schools that added storytelling courses (or parts of courses) were: Library School of Case Western Reserve University, 1904; Wisconsin Library School of the State Library Commission, 1909; New York Public Library, Library School, 1912; St. Louis Public Library School, 1917; Columbia University Library School, 1927.[39] The years given are not necessarily the first year of operation of the schools, but the first year for which a course description including storytelling could be located.

The last named university described its first storytelling course, taught by Alice Hazeltine, in this manner:

> A study of source material for the storyteller, with emphasis on folk and epic literature. Selection and adaptation of stories for children of different ages, especially cycles of stories for older children. Methods of learning and of presentation and practice in telling stories.[40]

This trend continues to the present day. Those library schools that give special courses on aspects of children's literature and library work with children also tend to offer a course in storytelling or oral narration. In addition, quite a number of universities or institutions of higher learning have placed such courses in the department of education or in the speech and drama department. If the library school does not offer a course, the library student can usually get credit for taking it in another department. By 1960 there were at least 211 institutions of higher learning in the United States offering some instruction in storytelling.[41] In 1979 among the 67 library schools granting degrees, 67 percent offered courses in storytelling.[42] At present, only one institution of higher learning, Dominican College in San Francisco, offers a major in storytelling.

A modern variation on the storytelling course is one that combines storytelling with other program techniques. Such courses concentrate on the planning and directing of film, video, picture-book, preschool, and story-hour programs, as well as covering the techniques of managing the content through selection and various forms of presentation.

## In-Service Training

In addition to the formal courses that were part of a curriculum leading to a professional degree or certificate, many public libraries also established short, in-service training seminars for their own staff. Some of these courses, such as those offered by the New York Public Library and the Carnegie Library of Pittsburgh, remain to this day a requirement for all new children's librarians entering the system. The New York Public Library in-service seminars were begun in 1951, under the direction of Eulalie Steinmetz.[43]

These in-service seminars usually consist of a series of four to eight lecture-demonstrations, spread out over as many weeks. The seminars are followed by active planning of several story hour programs. First might come "shared" story-hour programs in which a previously trained person does some of the telling and the new librarian may tell only one story. This number is gradually increased until the novice storyteller arranges to tell a full program.

By the end of the season, the training specialist, operating out of central administrative offices, will have observed all the new storytellers in action. In some library systems, the best of them are then selected to tell in a symposium or showcase of storytelling. Such a custom has been practiced annually in May by the New York Public Library. This has a precedent from the distant past. The medieval storytelling guilds in China often selected their best tellers to perform in a public display after an apprenticeship of anywhere from three to twelve years. Sometimes there were contests among the various guilds, to show off what each could accomplish in training.[44]

Recently, many library and school systems have instituted short workshops in storytelling for their professionals. A former children's librarian, Caroline Feller Bauer, has recently made a full-time career of conducting such workshops. Often, such training sessions are planned on an annual basis, and bring in new types of tellers to inform the teachers and librarians of techniques, story types, sources, and other aspects of storytelling. One manual even has a chapter on how to organize such a workshop.[45]

## Other Institutional Training Groups

Two organizations that influenced the training of storytellers in the United States and Canada during the earlier part of this century were the Chautauqua Institution and the National Story League. The former was at first a church-related summer school. Later it incorporated as a service organization providing adult education and cultural activities during the summer. It maintained a lecture bureau, sponsored social clubs in many communities, and carried out a wide variety of cultural and educational activities. The summer school in Chautauqua, New York (headquarters of the organization) had a storytelling course for many years. In 1904 it was taught by Marie Shedlock and in the decade following 1910 by Mabel C. Bragg.[46] Many librarians and others working with children were trained in these courses.

The National Storyteller's League was founded in 1903. Among its original purposes were:

> To encourage the art of storytelling and the use of classic and folklore stories in schools and other educational centers; to foster creative work in the arranging and re-writing of stories from various classic and historic sources; to serve as a medium of exchange of stories and experiences in the use of story; to discover in the world's literature, in history, and in life the best stories for education, and to tell them with love and sympathy for the children, and to bring together in story circles those who love to hear and tell a good story . . .[47]

Richard T. Wyche, a Tennessee educator, was the prime mover and organizer. The original members were not only educators, but also librarians, kindergarten teachers, playground workers, and ordinary interested persons. Wyche was determined to get the art of storytelling accepted as part of the programs of all kinds of organized work with children. He also stressed the importance of storytelling in the home. Although the League did have impact, it was never as strong as Wyche had hoped. The magazine he began, associated with the League, lasted only two issues. The most important contribution of the League was that it provided opportunity for storytellers of different styles and from different disciplines to hear and see each other.[48]

In 1923 the name and the purpose of the League were changed. It became the National Story League and its purpose was and still is stated thus: "to encourage the appreciation of the good and the beautiful in life and literature through the art of storytelling." This League still operates voluntary storytelling sessions in many public institutions, through local chapters in a number of cities. Courses for storytellers, if any are offered, are very informal. Most of the groups simply get together and compare storytelling techniques. The League has a membership of 45 state groups and 250 local groups, and publishes a magazine, *Story Art*.[49]

## NAPPS

Tennessee is obviously a state that encourages storytelling because in 1975, a group of tellers in Jonesborough got together and decided to develop an organizational umbrella under which to operate the storytelling festival which Jimmy Neil Smith had begun there a few years earlier. Six persons formed the National Association for the Preservation and Perpetuation of Storytelling, commonly known as NAPPS. They named a board of directors, elected Smith as the first chairman, and began searching for new members, mostly by word of mouth. Later, Connie Regan-Blake, another founding member, was named chairperson.[50] The association now has more than 3,700 members, many of whom are professional storytellers. The greater majority can be classed as institutional tellers, since they perform mostly in schools and libraries. The NAPPS festival will be described in Chapter 16.

A key component of NAPPS work is training and information exchange. An annual national congress, and sometimes regional conferences are held in addition to the festival. Every summer since 1977, there has been an institute devoted to storytelling. Most of these meetings are heavily oriented to demonstrating and teaching storytelling. NAPPS also issues periodicals that contain storytelling advice: *The Yarnspinner* and *Storytelling Magazine* (formerly *National Storytelling Journal*).

## Training Manuals

To cater to the needs of all these courses and workshops, formal and informal, there has been a constant stream of manuals and handbooks on storytelling. Usually these contained tips on the methods of selecting good stories to tell, on learning and reciting or telling the stories, and on how to set up a story session. Often this was followed by a collection of favorite stories to tell. The breakdown of the number published, by decade, gives a pretty fair idea of the steady demand for such material. Many have remained in print for five or more decades:

| Decade | No. of Storytelling Manuals Published in English[51] |
|--------|------------------------------------------------------|
| 1890s  | 2 |
| 1900s  | 1 |
| 1910s  | 11 |
| 1920s  | 8 |
| 1930s  | 3 |
| 1940s  | 4 |
| 1950s  | 9 |
| 1960s  | 4 |
| 1970s  | 12 |
| 1980s  | 14 |

Richard Alvey, in his dissertation on organized storytelling in the United States, gives an excellent analysis of the different approaches to storytelling that were to be found in many of the early manuals. He documents some of the ways in which they proved to be important in the training of storytellers. Of special interest are his comments contrasting the manuals of Marie Shedlock and Angela M. Keyes. In Alvey's view, Keyes had expressed in print five years before Shedlock "one of the most sophisticated of all models for storytelling to children in organized contexts." He cites the remarkable similarity of Shedlock's philosophy to that of Keyes, and speculates as to why the Shedlock book proved to be so much more popular and influential than the Keyes manual.

## Library Storytelling Training Outside the United States and Canada

Training for children's librarians in England, Australia, New Zealand, Sweden, Denmark, France, Greece, the Netherlands, Spain and the socialist countries of Eastern Europe all generally include some brief training in storytelling, either in separate courses or as a part of courses on introducing literature to children.[52] They have also developed local storytelling groups that operate in much the same way as the North American groups do, like informal guilds. And there are also a great deal of in-service training workshops, generally conducted by leading storytellers such as Eileen Colwell in England and Pat Scott in Australia.

In Japan, Momoko Ishii and later her assistant, Kiyoko Matsuoka, made a specialty of giving storytelling training to librarians in the home libraries movement. Ishii used as her model the in-service courses of the Toronto Public Library which she had observed on an extended training visit.[53]

Shigeo Watanabe, who received his in-service training at the New York Public

Library, returned to teach in Japan and included some storytelling in his courses at Keio University.[54]

Still another Japanese person who was influenced by library storytelling in the United States is Mitsue Ishitake. After seeing the pre-school and picture-book hours in the Westchester Public Library System and in the Weston Woods Studio traveling caravan, she returned to Japan and began training a staff that could function in a mobile unit specializing in storytelling, film and puppet programs for young children.[55] The Ohanashi Caravans (there are now several) still travel throughout Japan, to day-care centers, parks, libraries, and other places, giving programs that are a mixture of storytelling, puppetry, music, and films. In addition to the trained leaders, there are always some persons in training who go with the caravans, learning as apprentices do. The Ohanashi group has also given performances and training in other Asian countries.

In France, much of the storytelling training for children's librarians is given by the organization La Joie par les Livres or by L'Age d'Or, the national senior citizens group. Sometimes they jointly sponsor courses or workshops.

## Informal Training in the Home or Community

By far the majority of storytellers are trained in informal situations in their homes or communities. They learn by imitating the older tellers they admire, or occasionally they learn from their peer group. Margaret Brady spent considerable time observing how one group of Navajo children became increasingly competent, chiefly by practicing on their peers. As she pointed out: "No child is interested in how his or her narratives rate in a scientist's scale of cognitive development, but each and every child is acutely attuned to the ways in which peers evaluate and respond to his or her stories."[56]

Oftentimes, children learn in secret even though they are not supposed to be present at an adult session. Delargy mentioned an old man telling about this:

> The other boys thought I was too young to go with them to the house where Diarmuid the storyteller was staying, but I would give them the slip, and would hide under the table, where I could listen to the tales, undisturbed. There is not a word the storyteller would say that I had not off by heart the next morning.[57]

On the other hand, in some places they learned as children because training in storytelling was considered part of every child's upbringing, as in parts of Polynesia and Africa. Sometimes they learned easily, as did the Eskimo teller, Paul Monroe, who said: "When I heard stories they got in my head and I couldn't forget them."[58]

There does not seem to be any worldwide pattern of male parent, grandparent, or elder exclusively teaching the sons, and female parent or grandparent or elder teaching the daughters, as seems to be the case in many apprenticeships. There are many reverse situations mentioned in folk storytelling. Tirabutana as a girl in Thailand lived with her grandmother, but it was her father who told her stories and taught them to her.[59] Peig Sayers, the famous Irish storyteller from the Blasket Islands, also learned mostly from her father:

> ... he was the best teller of a tale that ever was in this countryside. ... My father had more tales than any man of his time, and if you had heard him telling them you would have wondered, for he never forgot anything. ...[60]

She speaks of only boys coming over to listen to the tales, but obviously she was also allowed to listen and learn.

Clementina Todesco of Faller, North Italy, learned most of her stories from an elderly neighbor (male) who "always had something to say." When she was eight or nine years old, she discovered that she remembered a story, "every word, . . . step by step." The old man noticed this also and would then challenge her to repeat the story. When she woke up the next morning, she would repeat the story again to herself, or to her younger brothers and sisters. In this way, she developed an extensive repertoire, and a lively style.[61]

Henssen, on the other hand, mentioned that the Dutch-German storyteller that he recorded, Egbert Gerrits, learned from the wife of the farmer to whom he was apprenticed as a young boy of eleven. In the evenings, she would sew, rock her child, and sing ballads or tell *märchen*.[62]

Jim Couch, one of the Sang Branch, Kentucky mountain tellers, recalled that he had learned all his tales from his mother:

> She was the storyteller in the family and would tell one about any time of a day or night. She would tell a story at the ends of corn rows while we was cooling and getting water and of an evening around a gnat smoke in the yard and of a night before bedtime. But . . . she wouldn't hardly tell stories when they was people at the house.[63]

Our most complete picture of the way in which a group of similar folk tellers from one small area form their repertoires comes from the fine research of Linda Dégh, particularly in her book *Folktales and Society: Storytelling in a Hungarian Peasant Community*. In it she shows how one family came to be famous for its three generations of storytellers, and how at the same time and in the same area, individuals who came from families with no particular history of storytelling could develop the art by listening to the rich body of oral narrative presented on many occasions.

The kind of talent that seemed to pass from one generation of a family to the next cannot be considered as conveying a hereditary position of storyteller in folk communities. It is true that the children of great storytellers will certainly have the advantage, so that if they have natural ability, they will then have the means of developing it by hearing outstanding story material told with frequency by a master. But often it will be the neighbor's child, or the outsider's, or a distant relative, who will carry forth the tradition of a well-known teller in the community. The children might express little or no interest in becoming narrators. The community often expects good storytelling to run in families, but if it does not, there are no sanctions. In fact, it seems as though it is considered *too* unusual when *many* members of the same family have some exceptional talent. In the Hungarian community of the Szeklers in Kakazd, the villagers tried to explain the unusual talents of the Zaicz family by saying their origins were from outside, or that "their grandmother was a Jewess, and the gift of stories came from her."[64]

Those who have access to the tales often hear them repeated on such frequent occasions that they unconsciously learn them by heart. They become tale-bearers whether they actually tell stories or not. This was the case with Mrs. Palkó, who did not tell stories while her brother was still living, because he was known to be the best storyteller around and it was unthinkable for her to infringe on his position. Yet when he died and she did begin to tell stories at large in the community, she told only some of the tales for which he had been famous and added others he had not told at all. As Dégh wrote, "She must have heard hundreds of tales during her long life; still, she adapted only a handful of them. The first encounter with these was so memorable, however, that she recalled it all her life."[65]

The remarkable memory of some storytellers is attested to over and over again. Apparently, quite a number of them could hear a story once and, if they liked it, it was "theirs" for life, for they remembered it in great detail. It would be easy to think that this was an exaggerated boast on the part of the storytellers, but it is a phenomenon reported in so many areas of the world and by so many types of storytellers, that one has to discount bragging as the reason behind the statement, "I heard it once and I could tell it." The only conclusion one can draw is that memory is an extraordinarily important factor in the training of a good storyteller.

## Training via Story Collections

Informal training could often take place via books as well. Some purists, such as O'Sullivan, expressed the belief that once a folk storyteller had learned from a book, his or her stories no longer had validity as oral tradition. "Be very cautious in dealing with a storyteller who can read," he warned.[66] Fortunately, most modern folklorists recognize the fact that it is inevitable in the modern world, just as it was occasional in the past, that storytellers (including folk tellers) will use any sources at their disposal to find stories that please them and spark their talent. This includes material from books and newspapers, other printed matter, films, and even television.

Dégh pointed out that it was often the storybook collection that inspired tellers to create new versions. In one part of *Folktales and Society*, there is an excellent summary of the opinions of various folklorists concerning the impact of written literature on the oral tale. Later Dégh lists all of the origins of the more than sixty tales recorded from Mrs. Palkó, at least insofar as she was able to remember them (fig. 46). Six of the tales Mrs. Palkó had heard first from someone who read them in a book. In her retellings she of course changed them into her own style.[67]

Other collectors whose informants mentioned that they got stories from reading books or listening to others read were Edwin Hall and H. R. Lynton. Hall recalled that one time, after the Eskimo storyteller Paul Monroe had recited a particularly dramatic and unusual story, he asked where Monroe had first heard it. Monroe's answer was that it had come from a copy of *True Confessions* magazine!

Lynton reported that the story appetite of the Nawab Fakh ul Mulk Bahadur, a Moslem noble who lived in Hyderabad at the turn of the century, was so great that one of the four night attendants, who was a storyteller, spent her days reading books so as to "increase or refresh her stock in trade."[68] On the other hand, Anna Liberata de Souza, an informant from India of the same period, did not like book versions of stories, calling them inferior and "all wrong." She believed they left out the "prettiest parts," and could not be counted on as good sources.[69]

Perhaps what Anna did not like was the same kind of thing objected to by modern Native Americans. Ella Clark writes:

**Figure 46**    *Zsuzsánna Palkó, gifted storyteller from the village of Kakasd, Hungary. Reproduced, with permission, from Linda Dégh,* Folktales and Society *(Bloomington: Indiana University Press, 1969).*

> College-educated Indians ... have told me or written me that they had been shocked by the caliber of many of the stories published from their own and other tribes. Such tales were never related around their firesides in their youth and, in their opinion, give an unfair impression of the literature of their people.[70]

The words of a recorded oral story without the accompanying actions, expressions, repetitions, gestures, and voice of the teller, and without the mood of the intimate occasion of storytelling, often do sound bald and not at all effective or beautiful. This is one of the important correctives current folklorists are trying to bring about: the description of context, audience interaction and response, and notation of all of the gestures and voice changes of the tellers, as well as their words.

Asbjørnsen must have believed that at least some storytellers would get their materials from the collections he recorded, because he left a special legacy for his editors. They were to be sure to change the language of the tales to correspond to the currently spoken Norwegian whenever a new edition appeared.[71]

Finally, the Japanese and Chinese traditions must be mentioned once again because, although the medieval storytelling guilds taught their apprentices through completely oral means and continued to do so up to modern times, it was not long before the best stories were put down in writing. These collections continued to be enriched so much over the centuries that it became obvious that the storytellers were no longer learning only from oral tradition, but from oral tradition that had been written and rewritten after many retellings. It was enjoyed by literate as well as non-literate people. Barbara Ruch calls this literature in Japan "vocal" rather than oral.[72] In fact, one of the common words for storytelling in Chinese, *shuo-shu*, literally means "to recite books."[73] For many storytellers today, this would be the correct interpretation.

## Ownership of Stories

There are some groups that consider stories to be so important to the entire life of the group that they treat them as property, often keeping them "secret" or not readily available to the outsider. This was probably true of the Easter Islanders, who hid their "story boards" upon the arrival of inquisitive strangers and unsympathetic missionaries to their shores (see Chapter 12). This attitude was found among many groups in the Pacific Islands.

The Winnebago, as mentioned in Chapter 3, placed a high value on *waikan*, their sacred stories, which could be inherited or sold.

The Palnādu epic singers in India claim the sole authority to sing the epic at festivals and other appropriate ritual times. They believe they have the right to press a civil suit against anyone who encroaches on their oral territory. They tolerate informal singing or telling of it, but not in the full ritual form.[74]

Laughlin mentions a common fear encountered by folklorists and ethnographers who are collecting tales: their informants believe that such tales are part of their group's treasure and property, and they have anxiety that this treasure might be misappropriated or incorrectly interpreted. They will share their tales, but they want assurances that they will be passed on correctly.[75] Darnell's Cree informant was also most concerned that his words be believed and respected. He spoke not as an individual but as "a performer of traditional material which is independent of his personal identity."[76] In other words, the stories belonged to all Cree; he was just the current transmitter.

Ron Evans, a Métis storyteller who frequently performs at festivals in the United States, invariably mentions the fact that he was given the "talking stick" simply as a current guardian of the stories he tells. The stories are owned by his people collectively.

In Egypt, some writers of folk ballads have been known to give a license to nonliterate performers, on condition they agree to memorize a certain number of lines, and perform them regularly.[77]

Recently, there has been much discussion about "ownership" of stories among professional storytellers who are members of the National Association for the Preservation and Perpetuation of Storytelling (NAPPS). Several articles and letters in *The National Storytelling Journal* (now *Storytelling Magazine*) indicate that there are strong feelings about this, with some tellers insisting that no story can be owned, while others believe stories are part of one's property, and still others follow a line somewhere down the middle.[78]

# CHAPTER 15

# Visuality, Orality, Literacy: Their Meaning in Relation to Storytelling for Entertainment, Education, and Health

In the past two decades there has been an explosion of research about the meaning and use of story, about orality, literacy, and "visual" literacy. Educators, psychologists, philosophers, folklorists, ethnologists, semioticians and many other specialists have attempted to explore such questions as:

Is the use of story (narrative) a universal human phenomenon?

Are those uses different in each culture? If so, how?

Can different genres of stories be classified on a universal basis or is the very concept of genre a western idea?

Is there a difference (in story itself, story giver, and receiver) when stories are told orally or read aloud or privately?

What differences exist between orally composed and written stories?

Is there a difference when story writing is alphabetic and phonetic?

Is there a difference when story writing is partly pictorial?

What is the effect of story when it is presented orally and visually, but by a live storyteller?

What is the effect of story when it is presented orally and visually in a medium such as film or television?

How much does the context (i.e. where and why a story is heard, read, seen, experienced) affect perception of the content of story?

Does a person have to learn the concept of "reading" pictures or symbols before learning to read?

Does the very fact of knowing how to read and write change a person's attitude to story?

These questions, and many related ones, have been explored not only for their own sake, but also because some of the answers might prove useful in the process of educating and socializing children and adults. It would be impossible in the limited space here to mention even briefly all the persons who have contributed to the research examining those questions. Here it will simply be accepted that all of the questions have some merit.

The previous chapters have shown that from earliest recorded history to the present, most cultures have used story for a variety of purposes and in a variety of ways. Whether the purposes were considered "good" or "bad" by the different authorities in each era, the average human obviously found something compelling, satisfying, validating, entertaining, informative or uplifting in any given encounter with story. To this very present time, one can find affirmations of the power of story (told or read or seen) made by all types of people. Cited here are just a few of these recent statements:

> When young people were asked "What would happen if there were no stories in the world?" they answered with replies like these—
> "People would die of seriousness."
> "When you went to bed at night it would be boring, because your head would be blank."
> "There wouldn't be a world, because stories made the world."
> Reported by Ellin Greene and Laura Simms, *Chicago Journal*, May 26, 1982.

> I think of that mountain called "white rocks lie above in a compact cluster" as if it were my maternal grandmother. I recall stories of how it once was at that mountain. The stories told to me were like arrows. Elsewhere, hearing that mountain's name, I see it. Its name is like a picture. Stories go to work on you like arrows. Stories make you live right. Stories make you replace yourself.
> Mr. Benson Lewis, Age 64, Western Apache, Cibecue, Arizona 1979[1]

> For the little ones who frolic in the moonlight, my tale is a fantastic story. For the cotton spinners during the long nights of the cold season, my tale is a delightful time passer. For the hairy chins and uneven heels, it's a genuine revelation. I am therefore all at the same time frivolous, useful and instructive.
> Peul (West African) storyteller[2]

> Their stories, yours, mine—it's what we all carry with us on this trip we take, and we owe it to each other to respect our stories and learn from them.
> William Carlos Williams, quoted by Robert Coles, psychiatrist[3]

Despite the numerous indications that story is a very important factor in the development of the healthy human personality, there are very few books or articles that discuss, in an integrated way, the comparative effectiveness of told stories, read-aloud stories, silently read stories, visual stories (in all formats) and stories presented in a combination of media. Where such studies exist, they invariably concentrate only on western (or westernized) stories in western contexts. Further, there has been even less published research and discussion about the use of story from one culture being adapted for use in a different context in another culture, and the changes that occur in the story itself and the different responses of its listeners or readers or viewers.

Since there are now many countries with heterogenous populations, often because of the arrival of groups of recent immigrants, there has been a renewed interest in using story to better understand the cultures of the different groups. More often than not, however, stories from non-European cultures have been put into formats that are western, and they are generally used in totally western contexts, rather than in the manner they might be used in their country or area of origin.

The average librarian, teacher, psychologist or other professional then asks:

1. What do I need to know about storytelling in the contexts that it is usually encountered in my own culture?
2. What are the other contexts of storytelling I need to know about, based on the different groups of people I work with?
3. What kinds of stories (and in what formats) are available to me?
4. When and where and how should I use storytelling?

There are no final or fixed answers to these questions, of course, but the information in this chapter and the other chapters of this book might help to point the way to partial answers.

Before getting into a discussion of various theories of visuality, orality, and literacy, and how they affect storytelling, we must first define these terms as they are being used here. They are defined specifically as they relate to story, although there are other forms of verbal and visual expression that they relate to as well. Those other forms are not under consideration here.

Primary visuality will mean here the ability to appreciate, interpret, and understand a local narrative depicted in two-dimensional pictures; it will also refer to the ability to draw, sketch, or paint such a narrative well enough for another person to be able to appreciate, interpret, and understand it. Secondary visuality will refer to the ability to appreciate, interpret, and understand a local narrative on television, film, filmstrip, or video.

Primary orality will mean the ability to appreciate, interpret, and understand a local narrative told by a live person to an audience listening in real time, and the ability to narrate well enough for that same audience to appreciate, interpret and understand most of a local narrative. Secondary orality will refer to the ability to do the above by means of listening or telling via telephone, radio, disc, cassette, video (but only showing the narrator), or some other mechanical means.

Primary literacy will mean the ability to read and write a local narrative in one's native language well enough to appreciate, interpret, and understand the major part of its generally accepted local meaning.

Local narrative refers to a story that is generally known by the people of a given locality.

There are some who believe that primary visuality was the first human method of experiencing story. Certainly, a number of narrative cave paintings predate by far the first written narrative records. But did these pictures tell a story to the people who painted them? And if they did, were such picture stories in existence before the first oral or pantomimed narratives?

It has been interesting for this writer to note that in informal questioning of numerous groups of schoolchildren around the world (usually prior to an oral storytelling session) the responses are roughly thus:

How did the earliest human beings first pass on their stories? Which of these came first?

They painted pictures of stories. (close to 50 percent)
They told them in human speech and gesture. (30 percent)
They sang and/or danced them. (20 percent)

There are hardly ever any respondents indicating early humans wrote them down. Children seem to sense, even though they may not know it as a historical fact, that scripts are a relatively recent part of human history.

Does their obvious preference for primary visuality indicate that children view the making of sequential pictures as a necessary prelude to alphabetic or phonetic writing? There are some who would be delighted with the perspicacity of these children in coming to a conclusion that has taken scholars enormous effort and time to reach, and then only tentatively.

There is still much disagreement about the early alphabets, and their impact on the human mind and consciousness. DeFrancis, for example, finds that there is an "essential oneness" in all full writing systems. He rejects the arguments of those who believe that logical and empirical modes of thought came about because of the uniqueness of the Greek alphabet, with its consonant plus vowel script, which was so easily learned and came so close to representing the totality of speech. On the contrary, he insists that the difficulty of script does not inhibit innovative thought, which is initiated by individuals, not society as a whole.[4]

DeFrancis and most other philologists and linguists do seem to agree that in the early stages of attempts to put speech into writing, virtually all societies used some type of pictographs. But there is almost no discussion of the possibility that pictures and pictographs came first and the words of human speech followed. Were the shapes, sounds, and structures of words for common objects invented to match the pictures of those objects? Did individual words of human speech first get put into narrative form because there were sequential pictures on a cave wall that some early human wanted to "interpret" for other humans? Could this possibility account for the preference among some societies for visual accompaniments to oral speech?

As mentioned in Chapter 12, among certain groups of aborigines in Australia and Eskimo in Alaska, it was and is common for virtually all narrative to be characterized by primary visuality as well as primary orality. When adults grow up in such a society, they often cannot carry out an ordinary conversation without making pictorial signs in the air with their fingers and hands.

In India, primary visuality has been as important as primary orality in conveying certain key myths, from the earliest recorded times to the present. Does this explain the equally strong development of secondary visuality there, where film production and film viewings are among the highest per capita in the world? And does this mean these myths could have evolved first from images, to which words were added only later?

On the other hand, there are societies where primary orality is extremely rich, but primary visuality is almost non-existent. Is this really because the ear is a better predictor of danger than the eye, as a number of scholars have suggested, and therefore humans developed and refined this sense first? Or is it because, as Walter Ong and others have stated so frequently, the human voice is the most effective way for one person to reveal interior thoughts and feelings to another, and also the best way for the listener to respond in kind?

Sometimes this primary orality is combined with music and dance, so that one could say primary motility is equally important among those groups. Is it the sound of this music (its aural quality) or its tendency to lead the human body into dance or motion that is most important in conveying narrative?[5] The few pre-historic records in those societies, as in most others, exist chiefly in pictorial form. There remains the question: did these societies have primary visuality and then lose it? If so, when and why?

Did primary literacy, especially that brought about by the Greek alphabet, really change human thought (and eventually the physiology of the brain) as much as Havelock and others suggest? Can this fact really explain the different ways of thinking that exist among peoples? Or is it, as DeFrancis insists, simply too facile an answer to suggest that differences in language and writing have created the enormously complicated problems regarding communication among societies. If, as he and others argue, discourse (and presumably story) can be carried out equally effectively in any language, then the problem is not one of mere translation, but of understanding the personal, moral and world views of the writer or teller and the context in which the words are written, sung, or spoken. Assuming an ideal and complete understanding of these views, we could then presumably have an exact translation of the words, gestures, music, and pictures, irrespective of language.

Yet we know there have been many difficulties caused by poor translation. And there have been many differences noted between societies that essentially use primary literacy for communication and those in which a majority use primary orality. Few studies have compared the variations that exist between societies that use primary orality and primary visuality (such as parts of rural India, for example, or certain Australian aborigine groups) and similar societies that use primary orality *and* primary literacy, so we know much less about those contrasts.

In the societies penetrated by primary literacy, there often remain large seg-ments of the population who continue to use primary and secondary visuality and orality as their chief media of communication. The usual reason given for this is that the means to acquiring and maintaining the skills of primary literacy are hard to come by. This reason does not hold up too well in places like the United States. Could it be that some of the present population actually *prefers* primary and secondary orality and visuality, and not primary literacy?

Or does this occur because children are raised and educated with such con-flicting advice and modeling? It is known that many parents and teachers will stress the importance of reading and writing to the children under their charge, but they themselves model chiefly primary and secondary visuality and orality. As Shirley Brice Heath has so convincingly pointed out in *Ways with Words*, the school and the formal education system, even when it uses teachers from the community, can have norms and expectations very different from those in the home.[6]

Is it for the above reasons that so many children today grow up without developing fluency and skill in *any* form of communication: speaking, writing, reading, or drawing? Or is it perhaps that they are educated and entertained chiefly by secondary visuality and orality?

These are some of the points professionals may wish to consider when evalu-ating the different ways of producing and using story:

1. There are children who grow up in an almost complete absence of primary visuality and primary literacy. Primary orality might be a better method to use with them for the first stages of their formal schooling, especially primary orality that gradually

introduces primary visuality. But this should be a genuine primary orality that is also well-modeled by the teachers and encourages children to work at and perfect their oral storytelling skills. In other words, such teachers would have to be very good storytellers.

2.  Teachers and children who have developed fairly good skills in both primary orality and primary literacy might be encouraged to do more comparing of the ways in which those skills differ, and learn to value each of them for the specific needs they seem to answer in human communication.

3.  In those formal and informal educational systems relying almost totally on literacy and secondary orality and visuality, some consideration might be given to incorporating primary orality and primary visuality, both on the part of teachers and those taught.

4.  The current attempts at primary visuality (that is, the heavy use of picture books or picture sequences with young children, often without words) might be expanded to include the skill that was once probably a part of general human communication in many parts of the world: the ability to sketch or draw a story in pictures. This skill could then be combined with primary orality or primary literacy.

5.  There is probably no single ideal mix of primary visuality, orality and literacy that could result in maximum educational effect everywhere, but it would seem useful to experiment more with all three formats, among children in schools in many different places, to determine whether there are combinations that are more effective than others; this might be especially helpful in places where children coming from widely differing cultural groups are placed in the same learning environment.

## Recognizing and Acknowledging the Contexts of Story

The experience of hearing stories told is universal. The contexts of that experience are not. It is difficult, if not impossible, to describe or recreate something one has not seen, heard, or felt. To attempt to tell stories "in an African style" or "in an Indian style" after reading only this book would be problematic. The intent of the author is not to be a substitute for the opportunity to see and hear stories told firsthand by the many individuals and groups mentioned in this book.

In virtually all school systems in the United States and Canada, and certainly in many other countries as well, there are textbooks, story books, films, filmstrips and videos that identify all or part of their contents as coming from a particular country or cultural group. There are also live storytellers who present their stories in that way, even though the sources of the stories might well be many times removed from the groups identified as the originators of the stories.

Is there any validity in telling a story from another culture, when one does not know that culture first hand? Of course, storytellers and writers have always picked up stories from whatever sources they could find. Throughout the ages, they either introduced the tales intact or changed them to suit their own personal tastes, most often not identifying where the tale came from. This is one of the reasons why we have such difficulty in tracing the origins of some of the old stories.

But this is not the kind of cross-cultural story exchange referred to here. The aspect that has changed about this process is the subtle but conscious addition of a pedagogical message. When a publisher prints, essentially for use in schools and libraries, an Ananse story from the Ashanti people of Ghana, and identifies it as such, the implication to the reader or audience is: here in this story you can learn something about the Ashanti people. The same is true when a storyteller announces to an audience of school children that "this is a story from the Ashanti of Ghana." In reality, the story might have had its entire context and meaning changed by the editor and storyteller, making it an American story with characters that have Ashanti names.

It is probably too much to expect that the habits built up over many years in the publishing industry and the educational purchaser institutions will change in the near future. The institutional teller can, however, learn enough to become skilled at recognizing authenticity in stories, especially those taken from printed collections. Let us say, for example, that a book of tales from Sierra Leone is being reviewed. It consists of long stories that have themes similar to European *märchen*, couched in very poetic language, but definitely set in West Africa and using personal and place names from the various groups in that country. There are no rhymes or songs included in the tales, and there is little use of onomatopeia. The compiler has given no source for the stories, except that they were written down in the last century. A check through the appropriate sections of this book will show that there have been a number of excellent studies of folktales in Sierra Leone, and a literary *märchen* style does not appear to be common to any of them, nor indeed in any West African folktales, as recorded by folklorists and anthropologists. It would be wise to review the collection as an original work, pointing out that the contents did not represent the traditional patterns of Sierra Leone folktales.

Let us further assume that in the collection are a few stories that strongly and immediately appeal to the teller. When telling stories such as those, it is better to introduce them by a general statement such as this: "Here are some stories I like; the author has set them in West Africa; she (he) has imagined what they would be like if they happened there." This allows the teller to use stories that are appealing, even though they are not "authentic" in the sense that they do not represent the oral traditions of the people with whom the editor or author has identified them. When feasible, of course, the best solution is to consult someone who has recorded and studied such stories first-hand, but this is seldom possible. If the text appears to be completely changed from the oral traditions with which it is identified by name, it is better to remove all place names and treat the story as an invented fiction.

For the stories that do appear to have authenticity, it is still challenging to create a storytelling event that might suggest some of the ambiance of the sessions in which the stories were recorded. This is especially the case if one has not been present at such a session. In such a situation the teller might try to describe briefly the atmosphere and occasions that might surround such a tale if it were being told in its place of origin. Many such descriptions can be culled from this book, and from items listed in the bibliography. And fortunately, there are now more and more folklorists who record the tales in such a way that it is easier to tell them in a manner that is at least similar to the original. An excellent example of such a book is Peter Seitel's *See So that We May See*. At a 1989 preconference of the American Library Association, the storyteller Margaret Read MacDonald told one of the stories in that book and was able to bring about, in an audience of librarians sitting in a modern hotel meeting room, a reaction that seemed not unlike that of a group of Haya villagers in Tanzania.

The storyteller presenting tales in an educational setting has a greater responsibility than one telling for sheer entertainment in a private situation. Learning about stories and the peoples from whom they were collected should be part of the preparation expected of any professional teller performing in institutions. Such tellers should be evaluated not only for their talent in keeping the audience involved and attentive, but also for their knowledge about story sources and contexts and the ways in which they convey this to the audience.

A good opening for those who have doubts about how closely they can recreate both the text and context of a story from another culture is to say something like this: "I cannot tell you the story in the way you would hear it from _____ or in _____. But I like the story so much I want to tell it for you in my own way." Some specific examples of story types when this teller has used such an opening include:

Stories from many different parts of Africa for which accompaniment to the musical segments should be an *mbira, sanza* or other instrument. One can show the instrument and pluck out a few sounds, but it would take years of practice to be a master player; yet the very showing of the instrument indicates there is more to the tale than just the words.

Stories in which the audience is expected to respond with words, phrases, or musical chants; teaching even a few words in the original language of the story is an enhancement.

Coyote tales and other Native American stories that should be told only in winter.

Stories from the *Ramayana, Mahabharata*, and other Hindu and Buddhist tradition, which have a rich visual counterpart in story cloths, scrolls, palm leaf books, and the like.

Picture-drawing stories from different cultures; learning and showing a few of the basic designs can give a hint of the complexity and richness of such unusual methods of telling.

## Publishing Folktales

Much as we might like to see more stories passed on through primary orality, it is not likely that a great number will reach the next generation in that manner, at least not in the United States. The majority will certainly be inherited, directly or indirectly, through some recorded form.

On the whole folktales that have been edited and published for popular, commercial sale have not been accorded the individual respect that is routinely given to stories with known authors. Rare is the folktale collection, or the individual picture-book folktale, that mentions the name of the original teller, even when it is known, or the original context of the tale as first recorded. This is partly the result of selecting stories from out-of-print nineteenth-century compilations, but mostly out of fear that if a source is cited, the copyright cannot be claimed by the reteller or the current publisher.

This situation could be remedied if editors and publishers insisted that every modern reteller or compiler provide at least a brief paragraph listing the specific source or sources. Some indication would also have to be given as to whether the tales have been modified or changed extensively, and how. There is nothing intrinsically wrong about taking a story and making it one's own through retelling. This is part and parcel of the storytelling process. What is dishonest, professionally if not legally, is to pretend that the story is close to the original recorded version. The reteller claims authenticity, but leaves out mention of the original source or sources, so there is no way to check whether the story does represent the genuine folklore of the people with whom it is identified.

Such a phrase as "Loosely based on a tale found in . . . or heard from . . ." can go a long way to helping the reader and user identify how much of the story is newly invented and how much is traditional. It should also be made clear when the illustrations are fantasy and when they are based on actual artistic motifs coming from the same culture as the story.

## Universality of Storytelling

It is not possible to claim for storytelling, as DeFrancis does for writing systems, an essential oneness. There is simply too much diversity of form, content, and purpose. But there is universality of storytelling, in that it continues to be used as a form of human expression in virtually all parts of the world. And the most common purpose, even though it might appear in varying degrees, is that of entertainment, especially entertainment that creates a sense of well-being. If this book can assist tellers and listeners to enjoy story more, it will have achieved its purpose.

# CHAPTER 16

# *Storytelling Festivals*

There have been showcase events for storytellers right down through the centuries. However, in recent times, the festival has become the favorite type of event for promoting storytelling. During the past decade there has been an explosion of storytelling festivals in the United States and Canada. In the 1989 edition of the *National Directory of Storytelling* published by NAPPS, there are more than one hundred festivals listed, most of them annual events. These take place in some thirty states, as well as the District of Columbia and Toronto, Canada. It is at these festivals that most professional storytellers in North America can be heard and seen on a regular basis.

Some of the annual festivals focus on a special type of story, such as the "Clever Gretchen" event sponsored by Syracuse University, where the feminist view of story is examined. Or they focus on a season to celebrate, such as the Olde Christmas Festival held at Callanwode Arts Center in Atlanta, Georgia, always near January 6, and the various storytelling festivals that emphasize ghost stories or scary stories to suit the period around Halloween.

Others serve as a showcase to celebrate the culture of particular groups. Examples are the National Festival of Black Storytelling, going on its tenth year in 1990, and the Jewish Storytelling Festival, which is in its sixth year.

One of the largest of festivals is that sponsored by NAPPS. It is held on the first weekend in October each year, in the picturesque town of Jonesborough, Tennessee. Storytelling by the featured tellers takes place in large tents especially set up for the purpose, but there are also smaller story sessions, some designed to allow tellers with less experience the opportunity to try out their skills. The festival is now a major tourist event for the area, drawing more than five thousand visitors each day (fig. 47).

Another long-running festival encompassing storytelling has been the Festival of American Folklife held each year in Washington, D.C., and other cities under the auspices of the Smithsonian Institution. There are many folk arts and crafts featured at this festival, but storytelling has always been a popular segment. Most of the tellers appearing in this festival come from purely oral folk traditions, and are not considered professional tellers.

A number of communities throughout the United States and Canada have begun annual ethnic festivals or Renaissance Fairs. The latter try to recreate, through music, costume, food, jousting tournaments and the like, an atmosphere resembling that of a weekly fair day in England some four or five hundred years ago. A professional storyteller is usually hired to give performances of the kind that minstrels once might have given. It must be noted, however, that current entertainment value is always considered as important as authenticity at these festivals, so they cannot be truly said to recreate or duplicate storytelling of the Renaissance period. One of the more elaborate of such fairs is held in Detroit each spring.

Some of the annual state fairs now have a component of storytelling added to the many other entertainments available to visitors. Again, these usually consist of professional storytellers hired to perform for the days of the fair. Sometimes they suit their stories to the theme of the state fair but in most cases they simply offer a type of storytelling that attempts a folk-like atmosphere.

There have been storytelling festivals in Europe for some time as well. Many towns in the British Isles have folk festivals on a regular basis. Some are highly structured and planned, but many are quite casual in format, and welcome participation by folk and professional storytellers. A typical example is the International Folk Festival in Sidmouth, in Devon, which includes a storytelling component.

The small town of Moncrabeau in Gascony, some 600 kilometers southwest of Paris, is the scene of an unusual storytelling festival that has taken place on a regular basis for several hundred years. There, some forty local members of a "Liars' Academy" accept the challenges of storytellers who agree to "twist the truth and nothing but the truth." The tellers come from all over France and other French-speaking countries. There are generally about twenty who are deemed good enough to have their challenges accepted.

They perform in a public square, facing the members of the "Academy," dressed in their seventeenth-century costumes. Townspeople and visitors sit behind, finding places where they can. Judging is by the ancient method of "passing out salt." Each academy member has a fixed amount of salt to disburse. If the members like the teller they give out a large amount of salt; if they are not too impressed, they disburse only a few grains. At the end of the telling sessions, the salt is weighed. The winner is the teller who ends up with the largest amount. He or she is crowned "King/Queen of Liars."

France also has festivals similar to the Renaissance Fairs in the United States. One of the largest takes place each summer in Avignon, where the ancient background does not have to be faked. The members of the Centre de Littérature Orale generally perform one of the great epics of past eras during the Avignon Festival.

Other festivals featuring storytelling in France are sponsored by such groups

**Figure 47**   Tents are used for the annual storytelling sponsored by the National Association for the Preservation and Perpetuation of Storytelling each year in Jonesborough, Tennessee, on the first weekend in October. Photo by Tom Raymond courtesy of NAPPS.

as L'Age d'Or and the Alliance Française. The former is an organization of persons who are retired and receiving government or private pensions. They are extremely active in all aspects of storytelling. The address of L'Age d'Or is 7 rue E. Poisson, Paris 75017. Alliance Française is the official branch of the French government that has as its mission the promotion of French language and culture. Their festival usually features a wide variety of tellers from many French-speaking countries around the world.

There have been regular gatherings of *märchen* tellers in Germany for some time, usually sponsored by the Europäische Märchengesellchaft (Schloss Bentlage, Postfach 328, D-4440 Rheine). That organization holds an annual congress at which the evenings are usually devoted to a festival of storytelling, mainly by tellers from German-speaking countries, but also occasionally from other countries. Recently, a festival modeled a bit on the NAPPS festival was begun by a group of independent tellers operating out of Cologne.

Australia is beginning to have storytelling festivals on a regular basis. These are generally sponsored by the storytelling guilds that have sprung up in almost every state during the past few years. Some of them feature mostly tellers from schools and libraries, while others include folk and theatrical tellers.

The Tel Aviv Public Library in Israel, starting in 1988, began an annual storytelling festival. It features tellers from the many different immigrant groups newly arrived in that country, as well as some international tellers.

In Japan, a newly founded storytelling hall and museum, named for Takehiko Kurushima, known as "the Andersen of Japan," was opened in Kusu, in Oita Prefecture on Kyushu Island in the south of Japan. It is hoped to have an annual storytelling festival there.

There are many other places one can hear and see storytelling in many parts of the world, but in most cases this must be specially arranged. For those wishing to experience such storytelling, the best tactic is to write to folklorists or ethnographers who have done recent work in the country. They can often suggest locations where one might be most likely to encounter storytelling. Other good sources are departments of folklore at the national universities in each country.

For those interested in library and institutional storytelling, the national sections of such organizations as IBBY (Nonnenweg 12, Postfach, CH-4003 Basel, Switzerland) or the International Reading Association (Newark, Delaware 19714) are often good sources of current information.

The most complete listing of current festivals, together with other storytelling events, can be found in the *National Directory of Storytelling*, published annually by NAPPS (P.O. Box 309, Jonesborough, Tennessee 37659).

# NOTES

Only the author and short form of title are given for most works cited. For complete bibliographic information on these items, consult the bibliography. A few items are cited in full in the notes, but not listed in the bibliography, because they have only very brief or passing references to storytelling and would not be of much general interest to the person looking for further information on the subject.

## NOTES TO CHAPTER 1 (pp. 1–18)

1 H. Frankfort, *The Art and Architecture of the Ancient Orient*, pp. 35–36.
2 "Tales of the Magicians," in *Egyptian Literature*, ed. and tr. by Epiphanius Wilson, pp. 159–169.
3 Ibid., pp. 173–176.
4 K. Ranke. "Volkserzählung," in *Die Religion in Geschichte und Gegenwart*, 3rd ed., vol. 6, p. 1451.
5 H. M. and N. K. Chadwick, *The Growth of Literature*, vol. 2, p. 753.
6 *The Sacred Books of the East* (S.B.E.), vol. 12, p. xxiv.
7 S.B.E., vol. 29, pp. 246–248.
8 S.B.E. vol. 30, p. 29.
9 V. Mair, *Painting and Performance*, pp. 17–37.
10 S.B.E., vol. 36, book 4, chap. 7, 1–7, pp. 92–96.
11 Euripides, *Complete Greek Tragedies*, vol. 5. New York: Modern Library, n.d., p. 132.
12 Aristophanes, *The Eleven Comedies*, vol. 1, New York: Liveright, 1943, p. 267.
13 Ibid., vol. 2, pp. 61–62.
14 W. C. Greene, ed., *The Dialogues of Plato*, New York: Liveright, 1927, p. 295.
15 Loeb Classical Library (L.C.L.), no. 257, 1932, p. 203.
16 L.C.L., no. 42, 1916, p. 181.
17 L.C.L., no. 49, 1917, pp. 67–69.
18 L.C.L., no. 268, 1933, p. 93.
19 New York: Everyman's Library, 1911, pp. 206–207.
20 New York: Modern Library, 1950, pp. 5ff.
21 L.C.L., no. 56, 1915, p. 329.
22 W. C. Greene, *The Dialogues of Plato*, p. 123.
23 S.B.E., vol. 41, p. 60.
24 L.C.L., no. 340, 1939, pp. 177–179.
25 L.C.L., no. 49, 1917, p. 65.
26 J. Huizinga, *Homo Ludens*, p. 1.
27 Ibid., p. 129.
28 H. M. and N. K. Chadwick, *Growth of Literature*, vol. 3, pp. 706ff.
29 A. Ransome, *A History of Storytelling*, pp. 6–7.
30 A. B. Lord, *The Singer of Tales*, pp. 137–138.

**31** E. Havelock, *The Muse Learns to Write*, p. 70.

**32** W. J. Ong, *Orality and Literacy*, p. 8.

**33** L.C.L., 1920, p. 157.

**34** *Panchatantra*, p. 16.

**35** *Geography*, xv, 3, 18, L.C.L., 8, p. 179.

**36** J. P. Losty, *The Art of the Book in India*, p. 14.

**37** For a map describing some of the possible ways that one type of storytelling may have spread in these directions, see the endpapers in Victor Mair's *Painting and Performance*.

**38** W. Bang, "Manichäische Erzähler."

**39** D. Durán, *Book of the Gods and Rites* and *The Ancient Calendar*, pp. 398–399.

**40** D. Ben-Amos, *Sweet Words*, pp. 30–31.

**41** L. Dégh, *Folktales and Society*, pp. 79, 171.

**42** I. Jan, *On Children's Literature*, p. 32.

**43** F. Bacon, *The Essays*, p. 64.

**44** F. Schiller, *Werke*, vol. 4, p. 107.

**45** E. S. Hartland, *The Science of Fairy Tales*, pp. 18–21.

**46** E. Greene, "Storytelling," *World Book Encyclopedia*, vol. 18 (1976 edition) p. 718.

**47** M. Gerhardt, *The Art of Storytelling*, p. 41.

**48** W. Benjamin, *Illuminations*, p. 91.

**49** A. Olrik, "Epic Laws of Folk Narrative," first published in 1908.

**50** W. H. Jansen, "Classifying Performance in the Study of Verbal Folklore," pp. 110–118.

**51** H. Scheub, "The Art of Nongenile Mazithathu Zenani," p. 115.

**52** D. Hymes, "Models of the Interaction of Language and Social Life," pp. 35–71.

**53** R. A. Georges, "Towards an Understanding of Storytelling Events," p. 313.

**54** Ibid., p. 317.

**55** L. Dégh, *Folktales and Society*, pp. 50–52.

**56** D. Tedlock, *The Spoken Word*, p. 3.

## Notes to Chapter 2 (pp. 20–43)

**1** S.B.E., vol. 44, p. 370.

**2** B. C. Law, *The Magadhas in Ancient India*, pp. 1–3.

**3** S. N. Kramer, *Sumerian Mythology*, p. 63.

**4** A. Parrot, *Sumer: The Dawn of Art*, pp. 126–127.

**5** C. Desroches-Noblecourt, *Ancient Egypt*, Plate 23.

**6** H. M. and N. K. Chadwick, *The Growth of Literature*, vol. 2, pp. 252ff; A. B. Lord, *The Singer of Tales*, pp. 19ff; see also W. Eberhard, *Minstrel Tales from Southeastern Turkey*, p. 2.

**7** L.C.L., no. 50, 1917, p. 245.

**8** Baltimore: Penguin, 1957, p. 38.

**9** L.C.L., no. 208, 1928, p. 195.

**10** *Leabhar na g-ceart*, p. 183.

**11** Cormac, *Sanas Chormaic*, p. 160.

**12** Ibid., p. 127.

**13** J. C. Walker, *A Historical Essay on the Dress of the Ancient and Modern Irish*, p. 20.

**14** Ibid., p. 8.

**15** A. W. Wade-Evans, *Welsh Medieval Law*, pp. 146, 167.

**16** Ibid., pp. 179–180.

**17** G. Williams, *An Introduction to Welsh Poetry*, pp. 7–8

**18** Encyclopedia Britannica, *Macropedia*, 1974, vol. 10, pp. 1114–1115.

**19** J. Toland, *A Critical History of the Celtic Religion*, p. 224.

**20** D. W. Nash, *Taliesin*, p. 33.

**21** G. Williams, *An Introduction to Welsh Poetry*, pp. 12–15.

**22** H. M. and N. K. Chadwick, *The Growth of Literature*, vol. 1, pp. 613–614.

**23** *Beowulf*, trans. by J. R. C. Hall, p. 74.

**24** *Runic and Heroic Poems of the Old Teutonic Peoples*, p. 77.

**25** Based on the translation of Charles S. Moncrieff, *Widsith*, New York: E.P. Dutton, 1921, p. 5, and on that of Francis B. Gummere, *The Oldest English Epic*, New York: Macmillan, 1929, p. 200.

**26** L. F. Anderson, *The Anglo-Saxon Scop*, pp. 25–26.

**27** H. M. and N. K. Chadwick, *The Growth of Literature*, vol. 1, pp. 618–621.

**28** W. A. Craigie, *Icelandic Sagas*, p. 11.

**29** Ibid.

**30** Ibid., p. 18.

**31** Abbé De La Rue, *Essais historiques sur les bardes*, vol. 1, pp. 110ff.

**32** Ibid., vol. 1, pp. 103ff.

**33** E. Faral, *Les Jongleurs en France au Moyen Age*, pp. 2–18.

**34** Ibid., pp. 25–43.

**35** Ibid., pp. 61ff.

**36** A. Bonner, *Songs of the Troubadours*, pp. 27–29, 223–224; see also A. Brandl, "Spielmanns-verhältnisse in frühmittelenglischer Zeit," pp. 873–892.

**37** Same as notes 32 and 34.

**38** H. M. and N. K. Chadwick, *The Growth of Literature*, vol. 2, p. 261.

**39** R. Zguta, *Russian Minstrels*, pp. 15–43.

**40** Ibid., pp. 64–65.

**41** S. Skendi, *Albanian and South Slavic Oral Epic Poetry*, p. 85.

**42** M. Boyce, "The Parthian Gosan," p. 18.

**43** Ibid., p. 22.

**44** W. Eberhard, *Minstrel Tales from Southeastern Turkey*.

**45** T. G. Winner, *Oral Art and Literature of the Kazakhs*, p. 27.

**46** A. Chodzko, *Specimens of the Popular Poetry of Persia*, pp. 12–13.

**47** S. Hoogasian-Villa, *100 Armenian Tales*, p. 21.

**48** G. N. Roerich, "The Epic of King Kesar of Ling," pp. 284–285.

**49** T. G. Winner, *Oral Art and Literature of the Kazakhs*, p. 29.

**50** S. A. Sowayan, *Nabati Poetry*, pp. 123–144.

**51** J. Darmesteter, *Chants populaires des Afghans*, pp. cxcii–cxciii.

**52** H. M. and N. K. Chadwick, *The Growth of Literature*, vol. 3, p. 178.

**53** I. W. Shklovsky, *In Far North-east Siberia*, p. 209.

**54** See, for example, A. K. Forbes, *Ras Mala*, vol. 1, p. 154.

**55** A. M. Shah and R. G. Shroff, "The Vahivanca Barots," pp. 42–70.

**56** [H. Ferguson and J. Ferguson] "Textiles That Tell a Story."

**57** O. P. Joshi, *Painted Folklore*, pp. 1–28.

**58** V. Hrdličková, "The Chinese Storytellers and Singers of Ballads," p. 103.

**59** V. Hrdličková, "The Professional Training of Chinese Storytellers," p. 242.

**60** B. Ruch, "Medieval Jongleurs," pp. 286–287.

**61** Ibid.

**62** C. J. Dunn, *The Early Japanese Puppet Drama*, p. 14.

**63** A. Waley, "Kutune Shirka: The Ainu Epic," pp. 235–236.

**64** C. Snouck Hurgronje, *The Achehnese*, p. 101.

**65** Ibid., p. 88.

**66** K. Luomala, "Polynesian Literature," p. 773.

**67** Ibid., p. 777.

**68** Ibid., p. 774.

**69** E. K. Maranda and P. Maranda, *Structural Models in Folklore*, p. 11.

**70** R. E. Mitchell, *Micronesian Folktales*, p. 16.

**71** R. E. Mitchell, "A Study of . . . the Repertoires of Two Trukese Informants," pp. 170–176.

**72** D. Durán, *Book of the Gods and Rites*, p. 299.

**73** J. H. Rowe, "Inca Culture at the Time of the Spanish Conquest," pp. 201–202.

**74** R. Finnegan, *Oral Literature in Africa*, p. 108–110.

**75** Quoted in A. Mafeje, "The Role of the Bard in a Contemporary African Community," p. 193.

**76** Ibid.; see also D. Biebuyck, "The Epic as a Genre of Congo Oral Literature"; I. Okpewho, *The Epic in Africa*; J. Opland, *Xhosa Oral Poetry*; S. A. Babalola, *The Content and Form of Yoruba Ijala*; H. F. Morris, *The Heroic Recitations of the Bahima of Ankole*; H. T. Norris, *Shinqiti Folk Literature and Song*; J. P. Clark, *The Ozidi Saga*.

**77** D. P. Biebuyck and K. C. Mateene, *The Mwindo Epic from the Banyanga*, pp. 12–15.

**78** Ibid., pp. 261–263.

**79** A. Mafeje, "The Role of the Bard in a Contemporary African Community," pp. 193–223.

**80** J. Opland, *Xhosa Oral Poetry*.

**81** J. Vansina, *Oral Tradition*, p. 189.

**82** Ibid., p. 119.

**83** Ibid., p. 32.

**84** L. Harries, *Swahili Poetry*, p. 24.

**85** R. Finnegan, *Oral Literature in Africa*, p. 174.

**86** J. H. Speke, *Journal of the Discovery of the Source of the Nile*, p. 344.

**87** J. Roscoe, *The Baganda*, p. 35.

**88** H. F. Morris, *The Heroic Recitations of the Bahima of Ankole*, p. 21.

**89** S. A. Babalola, *The Content and Form of Yoruba Ijala*, p. 18.

**90** Ibid., p. 3.

**91** C. Bird, "Heroic Songs of the Mande Hunters," p. 278.

**92** Ibid., p. 289.

**93** A. Mafeje, "The Role of the Bard," p. 195.

**94** S. Camara, *Gens de la Parole*.

**95** H. T. Norris, *Shinqiti Folk Literature*, p. 54.

**96** Kitab al-Wasit, quoted in H. T. Norris, Ibid., p. 65.

**97** H. M. and N. K. Chadwick, *The Growth of Literature*, vol. 3, pp. 524–526.

**98** M. Mondon-Vidailhet, "La Musique Éthiopienne," p. 3183.

**99** Same as note 98.

**100** M. Sulayman, quoted in B. Connelly, *Arab Folk Epic and Identity*, p. 4.

**101** B. Connelly, ibid., p. 12.

## NOTES TO CHAPTER 3 (pp. 44–65)

**1** S.B.E., vol. 44, p. xxiv.

**2** *The Vishnu Purana*, Publisher's Note, p. E.

**3** Ibid., pp. 17–18.

**4** V. Raghavan, "Methods of Popular Religious Instruction in South India," p. 130.

**5** Ibid., p. 133.

**6** L. K. A. Krishna Iyer, *The Cochin Tribes and Castes*, pp. 129–131.

**7** E. B. Cowell and F. Thomas, *The Harsa-Carita of Bana*, p. 119.

**8** A. Coomaraswamy, "Picture Showmen," pp. 182–187.

**9** J. Erickson, *Mata ni pachedi.* p. 48.

**10** H. Zimmer, *The Art of Indian Asia*, vol. 1, p. 367 and vol. 2, Plate 463.

**11** S. Blackburn, *Singing of Birth and Death*, p. 28.

**12** Ibid., p. 29.

**13** P. B. Mande, "Dakkalwars and Their Myths," pp. 69–76.

**14** [H. and J. Ferguson] "Textiles That Tell a Story."

**15** O. P. Joshi, *Painted Folklore*, pp. 34–36.

**16** A. Coomaraswamy, "Picture Showmen," p. 183; V. Raghavan, "Picture-Showmen: Mankha," p. 524.

**17** V. Mair, *Painting and Performance*, pp. 28–29.

**18** I. P. Singh, "A Sikh Village," pp. 286–291.

**19** S.B.E., vol. 21, pp. 120–129.

**20** S.B.E., vol. 36, pp. 92–96.

**21** J. Průšek, "The Narrators of Buddhist Scriptures," p. 376.

**22** Ibid., p. 377.

**23** Ibid., p. 388.

**24** V. Hrdličková, "The First Translations of Buddhist Sūtras in Chinese Literature and Their Place in the Development of Storytelling," pp. 114–144.

**25** A. Waley, *Ballads and Stories from Tun-huang*, pp. 242–243.

**26** V. Mair, *Painting and Performance*.

**27** P. Demiéville, "Tun-huang Texts," p. 186.

**28** P. Demiéville, "Translations of Buddhist Literature," p. 175.

**29** B. Ruch, "Medieval Jongleurs," pp. 294–299.

**30** Ibid.

**31** Ibid., p. 300.

**32** Ibid., p. 305.

**33** B. Gerhardsson, *Memory and Manuscript*, p. 62–78.

**34** Ibid., p. 89.

**35** M. Gaster, *The Exempla of the Rabbis*, p. 90, with minor stylistic changes for clarity.

**36** D. Noy, "The Jewish Theodicy Legend," p. 65; see also his article, "Is There a Jewish Folk Religion?"

**37** Y. Sabar, *The Folk Literature of the Kurdistani Jews*, p. xxix.

**38** J. R. Mintz, *The Legends of the Hasidim*, pp. 4–8.

**39** T. Shafter, *Storytelling for Jewish Groups*.

**40** B. Gerhardsson, *Memory and Manuscript*, p. 335.

**41** W. Kelber, *The Oral and the Written Gospel*, p. 207.

**42** T. F. Crane, *The Exempla . . . of Jacques de Vitry*, p. 162.

**43** L. Bødker, C. Hole, and G. D'Aronco, *European Folk Tales*, p. xix.

**44** S. Wenzel, "The Joyous Art of Preaching," p. 322.

**45** M. Avery, *The Exultet Rolls of South Italy*, vol. 2; J. P. Gilson, "Introduction," *An Exultet Roll Illuminated in the XIth Century at the Abbey of Monte Cassino*.

**46** L. Schmidt, "Geistlicher Bänkelsang," p. 7.

**47** R. W. Brednich, "Zur Vorgeschichte des Bänkelsangs," p. 85.

**48** H. M. and N. K. Chadwick, *The Growth of Literature*, vol. 2, pp. 270–283.

**49** Ibid., p. 271.

**50** D. S. Reynolds, "From Doctrine to Narrative"; B. A. Rosenberg, *Can These Bones Live?*

**51** H. G. Long, *Rich the Treasure*, pp. 48–49.

**52** E. P. St. John, *Stories and Storytelling in Moral and Religious Education*.

**53** R. G. Alvey, "The Historical Development of Organized Storytelling to Children in the United States," p. 57.

**54** *The Story Hour Leader*, begun in 1937 in Nashville, Tenn., by the Southern Baptist Convention.

**55** H. Küng, *On Being a Christian*, p. 52.

**56** M. Omidsalar, "Storytellers in Classical Persian Texts," p. 205.

**57** Ibn al-Jawzi, *Kitāb al quṣṣās*, p. 103.

**58** Ibid, pp. 109–114.

**59** I. Goldziher, *Muslim Studies*, vol. 1, p. 152.

**60** Based on personal observation of several Koranic schools in Morocco, Algeria, Nigeria, and Senegal.

**61** I. Shah, *Learning How to Learn*, p. 197.

**62** M. W. Beckwith, *Mandan-Hidatsa Myths and Ceremonies*, p. xvi.

**63** P. Radin, *The Trickster*, pp. 118–122.

**64** M. E. Opler, *Myths and Tales of the Jicarilla Apache*, p. ix.

**65** J. C. Andersen, *Myths and Legends of the Polynesians*, p. 445.

**66** E. Best, *The Maori*, vol. 1, p. 5.

**67** D. P. Biebuyck, and K. C. Mateene, *The Mwindo Epic*, p. 14.

## NOTES TO CHAPTER 4 (pp. 66–86)

**1** Julian, *Works*, L.C.L., p. 79.

**2** R. Benedict, *Zuni Mythology*. vol. 1, p. xii.

**3** J. H. Delargy, *The Gaelic Storyteller*, p. 19.

**4** T. S. Eliot, "Religion and Literature," p. 105.

**5** L. Dégh, *Folktales and Society*, p. 104.

**6** C. Béart, *Jeux et Jouets de l'Ouest Africain*, vol. 2, p. 767.

**7** E. Y. Egblewogbe, *Games and Songs as Education Media*, p. 47.

**8** J. Mbiti, *Akamba Stories*, pp. 23–24.

**9** H. T. Norris, *Shinqiti Folk Literature and Song*, p. 118.

**10** D. Ben-Amos, *Sweet Words*, pp. 23–24.

**11** H. Scheub, *The Xhosa Ntsomi*, pp. 12–13.

**12** D. J. Crowley, *I Could Talk Old-Story Good*, p. 12.

**13** B. Toelken, "The 'Pretty Languages' of Yellowman," p. 155.

**14** D. Hymes, *"In Vain I Tried to Tell You,"* p. 22.

**15** R. E. Mitchell, "A Study of . . . Two Trukese Informants," pp. 169–170.

**16** L. A. Allen, *Time Before Morning*, p. 23.

**17** L. Dégh, *Folktales and Society*, p. 118.

**18** L. Uffer, *Rätoromanische Märchen*, p. 63.

**19** Ibid., p. 73.

**20** H. Ammar, *Growing Up in an Egyptian Village*, p. 161.

**21** A. Al-Shahi, and F. C. T. Moore, *Wisdom from the Nile*.

**22** O. F. Raum, *Chaga Childhood*, pp. 217–218.

**23** G. Gorer, *Himalayan Village*, p. 266.

**24** N. Miller, *The Child in Primitive Society*, pp. 167–172.

**25** C. Bianco, "The Two Rosetos," pp. 127–137.

**26** A. Falassi, *Folklore by the Fireside*, p. xviii.

**27** M. Frere, *Hindoo Fairy Legends*, p. xxvii.

**28** J. Yolen, *Touch Magic*, pp. 48–49.

**29** NOVA Program No. 1002, WGBH, Boston; this is transcribed in A. Pellowski, *The Family Storytelling Handbook*, pp. 40–41.

**30** D. Chang, *Folk Treasury of Korea*, pp. 10–11.

**31** R. N. Umeasiegbu, *Words Are Sweet*, p. 9.

**32** N. Kipury, *Oral Literature of the Maasai*, p. 11.

**33** A. P. and T. E. Penard, "Surinam Folktales," pp. 242–243.

**34** F. M. Deng, *Dinka Folktales*, p. 30.

**35** P. Smith, *Le récit populaire*, p. 15.

**36** D. Hymes, *"In Vain I Tried to Tell You,"* p. 21.

**37** A. Cammann, *Westpreussische Märchen*, p. 63.

**38** Ibid., p. 19.

**39** A. Falassi, *Folklore by the Fireside*, p. 4.

**40** J. S. Goodman, "My Grandpa's Name Was Avraham"; P. Schram, *Jewish Stories: One Generation Tells Another*.

**41** J. H. Delargy, *The Gaelic Storyteller*, pp. 9ff.

**42** A. Carmichael, *Carmina Gadelica*, p. xxiii.

**43** H. Glassie, *Passing the Time in Ballymenone*, pp. 40–42.

**44** R. Gwyndaf, "The Welsh Folk Narrative Tradition."

**45** J. Cejpek, "Iranian Folk Literature," p. 653.

**46** R. Dorson, "Oral Styles of American Folk Narrators."

**47** J. M. Taggart, *Nahuat Myth and Social Structure*, p. 1.

**48** See, for example, his books *The Vanishing Hitchhiker* and *The Choking Doberman and Other Urban Folktales*.

**49** H. B. Schwartzman, "Stories at Work," pp. 80–93.

**50** R. J. Adams, "Social Identity of a Japanese Storyteller," pp. 6ff.

**51** E. Mathias and R. Raspa, *Italian Folktales in America*, pp. 37–45.

**52** J. Sherzer, *Kuna Ways of Speaking*, p. 108.

**53** L. Dégh, *Folktales and Society*, pp. 95–96.

**54** Ibid., pp. 102–103.

**55** O. Brinkmann, *Das Erzählen in einer Dorfgemeinschaft*, p. 9.

**56** G. Gorer, *Himalayan Village*, p. 266.

**57** R. East, *Akiga's Story*, pp. 308–309.

**58** M. Nebie, "Et si on disait un conte?" p. 43.

**59** S. Hoogasian-Villa, *100 Armenian Tales*, pp. 26–40.

**60** J. H. Delargy, *The Gaelic Storyteller*, p. 18.

**61** B. Gunda, "Die Funktion des Märchens," p. 101.

**62** L. Dégh, *Folktales and Society*, pp. 97–98.

**63** J. M. Taggart, *Nahuat Myth and Social Structure*, p. 1.

**64** Y. Pino-Saavedra, *Folktales of Chile*, p. xliii.

**65** S. A. Babalola, *The Content and Form of Yoruba Ijala*, p. 18.

**66** J. Cejpek, "Iranian Folk Literature," p. 653.

**67** G. Gorer, *Himalayan Village*, p. 265.

**68** M. W. H. Beech, *The Suk*, p. 38.

**69** L. Dégh, *Folktales and Society*, pp. 105–110.

**70** S.B.E., vol. 29, pp. 355–357.

**71** L. Lacourcière, "Canada," p. 450.

**72** J. H. Delargy, *The Gaelic Storyteller*, p. 20.

**73** E. Oring, "Ha-Chizbat," pp. 35ff.

**74** N. Z. Davis, *Fiction in the Archives*, pp. 7–35.

**75** R. Bauman, *Story, Performance and Event*, p. 12.

**76** P. B. Mullen, "A Traditional Storyteller," p. 22.

**77** L. Lacourcière, "Canada," p. 448.

**78** K. K. Das, *Burrakatha*, pp. 4–10.

**79** G. H. Roghair, *The Epic of Palnādu*, p. 35.

**80** M. I. Gerhardt, *The Art of Storytelling*, p. 382ff.

**81** M. Boyce, "The Parthian Gosan and the Iranian Minstrel Tradition," p. 34.

**82** A. H. Sayce, "Storytelling in the East," pp. 176–80.

**83** R. Heath, "Storytelling in All Ages," p. 199ff.

**84** V. C. S. O'Connor, "Beyond the Great Atlas," vol. 61, 1932, p. 285.

**85** S. Sen Gupta, *The Patas and the Patuas of Bengal*, p. 53.

**86** V. Hrdličková, "The Chinese Storytellers," p. 99.

**87** Ibid., p. 100.

**88** B. Ruch, "Medieval Jongleurs," pp. 301–302.

**89** S. Kako, "Kamishibai," pp. 6–7; K. Kata, *Machi no jijyoden (Autobiography of a Street-Person)*.

**90** S. Kako, "Kamishibai," p. 7.

**91** Ibid.

**92** M. Kita, *Nireke no Hitobito*, p. 231. New English translation by Dennis Keene, *The House of Nire*. Tokyo: Kodansha, 1984.

**93** W. A. Coupe, *The German Illustrated Broadsheet*, vol. l, pp. 13–17.

**94** H. Fehr, *Massenkunst*, p. 3.

**95** Same as note 88.

**96** Ibid.

**97** E. Janda and F. Nötzoldt, *Die Moritat vom Bänkelsang*, p. 9.

**98** C. Slater, *Stories on a String*, p. 191.

## Notes to Chapter 5 (pp. 88–95)

**1** Y. W. Ma, "The Beginnings of Professional Storytelling in China," pp. 226–237.

**2** V. Hrdličková, "The Professional Training of Chinese Storytellers," pp. 225–248.

**3** Ibid., p. 234; also, see her article "Some Questions Connected with Tun-huang pien-wen," and the item in note l above.

**4** J. Průšek, *The Origins and the Authors of the hua-pen*, pp. 22ff.

**5** Same as note 2, p. 234.

**6** Y. W. Ma, "The Beginnings of Professional Storytelling in China," p. 228.

**7** Ibid., p. 240.

**8** J. Průšek, "The Creative Methods of Chinese Mediaeval Storytellers," p. 265.

**9** V. Hrdličková, "The Chinese Storytellers," pp. 99–102.

**10** W. Eberhard, "Notes on Chinese Storytellers," pp. 1–31.

**11** G. Kara, *Chants d'un Barde Mongol*, p. 8.

**12** Ibid., p. 50.

**13** F. Brinkley, *Japan Described and Illustrated by the Japanese*, vol. 8, p. 286.

**14** J. Adam, *Japanese Storytellers*, and K. Meissner, "Die Yose."

**15** K. Meissner, "Die Yose," p. 233.

**16** Ibid., pp. 236–241.

**17** Ibid., p. 234.

**18** J. Barth, "Kodan und Rakugo," Teil D.

**19** Ibid., pp. 2–4.

**20** Ibid., p. 4.

**21** Ibid., p. 11.

**22** V. Hrdličková, "Japanese Professional Storytellers," and "The Zenza, the Storyteller's Apprentice."

**23** See first item in note 22 above, pp. 185–187 and Plate 23.

**24** C. Rougement, . . . *dann leben sie noch heute*, pp. 17–19.

**25** E. S. v. Kamphoevener, *An Nachtfeuern der Karawan-Serail*, p. 7.

**26** V. Gorog, "Qui Conte en France Aujourd'hui?" pp. 95–116.

**27** Ibid.

**28** Observed by the author in a performance at the College of Saint Teresa, Winona, Minnesota, and at a performance at the Hans Christian Andersen Monument in New York City.

**29** F. C. Sayers, *Anne Carroll Moore*, pp. 81ff.

**30** Y. M. Sokolov, *Russian Folklore*, pp. 416–417.

**31** P. B. McVicker, "Storytelling in Java"; V. Mair, *Painting and Performance*, pp. 73–79.

**32** Moebirman, *Wayang Purwa*, p. 14.

**33** A. Coomaraswamy, "Picture Showmen," p. 187.

**34** V. Mair, *Painting and Performance*, p. 108.

## NOTES TO CHAPTER 6 (pp. 96–108)

**1** E. P. Clarke, "Storytelling, Reading Aloud and Other Special Features," p. 189.

**2** J. B. Hardendorff, "Storytelling and the Story Hour," pp. 52–63.

**3** M. E. Dousman, "Children's Departments," p. 407.

**4** Ibid., p. 408.

**5** A. C. Moore, "The Story Hour at Pratt Institute," p. 210.

**6** Ibid., p. 206.

**7** A. Kennedy, "History of the Boys and Girls Department of the Carnegie Library," p. 23.

**8** Ibid.

**9** F. J. Olcutt, "Storytelling, Lectures and Other Adjuncts," p. 283.

**10** Ibid., p. 284.

**11** *Stories to Tell to Children*, 4th ed., 1926, p. 11.

**12** Same as note 7, pp. 23–24.

**13** R. G. Alvey, "The Historical Development of Organized Storytelling," pp. 400–401.

**14** F. J. Olcutt, "Storytelling, Lectures and Other Adjuncts," p. 284, mentions the fact that Omaha and Cedar Rapids, Iowa, had story hours of a similar nature; in addition to these were the story hours at Pratt Institute in Brooklyn, Carnegie Library in Pittsburgh, and the library in Buffalo.

**15** F. C. Sayers, *Anne Carroll Moore*, pp. 81ff. This entire section on Marie Shedlock and her influence on library storytelling is mostly a summary of this portion of Mrs. Sayers' book.

**16** Almost every other issue of *Library Journal* and of *Public Libraries* from 1902–1907 has a mention of a visit by Miss Shedlock to one or another of the libraries and library schools as a lecturer on storytelling.

**17** F. C. Sayers, *Anne Carroll Moore*, p. 83.

**18** M. H. Arbuthnot, *Children and Books*, 1st ed., p. 249.

**19** R. G. Alvey, "The Historical Development of Organized Storytelling," p. 244.

**20** J. Filstrup, "The Enchanted Cradle," p. 604.

**21** Ibid., p. 90.

**22** A. Kennedy, "History of the Boys and Girls Department," p. 24.

**23** F. C. Sayers, *Anne Carroll Moore*, pp. 81ff.

**24** J. Filstrup, "The Enchanted Cradle," p. 604.

**25** J. C. Dana, "Storytelling in Libraries," pp. 349–350.

**26** R. Gymer, "Storytelling in the Cleveland Public Library," pp. 417–418.

**27** American Library Association, *A Survey of Libraries*, vol. 3, p. 44.

**28** R. G. Alvey, "The Historical Development of Organized Storytelling," pp. 22–23.

**29** E. H. Gross, *Public Library Service to Children*, p. 96.

**30** A. Huls, "Pre-school Story Hour," pp. 726–727, 730.

**31** C. M. Chamberlin, "The Pre-School Story Hour," pp. 927–928.

**32** F. M. Foster, *A Round of Picture Book Programs*, 1944.

**33** A. Kane, "The Changing Face of the Story Hour," pp. 141–142.

**34** R. G. Alvey, "The Historical Development of Organized Storytelling," p. 638.

**35** E. Sheehan, and M. C. Bentley, "A Public Library Reassesses Storytelling," pp. 653–657.

**36** R. G. Alvey, "The Historical Development of Organized Storytelling," p. 313.

**37** Wisconsin Arts Board, *Artists in the Schools: Directory 1987, 1988, 1989.*

**38** See C. H. Farrell, *Word Weaving*; "Storytelling in Education," special issue of *The National Storytelling Journal*, Fall 1986.

**39** National Center for Education Statistics. *Services and Resources for Children in Public Libraries,*

*1988–1989. Survey Report. March 1990.* Data Series: FRSS-36; NCES 90-098. Washington, D.C., U.S. Department of Education, Office of Educational Research and Improvement, 1990.

**40** A. Carlson, *Early Childhood Literature Sharing Programs in Libraries.*

**41** See, for example, the manuals by J. Nichols and K. Roberts, cited in the Bibliography, Part 2, and the pamphlet produced by the Association for Library Services to Children, *Programming for Three- to Five-Year-Olds.*

**42** J. Filstrup, "The Enchanted Cradle," p. 605.

**43** A. C. Chandler, "Museum Story Hours," pp. 381–384.

**44** V. Haviland, *Ruth Sawyer*, p. 53.

**45** M. Lane, "Between Words and Steel," pp. 8–11.

## Notes to Chapter 7 (pp. 109–114)

**1** R. G. Alvey, "The Historical Development of Organized Storytelling," pp. 1–6.

**2** H. G. Long, *Rich the Treasure*, p. 8.

**3** J. A. Riis, *The Making of an American*, p. 16.

**4** J. Addams, *Twenty Years at Hull-House*, p. 101.

**5** Ibid., p. 103.

**6** M. Summers, "Storytelling in Playgrounds," p. 26.

**7** Ibid., p. 27.

**8** A. C. Moore, "Report of the Committee on Storytelling."

**9** G. Thorne-Thomsen, "The Practical Results of Storytelling," pp. 408–410.

**10** R. G. Alvey, "Historical Development of Organized Storytelling," pp. 18–19.

**11** A. C. Moore, "Report of the Committee on Storytelling," p. 169.

**12** J. Filstrup, "The Enchanted Cradle," p. 604.

**13** Ibid., p. 171.

**14** R. G. Alvey, "Historical Development of Organized Storytelling," p. 103.

**15** Ibid., p. 556; see also *Playground* 16 (January 1923): 479.

**16** Reported in a telephone conversation by David Wood, Professional Services Department, National Park and Recreation Association, August, 1989.

**17** Observed at several state and county nature centers in Wisconsin in the summer of 1989; also, a number of such events are highlighted in issues of the *National Storytelling Journal* and the *Yarnspinner.*

**18** J. Hamilton, "State Parks and Storytelling," pp. 7–9.

**19** Boy Scouts of America, *Handbook for Scoutmasters*, 1st ed., pp. 78ff.

**20** F. K. Mathiews, *Boy Scouts Book of Campfire Stories*, p. v.

## Notes to Chapter 8 (pp. 115–123)

**1** G. Olson, *Literature as Recreation*, p 78. This entire section is a summary taken from Olson's book.

**2** Ibid., p. 81.

**3** Ibid., pp. 82–83.

**4** *Aucassin et Nicolette*, trans. and quoted by G. Olson, *Literature as Recreation*, p. 134.

**5** B. J. Davis, *The Storytellers in Marguerite de Navarre's Heptameron.*

**6** *Consiglio contro a pistolenza*, trans. and quoted by G. Olson, *Literature as Recreation*, p. 175.

**7** See T. F. Crane, *The Exempla*, pp. x-xviii; S. Wenzel, "The Joyous Art of Preaching," p. 304.

**8** I. Shah, *Caravan of Dreams*, pp. 152–153.

**9** J. Sherzer, *Kuna Ways of Speaking*, pp. 110–111. All of the information that follows on the *ikar* comes from Sherzer. N. M. Holmer and S. H. Wassen give different terms for the chants and for the dolls in *The Complete Mu-Igala in Picture Writing.*

**10** Portion of "the *ikar* of the balsa wood" as performed by Pranki Pilos and recorded and trans. by J. Sherzer in *Kuna Ways of Speaking*, p. 126.

**11** Ibid., p. 134.

**12** V. de Mendoza,"El Mal de Espanto," and F. Rodriguez Rouanet, "Ojeo, Susto, Hijillo y Acuas."

**13** R. A. Gardner, *Therapeutic Communication with Children.*

**14** N. Kritzberg, *The Structured Therapeutic Game Method.*

**15** J. R. Brandell, "Stories and Storytelling in Child Psychotherapy."

**16** G. Constantino et al, *Cuento Therapy*, ERIC Document Ed. 257–902.

**17** E. Wynne, "Storytelling in Therapy and Counseling," and M. Freeman, "Tall Tales."

**18** R. Coles, *The Call of Stories*, p. 7.

**19** S. Rosen, *My Voice Will Go with You.*

**20** L. Wallas, *Stories for the Third Ear.*

**21** N. Peseschkian, *Oriental Stories as Tools in Psychotherapy.*

## NOTES TO CHAPTER 9 (pp. 127–137)

**1** J. H. Delargy, *The Gaelic Storyteller*, pp. 10, 19.

**2** M. W. Beckwith, *Mandan-Hidatsa Myths and Ceremonies*, p. xvi.

**3** O. Brinkmann, *Das Erzählen in einer Dorfgemeinschaft*, pp. 28–52.

**4** M. Kingsley, *West African Studies*, pp. 126–127.

**5** R. S. Rattray, *The Ashanti*, p. 162.

**6** V. Aardema, *Tales from the Story Hat*, New York: Coward-McCann, 1960.

**7** C. Meinhof, "Zur Entstehung der Schrift," pp. 1–14.

**8** K. v. d. Steinem, *Die Marquesaner und ihre Kunst*, pp. 63–66.

**9** H. A. Junod, *The Life of a South African Tribe*, vol. 1, p. 351.

**10** P. Seitel, *See So That We May See*, pp. 26–27.

**11** A. Sweeney, "Professional Malay Storytelling," p. 59.

**12** V. Hrdličkovà, "The Zenza," p. 39.

**13** E. C. Parsons, *Taos Tales*, p. 1.

**14** E. E. Clark, *Indian Legends from the Northern Rockies*, p 24.

**15** D. Tedlock, *The Spoken Word*, p. 68.

**16** T. Adamson, *Folktales of the Coast Salish*, pp. xii-xiii.

**17** J. Sherzer, *Kuna Ways of Speaking*, pp. 73–76.

**18** N. Munn, *Walbiri Iconography*, p. 69.

**19** H. A. Junod, *Life of a South African Tribe*, vol. 2, p. 209.

**20** H. Scheub, *The Xhosa Ntsomi*, pp. 9–11.

**21** M. Jackson, *Allegories of the Wilderness*, pp. 54–56.

**22** G. S. Kirk, *The Songs of Homer*, pp. 90ff.

**23** C. M. Bowra, *Heroic Poetry*, pp. 280–281.

**24** Ibid., p. 281; A. B. Lord, *The Singer of Tales*, pp. 68–98.

**25** M. Omidsalar, "Storytellers in Classical Persian Texts," p. 210.

**26** O. P. Joshi, *Painted Folklore*, p. 34.

**27** G. H. Roghair, *The Epic of Palnādu*, p. 33.

**28** B. Connelly, *Arab Folk Epic*, pp. 97–101.

**29** B, N'Diaye, *Veillées au Mali*, p. 8.

**30** A. Perera, *Sinhalese Folklore Notes.*

**31** K. Seki, *Folktales of Japan*, p. xv.

**32** W. S. Walker and A. E. Uysal, *Tales Alive in Turkey*, p. 10.

**33** M. Jacobs, *The Content and Style of an Oral Literature*, p. 220–221.

**34** G. Goodwin, *Myths and Tales*, p. 2.

**35** F. J. Newcomb, *Navajo Folk Tales*, p. xvi.

**36** A. F. Burns, *An Epoch of Miracles*, p. 17.

**37** D. Tedlock, *The Spoken Word*, p. 68.

**38** P. Smith, *Le récit populaire au Rwanda*, p. 25.

**39** F. M. Deng, *Dinka Folktales*, p. 25.

**40** H. Scheub, "South Africa," pp. 388–426.

**41** R. East, *Akiga's Story*, pp. 308–309.

**42** P. A. O'Connell, "Bandi Oral Narratives," p. 1.

**43** T. G. Winner, *The Oral Art and Literature of the Kazakhs*, p. 46.

**44** R. Jacobsen, "Commentary," in *Russian Fairy Tales*, by A. Afanas'ev, p. 645.

**45** P. A. Noss, "Description in Gbaya Literary Art," pp. 73–101.

**46** P. Seitel, *See So That We May See*, pp. 26–28.

**47** E. A. Magel, *Folktales from the Gambia*, p. 8.

**48** A. J. N. Tremearne, *Hausa Superstitions*, pp. 10–11; F. Edgar, *Hausa Tales*, p. xxiv.

**49** D. Ben-Amos, *Sweet Words*, pp. 50–51.

**50** R. Willis, *There Was a Certain Man*, p. 27.

**51** D. Tedlock, *The Spoken Word*, pp. 65–66.

**52** L. Dégh, *Folktales and Society*, pp. 75, 360.

**53** D. J. Crowley, *I Could Talk Old-Story Good*, pp. 19–22.

**54** G. Massignon, *Folktales of France*, p. xli.

**55** E. C. Parsons, *Folktales of Andros Island*, pp. xi-xii.

**56** Y. Pino-Saavedra, *Folktales of Chile*, p. 159.

**57** *Fairy Tales and Legends from Romania*, tr. by I. Sturdza, pp. 64, 75.

**58** J. S. Mbiti, *Akamba Stories*, p. v.

**59** S. L. Robe, *Amapa Storytellers*, pp. 1–10.

**60** A. F. Burns, *An Epoch of Miracles*, p. 20.

## NOTES TO CHAPTER 10 (pp. 138–157)

**1** J. Ball, "Style in the Folktale," pp. 170–172.

**2** R. A. Georges, "Toward an Understanding of Storytelling Events."

**3** D. Tedlock, *The Spoken Word* and D. Hymes, *"In Vain I Tried to Tell You."*

**4** M. Jacobs, *The Content and Style of an Oral Literature*.

**5** Ibid., pp. 266–267.

**6** Ibid., p. 5.

**7** D. Tedlock, *The Spoken Word*, pp. 38–42.

**8** Ibid., p. 47 and p. 63.

**9** G. A. Reichard, *An Analysis of Coeur d'Alene Indian Myths*, p. 26.

**10** E. C. Parsons, *Kiowa Tales*, p. x.

**11** B. Toelken, "The 'Pretty Languages' of Yellowman," p. 155.

**12** J. Sherzer, *Kuna Ways of Speaking*, pp. 21–35.

**13** D. Tedlock, *The Spoken Word* , pp. 169, 285–301.

**14** E. E. Clark, *Indian Legends from the Northern Rockies*, p. 317; and R. H. Lowie, *Myths and Traditions of the Crow Indians*, p.13.

**15** A. F. Burns, *An Epoch of Miracles*, p. 22.

**16** M. E. Opler, *Myths and Legends of the Jicarilla Apache*, pp. viii-ix.

**17** M. W. Beckwith, *Mandan-Hidatsa Myths and Ceremonies*, p. xviff; and T. Adamson, *Folktales of the Coast Salish*, pp. xii-xiii.

**18** E. S. Hall, *Eskimo Storyteller*, p. 412.

**19** H. M. Stanley, *My Dark Companions*, pp. 232ff.

**20** H. Chatelain, *Folktales of Angola*, pp. viiff. and 21ff.

**21** A. B. Ellis, *The Yoruba-Speaking Peoples*, pp. 243ff.

**22** E. W. Lane *An Account of the Manners and Customs of the Modern Egyptians*, p. 360.

**23** J. Torrend, *Specimens of Bantu Folklore*, p. 5.

**24** L. Sorin-Barreteau, "Gestes narratifs et langage gestuel," pp. 37–91.

**25** A. C. Jordan, "Tale, Teller and Audience," pp. 33–44.

**26** E. Beck, "Telling the Tale in Belize," p. 427.

**27** H. Scheub, *The Xhosa Ntsomi*, p. 6.

**28** Ibid.

**29** Ibid., pp. 7–8.

**30** E. E. Evans-Pritchard, *The Zande Trickster*, p. 34.

**31** C. Béart, *Jeux et Jouets de l'Ouest African*, vol. 2, p. 778.

**32** J. S. Mbiti, *Akamba Stories*, p. 24.

**33** M. Nebie, "Et si on disait un conte?" p. 48.

**34** M. Frost, "Inshimi and imilumbe."

**35** D. Cosentino, *Defiant Maids and Stubborn Farmers*, p. 7.

**36** D. Ben-Amos, *Sweet Words*.

**37** Ibid., pp. 49, 51.

**38** Ibid., pp. 52–53.

**39** Ibid., pp. 42–43.

**40** G. Calame-Griaule, "Pour une étude des gestes narratifs," p. 311.

**41** A. B. Ellis, *The Yoruba-Speaking Peoples*, p. 243.

**42** S. Johnson, *The History of the Yorubas*, pp. 125–126.

**43** Ibid., p. 58.

**44** E. J. Alagoa, "Oral Tradition among the Ijo," p. 410.

**45** A. A. Babalola, *The Content and Form of Yoruba Ijala*, p. vi.

**46** R. S. Rattray, *Religion and Art in Ashanti*, p. 219.

**47** D. P. Biebuyck and K. C. Mateene, *The Mwindo Epic*, pp. 6–14.

**48** C. S. Bird et al, *Song of Seydou Camara*, p. xiii.

**49** J. P. Clark, *The Ozidi Saga*, p. xxi.

**50** M. J. and F. S. Herskovits, *Dahomean Narrative*, p. 17.

**51** D. P. Biebuyck and K. C. Mateene, *The Mwindo Epic*, p. 8; H. F. Morris, *The Heroic Recitations of the Bahima*, pp. 19–39; A. C. Jordan, *Tales from Southern Africa*, pp. 2ff.

**52** S. A. Babalola, *The Content and Form of Yoruba Ijála*, p. 18; C. Bird, "Heroic Songs of the Mande Hunters," p. 278.

**53** T. Cope, *Izibongo*, p. 29.

**54** B. M. du Toit, *Content and Context of Zulu Folk-narratives*, p. x.

**55** O. F. Raum, *Chaga Childhood*, p. 222.

**56** I. Okpewho, *The Epic in Africa*, pp. 238–239.

**57** Ibid., pp. 202–210.

**58** Y. M. Sokolov, *Russian Folklore*, p. 311

**59** M. Azadovsky, *Eine Sibirische Märchenerzählerin*, pp. 36ff.

**60** Y. Sokolov, *Russian Folklore*, p. 405–406.

**61** C. H. Tillhagen, *Taikon Berättar*, pp. 11–12.

**62** K. Liestøl, *The Origin of the Icelandic Family Sagas*, p. 103.

**63** K. Haiding, *Von der Gebärdensprache*, pp. 9–10.

**64** O. Brinkmann, *Das Erzählen in einer Dorfgemeinschaft*, p. 11.

**65** U. Tolksdorf, *Eine ostpreussische volkserzählerin*, p. 30.

**66** L. Uffer, *Rätoromanische Märchen*, p. 81.

**67** L. Dégh, *Folktales and Society*, p. 227.

**68** Ibid., p. 253.

**69** Ibid., p. 183.

**70** Ibid., p. 184.

**71** A. Falassi, *Folklore by the Fireside*, pp. xviii; 30–33; 106; 148.

**72** G. Massignon, *Folktales of France*, pp. xli-xliii.

**73** J. H. Delargy, *The Gaelic Storyteller*, p. 16.

**74** A. Carmichael, *Carmina Gadelica*, p. xxii.

**75** K. H. Jackson, *The International Popular Tale*, p. 55.

**76** L. Millman, *Our Like Will Not Be There Again*.

**77** H. Glassie, *Passing the Time in Ballymenone*, pp. 47–50.

**78** O. P. Joshi, *Painted Folklore and Folklore Painters of India*, pp. 29, 34.

**79** S. Blackburn, *Singing of Birth and Death*, pp. 16–23.

**80** G. H. Roghair, *The Epic of Palnādu*, pp. 51–60.

**81** R. F. Barton, *The Mythology of the Ifugaos*, p. 11.

**82** E. K. and P. Maranda, *Structural Models in Folklore*, pp. 11–13.

**83** V. Hrdličková, "Japanese Professional Storytellers," pp. 171–190.

**84** "Japan: Dirty Stories," p. 51.

**85** W. Eberhard, *Minstrel Tales from Southeastern Turkey*, pp. 1ff.

**86** H. R. Lynton and M. Rajan, *The Days of the Beloved*, p. 140; K. Das, *A Study of Orissan Folklore*, p. 8; A. Perera, *Sinhalese Folklore Notes*.

**87** B. K. Walker, "The Folks Who Tell Folktales," pp. 636–642.

**88** R. E. Mitchell, "A Study of . . . Two Trukese Informants," p. 176.

**89** T. P. Fanua, *Po Fananga*, p. 7.

**90** G. Gorer, *Himalayan Village*, pp. 266–267.

**91** S. Lapai, "Burma," p. 277.

**92** Transcribed and translated by Kate Stevens from a videotaped performance recorded in Beijing.

**93** S. Hoogasian-Villa, *100 Armenian Tales*, pp. 535–537; L. Surmelian, *Apples of Immortality*, pp. 11ff.

**94** E. Mathias and R. Raspa, *Italian Folktales in America*, p. 59.

**95** C. Bianco, "The Two Rosetos," p. 137.

**96** B. Sklute, "Legends and Folk Beliefs in a Swedish-American Community," p. 174.

**97** B. Botkin, *A Treasury of Southern Folklore*, p. ix.

**98** M. Campbell, *Tales from the Cloud-Walking Country*; J. Frank Dobie, "Storytellers I Have Known," pp. 3–29.

**99** J. R. Mintz, *Legends of the Hasidim*, pp. 3–8.

**100** Y. Sabar, *The Folk Literature of the Kurdistani Jews*, p. xxxvii.

**101** D. S. Reynolds, "From Doctrine to Narrative," pp. 486–487.

**102** B. A. Rosenberg, *Can These Bones Live?*

**103** A. Kennedy, "History of the Boys and Girls Department," p. 23.

**104** A. B. Lord, *The Singer of Tales*, pp. 13–29; A. Parry, *The Making of Homeric Verse*.

**105** J. Dournes, "Scènes et récits de vie," pp. 142–143.

**106** P. B. Mullen, "A Traditional Storyteller," p. 27.

## NOTES TO CHAPTER 11 (pp. 158–168)

**1** S. Blackburn, *Singing of Birth and Death*, p. 11.

**2** H. T. Norris, *Shinqiti Folk Literature*, p. 61.

**3** *Berimbau*. 16 mm. film, dir. by T. Talbot.

**4** D. Ben-Amos, *Sweet Words*, pp. 25–29, 42–49.

**5** H. Frankfort, *Art and Architecture of the Ancient Orient*, pp. 35–36.

**6** G. S. Kirk, *The Songs of Homer*, pp. 90–91.

**7** Ibid., pp. 313–314.

**8** H. M. and N. K. Chadwick, *The Growth of Literature*, vol. 2, p. 271.

**9** L. F. Anderson, *The Anglo-Saxon Scop*, p. 13.

**10** H. T. Norris, *Shinqiti Folk Literature*, pp. 64–65.

**11** C. Bird, "Heroic Songs of the Mande Hunters," p. 279.

**12** C. Bird, *The Song of Seydou Camara*, vol. 1.

**13** H. T. Norris, *Shinqiti Folk Literature*, pp. 62–63.

**14** K. Meissner, "Die Yose," pp. 240–241.

**15** J. Barth, "Kodan und Rakugo," Teil 3, p. 3; B. Ruch, "Medieval Jongleurs," p. 287.

**16** C. Oppong, *Growing Up in Dagbon*, p. 57.

**17** H. M. and N. K. Chadwick, *The Growth of Literature*, vol. 2, p. 271; P. A. Bessonov, *Kalêki Perekhozhie*, Part 1 and Plates.

**18** T. G. Winner, *The Oral Art and Literature of the Kazakhs*, p. 29.

**19** Ibid.

**20** W. Eberhard, *Minstrel Tales*, pp. 1–8.

**21** G. S. Kirk, *The Songs of Homer*, p. 90; A. B. Lord, *The Singer of Tales*, p. 21.

**22** H. M. and N. K. Chadwick, *The Growth of Literature*, vol. 2, p. 22.

**23** G. Kara, *Chants d'un Barde Mongol*, pp. 46–47.

**24** There is a literary version in the beautiful children's book *Suho and the White Horse* by Yuzo Otsuka, tr. by Ann Herring. New York: Viking Penguin, 1981. See also C. R. Bawden's "Repertory of a Blind Mongolian Storyteller."

**25** G. Canova, as translated and quoted by B. Connelly, *Arab Folk Epic*, p. 61.

**26** S. Slyomovics, *The Merchant of Art*, p. 19.

**27** A. Sweeney, "Professional Malay Storytelling," pp. 47–55.

**28** M. Mondon-Vidhailet, "La Musique Éthiopienne," p. 3181.

**29** O. P. Joshi, *Painted Folklore*, p. 34.

**30** P. B. Mande, "Dakkalwars and Their Myths," p. 70.

**31** R. V. Russell and R. B. H. Lord, *Tribes and Castes of the Central Provinces*, p. 243.

**32** H. Tracey, "A Case for the Name Mbira," pp. 17–25.

**33** D. Ben-Amos, *Sweet Words*, pp. 25–29, 42–49.

**34** A. M. Jones, *African Music*, p. 29.

**35** M. Dias, *Instrumentos Musicais de Moçambique*, pp. 75–76.

**36** See also Tracey's son Andrew, as he demonstrates such a story in the film *Mapandangare*.

**37** D. Cosentino, *Defiant Maids and Stubborn Farmers*, p. 102.

**38** D. P. Biebuyck and K. C. Mateene, *The Mwindo Epic*, p. 13.

**39** Same as note 27.

**40** Same as note 1.

**41** Same as note 11.

**42** S. A. Babalola, *The Content and Form of Yoruba Ijala*, pp. 54–55.

**43** M. Jackson, *Allegories of the Wilderness*, p. 118.

**44** K. K. Das, *Burrakatha*, p. 6.

**45** Same as note 27.

**46** H. M. and N. K. Chadwick, *The Growth of Literature*, vol. 3, p. 423.

**47** R. Gingerich, "The Story of the Storytelling Drum," p. 6.

**48** Same as note 18.

**49** G. H. Roghair, *The Epic of Palnādu*, p. 33.

**50** M. G. Smith, "The Social Functions and Meaning of Hausa Praise Singing," p. 27.

## NOTES TO CHAPTER 12 (pp. 169–192)

**1** "Children Like Pictures," p. 589.

**2** L. H. Hedgbeth, "Extant American Panoramas," p. 28.

**3** A. Coomaraswamy, "Picture Showmen," p. 182.

**4** H. Lüders, "Die Śaubhikas," pp. 698–737.

**5** V. Mair, *Painting and Performance*, pp. 29–32.

**6** J. Mittal, "Kunepullalu Scroll," p. 51.

**7** G. Azarpay, *Sogdian Painting*, p. 102.

**8** V. Mair, *Painting and Performance*, p. 50.

**9** Ibid., p. 53.

**10** W. P. Groenevelt, "Notes on the Malay," p. 53.

**11** S. Kramrisch, *Unknown India*, p. 66.

**12** [H. and J. Ferguson] "Textiles That Tell a Story."

**13** Ibid.

**14** O. P. Joshi, *Painted Folklore*, p. 29.

**15** Ibid., pp. ix, 23–35.

**16** A. Bhattacharya, "Oral Tradition of the *Ramayana* in Bengal," pp. 593–616.

**17** J. Erickson, *Mata ni pachedi*, pp. 9ff.

**18** P. B Mande, "Dakkalwars and Their Myths," pp. 69–76.

**19** E. Ray, "Documentation for Paithan Paintings," pp. 239–282.

**20** See the excerpt from Morio Kita's novel, quoted in Chapter 4.

**21** K. Kata, *Machi no jijyoden*.

**22** Ibid.

**23** S. Peterson, "Translating Experience," pp. 6–22.

**24** J. P. Gilson, *An Exultet Roll*, pp. 5–7.

**25** R. W. Brednich, "Zur Vorgeschichte des Bänkelsangs," pp. 78–92.

**26** L. Schmidt, "Geistlicher Bänkelsang," pp. 1–16.

**27** Correspondence of the author and Fritz Nötzoldt.

**28** R. W. Brednich, "Zur Vorgeschichte des Bänkelsangs," p. 84.

**29** Goethe, *Werke*, vol. 51, p. 150.

**30** E. Janda and F. Nötzoldt, *Die Moritat vom Bänkelsang*, pp. 9ff.

**31** C. Slater, *Stories on a String*, pp. 192–193.

**32** A. Huls, "Pre-school Story Hour," p. 730.

**33** M. Shedlock, *The Art of the Storyteller*, pp. 13–14.

**34** G. M. Fannin, "A Resume," p. 10.

**35** Ibid., p. 14.

**36** F. Sanborn, "How to Use Picture-Story Books," pp. 272–274.

**37** F. M. Foster, *A Round of Picture Book Programs*.

**38** A. Corrigan, "The Next Step," pp. 2014–2016.

**39** A. Kane, "The Changing Face of the Story Hour," pp. 141–142.

**40** N. Munn, *Walbiri Iconography*, p. 59.

**41** T. G. Strehlow, "The Art of Circle, Line and Square," p. 46.

**42** W. H. Oswalt, "Traditional Storyknife Tales of Yuk Girls," pp. 310–336.

**43** See, among others, L. P. Ager, "Storyknifing: An Alaskan Girls' Game"; D. J. Ray, *Aleut and Eskimo Art*, pp. 40, 44–45, 61, 74 and Plate No. 74; E. W. Nelson, "The Eskimo About Bering Strait," pp. 345–346.

**44** W. H. Oswalt, "Traditional Storyknife Tales of Yuk Girls"; figures are also reproduced in A. Pellowski, *The Family Storytelling Handbook*, p. 120.

**45** J. DeFrancis, *Visible Speech*, pp. 24–32.

**46** A. Pellowski, *The Story Vine*, pp. 47–55, 76.

**47** Ibid., pp. 56–59; see also the two items in the bibliography on p. 76 of that book.

**48** Orally given to the author by several Japanese children; see also S. Kako, *Nihon Densho No Asobi Tokumon* and *Folk and Traditional Music of Asia for Children*, vol. 1, LP sound disc and booklet.

**49** Based on information from students in a library workshop, Administrative College of Papua New Guinea, Summer, 1983; see also D. Newton, *Art Styles of the Papuan Gulf*.

**50** Father Hippolyte Roussel, translated and quoted in *Reports of the Norwegian Archaeological Expedition to Easter Island*, vol. 2, p. 346.

**51** T. Q. Reefe, "Lukasa," p. 49.

**52** K. G. Lindblom, *String Figures in Africa*, p. 11.

**53** M. D. and L. S. B. Leakey, *Some String Figures from North East Angola*, p. 7.

**54** A. Pellowski, *The Family Storytelling Handbook*, pp. 62–73.

**55** See the page numbers cited in the index under "Dolls," in V. Mair's *Painting and Performance*.

**56** Observed by the author in a temple near Aomori, in northern Japan, where a monk used the twelve animal-year figures. A retelling of the story appears in A. Pellowski, *The Story Vine*, pp. 87–89. See also B. Ruch's "Medieval Jongleurs and the Making of a National Literature."

**57** A. Pellowski, *The Story Vine*.

**58** For a brief bibliography, see p. 90 in ibid.

**59** V. Hrdličková, "Japanese Professional Storytellers," p. 175.

**60** B. Ruch, "Medieval Jongleurs," pp. 286 and 305.

**61** Reported in a verbal conversation by Kate Stevens to the author, July 1989.

**62** G. Gorer, *Himalayan Village*, p. 267.

**63** D. J. Crowley, *I Could Talk Old-Story Good*, p. 28.

**64** H. M. and N. K. Chadwick, *The Growth of Literature*, vol. 2, p. 265.

**65** A. Sweeney, "Professional Malay Storytelling," p. 54.

**66** D. P. Biebuyck, "The Epic as a Genre in Congo Oral Literature," p. 262.

**67** G. Rouget, "Court Songs and Traditional History," pp. 39–41.

**68** L. Camara, *The Guardian of the Word*.

**69** H. F. Morris, *The Heroic Recitations of the Bahima of Ankole*, p. 21.

**70** I. Okpewho, *The Epic in Africa*, p. 233.

## NOTES TO CHAPTER 13 (pp. 193–200)

**1** B. K. Walker, "Folktales in Turkey," pp. 42–46.

**2** A. F. Burns, *An Epoch of Miracles*, p. 18.

**3** Reported to the author in a verbal conversation by Molly Melching, Dakar, September 1978.

**4** M. Jacobs, *Content and Style of an Oral Literature*, p. 220; D. Hymes, *"In Vain I Tried to Tell You,"* p. 323.

**5** O. P. Joshi, *Painted Folklore*, p. 34.

**6** S. Blackburn, *Singing of Birth and Death*, p. 14.

**7** J. H. Delargy, *The Gaelic Storyteller*, p. 20.

**8** G. Megas, *Folktales of Greece*, p. xlviii.

**9** D. J. Crowley, *I Could Talk Old-Story Good*, p. 32.

**10** A. Alpers, *Legends of the South Seas*, p. 41.

**11** K. Seki, *Folktales of Japan*, p. 125.

**12** P. Seitel, *See So That We May See*, pp. 29–30.

**13** D. Cosentino, *Defiant Maids and Stubborn Farmers*, pp. 91–92.

**14** P. Roulon and R. Doko, "Un pays de conteurs," p. 128.

**15** E. C. Parsons, *Taos Tales*, p. 1.

**16** A. P. and T. E. Penard, "Surinam Folk-tales," p. 243.

**17** P. Smith, *Le récit populaire au Rwanda*, p. 27.

**18** M. J. and F. S. Herskovits, *Dahomean Narrative*, pp. 53–54.

**19** E. E. Clark, *Indian Legends from the Northern Rockies*, p. 317; H. R. Lynton and M. Rajan, *Days of the Beloved*, p. 140; Mrs. Meer Hasan Ali, *Observations on the Mussulmauns of India . . .* , 2nd. ed. Oxford Univ. Pr., 1917 (First pub. 1832), pp. 251–252; R. E. Mitchell, "A Study of . . . Two Trukese Informants," p. 176; A. Perera, *Sinhalese Folklore*.

**20** T. Adamson, *Folktales of the Coast Salish*, p. xiii.

**21** M.E. Opler, *Myths and Tales of the Jicarilla Apache*, p. ix.

## Notes to Chapter 14 (pp. 203–221)

**1** L.C.L., 8, p. 179.

**2** V. Hrdličková, "The Professional Training of Chinese Storytellers," p. 228.

**3** H. M. and N. K. Chadwick, *The Growth of Literature*, vol. 1, p. 605.

**4** D. Corkery, "The Bardic Schools," pp. 19–24.

**5** H. M. and N. K. Chadwick, *The Growth of Literature*, vol. 1, p. 603.

**6** Same as note 4.

**7** C. Oppong, *Growing Up in Dagbon*, p. 54.

**8** Ibid., pp. 55–56.

**9** Ibid.

**10** Ibid., pp. 57–58.

**11** H. T. Norris, *Shinqiti Folk Literature*, p. 65.

**12** Ibid., p. 54.

**13** O. P. Joshi, *Painted Folklore*, pp. 31–33.

**14** E. S. Craighill Handy, *Marquesan Legends*, p. 20.

**15** E. Best, *The Maori*, pp. 57–84.

**16** P. Radin, *The Trickster*, p. 122.

**17** H. M. and N. K. Chadwick, *The Growth of Literature*, vol. 2, pp. 251–253.

**18** B. Malinowski, *Argonauts of the Western Pacific*, pp. 185–186, 291.

**19** J. H. Rowe, "Inca Culture," pp. 201–202.

**20** V. Hrdličková, "Japanese Professional Storytellers," and "The Zenza."

**21** V. Hrdličková, "The Professional Training of Chinese Storytellers," pp. 227ff.

**22** M. Omidsalar, "Storytellers in Classical Persian Texts," p. 208.

**23** J. Cejpek, "Iranian Folk Literature," p. 654.

**24** C. Bird, "Heroic Songs of the Mande Hunters," p. 279.

**25** J. Sherzer, *Kuna Ways of Knowing*, pp. 225–226.

**26** S. A. Babalola, *The Content and Form of Yoruba Ijala*, p. 41.

**27** D. P. Biebuyck and K. C. Mateene, *The Mwindo Epic*, pp. 11–12.

**28** Ibid.

**29** D. Ben-Amos, *Sweet Words*, pp. 37ff.

**30** B. Connelly, *Arab Folk Epic*, p. 60.

**31** H. Scheub, *The Xhosa Ntsomi*, p. 21.

**32** Ibid., p. 19.

**33** S. Blackburn, *Singing of Birth and Death*, pp. 14–15.

**34** A. Lord, *The Singer of Tales*, pp. 13–29.

**35** T. G. Winner, *The Oral Art and Literature of the Kazakhs*, pp. 33–34.

**36** Carnegie Library of Pittsburgh, *Annual Report*, 1900; Announcement of Pratt Institute, *Library Journal*, 24 (February 1899): 72.

**37** Announcement of Program of Study, *Library Journal* 26 (September 1901): 697.

**38** *Pratt Institute Monthly* 10 (December 1901): 46.

**39** Library School of Western Reserve University, *Catalog* 1904–1905; *Wilson Library Bulletin* 4(June 1908): 56; New York Public Library, Library School [*Catalog*] 1912; St. Louis Public Library, Library School, *Circular of Information* 1917–18; Columbia University, Library School, *Catalog*, 1928.

**40** Same as last item above.

**41** R. L. Abernethy, "A Study of . . . Storytelling for Children in the United States."

**42** B. L. Baker, "Storytelling, Past and Present," p. 26.

**43** G. M. Fannin, "A Resumé of the History . . . ," p. 13.

**44** V. Hrdličková, "Professional Training of Chinese Storytellers," p. 238.

**45** A. Baker and E. Greene, *Storytelling: Art and Technique*.

**46** Chautauqua Library School, *Handbook and Register 1901–1910.*

**47** *The Story Hour* 1 (1908):38.

**48** This short summary of the work of Richard T. Wyche and the National Storyteller's League is taken from R. G. Alvey, "The Historical Development of Organized Storytelling," pp. 182–220.

**49** *Encyclopedia of Associations*, 23rd ed. Detroit: Gale Reasearch, 1989, entry no. 9772.

**50** J. Oxendine, "An Interview with Connie Regan-Blake," pp. 4–5.

**51** Compiled from the bibliography of R. Alvey, "The Historical Development of Organized Storytelling," and from A. Pellowski, *The World of Children's Literature*; entries for the 1970s and 1980s were counted from items in the bibliography, part 2, of this book.

**52** Based on personal, first-hand observation.

**53** Reported in a personal conversation with the author, Tokyo, October 1975.

**54** Reported in a personal conversation with the author, Detroit, June 1977.

**55** A. Izard, "I Study Very Hard," pp. 130–132.

**56** M. K. Brady, "Narrative Competence," p. 181.

**57** J. H. Delargy, *The Gaelic Storyteller*, pp. 22ff.

**58** E. S. Hall, *The Eskimo Storyteller*, p. 38.

**59** P. Tirabutana, "A Simple One," pp. 10–11.

**60** R. Flower, *The Western Island*, p. 53.

**61** E. Mathias and R. Raspa, *Italian Folktales in America*, p. 45.

**62** G. Henssen, *Überlieferung und persönlichkeit*, pp. 1–3.

**63** L. Roberts, *Sang Branch Settlers*, p. 7.

**64** L. Dégh, *Folktales and Society*, p. 186.

**65** Ibid., p. 195.

**66** S. O'Sullivan, *Handbook of Irish Folklore*, p. 555.

**67** L. Dégh, *Folktales and Society*, pp. 192–194.

**68** H. R. Lynton and M. Rajan, *Days of the Beloved*, p. 140.

**69** M. Frere, *Hindoo Fairy Legends*, p. xxvii.

**70** E. E. Clark, *Indian Legends of the Northern Rockies*, p. xiii.

**71** Cited in R. T. Christiansen, *Folktales of Norway*, p. xli.

**72** B. Ruch, "Medieval Jongleurs," pp. 286–287.

**73** J. Průšek, "Creative Methods of Chinese Medieval Storytellers," p. 253.

**74** G. H. Roghair, *The Epic of Palnādu*, p. 32.

**75** R. M. Laughlin, *Of Cabbages and Kings*, p. 5.

**76** R. Darnell, "Correlates of Cree Narrative Performance," p. 325.

**77** P. Cachia, "Social Values Reflected in Egyptian Popular Ballads," p. 86.

**78** See, for example, in the *National Storytelling Journal*, "Copyright and Storytelling," by Michael E. Skinrud, in vol. 1, no. 1, (Winter 1984); "Ethics among Professional Storytellers" by Lee-Ellen Marvin and Doug Lipman, vol. 3, no. 4, (Summer 1986); "A Response to the Ethics Question" by Finley Stewart, vol. 4, no. 3, (Summer 1987); see also "Letters—and Ladies of the NSL" by Larry Johnson, in vol. 1, no. 1, (Summer 1989) of *Storytelling Magazine*.

## NOTES TO CHAPTER 15 (pp. 222–230)

**1** Quoted by K. H. Basso, "Stalking with Stories," p. 21.

**2** A. H. Bá , *Kaydara*, p. 17.

**3** R. Coles, *The Call of Stories*, p. 13.

**4** J. DeFrancis, *Visible Speech*, pp. 244–247.

**5** For an interesting extended discussion of these questions see K. B. Maxwell, *Bemba Myth and Ritual*, pp. 1–3 and W. J. Ong, *Orality and Literacy*.

**6** S. B. Heath, *Ways with Words*, pp. 157–189.

# BIBLIOGRAPHY
## PART I

## Books and Periodical Articles

Place of publication is not given for the following presses: Cambridge University Press, Oxford University Press, University of Chicago Press, and any other university press located in a city with the same name as the university.

Individual titles in the *Loeb Classical Library* and *The Sacred Books of the East*, mentioned in the text, are not given separate entries here.

Abernethy, Rose L. "A Study of Existing Practices and Principles of Storytelling for Children in the United States." Ph.D. dissertation, Northwestern University, 1964.

Abrahams, Roger D. *The Man-of-words in the West Indies: Performance and the Emergence of Creole Culture*. Baltimore: Johns Hopkins Univ. Pr., 1983.

Adam, Jules. *Japanese Storytellers*. Tr. from the French by Osman Edwards. Tokyo: T. Hasegawa, 1912.

Adams, Robert J. "Social Identity of a Japanese Storyteller." Ph.D. dissertation, Indiana University, 1972.

Adamson, Thelma. *Folktales of the Coast Salish*. Memoirs, 27. New York: American Folklore Society, 1934.

Addams, Jane. *Twenty Years at Hull-House*. New York: Macmillan, 1910.

Adler, Felix. *The Moral Instruction of Children*. New York: D. Appleton and Co., 1892.

Afanas'ev, Aleksandr. *Russian Fairy Tales*. New York: Pantheon, 1945.

Ager, Lynn Price. "Illustrated Oral Literature from Southwestern Alaska: Storyknifing, Storyknives and Knifestories." *Arts and Culture of the North* IV, 1 (Winter 1979–80): 199–202.

———. "Storyknifing: An Alaskan Eskimo Girls' Game." *Journal of the Folklore Institute* 11, 3 (1975): 187–198.

Al-Shahi, Ahmed, and Moore, F. C. T. *Wisdom from the Nile; A Collection of Folk-Stories from Northern and Central Sudan*. New York: Clarendon Press, 1978.

Alagoa, Ebiegberi Joe. "Oral Tradition among the Ijo of the Niger Delta." *Journal of African History* 7 (1966): 405–419.

Allen, Arthur T. "The Ethos of the Teller of Tales." *Wilson Library Bulletin* 40, 4 (December 1965): 356–358.

Allen, Louise A. *Time Before Morning: Art and Myth of the Australian Aborigines.* New York: Thomas Y. Crowell, 1975.

Alpers, Anthony. *Legends of the South Seas.* New York: Thomas Y. Crowell, 1970.

Alvey, Richard Gerald. "The Historical Development of Organized Storytelling to Children in the United States." Ph.D. dissertation, University of Pennsylvania, 1974.

American Library Association. *A Survey of Libraries in the United States.* Chicago: ALA, 1927.

Ammar, Hamed. *Growing Up in an Egyptian Village: Silwa, Province of Aswan.* New York: Octagon, 1966.

Anand, Mulk Raj et. al. *Homage to Kalamkari.* Bombay: Marg Publications, 1979.

Andersen, Johannes C. *Myths and Legends of the Polynesians.* Rutland, Vt.: Tuttle, 1969.

Anderson, L. F. *The Anglo-Saxon Scop.* Studies, Philosophical Series no. 1. Univ. of Toronto, 1903.

Andersson, Theodore M. *The Icelandic Family Saga.* Cambridge: Harvard Univ. Pr., 1967.

Anyumba, H. O. "The *Nyatiti* Lament Songs." In *East Africa Past and Present.* Paris: Presence Africaine, 1964.

Arbuthnot, May Hill. *Children and Books*, 1st ed. Chicago: Scott, Foresman, 1947.

Attagara, Kingkeo. "The Folk Religion of Ban Nai, a Hamlet in Central Thailand." Ph.D. dissertation, Indiana University, 1967.

Auerbach, Erich. *Literary Language and Its Public in Late Latin Antiquity and in the Middle Ages.* Tr. from the German by Ralph Manheim. Bollingen Series 74. New York: Pantheon, 1965.

Avery, Myrtilla. *The Exultet Rolls of South Italy.* 2 vols. The Hague: Martinus Nijhoff; Princeton Univ. Pr., 1936.

Azadovsky, Mark. *Eine Sibirische Märchenerzählerin.* Folklore Fellows Communications, no. 68. Helsinki, 1926.

Azarpay, Guitty. *Sogdian Painting: The Pictorial Epic in Oriental Art.* With contributions by A. M. Belenitskii, B. I. Marshak and Mark J. Dresden. Berkeley: Univ. of California Pr., 1981.

Azevedo, Warren L. d'. "Uses of the Past in Gola Discourse." *Journal of African History* 3 (1962): 11–34.

Bá, Amadou Hampaté. *Kaydara.* Abidjan and Dakar: Nouvelles Editions Africaines, 1978.

Babalola, Adeboye. "One Type of Yoruba Narrative Called Àrò." *Fabula* [Berlin] 14 (1973): 179–193.

Babalola, S. A. *The Content and Form of Yoruba Ijála*. Oxford Univ. Pr., 1966.

Bacon, Francis. *The Essays*, ed. by John Pitcher. New York: Penguin, 1986.

Bailey, Harold Walter. "Storytelling in Buddhist Central Asia." *Acta Asiatica* (Bulletin of the Institute of Eastern Culture) 23 (September 1972): 63–77.

Bain, R. Nisbet, ed. and tr. *Cossack Fairy Tales and Folk Tales*. New York: Frederick A. Stokes, n.d.

Baker, Augusta, and Greene, Ellin. *Storytelling: Art and Technique*. 2nd ed. New York: R. R. Bowker, 1987.

Baker, Barbara Lehfeldt. "Storytelling, past and present." Master's thesis, Graduate School of Library Science, Texas Woman's University, 1979.

Ball, John. "Style in the Folktale." *Folk-lore* 65 (1954): 170–172.

Bang, W. "Manichäische Erzähler." *Le Museon* 44 (1931): 1–36.

Barker, Theodore. *Using Metaphors in Psychotherapy*. New York: Brunner Mazel, 1986.

Barth, J. "Kodan und Rakugo." In *Mitteilungen*, vol. 22, Teil D. Tokyo: Deutsche Gesellschaft für Natur- und Völkerkunde Ostasiens, 1928.

Bartis, Peter, and Fertig, Barbara C. *Folklife Sourcebook: A Directory of Folklife Resources in the United States and Canada*. Washington, D.C.: American Folklife Center, Library of Congress, 1986.

Barton, Roy Franklin. *The Mythology of the Ifugaos*. Memoirs, 44. Philadelphia: American Folklore Society, 1955.

Bascom, William R. "The Forms of Folklore: Prose Narratives." *Journal of American Folklore* 78 (1965): 3–20.

Basso, Keith H. "Stalking with Stories: Names, Places, and Moral Narratives among the Western Apache." In *Text, Play, and Story: The Construction and Reconstruction of Self and Society*, ed. by Edward M. Bruner. Proceedings, 1983. Washington, D.C.: American Ethnological Society, 1984.

Bauer, Caroline Feller. *Handbook for Storytellers*. Chicago: American Library Association, 1977.

Baughman, Ernest Warren. *Type and Motif-index of the Folktales of England and North America*. The Hague: Mouton & Co., 1966.

Bauman, Richard. *Story, Performance, and Event*. Cambridge Univ. Pr., 1986.

———. *Verbal Art As Performance*. Rowley, Mass.: Newbury House, 1977.

———, and Sherzer, Joel. *Explorations in the Ethnography of Speaking*. Cambridge Univ. Press, 1974.

Bawden, Charles R. "The Repertory of a Blind Mongolian Storyteller." In: *Fragen der Mongolischen Heldendichtung*. Wiesbaden: Harrassowitz, 1981.

Béart, Charles. *Jeux et Jouets de l'Ouest African*. 2 vols. Dakar: IFAN, 1955.

Bechtum, Martin. *Beweggründe und Bedeutung des Vagantentums in der lateinischen*

*Kirche des Mittelalters.* Beiträge zur mittelalterlichen, neueren und allgemeinen Geschichte, 14. Jena: Gustav Fischer, 1941.

Beck, Ervin. "Telling the Tale in Belize." *Journal of American Folklore* 93 (1980): 417–434.

Beck, Jane C. *To Windward of the Land: The Occult World of Alexander Charles.* Bloomington: Indiana Univ. Pr., 1979.

Beckwith, Martha Warren. *Mandan-Hidatsa Myths and Ceremonies.* Memoirs, 32. New York: American Folklore Society, 1937.

Beech, Mervyn W. H. *The Suk.* New York: Negro Universities Press, 1966. (Originally pub. 1911 by Clarendon Press.)

Ben-Amos, Dan. *Sweet Words: Storytelling Events in Benin.* Philadelphia: Institute for the Study of Human Issues, 1975.

———, and Goldstein, Kenneth S. *Folklore: Performance and Communication.* The Hague: Mouton, 1975.

———, and Mintz, Jerome R. *In Praise of the Baal Shem Tov: The Earliest Collection of Legends about the Founder of Hasidism.* Bloomington: Indiana Univ. Pr., 1970.

Benedict, Ruth. *Zuni Mythology.* 2 vols. Contributions to Anthropology, 21. New York: Columbia Univ. Pr., 1935.

Benjamin, Walter, and Arendt, Hannah. *Illuminations.* Tr. by H. Zorn. New York: Harcourt, Brace, 1968.

*Beowulf.* Tr. by John R. Clark Hall. London: Allen and Unwin, 1911.

*Beowulf together with Widsith.* Tr. by Benjamin Thorpe. Great Neck, N.Y.: Barron's Educational Series, 1962.

Bessonov, Peter Alexseevich. *Kalêki Perekhozhie.* 6 parts. Moscow, 1861–4.

Best, Elsdon. *The Maori.* 2 vols. Polynesian Society, Memoirs, 5. Wellington: The Society, 1924.

Bettelheim, Bruno. *The Uses of Enchantment: The Meaning and Importance of Fairy Tales.* New York: Vintage, 1979.

Bhattacharya, Asutosh. "Oral Tradition of Ramayana in Bengal." In *The Ramayana Tradition in Asia*, ed. by V. Raghavan, pp. 593–616. New Delhi: Sahitya Akademi, 1980.

Bianco, Carla. "The Two Rosetos: The Folklore of an Italian-American Community in Northeastern Pennsylvania." Ph.D. dissertation, Indiana University, 1972.

Biebuyck, Daniel P. "The Epic as a Genre in Congo Oral Literature." In *African Folklore*, ed. by Richard Dorson. Bloomington: Indiana Univ. Pr., 1972.

———. *Hero and Chief: Epic Literature from the Banyanga, Zaire Republic.* Berkeley: Univ. of California Pr., 1978.

———. *Lega Culture: Art, Initiation, and Moral Philosophy among a Central African People.* Berkeley: Univ. of California Pr., 1973.

————, and Mateene, Kahombo C. *The Mwindo Epic from the Banyanga (Congo Republic)*. Berkeley: Univ. of California Pr., 1969.

Bird, Charles S. "Heroic Songs of the Mande Hunters." In *African Folklore* ed. by Richard Dorson. Bloomington: Indiana Univ. Pr., 1972.

————; Koita, Mamadou; and Soumaoro, Bourama. *The Song of Seydou Camara*; vol. 1, *Kambili*. Bloomington: African Studies Center, Indiana Univ., 1974.

Blacking, John. *Venda Children's Songs*. Johannesburg: Witwatersrand Univ. Pr., 1967.

Blackburn, Stuart H. "Oral Performance: Narrative and Ritual in a Tamil Tradition." *Journal of American Folklore* 94 (April-June 1981): 207–227.

————. *Singing of Birth and Death; Texts in Performance*. Philadelphia: Univ. of Pennsylvania Pr., 1988.

Boas, Franz. *Tsimshian Mythology*. Smithsonian Institution, U.S. Bureau of Ethnology, 31st Annual Report. Washington, D.C.: The Institution, 1916.

Bødker, Laurits; Hole, Christina; and D'Aronco, G. *European Folk Tales*. Copenhagen: Rosenkilde and Bagger, 1963.

Bolte, Johannes, and Polivka, Georg. *Anmerkungen zu den Kinder- und Hausmärchen der Brüder Grimm*. 5 vols. Leipzig: Dieterich, 1913–1932.

Bonner, Anthony, tr. *Songs of the Troubadours*. New York: Schocken, 1972.

Botkin, Benjamin. *A Treasury of Southern Folklore*. Foreword by Douglas Southall Freeman. New York: Crown, 1949.

Bowra, C. M. *Heroic Poetry*. London: Macmillan, 1952.

Boy Scouts of America. *Handbook for Scoutmasters*, 1st ed., 9th reprint. New York: Boy Scouts of America, 1919.

Boyce, Mary. "The Parthian Gosan and the Iranian Minstrel Tradition." *Journal of the Royal Asiatic Society* (1957): 10–45.

Brady, Margaret K. "Narrative Competence: A Navajo Example of Peer Group Evaluation." *Journal of American Folklore* 93 (1980): 158–181.

Brandell, Jerrold R. "Stories and Storytelling in Child Psychotherapy." *Psychotherapy; Theory, Research and Practice* 21 (Spring 1984): 54–62.

Brandl, Alois. "Spielmannsverhältnisse in frühmittelenglischer Zeit." In *Sitzungsberichte*, pp. 873–892. Berlin: Preussische Akademie der Wissenschaften, 1910.

Brednich, Rolf Wilhelm. "Zur Vorgeschichte des Bänkelsangs." Österreichisches Volksliedwerk, *Jahrbuch* 21 (1972): 78–92.

Breneman, Bren, and Breneman, Lucille N. *Once Upon a Time: A Storytelling Handbook*. Chicago: Nelson-Hall, 1983.

Briggs, Nancy E., and Wagner, Joseph A. *Children's Literature through Storytelling Drama*. 2nd ed. Dubuque: W. C. Brown Co., 1979.

Brinkley, F., ed. *Japan Described and Illustrated by the Japanese*. Written by eminent Japanese authorities and scholars. 10 vols. Boston: J. B. Millet Co., 1897.

Brinkmann, Otto. *Das Erzahlen in einer Dorfgemeinschaft.* Veröffentlichungen der Volkskundlichen Komission des Provinzialinstituts für Westfalische Landes- und Volkskunde. Erste Reihe, Heft 4. Münster: Aschendorffschen Verlagsbuchhandlung, 1931.

Bruford, Alan. *Gaelic Folktales and Medieval Romances.* Dublin: Folklore of Ireland Society, 1969.

Brunvand, Jan Harold. *Folklore: A Study and Research Guide.* New York: St. Martin's Press, 1976.

————. *The Choking Doberman and Other Urban Folktales.* New York: W. W. Norton, 1984.

————. *The Vanishing Hitchhiker.* New York: W. W. Norton, 1981.

Bryant, Sara Cone. *How to Tell Stories to Children.* Boston: Houghton Miffln, 1905; Detroit: Gale Research Co., 1973.

Burns, Allen F. *An Epoch of Miracles: Oral Literature of the Yucatec Maya.* Austin: Univ. of Texas Pr., 1983.

Burrell, Arthur. *A Guide to Storytelling.* London: Isaac Pitman & Sons, 1926; New York: Gryphon Books, 1971.

Bynum, David E. "The Generic Nature of Oral Epic Poetry." In *Folklore Genres,* ed. by Dan Ben-Amos, pp. 35–58. Austin: Univ. of Texas Pr., 1976.

Cachia, Pierre. "Social Values Reflected in Egyptian Popular Ballads." In *Studies in Modern Arabic Literature,* ed. by R. C. Ostler. Warminster: Aris and Phillips, 1975.

Calame-Griaule, Geneviève. "Pour une étude des gestes narratifs." In her *Langage et Culture Africaines: Essais d'Ethnolinguistique,* pp. 303–359. Paris: Maspero, 1977.

Caluwe, Gert de. *Vertellen en focaliseren.* Seminare voor Duitse Taalkunde. Gent: Studia Germanica Gandensia, 1985.

Camara, Laye. *The Guardian of the Word.* Tr. from the French by James Kirkup. New York: Vintage, 1984.

Camara, Sory. *Gens de la Parole: Essai sur la Condition et le Rôle des Griots dans la Societé Malinke.* Paris & The Hague: Mouton, 1976.

Cammann, Alfred. *Westpreussische Märchen.* Fabula. Supplement Series, Reihe A, Band 3. Berlin: W. de Gruyter, 1961.

Campbell, J. F. *Popular Tales of the West Highlands,* vol. 1. London: Alexander Gardner, 1890.

Campbell, Marie. *Tales from the Cloud-Walking Country.* Bloomington: Indiana Univ. Pr., 1958.

Cardinall, Allan Wolsey. *Tales Told in Togoland.* Oxford Univ. Pr., 1931; Westport, Conn.: Negro Universities Pr., 1970.

Carlson, Ann. *Early Childhood Literature Sharing Programs in Libraries.* Hamden, Conn.: Library Professional Publications, 1985.

Carlson, Ruth Kearney. *Folklore and Folktales Around the World.* Perspectives in Reading 15. Newark, Del.: International Reading Assn.,1972.

Carmichael, Alexander. *Carmina Gadelica,* 2nd ed. Edinburgh and London: Oliver and Boyd, 1928.

Carnegie Library. *Story Hour, 1915–16.* Atlanta, Ga.: Carnegie Library, 1915.

Carnegie Library of Pittsburgh. *Story Hour Courses for Children from Greek Myths, the "Iliad" and the "Odyssey."* Pittsburgh: Carnegie Library, 1906.

Carpenter, Inta Gale. *A Latvian Storyteller: the Repertoire of Janis Plavnieks.* New York: Arno, 1980.

Carvalho-Neto, Paulo de. *The Concept of Folklore.* Tr. by Jacques M. P. Wilson. Univ. of Miami Pr., 1965.

————. *Folklore and Psychoanalysis.* Tr. by Jacques M. P. Wilson. Coral Gables: Univ. of Miami Pr., 1972.

Cassel, Paulus S. *Aus Literatur und Symbolik.* Leipzig: W. Friedrich, 1884.

Cejpek, Jiří. "Iranian Folk Literature." In *History of Iranian Literature,* ed. by Jan Rypka. Dordrecht, Holland: D. Reidel Pub. Co., 1956.

Centner, Th. H. *L'enfant africain et ses jeux dans le cadre de la vie traditionelle au Katanga.* Elizabethville: CEPSI, 1963.

Cerulli, Enrico. *The Folk-Literature of the Galla of Southern Abyssinia.* Harvard African Studies, 3. Varia Africana 3. Harvard Univ. Pr., 1922.

Chadwick, H. Munro, and Chadwick, Nora Kershaw. *The Growth of Literature.* 3 vols. Cambridge Univ. Pr., 1932–1940.

Chadwick, Nora Kershaw. *Russian Heroic Poetry.* Cambridge Univ. Pr., 1932.

Chamberlin, Candace McDowell. "The Pre-School Story Hour." *Library Journal* 69 (November 1, 1944): 927–928.

Chambers, Dewey W. *The Oral Tradition; Storytelling and Creative Drama.* 2nd ed. Dubuque: Wm. C. Brown Co., 1977.

Chandler, Anna Curtis. "Museum Story Hours." *The Storytellers' Magazine* 5 (1917): 381–384.

Chang, Duk-soon. *The Folk Treasury of Korea: Sources in Myth, Legend and Folktale.* Seoul: Society of Korean Oral Literature, 1970.

Chatelain, Heli. *Folktales of Angola.* American Folklore Society, Memoirs, 1. Boston: Houghton Mifflin, 1894.

Chaudhury, P. C. Roy. *Folk Tales of Bihar.* New Delhi: Sahitya Akademi, 1968.

Chautauqua Library School. *Handbook and Register 1901–1910.* Chautauqua, N.Y., 1911.

"Children Like Pictures: The Wagko Story Hour Stimulates the Child's Interest." *Publisher's Weekly* 126 (Aug. 25, 1934): 589.

Chodzko, Alexander. *Specimens of the Popular Poetry of Persia as Found in the Adventures and Improvisations of Kurroglu.* . . . London: 1842.

Christiansen, Reidar Thoralf. *Folktales of Norway.* Univ. of Chicago Pr., 1964.

Clanchy, M. T. *From Memory to Written Record; England 1066–1307.* Cambridge: Harvard Univ. Pr., 1979.

Clark, Ella E. *Indian Legends from the Northern Rockies.* Norman: Univ. of Oklahoma Pr., 1966.

Clark, John Pepper. *The Ozidi Saga.* Coll. and transcribed from the Ijo of Okabou Ojobolo. Ibadan Univ. Pr., 1977.

Clarke, Elizabeth Porter. "Storytelling, Reading Aloud and Other Special Features of Work in Children's Rooms." *Library Journal* 27 (April 1902): 189–190.

Clarke, Kenneth, and Clarke, Mary. *A Concise Dictionary of Folklore.* Bowling Green: Kentucky Folklore Society, 1965.

———. *Introducing Folklore.* New York: Holt, Rinehart and Winston, 1965.

Coles, Robert. *The Call of Stories.* Boston: Houghton Mifflin, 1989.

Colum, Padraic. *A Treasury of Irish Folklore.* New York: Crown, 1967.

Colwell, Eileen H. *Storytelling.* London: Bodley Head, 1980.

"Competencies for Librarians Serving Children in Public Libraries." *Journal of Youth Services in Libraries* 2, 3 (Spring 1989): 219–223.

Connelly, Bridget. *Arab Folk Epic and Identity.* Berkeley: Univ. of California Pr., 1986.

Constantino, Giuseppe et al. *Cuento Therapy: Folktales as a Culturally Sensitive Psychotherapy for Puerto Rican Children.* New York: Fordham Univ., Hispanic Research Center, 1985. (ERIC Ed. 257–902)

Coomaraswamy, Ananda. "Picture Showmen." *Indian Historical Quarterly* 5, no. 2 (June 1929): 182–187.

Cope, Trevor. *Izibongo: Zulu Praise Poems.* Oxford Library of African Literature. Oxford Univ. Pr., 1968.

Corkery, Daniel. "The Bardic Schools of Munster." *The Blarney Annual* 1 (1948): 19–24.

Cormac. *Sanas Chormaic. Cormac's Glossary.* Tr. and annotated by John O'Donovan. Calcutta and Dublin: The Celtic Society, 1868.

Corrigan, Adeline. "The Next Step—the Picture Book Hour." *Library Journal* 81 (September 15, 1956): 2014–2016.

Cosentino, Donald. *Defiant Maids and Stubborn Farmers; Tradition and Invention in Mende Story Performance.* Cambridge Univ. Press, 1982.

Coupe, William A. *The German Illustrated Broadsheet in the Seventeenth Century.* Bibliotheca Bibliographica Aureliana, 17. Baden-Baden: Heitz, 1966–1967.

Courlander, Harold. *The Drum and the Hoe: Life and Lore of the Haitian People.* Berkeley: Univ. of California, 1960.

———. *A Treasury of African Folklore.* New York: Crown, 1975.

Cousins, Norman. *Anatomy of an Illness as Perceived by the Patient: Reflections on Healing and Regeneration.* New York: W. W. Norton, 1979.

Cowell, E. B., and Thomas, F. W. *The Harsa-Carita of Bana.* Oriental Translation Fund, New Series 2, 8. London: Royal Asiatic Society, 1897.

Craigie, William A. *Icelandic Sagas.* Cambridge Manuals of Science and Literature. Cambridge Univ. Press, 1913.

Crane, Thomas Frederick. *The Exempla or Illustrative Stories from the "Sermones Vulgares" of Jacques de Vitry.* London: D. Nutt for the Folk-lore Society, 1890.

Cronise, Florence M., and Ward, Henry W. *Cunnie Rabbit, Mr. Spider and the Other Beef: West African Folk Tales.* New York: E. P. Dutton, 1903; Chicago: Afro-Am Press, 1969.

Crosby, Ruth. "Oral Delivery in the Middle Ages." *Speculum* 11 (1936): 88–110.

Crowley, Daniel J. *I Could Talk Old-Story Good: Creativity in Bahamian Folklore.* Publications in Folklore Studies, 17. Berkeley: Univ. of California Pr., 1966.

Cundiff, Ruby Ethel, and Webb, Barbara. *Storytelling for You: A Handbook of Help for Storytellers Everywhere.* Yellow Springs, Oh.: Antioch Pr., 1957.

Damane, M., and Sanders, P. B. *Lithoko: Sotho Praise-Poems.* Oxford Library of African Literature. Oxford Univ. Pr., 1974.

Dana, John Cotton. "Storytelling in Libraries." *Public Libraries* 13 (November 1908): 349–350.

Dance, Daryl C. *Folklore from Contemporary Jamaicans.* Illus. by Murry N. DePillars. Knoxville: Univ. of Tennessee Pr., 1985.

Darmesteter, James. *Chants populaires des Afghans.* Paris: E. Leroux, 1888–1890.

Darnell, Regna. "Correlates of Cree Narrative Performance." In *Explorations in the Ethnography of Speaking,* ed. by Richard Bauman and Joel Sherzer, pp. 315–336, 464–467. Cambridge Univ. Pr., 1974.

Das, Kajal Kumar. *Burrakatha of Andhra Pradesh.* New Delhi: IIMC, 1980.

Das, Kunjabehari. *A Study of Orissan Folklore.* Santiniketan, India: Visvabharati, 1953.

Davis, Jack. "Story Traditions in Australian Aboriginal Cultures." In *Through Folklore to Literature,* ed. by Maurice Saxby, pp. 121–132. Sydney: IBBY Australia, 1979.

Davis, Betty J. *The Storytellers in Marguerite de Navarre's Heptameron.* Lexington, Ky.: French Forum Publishers, 1978.

Davis, Natalie Zemon. *Fiction in the Archives.* Palo Alto: Stanford Univ. Press, 1987.

Day, Cyrus Lawrence. *Quipus and Witches Knots; the Role of the Knot in Primitive and Ancient Cultures.* Lawrence: Univ. of Kansas Pr., 1967.

Day, Lal Behari. *Bengal Peasant Life; Folk-Tales of Bengal; Recollections of My School Days.* Calcutta: Editions Indian, 1969.

Dayrell, Elphinstone. *Folk Stories from Southern Nigeria West Africa.* London: Longmans, Green, 1910.

D'Da, Pierre. *Le conte africain et l'éducation.* Paris: L'Harmattan, 1984.

DeFrancis, John. *Visible Speech: The Diverse Oneness of Writing Systems.* Honolulu: Univ. of Hawaii Pr., 1989.

Dégh, Linda. "Folk Narrative." *In Folklore and Folklife,* ed. by Richard Dorson, pp. 53–83. Univ. of Chicago Pr., 1972.

————. *Folktales and Society: Storytelling in a Hungarian Peasant Community.* Tr. from the German by Emily M. Schlossberger. Bloomington: Indiana Univ. Pr., 1969.

————, ed. *Studies in East European Folk Narrative.* Publications, 30. Philadelphia: American Folklore Society, 1978.

————, and Vázsonyi, Andrew. "Legend and Belief." In *Folklore Genres,* ed. by Dan Ben-Amos, pp. 93–123. Austin: Univ. of Texas Pr., 1976.

Delargy, James H. *The Gaelic Storyteller.* Rhys Memorial Lecture for 1945. *Proceedings of the British Academy,* 31. London: The Academy, 1945.

Demiéville, Paul. "Translations of Buddhist Literature" and "Tun-huang Texts." In *Dictionary of Oriental Literatures,* ed. by Jaroslav Průšek and Zbigniew Słupski, vol. 1, pp. 174–175, 185–187. New York: Basic Books, 1974.

Deng, Francis Mading. *Dinka Folktales; African Stories from the Sudan.* New York: Africana Pub. Co., 1974.

Desroches-Noblecourt, Christiane. *Ancient Egypt.* Greenwich, Conn.: New York Graphic Society, 1960.

Dewdney, Selwyn. *The Sacred Scrolls of the Southern Ojibway.* Univ. of Toronto Press for the Glenbow-Alberta Institute, 1975.

DeWit, Dorothy. *Children's Faces Looking Up: Program Building for the Storyteller.* Chicago: American Library Association, 1979.

Dias, Margot. *Instrumentos Musicais de Moçambique.* Lisbon: Instituto de Investigação Cientifica Tropical, Centro de Antropologia Cultural e Social, 1986.

Dickey, Lyle A. *String Figures from Hawaii.* Bernice P. Bishop Museum, Bulletin 54. Honolulu: The Museum, 1927.

Diop, Birago. *Tales of Amadou Koumba.* Tr. by Dorothy S. Blair. Oxford Library of African Literature. Oxford Univ. Pr., 1966.

Dobie, J. Frank. "Storytellers I Have Known." In *Singers and Storytellers,* by Mody C. Boatright and others, pp. 3–29. Dallas: Southern Methodist Univ. Pr., 1961.

Doke, Clement M. *Lamba Folk-lore*. Memoirs, 20. New York: American Folklore Society, 1927.

Dorson, Richard. *Bloodstoppers and Bearwalkers: Folk Traditions of the Upper Peninsula*. Cambridge: Harvard Univ. Pr., 1952.

———. *Buying the Wind*. Univ. of Chicago Pr., 1964.

———. "Oral Styles of American Folk Narrators." In his *Folklore: Selected Essays*, pp. 99–146. Bloomington: Indiana Univ. Pr., 1972.

———, ed. *African Folklore*. Bloomington: Indiana Univ. Pr., 1972.

———, ed. *Folktales Told around the World*. Univ. of Chicago Pr., 1975.

Dournes, Jacques. "Scènes et récits de vie avec des conteurs indochinois." *Cahiers de Littérature Orale* 11 (1982): 135–143.

Dousman, Mary Ella. "Children's Departments." *Library Journal* 21 (September 1896): 406–408.

Dundes, Alan. "The Devolutionary Premise in Folklore Theory." *Journal of the Folklore Institute* 6 (1969): 5–19.

———. *The Study of Folklore*. New York: Prentice Hall, 1965.

Dunn, Charles James. *The Early Japanese Puppet Drama*. London: Luzac and Co., 1966.

Durán, Fray Diego. *Book of the Gods and Rites* and *The Ancient Calendar*. Tr. and ed. by Fernando Horcasitas and Doris Heyden. Norman: Univ. of Oklahoma Pr., 1971.

East, Rupert. *Akiga's Story; the Tiv Tribe As Seen By One of Its Members*. Oxford Univ. Pr., 1965. (First pub. 1939.)

Eberhard, Wolfram. *Folktales of China*. Univ. of Chicago Pr., 1965.

———. *Minstrel Tales from Southeastern Turkey*. Folklore Studies, 5. Berkeley: Univ. of California Pr., 1955.

———. "Notes on Chinese Storytellers." *Fabula* [Berlin] 11 (1970): 1–31.

———. *Studies in Taiwanese Folktales*. Asian Folklore and Social Life Monographs, 1. Taiwan: Orient Cultural Service, 1970.

Edgar, Frank. *Hausa Tales and Traditions*. Tr. and ed. from the Hausa by Neil Skinner, vol. 1. New York: Africana Pub. Co., 1969. (First pub. 1911.)

Egan, Kieran. *Teaching as Storytelling: An Alternative Approach to Teaching and Curriculum in the Elementary School*. Univ. of Chicago Pr., 1989.

Egblewogbe, E. Y. *Games and Songs as Education Media: A Case Study among the Ewes of Ghana*. Accra: Ghana Pub. Corp., 1975.

Eggleston, Margaret W. *The Use of the Story in Religious Education*. New York: G. H. Doran Co., 1920.

*Egyptian Literature*. Tr. and ed. by Epiphanius Wilson. London and New York: Colonial Pr., 1901.

Ehrlich, Konrad, ed. *Erzählen in Alltag*. Frankfurt/Main: Suhrkamp, 1980.

Elbert, Samuel H., and Monberg, Torben. *From the Two Canoes: Oral Traditions of Rennell and Bellona Islands.* Honolulu: Univ. of Hawaii; Copenhagen: Danish National Museum, 1965.

Eliot, T. S. "Religion and Literature." In his *Essays, Ancient and Modern.* London: Faber and Faber, 1936.

Elkin, Adolphus P.; Berndt, Catherine; and Berndt, Ronald. *Art in Arnheim Land.* Univ. of Chicago Pr., 1950.

Ellis, A. B. *The Yoruba-Speaking Peoples of the Slave Coast of West Africa.* London: 1894.

Ellis, Catherine J. *Aboriginal Music: Cross Cultural Experiences from South Australia.* St. Lucia: Univ. of Queensland Pr., 1985.

Emeneau, M. B. "Oral Poets of South India: the Todas." In *Traditional India*, ed. by Milton Singer, pp. 106–118. Philadelphia: American Folklore Society, 1959.

Emerson, Laura S. *Storytelling, the Art and the Purpose: A Manual on How to Tell Stories with Fifteen Typical Stories to Tell.* Grand Rapids, Mich.: Zondervan, 1959.

Ennis, Merlin. *Umbundu: Folktales from Angola.* Boston: Beacon Press, 1962.

Erickson, Joan. *Mata ni pachedi: A Book on the Temple Cloth of the Mother Goddess.* Ahmedabad: National Institute of Design, 1968.

Evans-Pritchard, E. E. *The Zande Trickster.* Oxford Library of African Literature. Oxford Univ. Pr., 1967.

Faik, Ala Yahya. "Theatrical Elements in Religious Storytelling of Medieval Islamic Culture." Ph.D. dissertation, University of Michigan, 1986.

*Fairy Tales and Legends from Romania.* Tr. by Ioana Sturdza, and others. New York: Twayne, 1972.

Falassi, Alessandro. *Folklore by the Fireside: Text and Context of the Tuscan Veglia.* Austin: Univ. of Texas Pr., 1980.

Fannin, Gwendolyn Marie. "A Resume of the History, Growth and Development of the Story Hour in the New York Public Library." Master's thesis, Atlanta University, School of Library Service, 1958.

Fanua, Tupou Posesi. *Po Fananga. Folktales of Tonga.* San Diego: Tofua Pr., 1975.

Farago, Jozsef. "Storytellers with Rich Repertoires." *Acta Ethnographica* 20 (1971): 439–443.

Faral, Edmond. *Les jongleurs en France au Moyen Age.* Paris: 1910; New York: Burt Franklin, 1970.

Farrell, Catherine Horne. *Word Weaving: A Guide to Storytelling.* San Francisco: Zellerbach Family Fund, 1983.

Fehr, Hans. *Massenkunst im 16. Jahrhundert.* Denkmale der Volkskunst, vol. 1. Berlin: Herbert Stubenrauch, 1924.

Felkin, Robert W. "Notes on the Waganda Tribe of Central Africa." In *Proceed-*

*ings, 1885–1886*, Royal Society of Edinburgh, pp. 699–770. Edinburgh: The Society, 1887.

[Ferguson, Henry, and Ferguson, Joan] "Textiles That Tell a Story." Series of three sheets accompanying cloths. Thompson, Conn.: InterCulture Associates, n.d.

Feynman, Richard P. "The Pleasure of Finding Things Out." Transcript, Program No. 1002, NOVA. Boston: WGBH, 1982.

Filstrup, Jane Merrill. "The Enchanted Cradle: Early Storytelling in Boston." *Horn Book* 52 (December 1976): 601–610.

Fine, Elizabeth C. *The Folklore Text*. Bloomington: Indiana Univ. Pr., 1984.

Finnegan, Ruth. *Oral Literature in Africa*. Oxford Library of African Literature. Oxford Univ. Pr., 1970.

Fitz-Gerald, Carolyn; and Gunter, Dolores. *Creative Storytelling, for Library and Teacher Aides*. Dallas: Leslie Pr., 1971.

Flerina, E. A., and Shabad, E. *Rasskazyvanie dlia doshkol'nogo vozrasta*. Moscow, 1937.

Flower, Robin. *The Western Island or the Great Blasket*. Oxford Univ. Pr., 1945.

Foley, John Miles. *Oral-Formulaic Theory and Research: An Introduction and Annotated Bibliography*. New York: Garland Books, 1985.

Forbes, Alexander Kinloch. *Rās Mālā or Hindu Annals of the Province of Goozerat in Western India*. 2 vols. Oxford Univ. Pr., 1924. (First pub. 1856.)

Foster, F. Marie. *A Round of Picture Book Programs*. Albany: Division of Adult Education and Library Extension, N.Y. State Education Dept., [1944].

Frankfort, Henri. *The Art and Architecture of the Ancient Orient*. Baltimore: Penguin Books, 1969.

Freeman, Douglas Southall. "Foreword" to *A Treasury of Southern Folklore*, ed. by B. A. Botkin. New York: Crown, 1949.

Freeman, Mark. "Tall Tales." *San Francisco Examiner*, September 15, 1985.

Frere, Mary. *Hindoo Fairy Legends (Old Deccan Days)*. New York: Dover, 1967. (First pub. 1881.)

Fretz, Rachel I. "Storytelling among the Chokwe of Zaire: Narrating Skill and Listener Responses." Ph.D. dissertation, Univ. of California at Los Angeles, 1987.

Fretz-Yoder, Rachel I. "Mwanoka, a Good Storyteller, 'Pours on the Oil.'" *Folklore and Mythology Studies* 5 (Spring 1981): 20–33.

Frey, Jaroslav. *Práce s dětským čtenářem*. Prague: Osveta, Vyd. Ministerstva informaci a osvety, 1951.

Frisbie, Charlotte J., and McAllester, David P. *Navajo Blessingway Singer: The Autobiography of Frank Mitchell 1881–1967*. Tucson: Univ. of Arizona Pr., 1978.

Frost, Mary. "Inshimi and imilumbe: structural expectation in Bemba oral imaginative performances." Ph.D. dissertation, University of Wisconsin, 1977.

Gardner, Richard A. *Therapeutic Communication with Children: The Mutual Storytelling Technique.* New York: Jason Aronson, 1971.

Gaster, Moses. *The Exempla of the Rabbis.* London and Leipzig: Asia Publishing Co., 1924.

Gaster, Theodor H. *The Oldest Stories in the World.* New York: Viking, 1952.

Gee, James Paul. "Orality and Literacy: From *The Savage Mind* to *Ways with Words.*" *TESOL Quarterly* 20, 4, (1986): 719–746.

Georges, Robert A. "Toward an Understanding of Storytelling Events." *Journal of American Folklore* 82 (1969): 313–328.

Gerhardsson, Birger. *Memory and Manuscript: Oral Tradition and Written Transmission in Rabbinic Judaism and Early Christianity.* Tr. by Eric J. Sharpe. Lund: C. W. K. Gleerup; Copenhagen: Ejnar Munksgaard, 1961.

Gerhardt, Mia I. *The Art of Storytelling.* Leiden: E. J. Brill, 1963.

*Gesta Romanorum.* Ed. by S. J. Heritage. Early English Text Series, Extra Series, vol. 33. Reprint of 1879 ed. Millwood, N.Y.: Kraus Reprint and Periodicals, 1962.

Gilson, J. P. "Introduction," in *An Exultet Roll Illuminated in the XIth Century at the Abbey of Monte Cassino.* Reproduced from Add. Ms. 30337. London: British Museum, 1929.

Gingerich, Robert. "The Story of the Storytelling Drum." *National Storytelling Journal* 5, 3 (Fall 1988): 6–7.

Giteau, Madeleine. *Khmer Sculpture and the Angkor Civilization.* New York: Harry Abrams, 1965.

Glassie, Henry. *Passing the Time in Ballymenone; Culture and History of an Ulster Community.* Philadelphia: Univ. of Pennsylvania Pr., 1982.

Gmelch, George, and Kroup, Ben. *To Shorten the Road.* Toronto: Macmillan of Canada, 1978.

Goethe, Johann Wolfgang von. *Wilhelm Meister's Theatralische Sendung,* vol. 51 of his *Werke.* Weimar, 1911.

Goldberg, Michael. *Theology and Narrative: A Critical Introduction.* Nashville: Abingdon, 1982.

Goldstein, Kenneth S. *A Guide for Field Workers in Folklore.* Hatboro, Pa.: American Folklore Society, 1964.

Goldziher, Ignaz. *Muslim Studies.* 2 vols. London: Allen & Unwin, 1971.

Goodman, James S. "My Grandpa's Name is Avraham." *National Storytelling Journal* 2, 4 (Fall 1985): 12.

Goodwin, Grenville. *Myths and Tales of the White Mountain Apache.* Memoirs, 33. New York: American Folklore Society, 1939.

Gorer, Geoffrey. *Himalayan Village: An Account of the Lepchas of Sikkim.* 2nd ed. New York: Basic Books, 1967. (First pub. 1938.)

Gorham, Rex. *The Folkways of Brazil.* New York: The New York Public Library, 1944.

Gorog, Veronika. "Qui Conte en France Aujourd'hui?" *Cahiers de Littérature Orale* 11 (1982): 95–116.

Gossen, Gary H. *Chamulas in the World of the Sun: Time and Space in a Maya Oral Tradition.* Cambridge, Harvard Univ. Pr., 1974.

Graham, David Crockett. *Songs and Stories of the Ch'uan Miao.* Smithsonian Institution, Miscellaneous Collections, vol. 123, no. 1. Washington, D. C.: The Institution, 1954.

Grant, James Augustus. *A Walk Across Africa.* Edinborough and London: William Blackwood, 1864.

Greene, Ellin, and Shannon, George. *Storytelling: A Selected, Annotated Bibliography.* New York: Garland, 1986.

Groeneveldt, Willem Pieter. *Notes on the Malay Archipelago and Malacca. Verhandelingen,* 39. Djakarta: Bataviaasch Genootschap van Kunsten en Wetenschappen, 1880.

Gross, Elizabeth Henry. *Public Library Service to Children.* Dobbs Ferry: Oceana Publications, 1967.

Guirma, Frederic. *Tales of Mogho.* Foreword by Elliott P. Skinner. New York: Macmillan, 1971.

Guma, S. M. *The Form, Content and Technique of Traditional Literature in Southern Sotho.* Hiddingh-Currie Publications, Univ. of South Africa, no. 8. Pretoria: J. L. Van Schaik, 1967.

Gunda, Bela. "Die Funktion des Märchens in der Gemeinschaft der Zigeuner." *Fabula* [Berlin] 6 (1964): 95–107.

Gunkel, Hermann. *Das Märchen im Alten Testament.* Die Religion des Alten Testaments, 2nd series, 23/6. Tübingen: J. S. B. Mohr, 1921.

Gwyndaf, Robin. "The Welsh Folk Narrative Tradition; Continuity and Adaptation." *Folk Life* [Leeds] 26 (1987–1988): 78–100.

Gymer, Rose. "Storytelling in the Cleveland Public Library." *ALA Bulletin* 3 (1909): 417–420.

Hadel, Richard E. "Five Versions of the Riding Horse Tale: A Comparative Study." *Folklore Annual* [Austin, Tx.] 2 (1970): 1–22.

Haiding, Karl. *Von der Gebärdensprache der Märchenerzähler.* Folklore Fellows Communications, no. 155. Helsinki, 1955.

Hall, Edwin S. *The Eskimo Storyteller.* Illus. by Clair Fejes. Knoxville: Univ. of Tennessee Pr., 1975.

Hamilton, Jim. "State Parks and Storytelling." *National Storytelling Journal* 3, 2 (Spring 1986): 7–9.

Handy, E. S. Craighill. *History and Culture in the Society Islands.* Bernice P. Bishop Museum, Bulletin 79. Honolulu: The Museum, 1930.

———. *Marquesan Legends.* Bernice P. Bishop Museum, Bulletin 69. Honolulu: The Museum, 1930.

Hannan, Jerome D. *Teacher Tells a Story: Story-lessons in conduct and religion for every day in the school year.* . . . Cincinnati: Benziger Bros., 1925.

Hardendorff, Jeanne B. "Storytelling and the Story Hour." *Library Trends* 12 (July 1963): 52–63.

Hardiman, James. *Irish Minstrelsy or Bardic Remains of Ireland.* 2 vols. London: J. Robins, 1831.

Harrell, John. *Origins and Early Traditions of Storytelling.* Kensington, Ca.: York House, 1983.

Harries, Lyndon. *Swahili Poetry.* Oxford Univ. Pr., 1962.

Harrison, Harry P. and Detzer, Karl. *Culture under Canvas: The Story of the Tent Chautauqua.* New York: Hastings House, 1958.

Härtel, Herbert, and Yaldiz, Marianne. *Along the Ancient Silk Routes; Central Asian Art from the West Berlin Museums.* New York: Metropolitan Museum of Art, 1982.

Hartland, Edwin Sidney. *The Science of Fairy Tales.* New York: Fred A. Stokes, [c.1891].

Havelock, Eric A. *The Literate Revolution in Greece and its Cultural Consequences.* Princeton Univ. Pr., 1982.

———. *The Muse Learns to Write.* New Haven: Yale Univ. Pr., 1986.

Haviland, Virginia. *Ruth Sawyer.* New York: Henry Z. Walck, 1965.

Hazeltine, Alice I. "Storytelling in the Carnegie Library of Pittsburgh." *ALA Bulletin* 3 (1909):413–415.

Heath, R. "Storytelling in All Ages." *Leisure Hour* 34 (1885): 199ff; 273ff.

Heath, Shirley Brice. *Ways with Words; Language, Life, and Work in Communities and Classrooms.* Cambridge Univ. Pr., 1983.

Hedgbeth, Llewellyn Hubbard. "Extant American Panoramas: Moving Entertainments of the Nineteenth Century." Ph.D. dissertation, New York University, 1977.

Henssen, Gottfried. *Überlieferung und persönlichkeit: Die Erzählung und Lieder des Egbert Gerrits.* Münster i. W.: Aschendorffsche Verlagsbuchhandlung, 1951.

Herman, Gail N. *Storytelling: A Triad in the Arts.* Mansfield Center, Ct.: Creative Learning Press, 1986.

Herskovits, Melville J., and Herskovits, Frances S. *Dahomean Narrative.* Evanston, Il.: Northwestern Univ. Pr., 1958.

———. *Suriname Folk Lore.* New York: Columbia Univ. Pr., 1936.

Herzfeld, Michael. *The Poetics of Mankind: Contest and Identity in a Cretan Mountain Village.* Princeton Univ. Pr., 1985.

Heusch, Luc de. *Le Roi ivre ou l'origine de l'État.* Paris: Gallimard, 1972. English tr. by Roy Willis: *The Drunken King or The Origin of the State.* Bloomington: Indiana Univ. Pr., 1982.

Hill, Janet. *Children Are People: The Librarian in the Community.* London: Hamish Hamilton, 1973.

Hodne, Bjarne. *Eventyret og tradisjonsbaererne: eventyrfortellere i en Telemarksbygd.* Oslo: Universitetsforlaget, 1979.

Hoffman, John C. *Law, Freedom, and Story: the Role of Narrative in Therapy, Society and Faith.* Waterloo, Ontario: Wilfred Laurier University Pr., 1986.

Hollis, A. C. *The Nandi: Their Language and Folklore.* Oxford Univ. Pr., 1909.

Holmer, Nils M., and Wassen, S. Henry. *The Complete Mu-Igala in Picture Writing: A Native Record of a Cuna Indian Medicine Song.* Etnologiske Studier, 21. Goteborg: Etnografiska Museum, 1953.

Holmes, Urban Tigner. *A History of Old French Literature from the Origins to 1300.* New York: F. S. Crofts, 1938.

Hoogasian-Villa, Susie, ed. *100 Armenian Tales and Their Folkloristic Relevance.* Detroit: Wayne State Univ. Pr., 1966.

Hopkins, E. Washburn. *India Old and New.* New York: Scribner's, 1901.

Horio, S., and Inaba, K., eds. *Kamishibai.* Tokyo: Doshinsha, 1972.

Hornell, James. *String Figures from Fiji and Western Polynesia.* Bernice P. Bishop Museum, Bulletin 39. Honolulu: The Museum, 1927.

Hrdličková, Věna. "The Chinese Storytellers and Singers of Ballads: Their Performances and Storytelling Techniques." Asiatic Society of Japan, *Transactions*, 3rd ser., vol. 10, pp. 97–115. Tokyo: The Society, 1968.

―――. "The First Translations of Buddhist Sutras in Chinese Literature and Their Place in the Development of Storytelling." *Archiv Orientální* 26 (1958): 114–144.

―――. "Japanese Professional Storytellers." In *Folklore Genres*, ed. by Dan Ben-Amos, pp. 171–190. Austin: Univ. of Texas Pr., 1976.

―――. "The Professional Training of Chinese Storytellers and the Storytellers' Guilds." *Archiv Orientální* 33 (1965): 225–248.

―――. "Some Questions Connected with *Tun-huang pien-wen.*" *Archiv Orientální* 30 (1962): 211–230.

―――. "The Zenza, the Storyteller's Apprentice." International Conference of Orientalists in Japan, *Transactions* 13 (1968): 31–41.

Htin Aung, Maung. *Burmese Monk's Tales.* New York: Columbia Univ. Pr., 1966.

Huizinga, Johan. *Homo Ludens.* Boston: Beacon Pr., 1955.

Huls, Ardis. "Pre-school Story Hour." *Wilson Library Bulletin* 16, 9 (May 1942): 726–727, 730.

Hultkrantz, Åke. "Religious Aspects of the Wind River Shoshoni Folk Literature." In *Culture in History*, ed. by Stanley Diamond, pp. 552–569. Pub. for Brandeis Univ. by Columbia Univ. Pr., 1960.

Hürlimann, Bettina. *Three Centuries of Children's Books in Europe.* Tr. from the German by Brian Alderson. Oxford Univ. Pr., 1967.

Hurreiz, Sayyid. "Afro-Arab Relations in the Sudanese Folktale." In *African Folklore*, ed. by Richard Dorson, pp. 157–163. Bloomington: Indiana Univ. Pr., 1972.

Hymes, Dell. *"In Vain I Tried to Tell You": Essays in Native American Ethnopoetics.* Philadelphia: Univ. of Pennsylvania Pr., 1981.

————. "Models of the Interaction of Language and Social Life." In *Directions in Sociolinguistics*, ed. by J. J. Gumperz and Dell Hymes, pp. 35–71. New York: Holt, Rinehart and Winston, 1972.

Ibn al-Jawzī, Abū al-Faraj 'Abd al-Rahmān ibn 'Alī. *Kitāb al quṣṣāṣ wa- al-mudhakkirīn.* Tr. and annotated by Merlin L. Swartz. Recherches de l'Institut de Lettres Orientales, Série 1, Pensée Arabe et Musulmane, Tome 47. Beirut: Dar el-Machreq, [1971].

Ives, Edward D. *The Tape-recorded Interview: A Manual for Field Workers in Folklore and Oral History.* Rev. ed. Knoxville: Univ. of Tennessee, 1980.

Izard, Anne. " 'I Study Very Hard. I Thank You Very Much.' " *Top of the News* 29 (January 1973): 130–132.

Jackson, Kenneth Hurlstone. *The International Popular Tale and Early Welsh Tradition.* Cardiff: Univ. of Wales Pr., 1961.

————. *The Oldest Irish Tradition: A Window on the Iron Age.* The Rede Lecture. Cambridge Univ. Pr., 1964.

Jackson, Michael. *Allegories of the Wilderness: Ethics and Ambiguity in Kuranko Narratives.* Bloomington: Indiana Univ. Pr., 1982.

Jacobs, Melville. *The Content and Style of an Oral Literature: Clackamas Chinook Myths and Tales.* Univ. of Chicago Pr., 1959.

Jan, Isabelle. *On Children's Literature.* New York: Schocken, 1974.

Janda, Elsbeth, and Nötzoldt, Fritz. *Die Moritat vom Bänkelsang: oder das Lied der Strasse.* Munich: Ehrenwirth Verlag, 1959.

Jansen, William Hugh. "Classifying Performance in the Study of Verbal Folklore." In *Studies in Folklore*, ed. by W. Edson Richmond, pp. 110–118. Bloomington: Indiana Univ. Pr., 1957.

"Japan: Dirty Stories." *Newsweek* 81 (June 4, 1973): 51.

Jayne, Caroline Furness. *String Figures and How to Make Them: A Study of Cat's Cradle in Many Lands.* New York: Dover, 1962. (First pub. 1906.)

Johnson, Samuel. *The History of the Yorubas*. London: Routledge and Kegan Paul, 1921.

Johnston, H. A. S. *A Selection of Hausa Stories*. Oxford Univ. Pr., 1966.

Jolles, André. *Einfache Formen*, 2nd. ed. Tübingen: Max Niemeyer, 1958.

Jones, A. M. *African Music in Northern Rhodesia and Some Other Places*. Rhodes-Livingstone Museum, Occasional Papers, new series, 4. Livingstone: The Museum, 1958. (Originally issued as no. 2 in 1943.)

Jordan, A. C. "Tale, Teller and Audience." In *Proceedings of a Conference on African Languages and Literature, Northwestern University, April 28–30, 1966*, pp. 33–44. Evanston, Il.: Northwestern Univ., n.d.

———. *Tales from Southern Africa*. Illus. by Feni Dumile; foreword by Z. Pallo Jordan; intro. and commentaries by Harold Scheub. Berkeley: Univ. of California Pr., 1973.

Joshi, Om Prakash. *Painted Folklore and Folklore Painters of India*. Delhi: Concept Pub. Co., 1976.

Junod, Henri A. *The Life of a South African Tribe*. 2 vols. New York: University Books, 1962.

Kabira, Wanjiku Mukabi. *The Oral Artist*. Nairobi: Heinemann Educational Books, 1983.

Kagan, R. M. "Storytelling and Game Theory for Children in Placement." *Child Care* 11 (1982): 280–290.

Kako, Satoshi. "Kamishibai—the Unique Cultural Property of Japan." Tokyo Book Development Centre, *Newsletter* 8, 2 (September 1976): 6–7.

———. *Nihon Densho No Asobi Tokumon*. Tokyo: Fukuinkan Shoten, 1967.

Kamphoevener, Elsa Sophia von. *An Nachtfeuern der Karawan-Serail: Märchen und Geschichten Alttürkischer Nomaden*. 2 vols. Hamburg: Christian Wegner, 1956.

Kane, Alice. "The Changing Face of the Story Hour." *Ontario Library Review* 49 (August 1965): 141–142.

Kara, György. *Chants d'un Barde Mongol*. Budapest: Akadémiai Kiadó, 1970.

Kata, Koji. *Machi no jiyoden (Autobiography of a Street-Person)*. Tokyo: Bansei-sha, 1977.

Kelber, Werner. *The Oral and the Written Gospel*. Philadelphia: Fortress Pr., 1983.

Kennedy, Audrey. "History of the Boys and Girls Department of the Carnegie Library of Pittsburgh." Master's thesis, Carnegie Institute of Technology, 1949.

Ker, Annie. *Papuan Fairy Tales*. New York: Macmillan, 1910.

Keyes, Angela M. *Stories and Storytelling*. New York: D. Appleton, 1911.

Kiefer, Emma E. *Albert Wesselski and Recent Folktale Theories*. Bloomington: Indiana Univ. Pr., 1947.

Killip, Margaret. *The Folklore of the Isle of Man.* Totowa, N. J.: Rowman and Littlefield, 1976.

Kilson, Marion. *Royal Antelope and Spider. West African Mende Tales.* Cambridge: Langdon Associates, 1976.

Kingsley, Mary. *West African Studies,* 3rd. ed. New York: Barnes and Noble, 1964. (First pub. 1899.)

Kipury, Naomi. *Oral Literature of the Maasai.* Nairobi: Heinemann Educational Books, 1983.

Kirk, G. S. *Myth: Its Meaning and Functions in the Ancient and Other Cultures.* Cambridge Univ. Pr.; Berkeley: Univ. of California Pr., 1971.

————. *The Songs of Homer.* Cambridge Univ. Press, 1962.

Kirshenblatt-Gimblett, Barbara. "Traditional Storytelling in the Toronto Jewish Community: A Study in Performance and Creativity in an Immigrant Culture." Ph.D. dissertation, Indiana University, 1972.

Kita, Morio. *Nireke no Hitobito (The Nine Families).* Tokyo: Shinchosha,1964.

Knowles, James Hinton. *Folk-Tales of Kashmir.* London: Trubner, 1888.

Kramer, Fritz W. *Literature Among the Cuna Indians.* Etnologiska Studier, 30. Göteborg: Etnografiska Museum, 1970.

Kramer, S. N. *Sumerian Mythology.* Philadelphia: American Philosophical Society, 1944.

Kramrisch, Stella. *Unknown India: Ritual Art in Tribe and Village.* Philadelphia Museum of Art, 1968.

Krishna Iyer, L. K. Anantha. *The Cochin Tribes and Castes.* Vol. 2. Madras: Higgenbotham, 1912; New York: Johnson Reprint, 1969.

Kritzberg, Nathan. *The Structured Therapeutic Game Method of Child Analytic Psychotherapy.* Hicksville, N. Y.: Exposition Pr., 1975.

Küng, Hans. *On Being a Christian.* Tr. by Edward Quinn. New York: Doubleday, 1976.

Lacourcière, Luc. "Canada." In *Folktales Told around the World,* ed. by Richard Dorson, pp. 429–467. Univ. of Chicago Pr., 1975.

Lane, Edward William. *An Account of the Manners and Customs of the Modern Egyptians . . . ,* 5th ed. London: John Murray, 1871.

Lane, Marcia. "Between Words and Steel: The Story of the Amtrak Storytelling Odyssey." *National Storytelling Journal* 5, 3 (Fall 1988): 8–11.

Lapai, Suzan. "Burma." in *Folktales Told around the World,* ed. by Richard Dorson, pp. 277–286. University of Chicago Pr., 1975.

La Pin, Deirdre Ann. "Story, Medium and Masque: the Idea and Art of Yoruba Storytelling." Ph.D. dissertation, Univ. of Wisconsin, 1977.

La Rue, Abbé Charles de. *Essais historiques sur les bardes, les jongleurs et les trouvères normands et anglo-normands.* 3 vols. Caen: 1854.

Laughlin, Robert M. *Of Cabbages and Kings: Tales from Zinacantan.* Contributions to Anthropology, 23. Washington, D.C.: Smithsonian Institution Pr., 1977.

Law, Bimala Churn. *The Magadhas in Ancient India.* Royal Asiatic Society Monographs, 24. Calcutta: The Society, 1946.

Lawrence, C. et al. *Storytelling for Teachers and School Media Specialists.* Minneapolis: Denison, 1981.

Laya, Dioulde. "Tradition orale et recherche historique en Afrique: méthodes, réalisations, perspectives." *Journal of World History* 12, 4 (1970): 560–587.

*Leabhar na g-ceart or The Book of Rights.* Tr. by John O'Donovan. Dublin: The Celtic Society, 1847.

Leach, MacEdward. "Problems of Collecting Oral Literature." *Publications of the Modern Language Association* 77 (1972): 335–340.

Leach, Maria, and Fried, Jerome, eds. *Standard Dictionary of Folklore Mythology and Legend.* New York: Funk and Wagnalls, 1972.

Leakey, M. D., and Leakey, L. S. B. *Some String Figures from North East Angola.* Lisbon: Companhia de Diamentes de Angola, Servicos Culturais, 1949.

Lenz, Rudolfo. "Un grupo de consejos chilenas." *Revista de Folklore Chileno* 3 (1912): 1.

Lequeux-Gromaire, Paulette. *L'Enfant et le conte: du réel à l'imaginaire.* Paris: L'École, 1974.

Lestrange, Monique de. "Contes et legendes des Fulakunda du Badyar." *Études Guinéennes*, no. 7 (1951): 6–7.

Licht, Jacob. *Storytelling in the Bible.* Jerusalem: Magnes Pr., Hebrew Univ., 1978.

Liestøl, Knut. *The Origin of the Icelandic Family Sagas.* Instituttet for Sammenlignende Kulturforskning. Serie A. Forelesninger, 10. Oslo: H. Aschehoug & Co., 1930.

Lindblom, K. G. *String Figures in Africa.* Populara Etnologiska Skrifter, Smarre meddelanden, 9. Stockholm: Riksmuseets Etnografiska Avdelning, 1930.

Lindell, Kristina; Swahn, Jan Ojvind; and Tayamin, Damrong. *Folk Tales from Kammu: II, A Storyteller's Tales.* Scandinavian Institute of Asian Studies, 40. London: Curzon Pr., 1980.

Livo, Norma J, and Rietz, Sandra A. *Storytelling Activities.* Littleton, Co.: Libraries Unlimited, 1987.

———. *Storytelling: Process and Practice.* Littleton, Co.: Libraries Unlimited, 1986.

*Loeb Classical Library.* Founded by James Loeb. Vol.1—. Cambridge: Harvard University Pr.; London: William Heinemann, 1912—.

Long, Harriet G. *Public Library Service to Children: Foundation and Development.* Metuchen, N.J.: Scarecrow Pr., 1969.

———. *Rich the Treasure: Public Library Service to Children.* Chicago: American Library Association, 1953.

Lord, Albert B. *The Singer of Tales*. Harvard Studies in Comparative Literature, 24. Cambridge: Harvard Univ. Pr., 1960.

Losty, Jeremiah P. *The Art of the Book in India*. London: British Library, 1982.

Lowie, Robert H. *Myths and Traditions of the Crow Indians*. Anthropological Papers, vol. 25, pt. 1. New York: American Museum of Natural History, 1918.

————. *Social Organization*. New York: Holt, Rinehart, 1948.

Lüders, Heinrich. "Die Śaubhikas: ein Beitrag zur Geschichte des indischen Dramas." Preussische Akademie der Wissenschaften, *Sitzungsberichte*, June 1916, pp. 698–737.

Luomala, Katherine. "Polynesian Literature." In *Encyclopedia of Literature*, ed. by Joseph T. Shipley, vol. 2, pp. 772–789. New York: Philosophical Library, 1946.

Lüthi, Max. *The European Folktale: Form and Nature*. Tr. by John D. Niles. Philadelphia: Institute for the Study of Human Issues, 1982. (First pub. 1947.)

Lutzker, John et al. "The Paradoxical Effects of 'Moral' Stories on Children's Behavior." *Education and Treatment of Children*, 4, 2 (Spring 1981): 115–124.

Lynton, Harriet Ronken, and Rojan, Mohini. *The Days of the Beloved*. Berkeley: Univ. of California Pr., 1974.

Ma, Yau-Woon. "The Beginnings of Professional Storytelling in China: A Critique of Current Theories and Evidence." In *Études d'Histoire et de Littérature Offertes au Professeur Jaroslav Průšek*. Bibliothèque de l'Institut des Hautes Études Chinoises, 24, pp. 227–245. Paris: The Institute, 1976.

MacDonald, Donald A. "Fieldwork: Collecting Oral Literature." In *Folklore and Folklife*, ed. by Richard Dorson, pp. 407–428. Univ. of Chicago Pr., 1972.

MacDonald, Margaret Read. *The Storyteller's Sourcebook: A Subject, Title, and Motif Index to Folklore Collections for Children*. Detroit: Gale, 1982.

————. *Twenty Tellable Tales*. New York: H. W. Wilson, 1985.

MacDonnell, Anne. *The Italian Fairy Book*. New York, Frederick Stokes, n.d.

McGinniss, Dorothy A., ed. *Oral Presentations and the Librarian*. Syracuse Univ. Pr., 1971.

MacManus, Seumas. *Donegal Fairy Book*. New York: Doubleday, 1932.

————. *A Renaissance in Storytelling*. Publications, 110. New York: National Recreation Association, 1912.

McVicker, Polly Bowditch. "Storytelling in Java." *Horn Book* 40 (December 1964): 596–601.

Mafeje, Archie. "The Role of the Bard in a Contemporary African Community." *Journal of African Languages* 6 (1967): 193–223.

Magel, Emil A. *Folktales from the Gambia*. Washington, D.C.: Three Continents Pr., 1984.

Maguire, Jack. *Creative Storytelling: Choosing, Inventing and Sharing Tales for Children*. New York: McGraw Hill, 1985.

Mair, Victor. *Painting and Performance; Chinese Picture Recitation and its Indian Genesis.* Honolulu: Univ. of Hawaii Pr., 1988.

———. *Tun-huang Popular Narratives.* Cambridge Univ. Pr., 1983.

Malinowski, Bronislaw. *Argonauts of the Western Pacific.* London: Routledge and Kegan Paul, 1922.

———. "Myth in Primitive Psychology." In his *Magic, Science and Religion and Other Essays,* pp. 93–148. New York: Doubleday, 1954. (First pub. 1926.)

Mallet, Karl-Heinz. *Fairy Tales and Children.* New York: Schocken, 1984.

Mande, Prabhaker B. "Dakkalwars and Their Myths." *Folklore* [Calcutta] 14 (January 1973): 69–76.

Mandler, Jean Matter. *Stories, Scripts and Scenes: Aspects of Schema Theory.* Hillsdale, N.J.: Erlbaum, 1984.

Maranda, Elli Köngäs, and Maranda, Pierre. *Structural Models in Folklore and Transformational Essays.* The Hague: Mouton, 1971.

*Märchenerzähler; Erzählgemeinschaft.* Veröffentlichungen der Europäische Märchengesellschaft 4. Kassel: Röth-Verlag, 1983.

Massignon, Geneviève. *Folktales of France.* Tr. by Jacqueline Hyland. Univ. of Chicago Pr., 1968.

Mathias, Elizabeth, and Raspa, Richard. *Italian Folktales in America: the Verbal Art of an Immigrant Woman.* Detroit: Wayne State Univ. Pr., 1985.

Mathiews, Franklin K., ed. *The Boy Scouts Book of Campfire Stories.* New York: Appleton, 1921.

Maus, Cynthia Pearl. *Youth and Storytelling.* Chicago: The International Council of Religious Education, 1928.

Maxwell, Kevin B. *Bemba Myth and Ritual; the Impact of Literacy on an Oral Culture.* American Univ. Studies, series 11, vol. 2. Frankfurt/Main: Peter Lang, 1983.

Mbiti, John S. *Akamba Stories.* Oxford Library of African Literature. Oxford Univ. Pr., 1966.

Megas, Georgios. *Folktales of Greece.* Tr. by Helen Colaclides. Univ. of Chicago Pr., 1970.

Meinhof, Carl. "Zur Entstehung der Schrift." *Zeitschrift für Aegyptische Sprache und Altertumskunde* 49 (November 1911): 1–14.

Meissner, Kurt. "Die Yose." Deutsche Gesellschaft für Natur- und Völkerkunde Ostasiens, *Mitteilungen* 14 (1913): 230–241.

Mendoza, Virginia de. "El mal de espanto y manera de curarlo en algunos lugares en México." *Boletín de la Sociedad de Folklore de Tucuman,* 5(1951).

Merkel, Johannes. *Erzählen: Die Wiederentdeckung einer vergessenen Kunst; Geschichten und Anregungen: ein Handbuch.* Frankfurt: ro ro ro, 1982.

Miller, Nathan. *The Child in Primitive Society.* New York: Brentano's, 1928.

Millman, Lawrence. *Our Like Will Not Be There Again: Notes from the West of Ireland.* Boston: Little, Brown, 1977.

Mills, Joyce, and Crowley, R. J. *Therapeutic Metaphors for Children and the Child Within.* New York: Brunner-Mazel, 1986.

*The Minnesingers: Portraits from the Weingartner Manuscript.* Basle: Amerbach Pub. Co., 1947.

Mintz, Jerome R. *The Legends of the Hasidim: An Introduction to Hasidic Culture and Oral Tradition in the New World.* Univ. of Chicago Pr., 1968.

Mitchell, Roger E. *Micronesian Folktales.* Asian Folklore Studies, 32. Nagoya: Asian Folklore Institute, 1973.

————. "A Study of the Cultural, Historical and Acculturative Factors Influencing the Repertoires of Two Trukese Informants." Ph.D. dissertation, University of Indiana, 1967.

Mittal, Jagdish. ["The Kunepullalu Scroll."] In *India: Art and Culture 1300–1900*, ed. by Stuart Cary Welch. New York: Metropolitan Museum of Art and Holt, Rinehart and Winston, 1985.

Moebirman. *Wayang Purwa: The Shadow Play of Indonesia.* Tr. from the French. Rev. ed. The Hague: Van Deventer-Maasstichting, 1960.

Mondon-Vidailhet, M. "La Musique Éthiopienne." In *Encyclopédie de la Musique*, ed. by Albert Lavignac, pt. 1, vol. 5, pp. 3179–3196. Paris: Delagrave, 1922.

Moore, Anne Carroll. "Report of the Committee on Storytelling." *Playground* 4 (August 1910): 162ff; reprinted in *Library Work with Children*, ed. by Alice I. Hazeltine, pp. 297–315. New York: H. W. Wilson Co., 1917.

————. "Ruth Sawyer, Storyteller." *Horn Book* 12 (January 1936): 34–38.

————. "The Story Hour at Pratt Institute Free Library." *Library Journal* 30 (April 1905): 204–211.

Moore, Vardine. *The Pre-School Story Hour.* 2nd ed. Metuchen, N.J.: Scarecrow Pr., 1972.

Morris, Henry F. *The Heroic Recitations of the Bahima of Ankole.* Oxford Library of African Literature. Oxford Univ. Pr., 1964.

Motherwell, William. *Minstrelsy: Ancient and Modern.* Boston: W. D. Ticknor, 1846.

Mountford, Charles P. "Exploring Stone Age Arnheim Land." *National Geographic* 96 (December 1949): 745–782.

Mullen, Patrick B. "A Traditional Storyteller in Changing Contexts." *National Storytelling Journal*, 4, 2 (Spring 1987): 22–27.

Muller, F. Max, ed. *The Sacred Books of the East.* Tr. by various Oriental scholars. 50 vols. Oxford Univ. Pr., 1879; Delhi: Motilal Banarsidass, 1965.

Munn, Nancy D. *Walbiri Iconography.* Ithaca: Cornell Univ. Pr., 1973.

Nagler, Michael N. *Spontaneity and Tradition; A Study of the Oral Art of Homer.* Berkeley: Univ. of California Pr., 1974.

Nahmad, H. M. *A Portion in Paradise and Other Jewish Folktales.* New York: W. W. Norton, 1970.

Nash, D. W. *Taliesin; or the Bards and Druids of Britain.* London: John Russell Smith, 1858.

N'Diaye, Bokar. *Veillées au Mali.* Bamako, Mali: Editions Populaires, 1970.

Nebie, Marc. "Et si on disait un conte?" *Cahiers de Littérature Orale* 16 (1984): 35–58.

Nelson, Edward William. *The Eskimo about Bering Strait.* Bureau of American Ethnology, Annual Report 1896–97. Washington, D.C.: 1899.

Nesbitt, Elizabeth. "The Art of Storytelling." *Horn Book* 21 (November-December 1945): 439–444.

———. "Hold to That Which Is Good." *Horn Book* 16 (January-February 1940): 7–15.

Newcomb, Franc J. *Navajo Folk Tales.* Santa Fe: Museum of Navajo Ceremonial Art, 1967.

Newton, Douglas. *Art Styles of the Papuan Gulf.* New York: Museum of Primitive Art, 1961.

Nichols, Judy. *Storytimes for Two-year-olds.* Chicago: American Library Association, 1987.

Norris, H. T. *Shinqiti Folk Literature and Song.* Oxford Library of African Literature. Oxford Univ. Pr., 1968.

Noss, Philip A. "Cameroun (Gbaya People)." In *Folktales Told around the World,* ed. by Richard Dorson, pp. 360–379. Univ. of Chicago Pr., 1975.

———. "Description in Gbaya Literary Art." In *African Folklore,* ed. by Richard Dorson, pp. 73–101. Bloomington, Indiana Univ. Pr., 1972.

Noy, Dov. "Is There a Jewish Folk Religion?" In *Studies in Jewish Folklore,* pp. 273–285. Cambridge: Harvard Univ. Pr., 1980.

———. "The Jewish Theodicy Legend." in *Fields of Offering; Studies in Honor of Raphael Patai,* ed. by Victor D. Sanua, pp. 65–84. Cranberry, N.J.: Associated Univ. Pr./Fairleigh Dickinson Univ. Pr.; New York: Herzl Pr., 1983.

Nwokah, Evangeline. "Once Upon a Time—Aspects of Storytelling in Normal and Retarded Children." *Language and Speech* 25 (July-August 1982): 293–298.

O'Connell, Patricia Ann. "Bandi Oral Narratives." Master's thesis, Indiana University, 1976.

O'Connor, V. C. Scott. "Beyond the Grand Atlas." *National Geographic* 61 (March 1932): 261–320.

Okeke, Uche. *Tales of the Land of Death: Igbo Folk Tales.* New York: Doubleday, 1971.

Okpewho, Isidore. *The Epic in Africa: Towards a Poetics of the Oral Performance.* New York: Columbia Univ. Pr., 1979.

Olcutt, Frances J. "Storytelling, Lectures and Other Adjuncts of the Children's Room." *Public Libraries* 5 (July 1900): 282–284.

O'Lochlainn. *Irish Street Ballads.* New York: Citadel, 1960.

Olrik, Axel. "Epic Laws of Folk Narrative." In *The Study of Folklore,* ed. by Alan Dundes, pp. 129–141. New York: Prentice-Hall, 1965.

Olson, Glending. *Literature as Recreation in the Late Middle Ages.* Ithaca: Cornell Univ. Pr., 1982.

Omidsalar, Mahmoud. "Storytellers in Classical Persian Texts." *Journal of American Folklore* 97 (1984): 204–212.

Ong, Walter J. *Orality and Literacy: The Technologizing of the Word.* New York: Methuen, 1982.

Onyango-Oguto, Benedict, and Roscoe, Adrian A. *Keep My Words.* Nairobi: East African Pub. House, 1974.

Opland, Jeff. *Anglo-Saxon Oral Poetry: A Study of the Traditions.* New Haven: Yale Univ. Press, 1980.

———. *Xhosa Oral Poetry: Aspects of a Black South African Tradition.* Cambridge Univ. Pr., 1983.

Opler, Morris Edward. *Myths and Tales of the Jicarilla Apache Indians.* Memoirs, 31. New York: American Folklore Society, 1938.

Oppong, Christine. *Growing Up in Dagbon.* Accra: Ghana Pub. Corp., 1973.

Orbell, Margaret. *Maori Folktales in Maori and English.* Auckland: Blackwood and Janet Paul Ltd., 1968.

Oring, Elliott. "Ha-Chizbat: The Content and Structure of Israeli Oral Tradition." Ph.D. dissertation, Indiana University, 1974.

O'Sullivan, Sean. *The Folklore of Ireland.* New York: Hastings House,1974.

———. *A Handbook of Irish Folklore.* Detroit: Singing Tree Pr., 1970.

Oswalt, Wendell H. "Traditional Storyknife Tales of Yuk Girls." *Proceedings of the American Philosophical Society* 108, 4 (August 1964): 310–336.

Page, Mary Ellen. "Professional Storytelling in Iran: Transmission and Practice." *Iranian Studies* 12, 3–4 (1979): 195–217.

Pakrasi, Mira. *Folk Tales of Assam.* Folk Tales of India, no. 3. Delhi and Jullundur: Sterling Pub. Co., 1969.

*The Panchatantra.* Tr. from the Sanskrit by Arthur W. Ryder. Univ. of Chicago Pr., 1956.

Parrot, Andre. *Sumer: The Dawn of Art.* Tr. by Stuart Gilbert and James Emmons. New York: Golden Press, 1961.

Parry, Adam, ed. *The Making of Heroic Verse: The Collected Papers of Milman Parry.* Oxford Univ. Pr., 1971.

Parsons, Elsie Clews. *Folklore of the Sea Islands, South Carolina.* Cambridge, Mass., and New York: American Folklore Society, 1923.

———. *Folktales of Andros Island, Bahamas.* Memoirs, 13. New York: American Folklore Society, 1918.

———. *Kiowa Tales.* Memoirs, 22. New York: American Folklore Society, 1929.

———. *Taos Tales.* Memoirs, 34. New York: American Folklore Society, 1940.

Pastoriza de Etchebarne, Dora. *El Oficio Olvidado; El Arte de Narrar.* Buenos Aires: Edit. Guadalupe, 1972.

Patai, Raphael. *On Jewish Folklore.* Detroit: Wayne State Univ. Pr., 1983.

———; Utley, Francis Lee; and Noy, Dov. *Studies in Biblical and Jewish Folklore.* Bloomington: Indiana Univ. Pr., 1960.

Patte, Geneviève. *Laissez-les lire! Les enfants et les bibliothèques.* Paris: Éditions Ouvrières, 1978.

Pellowski, Anne. *The Family Storytelling Handbook.* Illus. by Lynn Sweat. New York: Macmillan, 1987.

———. *The Story Vine; A Source Book of Unusual and Easy-to-Tell Stories from around the World.* Illus. by Lynn Sweat. New York: Macmillan, 1984.

———. *The World of Children's Literature.* New York: Bowker, 1968.

Penard, A. P., and Penard, T. E. "Surinam Folk-tales." *Journal of American Folklore* 30(1917): 239–250.

Pentikainen, Julia. *Oral Repertoire and World View: An Anthropological Study of Marina Takalo's Life History.* Helsinki: Suomalainen Tiedeakatemia, 1978.

Perera, Arthur. *Sinhalese Folklore Notes.* Bombay, 1917.

Peseschkian, Nossrat. *Oriental Stories as Tools in Psychotherapy: The Merchant and the Parrot; with 100 Case Examples for Education and Self-Help.* Berlin and New York: Springer-Verlag, 1985.

Peterson, Sally. "Translating Experience and the Reading of a Story Cloth." *Journal of American Folklore* 101 (1988): 6–22.

Petzoldt, Leander. *Die freudlose Muse: Texte, Lieder und Bilder zum historischen Bänkelsang.* Stuttgart: J. B. Metzler, 1978.

Phillips, Herbert P. *Thai Peasant Personality.* Berkeley: Univ. of California Pr., 1966.

Phillott, D. C. "Some Current Persian Tales." Asiatic Society of Bengal [Calcutta], *Memoirs* 1, no. 18 (1906): 375–412.

Pickard, P. M. *I Could a Tale Unfold: Violence, Horror and Sensationalism in Stories for Children.* New York: Humanities Pr., 1961.

Pino-Saavedra, Yolando. *Folktales of Chile.* Tr. by Rockwell Gray. Univ. of Chicago Pr., 1967.

Platiel, Suzanne. *La fille volage & autres contes du pays San (Burkina, anciennement Haute-Volta)*. Paris: Armand Colin, 1984.

Plüss, Jean-Daniel. *Therapeutic and Prophetic Narratives in Worship: A Hermeneutic Study of Testimonies and Visions; Their Potential Significance for Christian Worship and Secular Society*. Frankfurt/Main: Verlag Peter Lang, 1988.

*Polish Folklore*. Vol. 3 (1958)–Vol. 5 (1960). Cambridge Springs, Pa.: Alliance College.

Poppe, Roger Louis. "Narrative folklore and its transmission in a Northern Wisconsin Indian family." Master's thesis, Anthropology, University of Wisconsin, 1968.

Postma, Minnie. *Tales from the Basotho*. Austin: Univ. of Texas Pr., 1974.

Power, Effie Lee. "Syllabus for the Study of Storytelling for Use in Connection with Library Service S178." New York: Columbia Univ., School of Library Service, 1936.

Powlison, Paul Stewart. "Yagua Mythology and Its Epic Tendencies." Ph.D. dissertation, Indiana University, 1969.

Pratt Institute. *Report of the Free Library for the Year Ending June 30, 1900*. Brooklyn: The Institute, 1900.

Praz, Mario. *Mnemosyne: The Parallel between Literature and the Visual Arts*. Princeton Univ. Pr., 1970.

*Programming for Three- to Five-year-olds*. ALSC Program Support Publications, 8. Chicago: Association for Library Services to Children, American Library Association, 1983.

Průšek, Jaroslav. "The Creative Methods of Chinese Mediaeval Storytellers." In *Charisteria Orientalia*, by Felix Tauer and others, pp. 253–273. Prague: Nakladatelstvi Československe Akademie Věd, 1956.

———. "The Narrators of Buddhist Scriptures and Religious Tales in the Sung Period." *Archiv Orientálni* 10 (1938): 375–388; 23 (1955): 620ff.

———. *The Origins and the Authors of the hua-pen*. Dissertationes Orientales 14. Prague: Academia, 1967.

———. "Shuo-ch'ang wen-hsüeh." In *Dictionary of Oriental Literatures*, vol. 1, pp. 161–162. New York: Basic Books, 1974.

Radin, Paul. *The Trickster: A Study in American Indian Mythology*. New York: Greenwood Pr., 1969.

Raghavan, V. "Methods of Popular Religious Instruction in South India." In *Traditional India*, ed. by Milton Singer, pp. 130–138. Philadelphia: American Folklore Society, 1959.

———. "Picture-Showmen: Mankha." *Indian Historical Quarterly* 12, 3 (1936): 524.

———. *The Ramayana Tradition in Asia*. New Delhi: Sahitya Akademi, 1980.

Raine, Kathleen. "Foreword," in *Fairy and Folk Tales of Ireland*, by William Butler Yeats. New York: Macmillan, 1973.

Ramakrishna Pillai, Thottakadu. *Life in an Indian Village*. London: T. F. Unwin, 1891.

Ranke, Kurt. "Volkserzählung." In *Die Religion in Geschichte und Gegenwart*, 3rd ed., vol. 6. Tübingen: J. C. B. Mohr, 1965.

Ransome, Arthur. *A History of Storytelling: Studies in the Development of Narrative*. London: T. C. & E. C. Jack, 1909.

Rattray, Robert S. *The Ashanti*. Oxford Univ. Pr., 1923.

———. *Religion and Art in Ashanti*. Oxford Univ. Pr., 1927.

Raum, O. F. *Chaga Childhood: A Description of Indigenous Education in an East African Tribe*. Oxford Univ. Pr., 1940.

Ray, Dorothy Jean. *Aleut and Eskimo Art: Tradition and Innovation in South Alaska*. Seattle: Univ. of Washington Pr., 1981.

Ray, Eva. "Paithan Paintings." *Artibus Asiae* 40, 4 (1978): 239–282.

Ray, Sudhandu Kumar. *The Ritual Art of the Bratas of Bengal*. Calcutta: K. L. Mukhopadhyay, 1961.

Read, Margaret. *Children of their Fathers: the Ngoni of Nyasaland*. New Haven: Yale Univ. Pr., 1960.

*Reallexikon der deutschen Literaturgeschichte*. Berlin: Walter de Gruyter, 1958.

Reefe, Thomas Q. "Lukasa: A Luba Memory Device." *African Arts* 10, 4 (1977): 49–50.

Reichard, Gladys A. *An Analysis of Coeur d'Alene Indian Myths*. Philadelphia: American Folklore Society, 1947.

*Die Religion in Geschichte und Gegenwart*, 3rd. ed. Tübingen: J. C. B. Mohr, 1965.

*Reports of the Norwegian Archaelogical Expedition to Easter Island and the Pacific*. Vol. 2. Chicago: Rand McNally, 1965.

Reventberg, E. "Böcker på lekplatsen." *Biblioteksbladet* 40, 3 (1955):170–171.

Rey-Hulman, Diana. *Les Bilinguismes Littéraires. Signification sociale de la littérature orale tyokossi (Togo)*. Paris: Centre National de la Recherche Scientifique, 1982.

Reynolds, David S. "From Doctrine to Narrative: the Rise of Pulpit Storytelling in America." *American Quarterly* 32, 5 (1980): 479–498.

Riis, Jacob A. *The Making of an American*. New York: Macmillan, 1901.

Ritschl, Dietrich, and Jones, Hugh O. *"Story" als Rohmaterial der Theologie*. Munich: Kaiser, 1976.

Robe, Stanley L. *Amapa Storytellers*. Folklore Studies, 24. Berkeley: Univ. of California Pr., 1972.

Roberts, Ken. *Pre-school Storytimes*. Ottawa: Canadian Library Association, 1987.

Roberts, Leonard. *Sang Branch Settlers: Folksongs and Tales of a Kentucky Mountain Family*. American Folklore Society, Memoirs, 61. Austin: Univ. of Texas Pr., 1974.

Rodari, Gianni. *Grammatica della fantasia; introduzione all' arte di inventare storie*. Turin: Einaudi, 1973.

Rodriguez Rouanet, Francisco. "Ojeo, Susto, Hijillo y Acuas: Enfermedades del Indigena Kekchi." *Tradiciones de Guatemala* 1 (1968): 43–46.

Roerich, George N. "The Epic of King Kesar of Ling." *Journal of the Royal Asiatic Society of Bengal, Letters* 8 (1942): 277–311.

Roghair, Gene H. *The Epic of Palnādu: A Study and Translation of "Palnāti Virula Kātha," a Telugu Oral Tradition from Andhra Pradesh, India*. Oxford Univ. Pr., 1982.

Röhrich, Lutz. *Märchen und Wirklichkeit; eine volkskundliche Untersuchung*, 2nd ed. Wiesbaden: F. Steiner, 1964.

Rooth, Anna Birgitta. *The Importance of Storytelling: A Study Based on Field Work in Northern Alaska*. Studia ethnologica uppsaliensia 1. Stockholm: Almqvist & Wiksell, 1976.

Roscoe, John. *The Baganda*, 2nd ed. New York: Barnes and Noble, 1966. (First pub. 1911.)

Rosen, Sidney. *My Voice Will Go with You; The Teaching Tales of Milton Erickson*. New York: Norton, 1982.

Rosenberg, Bruce A. *Can These Bones Live? the Art of the American Folk Preacher*. Urbana: Univ. of Illinois Pr., 1988.

Ross, Ramon. *Storyteller*. 2nd ed. Columbus: Charles E. Merrill, 1980.

Rossell, Mary E. "History of Storytelling in England, Germany, and France." Thesis, The New York Public Library, Library School, 1915.

Rougemont, Charlotte. . . . *dann leben sie noch heute: Erlebnisse und Erfahrungen beim Märchenerzählen*. Münster: Verlag Aschendorff, 1962.

Rouget, Gilbert. "Court Songs and Traditional History in the Ancient Kingdoms of Porto-Novo and Abomey." In *Essays on Music and History in Africa*, ed. by Klaus P. Wachsmann, pp. 27–64. Evanston: Northwestern Univ. Pr., 1971.

Roulon, Paulette and Doko, Raymond. "Un pays de conteurs." *Cahiers de littérature orale* 11 (1982): 123–134.

Rowe, John Howland. "Inca Culture at the Time of the Spanish Conquest." In *Handbook of South American Indians*, ed. by Julian H. Steward, pp. 183–330. Smithsonian Institution, Bureau of Ethnology, Bulletin 143. Washington, D.C.: The Institution, 1946.

Royal, Claudia. *Storytelling*. Nashville: Broadman Pr., 1956.

Ruch, Barbara. "Medieval Jongleurs and the Making of a National Literature." In *Japan in the Muromachi Age*, ed. by John W. Hall and Toyoda Takeshi, pp. 279–309. Berkeley: Univ. of California Pr., 1977.

*Runic and Heroic Poems of the Old Teutonic Peoples.* Cambridge Univ. Pr., 1915.

Russell, R. V., and Rai Bahadur Hira Lal. *The Tribes and Castes of the Central Provinces of India.* Vol. 2. Oosterhuit, Netherlands: Anthropological Publications, 1969. (First pub. 1916.)

Sabar, Yona. *The Folk Literature of the Kurdistani Jews: An Anthology.* Yale Judaica Series, 23. New Haven: Yale Univ. Pr., 1982.

Sadwelkar, Baburao. "Chitrakathi Tradition of Pinguli and the Environment." In *Calendar 1978.* Bombay: Government Central Press, 1978.

Sahagun, *Historia de las cosas de Nueva España.* In *Antiquities of Mexico* by Lord Kingsborough. Vol. 4 and vol. 7. London: Robert Havell, 1831.

St. John, Edward Porter. *Stories and Storytelling in Moral and Religious Education.* Boston: The Pilgrim Press, 1910.

Sanborn, Florence. "How to Use Picture-Story Books." *Library Journal* 74 (February 15, 1949): 272–274.

Saul, George Brandon. *Traditional Irish Literature and Its Backgrounds: A Brief Introduction.* Lewisburg: Bucknell Univ. Pr., 1970.

Sawyer, Ruth. *The Way of the Storyteller.* New York: Viking, 1965. (First pub. 1942.)

Sayce, A. H. "Storytelling in the East." *Living Age,* 5th series, 64 (Oct. 20, 1888): 176–180.

Sayers, Frances Clarke. *Anne Carroll Moore: A Biography.* New York: Atheneum, 1972.

———. "Notes on Storytelling." *Top of the News* 14 (March 1958): 10–11.

Schapera, I. *Praise-Poems of Tswana Chiefs.* Oxford Library of African Literature. Oxford Univ. Pr., 1965.

Scheub, Harold. "The Art of Nongenile Mazithathu Zenani, a Gcaleka *Ntsomi* Performer." In *African Folklore,* ed. by Richard Dorson, pp. 115–142. Bloomington: Indiana Univ. Pr., 1972.

———. "South Africa." In *Folktales Told around the World,* ed. by Richard Dorson, pp. 388–426. Univ. of Chicago Pr., 1975.

———. *The Xhosa Ntsomi.* Oxford Library of African Literature. Oxford Univ. Pr., 1975.

Schiller, Friedrich von. *Werke,* vol. 4. Berlin & Weimar: Aufbau Verlag, 1967.

Schimmel, Nancy. *Just Enough to Make a Story: A Sourcebook for Storytelling.* 2nd ed. Berkeley: Sisters' Choice Pr., 1982.

Schmidt, Leopold. "Geistlicher Bänkelsang." Österreichisches Volksliedwerk, *Jahrbuch* 12 (1963): 1–16.

Schneiderman, Leo. *The Psychology of Myth, Folklore, and Religion.* Chicago: Nelson-Hall, 1981.

Schram, Peninnah. *Jewish Stories: One Generation Tells Another*. Northvale, N.J.: Jason Aronson, 1987.

Schröcke, Kurt. *Märchen und Kind; eine pädagogische Studie*. Leipzig, 1911.

Schwartz, Howard. *Miriam's Tambourine: Jewish Folktales from around the World*. Illus. by Lloyd Bloom. Foreword by Dov Noy. New York: Seth Pr., 1986.

Schwartzman, Helen B. "Stories at Work: Play in an Organizational Context." In *Text, Play and Story: The Construction and Reconstruction of Self and Society*, ed. by Edward M. Bruner, pp. 80–93. Proceedings 1983. Washington, D.C.: American Ethnological Society, 1984.

Schwarzbaum, Haim. *Studies in Jewish and World Folklore*. Berlin: Walter de Gruyter, 1968.

Scott, Edna Lyman. *Storytelling: What to Tell and How to Tell It*. Rev. ed. Chicago: A. C. McClurg, 1923.

Scribner, Sylvia and Scribner, Cole. *The Psychology of Literacy*. Cambridge: Harvard Univ. Pr., 1981.

Seitel, Peter. *See So That We May See: Performances and Interpretations of Traditional Tales from Tanzania*. Bloomington: Indiana Univ. Pr., 1980.

Seki, Keigo. *Folktales of Japan*. Chicago Univ. Pr., 1963.

Sen, Dineshchandra. *Folk Literature of Bengal*. Univ. of Calcutta, 1920.

Sen Gupta, Sankar. *The Patas and the Patuas of Bengal*. Foreword by Niharranjan Ray. Calcutta: Indian Publications, 1973.

Shafter, Toby. *Storytelling for Jewish Groups*. New York: National Jewish Welfare Board, 1946.

Shah, A. M. and Schroff, R. G. "The Vahīvancā Bārots of Gujarat: A Caste of Genealogists and Mythographers." In *Traditional India*, ed. by Milton Singer, pp. 40–70. Philadelphia: American Folklore Society, 1959.

Shah, Idries. *Caravan of Dreams*. London: Octagon Press, 1968.

———. *Learning How to Learn; Psychology and Spirituality in the Sufi Way*. London: Octagon Press, 1982.

Shaw, Mary, ed. *According to Our Ancestors: Folk Texts from Guatemala and Honduras*. Illus. by Patricia Ingersoll. Norman: Univ. of Oklahoma Pr., 1971.

Shedlock, Marie L. *The Art of the Storyteller*. New York: Dover, 1951. (First pub. 1915.)

Sheehan, Ethna, and Bentley, Martha C. "A Public Library Reassesses Storytelling." *Illinois Libraries* 44 (December 1962): 653–657.

Shepard, Leslie. *The Broadside Ballad: A Study in Origins and Meaning*. London: H. Jenkins, 1962.

Sherzer, Joel. *Kuna Ways of Speaking: An Ethnographic Perspective*. Austin: Univ. of Texas Pr., 1983.

Sherzer, Dina, and Sherzer, Joel. "Literature in San Blas: Discovering the Cuna Ikala." *Semiotica* 6, 2 (1972): 182–199.

Shklovsky, I. W. *In Far North-east Siberia*. London: Macmillan, 1916.

Shuman, Amy. *Storytelling Rights: The Uses of Oral and Written Texts by Urban Adolescents*. Cambridge Univ. Pr., 1986.

Sidahome, Joseph E. *Stories of the Benin Empire*. Ibadan, Nigeria: Oxford Univ. Pr., 1964.

Sidhanta, N. K. *The Heroic Age of India*. London: Kegan, Paul, Trench, Trubner, 1929.

Simmons, D. C. "Specimens of Efik Literature." *Folklore* 66 (1955):417–418.

Simpson, Jacqueline. *Icelandic Folktales and Legends*. Berkeley: Univ. of California Pr., 1972.

Singer, Milton, ed. *Traditional India: Structure and Change*. Philadelphia: American Folklore Society, 1959.

Singh, Indira P. "A Sikh Village." in *Traditional India*, ed. by Milton Singer, pp. 273–297. Philadelphia: American Folklore Society: 1959.

Skendi, Stavro. *Albanian and South Slavic Oral Epic Poetry*. Philadelphia: American Folklore Society, 1954.

Sklute, Barbro. "Legends and Folk Beliefs in a Swedish American Community: A Study in Folklore and Acculturation." Ph.D. dissertation, Indiana University, 1970.

Slater, Candace. *Stories on a String: The Brazilian "Literatura de Cordel."* Berkeley: Univ. of California Pr., 1982.

———. *Trail of Miracles: Stories from a Pilgrimage in Northeast Brazil*. Berkeley: Univ. of California Pr., 1986.

Slyomovics, Susan. *The Merchant of Art: An Egyptian Hilali Oral Epic Poet in Performance*. Publications in Modern Philology, 120. Berkeley: Univ. of California Pr., 1987.

Smardo, Frances A. and Curry, John F. *What Research Tells Us about Story Hours and Receptive Language*. Dallas Public Library, 1982.

Smith, Mary F., ed. *Baba of Karo: A Woman of the Muslim Hausas*. London: Faber and Faber, 1954.

Smith, M. G. "The Social Functions and Meaning of Hausa Praise Singing." *Africa* 27 (1957): 27.

Smith, Pierre. *Le récit populaire au Rwanda*. Classiques africains, 17. Paris: Armand Colin, 1975.

Snouck Hurgronje, Christiaan. *The Achehnese*. Tr. by A. W. S. O'Sullivan. London: 1906.

Sokolov, Yuri M. *Russian Folklore*. Tr. by Catherine Ruth Smith. New York: Macmillan, 1950.

Sorin-Barreteau, Liliane. "Gestes narratifs et langage gestuel chez les Mofu-Gudur (Nord-Cameroun)." *Cahiers de Littérature Orale* 11 (1982): 37–91.

Sowayan, Saad Abdullah. *Nabati Poetry; the Oral Poetry of Arabia.* Berkeley: Univ. of California Pr., 1985.

Speke, J. H. *Journal of the Discovery of the Source of the Nile.* Edinburgh, 1863.

*Spirit Mountain: An Anthology of Yuman Story and Song,* ed. by Leanne Hinton and Lucille J. Watahomigie. Tucson: Sun Tracks and Univ. of Arizona Pr., 1984.

Srivastava, Sahab Lal. *Folk Culture and Oral Tradition.* New Delhi: Abhinav Publications, 1974.

Stanley, Henry M. *My Dark Companions and Their Strange Stories.* New York: Charles Scribner's Sons, 1893.

Stefaniszyn, B. "The Hunting Songs of the Ambo." *African Studies* 10 (1951): 1–12.

Steinen, Karl von den. *Die Marquesaner und ihre Kunst.* 2 vols. Berlin: Dietrich Reimer, 1925.

Stevenson, Robert H. ed. and tr. *Amiran-Darejaniani; a cycle of medieval Georgian tales traditionally ascribed to Mose Khoneli.* Oxford Univ. Pr., 1958.

Stevenson, Tilly E. "The Religious Life of the Zuni Child." Smithsonian Institution. American Bureau of Ethnology. *Annual Report,* vol. 5, pp. 533–555. New York, 1897.

*Stories: A List of Stories to Tell and to Read Aloud,* ed. by Marilyn Berg Iarusso. 7th ed. The New York Public Library, 1977.

*Stories to Tell: A List of Stories with Annotations,* ed. by Jeanne Hardendorff. 5th ed. Baltimore: Enoch Pratt Free Library, 1965.

*Stories to Tell to Children.* 4th ed. Pittsburgh: Carnegie Library, 1926; 8th ed., ed. by Laura Cathon. Univ. of Pittsburgh Pr., 1974.

*The Story Hour Leader.* Quarterly. Nashville, Tn., Southern Baptist Convention, 1937–.

*Storytelling: Practical Guides.* Birmingham, Eng.: Library Association, Youth Libraries Group, 1979.

"Storytelling around the World: A Symposium." *Library Journal* 65 (April 1, 1940): 285–289.

Strehlow, Theodor Georg H. *Aranda Traditions.* Melbourne Univ. Pr., 1947; New Haven: Human Relations Area Files, 195_.

———. "The art of circle, line and square." In *Australian Aboriginal Art,* ed. by Ronald M. Berndt, pp. 44–49. Sydney: Ure Smith, 1964.

Summers, Maud. "Storytelling in Playgrounds." *The Story Hour* 1, 1 (1908): 24–27.

Surmelian, Leon. *Apples of Immortality; Folktales of Armenia.* UNESCO Collection of Representative Works. Berkeley: Univ. of California Pr., 1968.

Sweeney, Amin. "Professional Malay Storytelling: Some Questions of Style and Presentation." In *Studies in Malaysian Oral and Musical Traditions*, pp. 47–99. Ann Arbor: Univ. of Michigan, Center for South and Southeast Asian Studies, 1974.

Sydow, C. W. von. "Folktale Studies and Philology: Some Points of View." In *The Study of Folklore*, ed. by Alan Dundes, pp. 219–242. New York: Prentice-Hall, 1965.

Taggart, James M. *Nahuat Myth and Social Structure*. Austin: Univ. of Texas Pr., 1983.

Tallman, Richard S., and Tallman, A. Laurna. *Country Folks: A Handbook for Student Folklore Collectors*. Batesville, Ak.: Arkansas College Folklore Archive, 1978.

———. "Where Stories Are Told: A Nova Scotia Storyteller's Milieu. *American Review of Canadian Studies* 5 (1975): 17–41.

Tanna, Laura. *Jamaican Folktales and Oral Histories*. Kingston: Institute of Jamaica, 1984.

Tannen, Deborah. *Spoken and Written Language; Exploring Orality and Literacy*. Norwood, NJ: ABLEX Pub. Co., 1980.

Taylor, Loren E. *Storytelling and Dramatization*. Minneapolis: Burgess, 1965.

Tedlock, Dennis. *Finding the Center: Narrative Poetry of the Zuni Indians*. New York: Dial, 1972.

———. *The Spoken Word and the Work of Interpretation*. Philadelphia: Univ. of Pennsylvania Pr., 1983.

Tetzner, Lisa. *Vom Märchenerzählen im Volke*. Jena: Verlag Eugen Diederichs, 1925.

Thompson, Stith. *The Folktale*. New York: Dryden Press, 1946.

———. "Story-Telling to Story-Writing." In *Proceedings of the 5th Congress of the International Comparative Literature Association*," pp. 433–442. Amsterdam: Swets and Zeitlinger, 1969.

Thomson, James Alexander Ker. *The Art of the Logos*. London: George Allen and Unwin, 1935.

Thorne-Thomsen, Gudrun. "The Practical Results of Storytelling in Chicago's Park Reading Rooms." *ALA Bulletin* 3 (1909): 408–410.

Thornton, Robert J. *Space, Time, and Culture among the Iraqu of Tanzania*. New York: Academic Press, 1980.

Tiger, Rebecca. "Narrative Folk Pat-s of West Bengal: Approaches to the Analysis of Painted Scrolls in Village India." Master's thesis, University of Pennsylvania, 1975.

Tillhagen, Carl-Herman. *Taikon Berättar*. Stockholm: P. A. Norstedt Söners, 1946.

Tirabutana, Prajuab. "A Simple One: The Story of a Siamese Girlhood." Data Paper no. 30. Ithaca: Southeast Asia Program, Dept. of Far Eastern Studies, Cornell Univ., 1958.

Tod, James. *Annals and Antiquities of Rajasthan.* 3 vols. Oxford Univ. Pr., 1920. (First pub. 1829–32.)

Todd, Loreto. *Some Day Been Dey; West African Pidgin Folktales.* London: Routledge & Kegan Paul, 1979.

Toelken, Barre. *The Dynamics of Folklore.* Boston: Houghton Mifflin, 1979.

———. "The 'Pretty Languages' of Yellowman: Genre, Mode and Texture in Navajo Coyote Narratives." In *Folklore Genres,* ed. by Dan Ben-Amos, pp. 93–123. Austin: Univ. of Texas Pr., 1976.

Toit, Brian M. du. *Content and Context of Zulu Folk-narratives.* Gainesville: Univ. of Florida, 1976.

Toland, John. *A Critical History of the Celtic Religion and Learning . . .* London: Lackington, Hughes, Harding and Co., 1815. (First pub. 1719.)

Tolksdorf, Ulrich. *Eine ostpreussische volkserzählerin; Geschichten-Geschichte-Lebensgeschichte.* Marburg: N. G. Elwert Verlag, 1980.

Tooze, Ruth. *Storytelling.* Englewood Cliffs, N.J.: Prentice Hall, 1959.

Torrend, J. *Specimens of Bantu Folklore from Northern Rhodesia.* New York: Negro Universities Pr., 1969. (First pub. 1921.)

Towo-Atangana, Gaspard. "Le mvet, genre majeur de la littérature orale des populations pahoines (Bulu, Beti, Fang-Ntumu)." *Abbia* 9/10 (1965): 163–179.

Tracey, Hugh. "A Case for the Name Mbira." *African Music* 2,4 (1961): 17–25.

———. *The Lion on the Path and Other Stories.* London: Routledge & Kegan Paul, 1967; New York: Praeger, 1969; Pacific Palisades, Ca.: P. Tracey, 340 Las Casas, 198_.

Tremearne, A. J. N. *Hausa Superstitions and Customs: An Introduction to the Folklore and the Folk.* London: Frank Cass, 1970. (First pub. 1913.)

Uffer, Leza. *Rätoromanische Märchen und ihre Erzähler.* Schriften, Band 29. Basel: Schweizerische Gesellschaft für Volkskunde, 1945.

Umeasiegbu, Rems Nna. *Words Are Sweet; Igbo Stories and Storytelling.* Leiden: F. J. Brill, 1982.

Upadhyaya, K. D. "The Classification and Chief Characteristics of Indian (Hindi) Folk Tales." *Fabula* 7 (1965): 225–229.

Vaillant, G. C. *The Aztecs of Mexico.* New York: Doubleday, 1962.

Van Wyke, P. E. "Covert Modeling in the Context of Storytelling; Observational Learning in Therapy with Children." *Imagery: Concepts, Results, Applications* 2 (1981): 333–345.

Vansina, Jan. *Oral Tradition.* Tr. from the French by H. M. Wright. Chicago: Alsine Pub. Co., 1965.

*Vishnu Purana: A System of Hindu Mythology and Tradition.* Tr. by H. H. Wilson. Intro. by R. C. Hazra. 3rd ed. Calcutta: Punthi Pustak, 1972.

Wade, Barrie. *Story at Home and School.* Educational Review Occasional Publications 10. Edgbaston: Univ. of Birmingham, 198_.

Wade-Evans, A. W. *Welsh Medieval Law: Being a Text of the Laws of Howel the Good.* Oxford Univ. Pr., 1909.

Wagner, Joseph Anthony and Smith, Robert W. *A Teacher's Guide to Storytelling.* Dubuque: Wm. C. Brown, 1958.

Waley, Arthur. *Ballads and Stories from Tun-huang.* New York: Macmillan, 1960.

———. "Kutune Shirka: The Ainu Epic." In *Botteghe Oscure* 7 (1951): 214–236.

Walker, Barbara K. "The Folks Who Tell Folktales: Field Collecting in Turkey." *Horn Book* 47 (December 1971): 636–642.

———. "Folktales in Turkey." *Horn Book* 40 (February 1964): 42–46.

Walker, Joseph C. *A Historical Essay on the Dress of the Ancient and Modern Irish*, 2nd ed. 2 vols. Dublin: J. Christie, 1918. 1st ed., Dublin: 1788.

Walker, Warren S., and Uysal, Ahmet E. *Tales Alive in Turkey.* Cambridge: Harvard Univ. Pr., 1966.

Wallace, Phyl, and Wallace, Noel. "Milpatjunanyi, the Story Game." In their *Children of the Desert*, pp. 24–26. Melbourne: Thomas Nelson, 1968.

Wallas, Lee. *Stories for the Third Ear.* New York: W. W. Norton, 1985.

Wandira, Asavia. *Indigenous Education in Uganda.* Kampala: Makerere Univ. Dept. of Education, 1971.

Wenzel, Siegfried. "The Joyous Art of Preaching; or the Preacher and the Fabliau." *Anglia* 97 (1979): 304–325.

Westermann, Diedrich. *The Shilluk People: Their Language and Folklore.* Westport, Ct.: Negro Universities Pr., 1970. (First pub. 1912.)

Wheeler, Howard T. *Tales from Jalisco Mexico.* Memoirs, 35. Philadelphia: American Folklore Society, 1943.

Wheeler, Post. *Tales from the Japanese Storytellers.* Ed. by Harold G. Henderson. Rutland, Vt.: Charles E. Tuttle, 1964.

Wiggin, Kate Douglas. *Children's Rights.* Boston: Houghton Mifflin, 1892.

Williams, Gwyn. *An Introduction to Welsh Poetry: From the Beginnings to the 16th Century.* Philadelphia: Dufour, 1952.

Willis, Roy, ed. *There Was a Certain Man: Spoken Art of the Fipa.* Oxford Univ. Pr., 1978.

Wilson, Jane B. *The Story Experience.* Metuchen, N.J.: Scarecrow Pr., 1979.

Winner, Thomas G. *The Oral Art and Literature of the Kazakhs of Russian Central Asia.* Durham: Duke Univ. Pr., 1958.

Wintgens, Hans-Herbert. *Das Erzählen im Religionsunterricht*. Gutersloh: Gerd. Mohn, 1971.

Wisconsin Arts Board. *Artists in the Schools. Directory 1987, 1988, 1989*. Madison: The Board, n.d.

Wisser, Wilhelm. *Auf der Märchensuche; die Entstehung meiner Märchensammlung*. Hamburg und Berlin: Hanseatische Verlagsanwalt, 1920.

Wolkstein, Diane. *The Magic Orange Tree*. Illus. by Elsa Henriquez. New York: Knopf, 1978.

*The Work of the Cleveland Public Library with the Children and the Means Used to Reach Them*. Cleveland Public Library, 1908.

Wynne, Elaine. "Storytelling in Therapy and Counseling." *National Storytelling Journal* 6 (Winter 1989): 3–6.

Yolen, Jane. *Touch Magic*. New York: Philomel, 1981.

Young, Frances. "Primitive Storytelling in Greece." Thesis, New York Public Library, Library School, 1915.

Zeitlin, Steven J.; Kotkin, Amy J.; and Baker, Holly Cutting, eds. *A Celebration of American Family Folklore; Tales and Traditions from the Smithsonian Collection*. New York: Pantheon, 1982.

Zguta, Russell. *Russian Minstrels: A History of the Skomorokhi*. Philadelphia: Univ. of Pennsylvania Pr., 1978.

Zimmer, Heinrich. *The Art of Indian Asia; Its Mythology and Transformations*. Completed and ed. by Joseph Campbell. 2 vols. Bollingen Series, 39. Princeton Univ. Pr., 1960.

Ziskind, Sylvia. *Telling Stories to Children*. New York: H. W. Wilson Co., 1976.

## Nonprint Materials

Only items cited in the text are included in this bibliography of nonprint materials. There are numerous films, videos, cassettes and discs related to storytelling. They can be located by consulting past issues of *The National Storytelling Journal* as well as catalogs issued by the National Association for the Preservation and Perpetuation of Storytelling, P. O. Box 112, Jonesborough, Tn. 37659.

*Berimbau*. 16 mm film. 12 minutes. Color. Directed by Tony Talbot. Narrated by Emile de Antonio. New York: New Yorker Films, 1971.

*Folk and Traditional Music of Asia for Children*. Vol. 1. LP sound disc and booklet. Tokyo: Asian Cultural Centre for UNESCO, 1975.

*The Griots; ministers of the spoken word*. Recorded by Samuel Charters. 2 LP sound discs. New York: Folkways, 1975.

*Index of Films and Videotapes on American Folklore*. Memphis: Center for Southern Folklore, 1976.

*Mapandangare, the Brave Baboon*. 16 mm film. 12 min. color. Los Angeles: Film Fair Communications, n.d.

*The Pleasure Is Mutual: How to Conduct Effective Picture Book Presentations.* 16 mm film. 26 minutes. Color. Prod. and directed by Joanna Foster and William D. Stoneback. Stamford: Connecticut Films, 1966.

"Recordings: Phonodisc. Cassette." In *Stories: A List of Stories to Tell and to Read Aloud,* 7th ed., comp. by Marilyn Berg Iarusso, pp. 64–67. The New York Public Library, 1977.

*There's Something About a Story.* 16 mm film. 27 min. Color. Dayton: Public Library of Dayton and Montgomery County, 1969.

# BIBLIOGRAPHY
## PART II

## Training Manuals of the 1970s and 1980s

The following are authors of handbooks of storytelling published in English during the past two decades and of handbooks used in the collection of stories. For the former group, each author is listed only once, in the decade during which the first edition of the handbook was published, even though there might be several editions. Only books that have fairly extensive information on the art or craft of telling are included here. Collections of stories, with suggestions for telling each story, do not fall into this category unless they also have general, "how-to" chapters on storytelling. There was no attempt to be selective here. Some of the handbooks are self-published. Full information on each can be found by looking under the author's name in the general bibliography.

1970s

Baker, A., and Greene, E.
Bauer
Briggs
Chambers
DeWit
Fitz-Gerald and Gunter
Moore, V.
Ross
Schimmel
Storytelling: Practical Guides
Wilson
Ziskind

1980s

Breneman
Colwell
Egan
Farrell
Herman
Lawrence
Livo and Rietz (2 titles)
Maguire
MacDonald, M. *Twenty* . . .
Nichols

Pellowski, *Family* . . .
Roberts, K.
Wade, B.

## Story Collecting Handbooks

Handbooks published in other languages include:

Frey
Lequeux-Gromaire
Merkel
Pastoriza de Etchebarne
Rodari
Schröcke

Handbooks published for the guidance of folklorists and others wishing to learn how to record folktales, legends and other stories include:

Bartis, P., and Fertig, B.C.
Brunvand, J. *Folklore* . . .
Clarke, K. and M. *Introducing* . . .
Fine
Goldstein, K. *A Guide* . . .
Ives

# INDEX